GUARANTEED INCOME FOR THE UNEMPLOYED

THE STORY OF SUB

GUARANTEED INCOME
FOR THE UNEMPLOYED
THE STORY OF SUB

JOSEPH M. BECKER, S.J.

THE JOHNS HOPKINS PRESS
BALTIMORE, MARYLAND

This report was prepared under a contract with the Manpower Administration, U.S. Department of Labor, under the authority of the Manpower Development and Training Act. Researchers undertaking such projects under U.S. Government sponsorship are encouraged to express their own judgment. Interpretations or viewpoints stated in this document do not necessarily represent the official position or policy of the Department of Labor. Reproduction in whole or in part permitted for any purpose of the U.S. Government.

Copyright © 1968
by The Johns Hopkins Press
Baltimore, Maryland 21218
All Rights Reserved

Manufactured in the United States of America

Library of Congress Catalog Card. No. 68-21864

LIBRARY
FLORIDA STATE UNIVERSITY
TALLAHASSEE, FLORIDA

To my brothers,
Clarence and Frank

CONTENTS

PART III. EXPERIENCE OF SUB

APPENDIXES

Tables

Appendixes

Table   Page

PREFACE

One of the perennial issues debated in modern society is the proper division of social tasks between the private and the public spheres. It was a concern with this issue that prompted the present study of private unemployment-benefit plans. More information was needed than was currently available on how the public and private spheres should share the task of providing benefits for the unemployed.

A prerequisite for determining the proper division of these tasks is knowledge of what unemployment-benefit programs are currently operative in the public and private spheres and what their experience has been. When this study was undertaken, a great deal was known regarding the public program of unemployment insurance, since the state agencies administering this program are required by law to report regularly and in considerable detail. By contrast, there was little current information available on the existence, extent, and characteristics of private unemployment-benefit plans and practically no assembled data on their operations. While this investigation was in progress, the Bureau of Labor Statistics published an extensive and very useful bulletin detailing the provisions of the major plans that were functioning in 1962–1963. Even this bulletin, however, provided no account of origins of the plans, the stages of their development, or the history of their operations. It was to supply this lack that the present study was undertaken.

A characteristic of the private sphere is variety, and there are a great many different kinds of private unemployment-benefit plans. This investigation has concentrated on the group of plans called Supplemental Unemployment Benefits. SUB was chosen partly because it was the largest family of private unemployment-benefit plans, covering between two and three million workers, but principally because by its provisions SUB was directly related to the public program and thus brought the public-private issue into sharp focus.

The phrase "guaranteed income" in the title reflects the close relation of SUB to labor's long-term goal, the guaranteed annual wage. In both origin and nature, SUB is the milk-cousin of GAW. At a press conference held to announce the negotiation of the first SUB plan in 1955, Walter Reuther said of the plan: "It provides the principle upon which we are going to build the guaranteed annual wage." A dozen years and four

xvii

contract negotiations later, Reuther was able to say that the goal had been reached: "Ford workers have led the way by winning a guaranteed annual income."

This study covers the first decade of SUB's operations, 1955 through 1965. The essential details of major contracts negotiated since 1965 are provided in an appendix; reports of experience under these recently negotiated provisions will not be available for some time. The goal of this investigation was less quantitative than qualitative; that is, it aimed less at providing a complete history of all SUB plans than at providing such information as would best illuminate key issues and answer such questions as why did SUB plans come into existence; how and why have they changed over time; how successful have they been in attaining their objectives; how much have they cost; what impact, if any, have they had on other social goals; and in particular, how are they related to the public program of unemployment insurance.

The research staff available for finding answers to these questions was limited—one principal researcher and an assistant. This limitation precluded a full investigation of all SUB plans. As explained in the introductions to Parts II and III, a selection was made of "core" plans. Even within these core plans, the qualitative nature of the goal and the uneven availability of data precluded a uniform treatment of each plan. Instead, the investigation made the best use of scarce resources by concentrating on areas where significant data were most abundant.

This method was not designed to produce complete and balanced histories of the individual SUB plans. Far from being an exhaustive work on SUB, this is only an introduction to the subject. It is a one-man scouting expedition into a relatively unknown area and must be followed by larger expeditions before the region can be adequately mapped. But until the definitive account is written (if it ever is), this scouting report should be helpful as a general guide.

The study will have different interests for different groups. The union and employer representatives who negotiate and administer labor contracts may find this a useful handbook on the generation and nurture of supplemental unemployment-benefit plans. Students of industrial relations will find new information here on such perennial issues as the choice of fringe benefits in place of money wages, the search for salaried status on the part of the hourly-paid worker, the scope of seniority provisions, and the implications of these issues for the most efficient allocation of labor. Finally, students of government and of governmental programs for income redistribution, especially unemployment insurance, will find this a recent investigation of an ever-contemporary political problem—the proper division of a social task between the private and the public spheres.

The parts of the book follow a biological analogy. After discussing the birth of SUB plans (Part I), the study describes the developing body of the growing child (Part II), and finally narrates the history of its activities (Part III). The general reader can get the gist of the book by reading the first three chapters and Chapter 12.

I wish to express my appreciation to the Office of Manpower Policy, Evaluation, and Research, United States Department of Labor, and to the Institute for Social Science Research for their financial assistance in carrying through this study. Neither of the financial sponsors is in any way responsible for the views expressed herein.

I am deeply indebted to the many companies and labor unions whose cooperation provided the "stuff" of the study: I wish I could acknowledge my indebtedness to each by name. The entire project owes much to the work of Virginia K. Boman in the earlier stages and to Mary E. Wilcox in the later stages. Without the contributions of these two assistants, the task could not have been accomplished. The Cambridge Center for Social Studies provided indispensable facilities for the work.

JOSEPH M. BECKER, S.J.

Cambridge Center for Social Studies
Cambridge, Massachusetts
October 9, 1967

Part I
BIRTH OF SUB

1

BIRTH OF THE FIRST SUB PLAN

Background of SUB

The worker's persistent search for employment security has taken many forms, of which one is the program of supplemental unemployment benefits called "SUB." This program is part of a large family of private arrangements that provide some guarantee of income to current jobholders. Although our concern is only with SUB plans, it may facilitate understanding of these plans to view them against the background of the larger family to which they belong. Schematically, the family tree of private plans of employment security looks like this:

A. Protection is measured from the time of hire.
B. Protection is measured from the time of layoff.
   1. Unemployment is not a condition for receipt of benefits.
   2. Unemployment is a condition for receipt of benefits.
      a. Benefit funds are vested in individuals.
      b. Benefit funds are pooled.

Private programs which provide a guarantee of income to current jobholders are thus divided into two main branches, differentiated by the point of time at which the guarantee of protection begins to operate. In the first branch (A), protection is measured from the time of hire. To this branch belongs the seniority system, perhaps the most effective of all protections against unemployment — for those who have seniority. To this branch also belong call-in pay and the short-week benefit of the SUB plans. Here also belong schemes for wage-rate retention, whereby a worker demoted to a job which normally pays a lower rate still retains his original rate of pay. The most widely known plan in this category is the guaranteed annual wage (GAW), which attracted much attention during the decade immediately following World War II but which by 1955 had undergone a gradual, almost imperceptible, transformation into SUB. Some of the old GAW plans have continued to operate, in companies like Hormel and Nunn-Bush, and occasionally new ones have been negotiated.

Some contracts guarantee employment not merely for a year, but indefinitely. They provide that a reduction of force will take place only by attrition — through deaths, retirements, and voluntary quits. Such contracts are usually negotiated in situations where technological changes threaten an

3

entire occupation — as, for example, those of firemen and telegraphers on the railroads. Unemployment programs that pay very high benefits for very long periods of time — as in the Alan Wood Steel Company plan described later — are the equivalent of guaranteed employment plans, inasmuch as the high cost of terminating an employee under such plans discourages an employer from doing so. In such cases, the GAW proposals that became SUB plans a decade ago have completed a cycle.

In the second branch of the family of private programs (B), protection is measured from the point of layoff; the guarantee becomes operative at the time of separation instead of at the time of hire. This branch is much larger than the other and itself has two subdivisions, differentiated by whether unemployment is or is not a necessary condition for receipt of benefits.

Unemployment not a necessary condition. Plans belonging to this branch of the family (B1) look only to the past employment relationship. If this connection is broken and is expected to remain broken, the employee receives a benefit whether or not he actually experiences unemployment.

A leading member of this branch is the severance-pay plan,[1] which may serve two related but distinct functions in connection with layoffs. First, severance pay may serve as indemnification for what is equivalent to a property loss. So much of an employee's time and talent may have been invested in a particular job, with all its rights and perquisites, that termination of employment represents the loss of a valuable capital good. Second, separation pay may serve the function of replacing some of the income lost during a period of unemployment. In this latter function, severance pay is particularly appropriate for situations where the employment relationship is terminated permanently. Since the benefit is paid independent of actual unemployment, the recipient has no reason to delay his search for another job. Most severance-pay plans pay the benefit in a lump sum; a few plans (for example, some of those in the meat-packing industry) permit payments to be made in installments and thus have a deceptive resemblance to SUB payments.

Early-pension plans belong to this same branch. Provisions for early retirement are in most instances just a concealed form of unemployment benefits payable until retirement age is reached. Contributory pension plans, which are common in large, conservative industries like oil and public utilities, frequently perform the function of unemployment benefits. If the

---

1. The most comprehensive survey of severance-pay plans is a recent report of the Bureau of Labor Statistics; see reference [1].

employee is terminated before retirement age, he receives his contributions with interest. The provision for thirteen weeks of sabbatical leave negotiated by the United Steelworkers of America in 1963 (effective January 1, 1964) should probably also be considered a form of concealed unemployment benefits.

The Extended Layoff Benefit Plan of the aerospace industry is a hybrid. Although this plan does not require that the employment relationship be severed permanently (beneficiaries retain their seniority rights) and therefore it is not strictly a severance-pay plan, neither does it require that the recipient be unemployed, and therefore it is not a pure unemployment-benefit plan.

Unemployment a necessary condition. The second branch (B2) represents the purest form of unemployment benefits inasmuch as the benefits are paid only to those actually unemployed. It has many subspecies, of which the principal ones are the individual-account, or vested, plan and the pooled-fund plan.

The individual-account, or vested, plan does not pool risks and resources but establishes an individual account for each employee on which he may draw when he becomes unemployed, with any unused balance refundable to him when his attachment to the employer has been severed permanently. Most of these plans are simply forms of compulsory saving; that is, the amount which the employer puts into each employee's account would probably have gone to the employee in the form of higher wages if the union had not negotiated the unemployment-benefit plan. But in some instances, as in the plan negotiated in 1965 by the International Association of Machinists with the Douglas Aircraft Company, there is a degree of individual choice: the employee authorizes a certain amount, which is variable, to be deducted from his pay, and the employer matches this amount, at least in part (Douglas, for example, matches half of the amount). There are also various forms of profit sharing which produce an account on which the employee may draw when unemployed. Few individual account plans are SUB plans as defined in this study.

The pooled-fund plan, as its name indicates, combines risks and resources on behalf of all the employees who are covered by the plan. It is an insurance, not a savings, plan. Usually the employer contributes a specified number of cents per hour worked to a central fund, out of which specified benefits are paid to employees. The great variety possible under such a plan is exemplified later (see Part II below).

The present study is concerned only with plans in the branch B2, and not with all such plans. The concern of this study is with private plans of unemployment benefits only insofar as they are supplemental to the public program of unemployment insurance. In a wide sense, every private plan of unemployment benefits is "supplemental" to the public program. However, the present study is concerned only with the type of private plan whose eligibility requirements or benefit provisions are linked directly with the public program.

For the purposes of this study, therefore, the term "supplemental unemployment benefits" (SUB) is defined as a *private plan of unemployment benefits whose eligibility or benefit requirements are linked directly with the public program of unemployment insurance (UI).*

There are two reasons for selecting this particular type of plan for special study. In addition to being the largest member of the family of private unemployment benefit plans — in terms of number of plans and number of workers covered — SUB is also the most interesting member of the family. SUB is the workaday moth that emerged from the fascinating cocoon called the guaranteed annual wage, and it retains much of the interest that attended the earlier stage of its development.

In the postwar period, the guaranteed annual wage was one of the most discussed issues in the area of labor-management relations. As the National Association of Manufacturers said in a memorandum to its members: "Seldom, if ever, has an economic issue engaged as much public attention as the guaranteed annual wage." A part of the reason was the massive educational effort put forth by the unions, especially the United Auto Workers, to inform their membership of the meaning and value of their drive for GAW. This effort included formal courses for local union committeemen, handbooks, millions of bumper stickers, millions of handbills, and a long series of radio, newspaper, and television advertisements. Brendon Sexton, the director of education for the UAW, summed it up: "The drive for the guaranteed annual wage was the most concerted effort we have ever made."

SUB is of particular interest for another and more fundamental reason. It involves a key issue of political economy, namely, the "proper" division of a given task between the public and private spheres. Decisions on this issue, made in area after area of its life, largely determine a nation's political and economic character. This key issue is posed directly by SUB because the provisions of SUB plans are directly related to the public program of unemployment insurance.

By 1966, SUB had been in existence for a decade. Its tenth birthday offers an appropriate occasion for a review of its birth, growth, and life experience.

Ancestors of SUB

Nothing under the sun is entirely new, and SUB had its antecedents. Although a complete history of the evolution of SUB is beyond the scope of this study, it may be useful to note a few events that are directly related to the development of modern SUB in the United States.[2]

In Europe, the Ghent plan, established about 1900, involved the supplemental process, but in reverse; that is, public funds were used to supplement private funds. Under this plan (named after the city in Belgium where it began), the government sought to encourage the establishment of private programs by offering to subsidize any voluntary organization (usually a labor union) that paid unemployment benefits to its members. The Ghent plan spread to many countries of Europe; even at its peak, however, it covered only a small fraction of all workers.

Much more closely resembling modern SUB were the private plans established in England about a decade after the first public unemployment insurance system had been set up there in 1911. During the very heavy unemployment of the 1920's, a few English firms decided that their employees needed more liberal unemployment benefits than those provided by the public program and that the firms could afford to supplement the public benefits. Among these firms was Rowntree and Company, a manufacturer of cocoa products, which installed a plan almost identical in its fundamentals with the SUB plans established in the United States in 1955.

In the Rowntree plan [4], the company at the outset established a fund of £10,000 and obligated itself to keep the fund at this level by making regular payments at a rate not to exceed 1 percent of the payroll. The company's liability was thus limited by the size of the fund and by the rate of payment needed to replenish it. Eligible employees were those with six months or more of service. The supplemental weekly payment under the company's scheme was the difference between the unemployment benefit payable under the national scheme and an amount computed as follows: 50 percent of average weekly earnings, plus 10 percent for a dependent wife, plus 5 percent for each dependent child under 16 years of age. The combined weekly benefit, public plus private, could not exceed 75 percent of the employee's average weekly earnings. Duration of benefits was determined by the length of service, with a maximum of 15 weeks. Here were contained most of the essentials of the SUB plan negotiated by Ford and

---

2. A detailed survey of private guarantees of employment and wages can be found in references [2] and [3].

the UAW in May of 1955.[3] Since Rowntree is in the food industry, with relatively steady employment, its experience probably has the same limited significance for modern SUB as the plan of Bristol-Myers mentioned below.

In the United States there were also prototypes of modern SUB. The Armstrong Cork Company adopted a plan of unemployment benefits in 1935, before the general enactment of state unemployment insurance laws. In 1939, when the state unemployment insurance programs were generally operative, the company modified its plan so as to fit the company benefits into the states' waiting periods — then generally three weeks — and to supplement the amount of state benefits if the latter was less than 60 percent of wages. The Armstrong plan was discontinued in 1950, but according to the company, the Ford Motor Company "drew on our experience in their preliminary study of SUB that they offered the United Automobile Workers" [6].

For another example, in 1947 the Bristol-Myers drug company inaugurated a plan which paid unemployment benefits equal to 60 percent of wages up to $100 per week, "less benefits payable under any government program." The last condition relates the private plan directly to the public program and thus brings it under the definition of SUB. Experience under this plan, however, could not have been very useful to the progenitors of modern SUB. In this company, labor costs were a small part of total costs and employment was so steady that almost the only occasion for the payment of benefits under the plan was the employee's permanent separation from the company. This kind of experience could hold few helpful lessons for such mass-production industries as basic steel and autos, where labor costs are a large part of total costs and employment is much less stable.

Many early plans which paid benefits to employees who might also be receiving unemployment insurance do not come under the definition of SUB because the plans did not explicitly relate their benefits to those of the public program. For example, in 1934 the Quaker Oats Company adopted a plan whereby the company paid employees on layoff a benefit equal to 70 hours of work per month. This provision was retained even after the enactment of public unemployment insurance in 1935 and thus raised the characteristic SUB issue — the legality of simultaneous payment of private and public benefits. The issue was resolved in New York by a ruling that the company's benefits constituted wages for the first two weeks of the month and that state benefits could be paid for the remaining two weeks. Other states decided the issue differently, but since in any case the Quaker Oats plan was entirely independent of the public program, it was not, strictly speaking, a prototype of SUB.

3. As of late 1966, the Rowntree scheme was still in existence, although, partly because of changes in the national scheme, some revisions had been made [5].

The Conception of Modern SUB

When and where was modern SUB conceived? It is as difficult to locate the exact beginning of SUB as it is to point to the exact spot at which the Mississippi River rises. Which of the tiny springs that join to form the little ponds, that in turn unite to form the headwaters, is the "real" head? Likewise, of the many private programs that preceded SUB, it is impossible to say which was the "real" head of the family.

However, there is one particular development which can be identified in a special way with the beginning of modern SUB. It is the demand made in the postwar period by some CIO unions for a guaranteed annual wage. In the course of a decade of successive proposals, this demand for GAW was gradually transformed into a plan which, while it still bore the old name, was essentially the plan which the Ford Motor Company negotiated with the United Auto Workers in 1955 and which came to be known as SUB.

The CIO

In 1943, as the end of World War II came in sight, a number of unions turned their attention to the problem of the unemployment anticipated during the reconversion period and demanded some form of guaranteed income. They argued that since the profits of corporations had been guaranteed through governmental regulations allowing rapid amortization of the cost of defense plant equipment, carry-forward and carry-back provisions affecting income taxes, a contract renegotiation law, and similar aids, and since the income of farmers had been guaranteed by the enactment of price supports, the income of wage earners also should be guaranteed. The unions advanced the additional argument that such a guarantee would stabilize employment and increase the gross national product, and would therefore cost nothing.

This demand for guaranteed employment came chiefly from the unions in the mass-production industries of steel, autos, rubber, and aluminum. It came also from workers in the maritime and meat-packing industries, as well as from the Bakery Workers, Teamsters, and a few others. In 1943, demands for guaranteed wages were pending before the War Labor Board on the part of five groups of workers. In addition to the Steelworkers and the Auto Workers, there were the Aluminum Workers of America, the United Electrical, Radio and Machine Workers of America (UE, the union later expelled from the CIO), and two unions in the meat-packing industry.

The unions in the meat-packing industry were asking for a liberalization of the weekly guarantee they already had, and the War Labor Board had partially granted their request. Since this development had no connection with the development of SUB, it need not be followed here. The demands of the Aluminum Workers were essentially similar to those of the Steelworkers, and the demands of the UE were essentially similar to those of the UAW. Hence it suffices to follow developments in the two key unions, the Steelworkers and the Auto Workers.

The Steelworkers

As far back as 1937, at the first annual convention of the union, Philip Murray had voiced a demand for the guaranteed annual wage. This demand was muted during the succeeding years in favor of other more desirable and more feasible objectives, but, largely due to the efforts of the union's counsel during that period, Arthur Goldberg, it was not forgotten. In 1943, the union resumed the demand more seriously and the case came before the War Labor Board. The Board decided that it could not impose GAW on the steel industry because not enough was known of the effects of such a guarantee and because it was contrary to the Board's policy to introduce by order a major innovation in collective bargaining. However, the Board recognized merit in the demand and recommended to President Roosevelt "that the whole question of guaranteed wage plans... should be comprehensively studied on a national scale" [7, p. 5].

This recommendation resulted in the 1947 report entitled *Guaranteed Wages* produced by the Advisory Board of the Office of War Mobilization and Reconversion, with Murray W. Latimer as research director [3]. The Advisory Board concluded: "The study shows clearly that plans guaranteeing wages or employment, when suitably adapted to the needs and conditions of the industry or establishment, are valuable to the entire Nation and afford a wholesome and desirable means for improving both worker and employer security" [3, p. xviii]. However, the Board also concluded: "Adoption of guaranteed wage plans should not be the subject of legislative action, but should be referred to free collective bargaining" [3, p. xviii].

Recognizing the basic unity of labor's varied strivings for employment security, the Latimer Report, as it came to be known, reviewed the many forms this effort had taken in the past, and thus gave the "guaranteed annual wage" its proper setting in the total picture. From this review, the Latimer Report concluded that, while such a guarantee was feasible in some circumstances, it was not practicable for an industry like steel, which had wide and unpredictable fluctuations in employment. The report suggested that a more promising approach would be to start with the existing unemployment insurance system and negotiate private supplements to the

4. Guarantee payments should be integrated with state unemployment compensation benefits so that employers can reduce their liabilities by effectively working toward the improvement of state laws.

5. The plan should be administered by a Joint Board of Administration having equal representation from the Union and from management, with an impartial chairman to break deadlocks. Decisions of the Joint Board with respect to eligibility and disqualification would be made independent of decisions made by state agencies with regard to unemployment compensation.

6. Financing should combine a pay-as-you-go requirement, to provide employers with an incentive to stabilize employment, with a reserve trust fund to meet abnormal costs. Provision should be made for reinsurance to reduce the size of required reserves and to spread the risks of abnormal unemployment over the widest possible area of the economy.

In discussing the first principle, the union explained the title of the brochure: "The UAW's purpose is really to develop a *Guaranteed Employment* plan. We use the phrase 'guaranteed wage' because it is widely used and understood. But it is not a completely accurate description of what our union will propose in collective bargaining. *Our main objective is steady full-time employment, week by week, the year round*" [10, p. 5]. It was a characteristic UAW emphasis at the time to make this the first principle.

The union's explanation of the second and third principles contained the substance of the guarantee, which was in two parts. First, all workers were to be salaried in the sense that they would receive a full week's salary if they worked at all in any week. Second, workers with seniority, which could be acquired in three months, were to receive guarantee payments for each week of layoff — in amounts equal, apparently, to 100 percent of take-home pay.

The desirable duration of benefits was specified in the third principle, which also included a choice of variable over uniform duration. The choice of variable duration represented a long step in the direction of realism as compared with the 1943 proposal. The UAW explained the choice to its membership as follows: "If an employer were required to guarantee fifty-two weeks pay to any new worker from the date of hire, the employer would avoid hiring new workers if there was any uncertainty at all about the amount of work available in the year ahead. Employers might turn down orders, or work their existing labor force excessive overtime, rather than take risks involved in hiring additional workers. Formation of new businesses would be made too risky because of the heavy possible guarantee liabilities, and the number of job opportunities in the economy would tend to diminish" [10, p. 13].

In explaining the fourth principle, the UAW said: "Through proper integration, a guaranteed annual wage plan can be as effective in bringing about higher unemployment compensation benefits for all workers as our integrated pension plans were in bringing about higher federal pension payments for workers covered by the federal law. . . . The higher state unemployment compensation benefits are raised, the greater the number of weeks for which they are paid, and the fewer the unjust excuses for disqualifying workers from eligibility for benefits, the lower will the cost of the guaranteed wage be to the corporation" [10, p. 17]. Three years later, Walter Reuther was to claim that SUB was actually producing this anticipated effect. The evidence for this evaluation is reviewed below, in Chapter 11.

In explaining the fifth principle, the union said that, while laid-off employees would be required to register with the public employment service, they would not be bound by the state's decisions on availability for suitable work. A joint board of administration composed of union and company representatives would make its own decisions and apply its own standards.

> If a job is considered suitable under the state law but unsuitable under the guaranteed wage agreement, the worker will be able to refuse it without loss of guarantee rights or payments. If refusal of a job considered "unsuitable" under the agreement results in denial of unemployment compensation benefits to the worker, he will nevertheless receive the same total amount in guarantee payments except that the entire amount will come from the employer rather than part from unemployment compensation. Employers will, therefore, have an incentive to seek improvements in definitions of suitable work in the state laws and to work for more reasonable administration of the suitable work provisions [10, p. 19].

> The requirement that the Joint Board of Administration make its own determinations independently of decisions made under state unemployment compensation laws is of the utmost importance [10, p. 37].

This issue, which touches the public-private relationship at its most sensitive point, generated much heat at the time and has remained a center of controversy ever since.

The sixth principle made use of the distinction employed in the second principle, that is, between partial and full weeks of layoff. Short-week benefits were to be met entirely by pay-as-you-go financing: "Since proper scheduling of work is almost fully within management's control, management should be required to bear directly the full cost of its failures to plan a full week of work for all the workers it calls in to work in any week" [10, p. 21].

For the same reason — to give employers an incentive to stabilize employment — some of the costs of full weeks of layoff also were to be met by pay-as-you-go financing. The union called this "a key provision of the plan" and explained: "It penalizes management at the point where workers are laid off and enables management to reduce its costs by avoiding layoffs" [10, p. 21]. But, in addition, a reserve trust fund was to be set up to finance abnormal layoffs. The union recognized that the employer's ability to support the guarantee would be least at the time when it would be needed most, that is, when the largest number of workers were laid off. "Accordingly, if the plan relied entirely on pay-as-you-go, there would be no real security for laid-off workers at the time when the number of such workers was largest" [10, p. 23]. It was therefore necessary to provide a reserve to meet the heavy guarantee liabilities that would result from large layoffs.

The union recognized that the employer's contribution for all purposes must be limited to a "specific maximum percentage of payroll" and explained to its membership: "A ceiling on the employer's liability is essential to enable the employer to anticipate his maximum possible costs under the guarantee agreement. If the employer was unable to estimate what the outside limit of his costs would be, it would be impossible to negotiate a guaranteed wage agreement in our industries" [10, p. 21].

The union also advocated the use of reinsurance as "a method of decreasing the size of the reserves that would otherwise be necessary to assure maximum security to the workers." It did not advocate any particular form of reinsurance, since "this is more the employer's problem than it is a union problem." However, it did express a preference for a system in which the federal government would reinsure approved trust funds [10, pp. 27–29].

Auto Workers' Plan versus Steelworkers' Plan

At this time the Auto Workers' proposals differed from those of the Steelworkers in at least four important respects:

(1) Where the Steelworkers proposed to pay the unemployed worker only 75 percent of his regular wage, the Auto Workers refrained from setting a figure but described a benefit which generally was interpreted to mean 100 percent of take-home pay.

(2) Where the Steelworkers restricted the plan to the core of the company's labor force (employees with three years of seniority), the Auto Workers included everyone who had been with the company for as short a period as three months.

(3) Where the Steelworkers envisaged a plan integrated administratively

with the public program of UI, the Auto Workers proposed to set up parallel administrative machinery and establish definitions of availability for suitable work which would be less strict than those used in the public program.

(4) The sole source of financing in the Steelworkers' plan was the reserve fund, but the Auto Workers' plan provided for a combination of pay-as-you-go and reserve fund financing. This difference reflected the preoccupation of the Auto Workers with employer incentives.

During this period, the two unions were collaborating in their respective approaches to the common goal of a guaranteed annual wage plan. Substantively there was more agreement than disagreement between them; however, there was also rivalry. In addition to the personal rivalry between MacDonald and Reuther, there seem to have been some strongly held differences regarding principles.

Although Murray Latimer did not speak officially for the Steelworkers, his close relationship with that union makes his position significant. In a debate with Edward Maher of the National Association of Manufacturers in November of 1955, Latimer said: "I think most of the unkind things that Mr. Maher has found about the GAW idea are more properly addressed to other quarters of the labor movement than that particular labor organization which I represent. I think it is not altogether unknown that the United Steelworkers of America do not follow the lead of Mr. Walter Reuther. And they do not follow him in his advocacy of extreme guaranteed wage measures because those measures, as correctly said — taking Mr. Reuther at his word — are socialism. The United Steelworkers of America are not Socialists" [11].

The Ford Motor Company

According to Malcolm L. Denise, later the Industrial Relations Manager of Ford, the company had anticipated that it would be the target in the 1955 negotiations: "It was already quite apparent that ours was the key bargaining table in our industry this year, and, of course, a key economic issue at that bargaining table was the guaranteed annual wage demand. We assumed that this issue had been scheduled for resolution at this particular time and table for several years; that in these negotiations there would be no more waiting to see what somebody else would do with it" [12, p. 6].

In a booklet published shortly after the completion of negotiations, the company revealed the extent of its preparation:

The Ford Motor Company spent three years intensively researching the whole field encompassing the UAW's "Guaranteed Annual Wage" demands. The outlines of its demands were known more than two years ago, and many details were known more than a year ago. The study was continuous throughout that period of time, but increased in tempo and intensity as negotiations approached in the spring of 1955. This research included much analysis within the Company, and all interested components of the Company participated. It also included many and wide discussions with outside companies, organizations, individuals, technicians, economists, actuaries, and others [13].

This long and intensive research effort on the part of the Ford Motor Company was one of the three most decisive factors in the birth of SUB, ranking with the Latimer Report of 1947 and with the Auto Workers' campaign of study and publicity in the period 1953–1955. Because Ford had prepared itself so thoroughly, it was able to quantify the union's proposals where these were only general goals or principles;[6] it was also able to propose constructive alternatives for those provisions of the UAW plan which it felt it could not accept.

In this way, Ford was able to exert an active, detailed influence on the final structure of the plan negotiated. Since this first SUB plan became the pattern for subsequent negotiations in the other industries (basic steel, can, agricultural implements, rubber), the three-year research effort of the Ford Motor Company left a deep imprint on the development of most SUB plans in the United States. Although each successive negotiation between other unions and other companies left SUB somewhat changed, the original Ford-UAW contract set the basic mold, which perdured.

Birth of the First SUB Plan

Normally the UAW would have started negotiations in 1955 with General Motors Corporation, whose contract expired first. The union did hold a preliminary meeting with General Motors in which it learned that the corporation was absolutely opposed to SUB but was prepared to offer a combination of severance pay, a loan plan, and a stock savings plan worth more in dollars than the union's SUB plan. In rejecting the offer, Walter Reuther said, half seriously; "That plan is fine for the provident; this year we are taking care of the improvident."

After this exploratory meeting with General Motors, the UAW settled on Ford as the target company. There seem to be two main reasons for the choice. As the union later explained, it was easier to get money from General Motors but easier to gain acceptance of a principle from Ford,

6. Within the company, Richard L. Johnson (finance) and Malcolm L. Denise (industrial relations) were chiefly responsible for preparing the plan which Ford unveiled during negotiations.

and a controversial innovation was involved in these negotiations. Secondly, in the first quarter of 1955, license registrations had been filed on 332,401 Ford sales, just 593 above the Chevrolet total. The union anticipated that Ford would be most reluctant to jeopardize this newly won leadership by taking a strike while General Motors continued to produce.

After Ford had offered, and the union had refused, the same stock savings plan that General Motors had offered, negotiations proceeded to the point where all other major problems had been solved except that of the proposed SUB plan. The overall cost of the package had also been determined. The only question was whether the money should be paid out in the form of contributions to a SUB plan or in some other form. When the union insisted upon SUB and would accept no substitute, the company finally yielded and the contract was signed.[7]

The plan that emerged from the negotiations differed significantly from the plan originally proposed by the union. It was restricted to employees with 1 year of seniority instead of 90 days; it paid 60 to 65 percent of take-home pay for 26 weeks instead of 100 percent for 52 weeks; it provided a method for assuring that some of the fund would still be available if and when long-service employees were laid off;[8] and it did not allow the union a direct voice in disqualification decisions. In comparison with state unemployment insurance programs, it might be described as a plan paying somewhat higher benefits to a more select group of employees under stricter conditions.

Ford stated publicly (apparently in order to defend itself against the charge by other employers that it had failed to hold the line against the union) that the SUB plan had not increased total labor costs: "The over-all size of the package had already been established by a prior offer of another company in the industry" [12, p. 6], namely, General Motors. In agreeing to the SUB plan, therefore, Ford was merely agreeing to allocate to SUB part of the money its employees would receive in any case. As a matter of fact, at one point in the negotiations Ford offered to contribute somewhat more to the SUB fund, and it was the union that limited the contribution to 5 cents per hour, preferring to take the difference in another form.

It was unusually clear in the case of this first SUB plan that its immediate effect would be to redistribute income between the employed and the unemployed members of the union. Given the order of developments in

7. A colorful, detailed, and substantially accurate account of the tactical maneuvers employed by the two sides in the course of the negotiations was published by the Detroit Free Press under the headline, "Now It Can Be Told" [14].

8. See Chapter 5 for the description of the method. Its invention by Ford removed a serious barrier to the company's acceptance of the plan.

the negotiations, it was obvious that the additional income accruing to the unemployed would be diverted not from the purchasers of autos (in the form of higher prices), nor from the owners and creditors of the auto industry (in the form of lower profits and interest payments), but from the employed workers in the auto industry (in the form of lower wages, or lower fringe benefits other than unemployment benefits).

There is general agreement that in this instance labor and management were models of responsible behavior in their approach to the negotiating table. The UAW had given the auto companies three years' warning that a plan was in the making. As the union developed its successive versions of the plan, it made them public and invited criticism. Union spokesmen presented and defended the plan before learned societies and wrote articles about it in technical journals. The union even established a Public Advisory Committee and submitted the plan to them for criticism.

When the union was finally ready, it announced that, though it was determined to strike for the principle of the guaranteed wage, it was not wedded to the details of its plan and would accept reasonable modifications by way of compromise. The country has probably never seen a more thorough preparation or a more reasoned approach by labor to a new proposal.

Management, also, showed a notable sense of responsibility. The Ford Motor Company had not ignored the union's three years' warning but had used the interval to prepare a constructive alternative plan. Without such an alternative, negotiations would probably have degenerated into a stalemate. As it was, a precedent-setting plan in a major industry was established without a strike. Commentators on the negotiations generally agreed that this was free American collective bargaining at its best.

2

BIRTH OF LATER SUB PLANS

The Ford-UAW agreement had a significance that transcended, of course, the particular negotiations from which it resulted. The agreement marked the beginning of a trend, and the first-born SUB plan was followed by a multitude of siblings.

It is not possible from readily available data to present a complete picture of the chronological growth in the number of SUB plans, nor even of the present extent of the plans. The general outline, however, of the major developments is discernible in the following narrative, which, after briefly recounting the changes which took place in the legal status of SUB payments, sketches the activities of the principal unions in establishing SUB plans and summarizes the present extent of such plans. (Additional details on the growth of SUB plans may be found in Chapter 3.)

Legal Status of SUB Payments

With the birth of the first SUB plan in 1955, the state UI agencies were faced with the question whether receipt of a benefit under a SUB plan would affect the worker's eligibility for UI benefits. The public issue involved in this question was very widely debated. Here it suffices to chronicle the facts of the states' answers to the question.[1]

In the periods immediately before and after the negotiation of the first SUB plans, many responsible persons, including some attorneys general, stated that under existing state legislation it was illegal to pay both benefits simultaneously. But once the plans had been negotiated by powerful unions and corporations, political forces came into play that soon started a trend toward the opposite interpretation.

The situation as of late August 1957 was summarized in a bulletin issued by the Department of Labor in September of that year [15]. By that date, of the 44 states which had acted on the question, only 4 did not permit supplementation: Indiana and Virginia had amended their statutes to deny such supplementation and the employment security agencies of North Carolina and Ohio had ruled against it. The 7 remaining states had not passed upon the question up to that time.

---

1. Further details of this development may be found in the sources listed in [15].

In states which had originally forbidden supplementation, various alternative methods of payment under SUB plans were employed. Such alternative methods included the payment of three or four times the regular weekly private benefit after two or three weeks of state UI benefits without supplementation, lump-sum substitute payments when the layoff ended or when state benefits were exhausted (whichever occurred earlier), and payments through other special arrangements.

In July 1957, the administrator of the Ohio Bureau of Employment Security ruled not to permit supplementation under a lump-sum substitute payment arrangement, holding that any such supplemental payment was to be considered remuneration to be allocated to previous weeks of unemployment. After successive appeals to the courts, culminating in an adverse decision by the Ohio Supreme Court in December of 1958,[2] the issue was finally resolved in March 1959 by the Ohio legislature, which amended the state law to permit supplemental unemployment benefits and unemployment insurance benefits to be paid concurrently. The Indiana law was similarly amended in the same month.

By the end of 1965, all states except New Hampshire, New Mexico, South Carolina and South Dakota, and Puerto Rico had taken action on the question. Only in Virginia was such supplementation still definitely denied, by statute [17].

Chronology of SUB Births

Single-Employer SUB Plans

Auto Workers (UAW). Following the successful conclusion of the Ford contract, the UAW negotiated almost identical SUB plans with the other auto companies and with the major firms manufacturing agricultural implements. Although General Motors had insisted that Ford should have taken a strike rather than agree to the plan, when its turn came, it also agreed. The corporation recognized that, once the UAW members employed by Ford had secured the SUB plan, it was impracticable to try to deny the same benefit to its own employees who were UAW members. By the end of 1955, the UAW had negotiated SUB plans with all the auto companies, although it had granted American Motors Corporation, then

2. The Court held that it was not within the lower court's province to interpret the intent of the law and that the matter should be clearly spelled out through legislation or by an amendment to the state constitution. Michael V. DiSalle campaigned successfully for the governorship on a platform which included a promise to recommend to the next (1959) session of the Ohio legislature legislation permitting laid-off workers to receive both types of payment at the same time [16].

newly established by merger of the Nash and Hudson companies, a year's delay in the commencement of the program.

During 1955, the UAW also succeeded in negotiating SUB plans with all the major agricultural implement companies except the J. I. Case Company. (A SUB plan was not to be negotiated with this company until 1964, when a new and more harmonious era of labor-management relationships commenced.) In the Allis-Chalmers contract, which was negotiated last, the union succeeded in liberalizing some SUB provisions, as described in Part II, and thus took the first step toward the announced goal of eventually negotiating a guaranteed employment plan like the one the union had originally demanded.

SUB was a decade old before the UAW succeeded in introducing it into the aerospace industry in the United States. That industry had countered the first SUB thrust by offering an alternative, the Extended Layoff Benefit Plan, which is more like a severance-payment than an unemployment-benefit plan.[3] The industry argued that the employment pattern of the aerospace industry differed from that of the auto industry and required a different type of plan. In the aerospace industry, unemployment due to cyclical, seasonal, and frictional causes was not so important as in the auto industry. Most of the aerospace unemployment occurred when government contracts were completed or canceled, causing large numbers of employees to be permanently laid off.

The UAW nevertheless preferred SUB, and in 1962 it persuaded the Douglas Aircraft Company to start contributing 2 cents per man-hour to a fund toward the establishment of a SUB plan when the next contract was negotiated. In the period 1965–1966, the UAW succeeded in negotiating SUB plans with the Douglas Aircraft Company, the Vertol Division of Boeing Company, the Martin Company, and the Ling-Temco-Vought Company. The rest of the aerospace companies, with the approval of the Machinists, who have organized a large part of the industry, chose instead to liberalize the Extended Layoff Benefit Plan or to establish individual-account savings plans.

The UAW has had less success in negotiating SUB plans with firms in other industries. Most of these other firms were smaller, were less profitable, had a larger labor component of total costs, and were more exposed to the competition of nonunionized firms. As of 1966, the UAW did not have a complete current list of contracts containing SUB plans; union headquarters has never been able to get all the locals to report

3. The Extended Layoff Benefit Plan pays a lump sum based on years of service to employees whose layoff has lasted for four weeks.

faithfully all contract changes. However, in 1962 the union had compiled a partial list which covered about three fourths of the union membership. At that time, out of 782 contracts, 188 (24 percent) contained SUB plans. These 188 contracts, however, covered 89 percent of the union members represented by the 782 contracts. Of the 188 SUB contracts, 12 percent had been negotiated with small firms having less than 50 employees.

Not all the SUB plans negotiated by the UAW were identical in their provisions. Where the UAW represented only a small part of the total labor force of a firm that had negotiated a different type of SUB plan with the dominant union, the UAW accepted the plan of the dominant union. Contrariwise, the UAW negotiated the auto-type plan to cover industrial activities other than automaking — for example, steelmaking or glass-making — where the UAW was the dominant union in a corporation that engaged in these other activities. Furthermore, as time went on, differences developed among the plans that first had been set up in 1955–1956, chiefly because some of these early plans did not adopt all the liberalizations negotiated in successive contracts. (The year-by-year growth in the number of SUB plans negotiated by the UAW cannot be shown because, as indicated above, the necessary data are not available.)

Steelworkers (USWA). In late 1955, when the contracts of the American Can Company and the Continental Can Company expired, the Steelworkers were presented with their first opportunity to negotiate a SUB plan. The plans negotiated with these two companies showed the influence of the early Steelworkers' proposals, but they also inevitably reflected the recently completed auto contracts — "inevitably" because the negotiators found it convenient to adopt the solutions already arrived at for the complex technical problems encountered in any SUB plan.

In early summer of the following year, 1956, the Steelworkers commenced negotiations with the basic steel companies. As an alternative to SUB, the companies offered the union a savings fund plan by which the company would contribute a dollar for every two dollars saved by the employee. The union rejected the offer and, after a strike of five weeks, proceeded to negotiate SUB plans with the major basic steel companies and with some of the steel fabricators. These plans were generally similar to those established in the can industry. Within this general type, the SUB plans negotiated by the Steelworkers varied in much the same way and for much the same reasons as did the plans of the Auto Workers.

As of 1964, the Steelworkers had negotiated 2,483 contracts, of which 487, or 20 percent, contained a SUB plan. These 487 SUB contracts covered about 750,000 employees, or about 85 percent of the union membership. Of the 487 SUB contracts, 51 percent were with small firms (less than 200 employees), while 16 percent were with major firms (more than 1,000 employees). The incidence of SUB was much higher among the larger firms: of the 112 major contracts, 71 percent provided SUB, while of the 1,918 small contracts, only 13 percent provided SUB. The union's early policy, partly influenced by Murray Latimer, was not to negotiate SUB plans with firms having less than 500 employees.

Table 2–1 shows the industrial distribution of the 2,483 Steelworkers' contracts. As is to be expected, the great bulk of the contracts (65 percent)

TABLE 2–1

Industrial Distribution of Contracts of United Steelworkers of America in Effect during 1963–1964, and Percent Providing for SUB

Industry group	Total contracts	Contracts providing for SUB	
		No.	% of total contracts
Mining			
Metal mining	59	21	35.6
Mining and quarrying of nonmetallic minerals, except fuels	20	3	15.0
Construction			
Building construction—general contractors	2	1	50.0
Construction—special trade contractors	5	0	0.0
Manufacturing			
Ordnance and accessories	6	1	16.7
Food and kindred products	17	0	0.0
Textile mill products	4	0	0.0
Apparel and other finished products made from fabrics, etc.	1	0	0.0
Lumber and wood products, except furniture	15	3	20.0
Furniture and fixtures	55	4	7.3
Paper and allied products	14	0	0.0
Printing, publishing, etc.	4	1	25.0
Chemical and allied products	55	9	16.2
Petroleum refining and related industries	5	0	0.0
Rubber and miscellaneous plastic products	17	0	0.0
Leather and leather products	3	0	0.0
Stone, clay, and glass products	106	13	12.3
Primary metal industries	570	208	36.5
Fabricated metal products, except ordnance, machinery, and transportation equipment	616	86	14.0
Machinery, except electrical	440	54	12.3
Electrical machinery, equipment, and supplies	60	6	10.0
Transportation equipment	88	18	20.5
Professional, scientific, and controlling instruments; photographic and optical goods	20	2	10.0
Miscellaneous manufacturing industries	37	2	5.4

TABLE 2-1 (*Continued*)

Industry group	Total contracts	Contracts providing for SUB	
		No.	% of total contracts
Transportation, Communications, and Utilities			
Railroad transportation	17	11	64.9
Motor freight transportation and warehousing	14	2	14.3
Water transportation	17	12	70.6
Transportation services	1	0	0.0
Electric, gas, and sanitary services	4	1	25.0
Wholesale and Retail Trade			
Wholesale trade	143	26	18.2
Retail trade—building materials, hardware, and farm equipment	4	0	0.0
Wholesale and Retail Trade (Cont.)			
Retail trade—general merchandise	4	1	25.0
Automotive dealers and gasoline service stations	1	0	0.0
Retail trade—furniture, home furnishings, and equipment	1	0	0.0
Retail trade—eating and drinking places	25	1	4.0
Finance, Insurance, and Real Estate			
Credit agencies other than banks	1	0	0.0
Service Industries			
Miscellaneous business services	10	1	10.0
Automobile repair, automobile services, and garages	9	0	0.0
Miscellaneous repair services	8	0	0.0
Amusement and recreation services, except motion pictures	1	0	0.0
Medical and other health services	3	0	0.0
Educational services	1	0	0.0
Total, all industries	2,483	487	19.6

SOURCE: Unpublished tabulations furnished by United Steelworkers of America.

were in three industrial groups: primary metals, fabricated metal products, and nonelectrical machinery. The incidence of SUB varied among these three from 36.5 percent in primary metals to 12.3 percent in nonelectrical machinery. Among all industries, incidence varied from 70.6 percent to zero. The wide variety of industries represented in the 487 SUB contracts shows that SUB is at least possible in many different situations.

About three quarters of the SUB plans in the Steelworkers' contracts had been negotiated in 1956. During the next three years, through 1959, new plans were added at the rate of about 30 per year. Thereafter, the average number of new plans per year declined to about half that number. In the meantime, a few SUB plans had been discontinued, most of them because a plant was closed or the company went out of business. But in at least one case the plan was discontinued because the local union and the firm, a metal fabricator, dropped SUB from the contract. According to the firm, it was dropped in 1961, after five years of operation, because "older workers, who had steady employment, discovered they were supporting those on the lower end of the seniority list" [18].

Brick and Clay Workers (UBCW). This union negotiated SUB plans with the major refractories in 1956 and 1957. Because the steel industry is the principal customer of the refractories, the latter tend to follow the pattern set in steel. As of 1965, about 4,500, or 18 percent, of the union's total membership of 24,000 were covered by SUB under agreements negotiated with 20 companies. The SUB plans of the refractories followed the provisions of the steel plans until 1961–1962, when, because of heavy unemployment at that time, most of the refractories refused to adopt the liberalized provisions negotiated by the Steelworkers with the steel companies.

Rubber Workers (URW). The United Rubber, Cork, Linoleum and Plastic Workers of America was among the unions actively engaged in the postwar campaign of the CIO for the guaranteed annual wage. The chief force back of the union's activity in this area was its vice-president, the late Joseph W. Childs, who persuaded the URW's 1954 convention to adopt as a prime objective the guaranteed employment plan of the Auto Workers. His most effective argument was that of the increased unemployment which the rubber industry began to experience after the Korean War ended.

In September of 1956, the URW succeeded in negotiating auto-type SUB plans with the Big Four basic rubber companies — Firestone, Goodrich, Goodyear, and United — and thereafter with some of the other rubber fabricators. By the end of 1965, according to information furnished to this writer by the union, 129 SUB agreements had been negotiated, distributed by year of negotiation as follows:

1956	66	1961	1
1957	29	1962	5
1958	2	1963	8
1959	0	1964	11
1960	3	1965	4

Because bargaining in the rubber industry is on a local basis, there is even less correspondence than usual between the number of agreements and the number of companies or the number of funds. The 129 agreements were with 37 companies and established about 50 funds, or plans.

As of December 1960, over 68 percent of the union's membership was covered by SUB, but the incidence of SUB varied widely by region, as is shown by Table 2–2. The high percentage of coverage in District 8, in the south, is explained by the prevalence of large plants and company-wide bargaining, just as the low percentages in Districts 2 and 7, in the east, are explained by the prevalence of small, independent firms. As of the end of 1965, 72 percent of the union's membership was covered by SUB; data on the incidence of the plans by region were not available for this later date.

Cement Workers (CLGW). The international union of United Cement, Lime, and Gypsum Workers was unable to secure a SUB plan for its members until 1959. Of the union's four constituent groups — one each in cement, lime, gypsum, and miscellaneous — the workers in cement are the most numerous, comprising two thirds of the total membership. As of the end of 1965, 98 percent of the cement workers were covered by SUB, but none of the other groups in the union had been able to negotiate a SUB plan on its own strength. The handful among the other groups who were covered by SUB were in the employ of steel companies and had come under the general umbrella of the steel SUB plan.

TABLE 2–2

Percent of Membership of United Rubber, Cork, Linoleum and Plastic Workers of America Covered by SUB Plans, December 1960, by District

District	Total members	Members covered by SUB plans			
		No.	Rank	% of total	Rank
Central (District 1)	70,395	53,518	1	76.0	2
Midwest (District 4)	27,633	20,734	2	75.0	3
New England (District 2)	26,316	15,347	3	58.3	6
East (District 7)	21,822	8,089	6	37.1	7
West (District 5)	16,123	11,342	4	70.3	5
South (District 8)	12,301	10,653	5	86.6	1
Canada (District 6)	11,120	7,943	7	71.4	4
Total, all districts	185,710	127,626		68.7	

SOURCE: Unpublished tabulation furnished to the writer by the union from its membership record.

NOTE: Originally there was a District 3, but it was eliminated some years ago and its territory taken over by District 1.

Bargaining in the cement industry is local in character but follows a general pattern so uniformly as to be equivalent to industry-wide bargaining. Usually the first contract is negotiated with the Ideal Cement Company and then extended to the other firms in the industry. By way of exception, opening negotiations in 1965 were held with a group of firms in California, and the resulting contract was then extended to Ideal and the other companies.

Although unemployment in the cement industry generally runs higher than in the steel and auto industries, in 1955 and 1956, when the Auto Workers and the Steelworkers were negotiating SUB plans, unemployment in cement was relatively low. The 1954 recession had not affected the industry severely, nor had excess capacity — the result of technological improvements — become a serious problem as yet. Modernization began to affect the industry in a marked way in 1956, and by 1957 layoffs connected with such changes had begun to be significant.

In 1957, and again in 1958, the union asked the cement companies for the individual-account type of unemployment-benefit plan. The union preferred this type of plan for its administrative simplicity and because it gave the individual employee maximum flexibility in determining the amount and duration of his own benefits. There was also widespread apprehension among the union members that a pooled SUB fund would be drained by those laid off early and that little would be left for the higher seniority employees. This fear was linked with the incorrect assumption that, since bargaining in the cement industry was by local units, a separate SUB fund would be established for each plant. The cement companies rejected the union's proposed plan on the ground that it was merely a form of forced savings and argued: "Cannot grown men do their own saving?"

By 1957, there was an increasing but not decisive interest on the part of the CLGW members in unemployment benefits. Severe unemployment was mostly confined to isolated areas and was not yet a widespread threat throughout the industry. By 1958, interest had increased, but not to the point of willingness to support a strike over the issue. By 1959, the interest of the members was intense, and they were ready to strike, if necessary, for some form of unemployment benefits.

In 1959, negotiations began, as usual, with the Ideal Cement Company. The union demanded an individual-account plan and the company countered with a proposal for SUB. This is the only instance encountered in the course of this study of a company's preferring SUB to the individual-account type of plan. According to Ideal, it saw SUB as inherently superior as a protective device. According to the union, the company expected SUB to be less expensive. Also, the company could not logically accept the individual-account plan after it had rejected such a plan repeatedly on the basis of principle.

The SUB plan negotiated in 1959 was generally similar to the auto plan but it also had many features of the steel plan. The choice of the basic auto plan was no doubt influenced by the fact that both the actuarial consultant retained by the company and the technical adviser of the union had formerly been connected with the UAW. After the pattern had been set in these negotiations between the union and Ideal Cement, the plan was adopted throughout the industry. Because many of the other companies and their local unions were not familiar with the technical details of the SUB contract they had negotiated, the plan had to be explained to them after they had adopted it.

Electrical Workers (IUE). The International Union of Electrical, Radio and Machine Workers is another of the CIO unions[4] which early showed interest in plans of guaranteed employment, but it has had only modest success in negotiating such plans. As of the end of 1965, the IUE had negotiated SUB plans of the auto-steel type for about 30,000 members, something more than 10 percent of its total membership. About 25,000 of these were General Motors employees, and the rest were employees of half a dozen other auto and steel companies. All of these companies had freely extended SUB to the IUE after negotiating the plan with either the UAW or the USWA.

In addition, the IUE had accepted a limited form of SUB called an Income Extension Plan, which covered employees of the General Electric Company (80,000), the Westinghouse Electric Corporation (40,000), and the Radio Corporation of America (25,000). These companies were opposed to SUB plans of the auto-steel type. The Income Extension Plan is of the individual-account type; under its provisions unemployed workers who have exhausted their state unemployment insurance benefits can draw supplemental benefits equal to 50 percent of wages as long as there is a balance in their individual accounts.

Because the industry is multi-product rather than homogeneous, with varying occupational and sex mixes, the union has not found it possible or desirable to follow a uniform pattern in negotiating SUB plans. Most of the smaller companies with which the union deals have not established SUB plans. Among the reasons given by the employers for rejecting SUB is the competitive pressure exerted by the numerous unorganized firms in the industry.

4. The members of the IUE are engaged principally in manufacturing, while the members of the IBEW, discussed below, work chiefly in construction and maintenance.

Multi-Employer Plans

Since practically all SUB plans work on the insurance principle of spreading risks and combining resources, to be able to provide security at reasonable cost, they need a large number of members. Also, since SUB is a complex program with relatively high overhead costs, a large membership is desirable in order to lower the per capita cost of administration.[5] The smallness of a firm generally constitutes a serious obstacle to the establishment of a SUB plan.

A way around this obstacle has been found in the multi-employer plan. In such a plan a union negotiates an identical agreement with a number of employers. Under this agreement, each employer contributes a uniform percentage of payroll or a uniform number of cents per man-hour to a common fund, out of which benefits are paid to eligible employees of all the contracting employers. The fund is usually managed by a board of trustees, with a full-time administrator.

Garment Workers (ILGWU). The largest of these multi-employer plans has been negotiated by the International Ladies' Garment Workers Union.[6] As of 1965, the plan covered about 430,000 employees in over 10,000 firms. The plan grew out of an unemployment problem peculiar to the industry. The ladies' garment industry is characterized by a high mortality rate among firms. An average of 17 percent go out of business each year. Some are unprofitable; among the profitable firms some go out of business for a year or two, only to reopen under another name; in the case of others that are family-owned, the son does not want to continue to carry on the enterprise, so he sells the machinery and closes down the business. In his presidential report to the union membership in 1950, David Dubinsky stressed the need for severance pay as a way of preventing firms from running away from their obligations to the unemployed.

In 1956, Local 105 negotiated a severance-pay plan, and two years later a general strike by the dressmakers won an agreement from most firms to contribute to a central fund for such benefits. As in most multi-employer plans, the agreement gave the trustees of the fund authority to determine the benefit structure. In 1960, the trustees announced that thereafter the fund would pay two kinds of benefits, both restricted to situations where the employing firm had gone out of business. The plan would pay a rela-

5. In the auto-type plan as first negotiated by the Ford Motor Company, procedures were developed that kept administrative costs to a minimum; hence the differential cost between plans with many and those with few members was also minimized.
6. This union has a long history of employment guarantees. In 1921, it negotiated an annual wage guarantee with the garment manufacturers of Cleveland, Ohio [19].

tively small severance payment (the maximum was $400 for 16 years of work with one employer) and, in addition, a potentially larger supplemental unemployment benefit.

There were several reasons for the decision to use most of the money for SUB rather than for severance payments. (1) Some state UI laws considered severance payments to be wages and deducted them from the UI benefits otherwise due the employee, whereas most states had decided by this time that SUB was not wages and was not to be deducted from UI benefits. (2) At the time, there was some uncertainty about the tax status of a group-owned fund established to pay severance benefits, while SUB funds had already received a favorable ruling from the Bureau of Internal Revenue. (3) Finally, and principally, too much of the money contributed to the fund had been going to employees who had experienced no unemployment because they went immediately to another job, and a fund of a given size would go further if it paid benefits only to those actually unemployed. For these reasons, the original severance-pay plan was changed into a predominantly SUB plan. A severance payment was retained in the plan to satisfy the complaints of those who feared they would otherwise get nothing from the fund. Every eligible separated employee receives a severance payment; in addition, the employee who remains unemployed receives SUB. The only employment which counts toward either benefit is continuous employment with the terminating employer; this requirement can be a serious limitation.

The fund is maintained by employer contributions of 0.5 percent of covered payrolls. For administrative simplicity, the plan pays flat benefits. It sets up six wage classes and pays to each class a flat benefit equal to about 25 percent of the average wage in that class. (Some long-term unemployed may receive a somewhat higher weekly benefit.) Duration of benefits is variable. The employee is credited with (only) three weeks of benefits for each year he was employed with the terminated employer up to a maximum of 48 weeks. The plan is a true SUB plan because its eligibility conditions are directly related to the unemployment insurance program. To receive these private benefits, an employee must be eligible for the state unemployment insurance benefit and, barring a special contrary decision by the trustees, must accept employment deemed suitable under the state system.

Why is the plan limited to unemployment resulting from the closing of firms? There are probably several reasons. (1) The plan started as a severance-pay plan to meet the specific problem caused by firms going out of business. (2) There is a great deal of seasonal unemployment in the industry, and a full SUB plan would be very expensive (under SUB plans, benefit costs are not shared by other industries as they are in unemployment insurance, but have to be borne entirely by the contracting employers). (3) The policing of unemployment benefits in a full SUB plan would be difficult in an industry characterized by a multitude of small firms and a preponderance of female employees. Since the contribution rate is uniform — that is, there is no individual experience rating at work — employers would have little financial incentive to assist in the policing task.

Maritime Workers (NMU). One of the earliest of the multi-employer plans was negotiated by the National Maritime Union of America (NMU) in June of 1955, shortly after the conclusion of the Ford-UAW negotiations. At that time, the NMU was keenly aware of the problem of unemployment among its members. From 1951 to 1955, the number of seafaring jobs[7] had declined from 93,000 to 56,000, a drop of 40 percent. The union expected unemployment to be a continuing problem as ships under the American flag stepped up the pace of automation to meet foreign competition, and as competition from aircraft grew.[8] A demand for some form of private unemployment benefits was at the top of the union's list in the 1955 negotiations.

After a short strike over this issue, the union negotiated an "Employment Security Plan" which required all employers to contribute 25 cents per man-day worked. These contributions would go into a central fund out of which unemployment benefits would be paid according to conditions determined by the fund trustees. President Joseph Curran announced to the union's membership: "No other employment security plan signed by any union anywhere is industry-wide like ours. It is this feature which makes our Plan outstanding" [21].

As of the end of 1965, the fund was paying a weekly benefit of $25 to applicants who were entitled to state unemployment insurance benefits and $40 to those who were not. Duration was limited to eight weeks. Eligibility was limited to seamen who were "entitled to permanent employment," that is, who had a right to a particular job. This right is established by agreement between the union and a particular employer. The right may be gained on a first voyage. On the other hand, a seaman may ship out on a number of voyages over a period of a year or more and not gain this

7. Jobs aboard oceangoing merchant ships of 1,000 tons or more registered under the United States flag.
8. In November 1960, the National Maritime Union protested to the United States Government against the discontinuance of the use of ships for transporting military personnel and dependents. The government replied regretfully that travel by air was only one third as costly as travel by water [20].

right if in each case he ships out as a relief man. (Two significant changes were made in this plan in 1967. The weekly benefit was changed to a flat rate of $28.50 for everyone. Also, all connection with UI was eliminated. The chief object of both changes was simplification of administration with a consequent saving in costs.)

Electrical Workers (IBEW). In the construction industry, where SUB plans might be thought particularly difficult to administer because of the frequent changes of employer, plans nevertheless have been negotiated by at least three unions. The earliest plan was established in New York City by the International Brotherhood of Electrical Workers. In 1954, Local 3 of the IBEW negotiated an individual-account plan with the electrical contracting industry of New York City. The plan covered about 8,000 of the local's 30,000 members. According to the original provisions of the plan, which have never been changed, each employer pays into a trust fund the sum of $4 for each day worked by an employee. The fund is used to supplement the public benefits provided by three New York State programs — Unemployment Insurance, Disability Insurance, and Workmen's Compensation. Although the plan was of the individual-account type, and any benefits a union member received came from his own money, the plan specified that an applicant had to be eligible for UI benefits. "After January 1, 1955, in the event any Participant becomes unemployed...such Participant shall receive $25.00 each week for the period that such Participant receives a full week's payment under the New York State Unemployment Insurance law."

The circumstances that led to the negotiation of this early plan are not entirely clear, but according to Maurice F. Neufeld the union was principally motivated by the tax advantage they thought they saw in the plan [22]. Whatever the reasons for its negotiation at this time, this early plan probably was influential in the history of SUB. Coming at a time when talk of the guaranteed annual wage filled the air and when unions were faced with a choice among various roads leading in the direction of this goal, Local 3's selection of the individual-account scheme probably influenced other unions, such as the Glass Workers, to make the same choice.

Much later, another IBEW local, with a membership of about 4,000, selected a different method. In 1962, Local 58 in Detroit negotiated a pooled-fund plan with the Southeastern Michigan Chapter of the National Electrical Contractors' Association. From 1955 to 1962, the electrical industry in the Detroit area had never operated at the level of full employment. Even at seasonal peaks there had been some unemployment. In 1962, the union took a dispute with the association to arbitration, and the arbitrator awarded the union a wage increase of 25 cents per hour. The union then secured agreement from the association to allocate 15 cents of this amount to the establishment of a SUB plan. With little or no dissension, the union members accepted the recommendation of their leaders that the plan be of the pooled rather than of the individual-account type.

The plan pays a flat unemployment benefit of $30 weekly for variable periods up to 26 weeks. It has just enough connection with the state unemployment insurance program to qualify as a SUB plan. The plan specifies: "In the absence of any contradictory evidence, the Trustees may accept as prima facie, but not conclusive, evidence of a layoff the fact that the employee is entitled to receive weekly unemployment benefits from the Michigan Employment Security Commission." And the booklet prepared for the membership explains: "The Trustees will be relying heavily on the fact that you are entitled to state unemployment benefits." Nevertheless, the trustees may, if they wish, dispense with the requirement that the applicant for SUB be eligible for unemployment insurance.

The Detroit plan explicitly provided that a member could refuse one job offer without penalty: "During any period of unemployment, an Employee may refuse one job opportunity without losing his status of being unemployed but available for work; however, should an Employee refuse more than one job opportunity during a particular period of unemployment, he shall lose his status of being unemployed but available for work and shall also lose his right to receive any further benefits under the Plan for the duration of that particular period of unemployment." The plan excludes from benefits any employee who is receiving a pension, private or governmental, even though he may be registered with the union as available for work [23].

Unemployment disappeared at about the time that the plan was ready to make payments, and during the next two years, 1964 through 1965, no benefits were paid. One union official opined in mid-1966: "If the membership had to vote now on whether to have a SUB plan, the proposal would not have the chance of a snowball in Hades."

Plumbers and Pipefitters (PPF). An early multi-employer SUB plan was established in New York City by Local 2 of the United Association of Journeymen and Apprentices of the Plumbing and Pipefitting Industry. In 1956, when unemployment among the local's members was very high, the plumbers' Local 2 (New York City), with about 3,800 members, negotiated an Additional Security Benefit Fund (ASBF) with two associations of contractors along with some independent contractors. The plan was of the individual-account type, so that whatever benefits the union member received came from his own money. Nevertheless, in order to be eligible for these supplemental unemployment benefits, the member had to be eligible also for state UI benefits. This eligibility requirement was intended to limit the use of the fund to genuine unemployment. To escape the difficult administrative task of defining genuine unemployment, the union simply adopted the state's definition and in effect made use of the state's administrative machinery. Actually, the state's administrative control over UI benefits going to these workers was minimal. Normally only union jobs carrying the union rate of pay would be considered suitable work for these union members by the UI agency; but the state employment service had very little contact with these jobs. As in most of the construction industry, practically all such jobs were controlled by the union itself.

Following the lead of Local 2, other plumbers' locals in the New York area have negotiated similar plans. They include local unions 1, 371, 457, and 775. The pipefitters' Local 638 (New York City) negotiated a very similar plan with the Mechanical Contractors Association in 1960.

In 1962 the Detroit plumbers (Local 98) and in 1963 the pipefitters (Local 636) followed the example of their New York brethren, but with a significant difference. The Detroit unions negotiated pooled-fund plans. Both unions, but especially the plumbers, had experienced heavy unemployment in the years 1959–1961, and all members felt unemployment as a personal threat at the time of the 1962–1963 negotiations. The choice of the pooled fund was made under the strong leadership of the unions' officers and met with little opposition.

As of 1965, the plan of the plumbers' Local 98 covered about 2,500 members and paid uniform weekly benefits of $35 for 26 weeks. The plan of the pipefitters' Local 636 covered about 1,700 members and paid uniform weekly benefits of $25 for 52 weeks. Each plan was negotiated with two groups of employers, the Detroit Association of Plumbing Contractors and the Mechanical Contractors' Association of Detroit. The employer contribution of 10 cents per man-hour goes into a common fund out of which are paid three types of supplemental benefits: occupational injury, nonoccupational illness, and unemployment.

Although these plans require that, in general, the applicant be eligible for state unemployment insurance benefits, they provide for a possible exception. The agreements stipulate: "In the event that an employee is denied a State benefit on the ground that he had refused suitable employment or has voluntarily left his employment, the Trustees shall have the power to authorize the payment of benefits notwithstanding a disqualification for State benefits, after submission by the employee of a petition to the Trustees and consideration of the petition by the Trustees." This stipulation comes close to establishing the "independent joint board of administration" sought originally by the UAW when it negotiated with the auto companies in that same city seven years earlier.

In 1963, after a strike of 11 weeks' duration, the St. Louis pipefitters' Local 562 negotiated a contract which included an unemployment benefit plan. The members of the employers' association agreed to contribute 30 cents per man-hour to an unemployment-benefit fund. As of the end of 1965, however, the union membership had not reached agreement on the kind of plan — pooled or individual-account — to be established. The plumbers of St. Louis have not been interested in any kind of unemployment-benefit plan.

Carpenters (CJA). The United Brotherhood of Carpenters and Joiners of America (CJA) is a third union in the construction industry to establish a SUB plan (the other two are the PPF and the IBEW). The first Carpenters' plan seems to have been negotiated by Local 964 (New York City) in 1957. It is a pooled-fund type of plan paying, as of 1965, a flat weekly benefit of $25 for 26 weeks. To be eligible, an applicant must be entitled to state unemployment insurance benefits. The plan covers about 400 employees.

A larger SUB plan covering about 800 employers and 2500 employees was established in 1960 by the Carpenters of the Buffalo District, which comprises 13 locals and negotiates with the Construction Industry Employers Association. In type the plan is similar to that of the New York local described above. As of 1965, the plan paid a weekly benefit of $35 for the first 26 weeks and $50 for the next 26 weeks. Shortly after the Buffalo SUB plan became operative, the Carpenters of Niagara, New York, negotiated a similar plan.

The Construction Industry Employers Association has negotiated similar SUB plans with three other construction unions in the state of New York — the Bricklayers (BMP), the Laborers (HLC), and the Operating Engineers (IUOE). The plan of the Operating Engineers is small now but could easily develop into a statewide plan, since both the union and the contractors have statewide organizations and conduct some negotiations on a statewide basis.

Tool and Die Workers (UAW). Locals 155 and 157 in Detroit are composed of tool and die workers who negotiate with the Detroit Tooling Association. Although these locals belong to the UAW, they did not establish a SUB plan in 1955. At that time, these locals had experienced very little unemployment, and, although under the prodding of the international union they had made a *pro forma* demand for SUB, they were not seriously interested in it. After some indecisive bargaining, they eventually accepted a supplemental pension plan instead.

Beginning in the latter half of 1957 and continuing through 1961, the tool industry experienced extremely heavy unemployment. A number of factors contributed to the upward trend in unemployment, most of them connected with the auto industry. During 1955 and 1956, the auto companies were producing in highly concentrated patterns, and as a consequence were paying overtime wages. After 1956, the auto manufacturers took a number of steps to reduce this cost. They decentralized operations (some plants were moved out of Detroit), increased the size of their own tool rooms, and extended use of uniform tools that could be utilized on a number of different car models. Moreover, at this time the level of automobile production was low. Technological change, according to the Detroit Tooling Association, has not been an important cause of unemployment.

In the 1961 negotiations, the two locals were serious in their demand for SUB, and they succeeded in negotiating a pooled-fund plan over relatively light employer opposition. Because 1961 was a recession year, the start of employer contributions was delayed until October 1963; benefits became payable a year later. As of 1965, the plan paid a flat weekly benefit of $25 for a maximum of 26 weeks. To be eligible for SUB the applicant must be eligible for unemployment insurance.

Retail Clerks (RCIA). In 1959, Local 770 (Los Angeles) of the Retail Clerks International Association went on strike against the Food Employers Council. One of the issues in dispute was the union's demand for a SUB fund. The employers were opposed to the demand, not on principle, but simply because the demand added to the overall cost of the package. They argued that since unemployment was not a pressing problem in their industry the available money could be better used in other forms. The union, however, was insistent: protection against unemployment was part of its grand design of total security for all its members.[9] In the end, a SUB plan of the pooled type was established. As of 1965, the plan covered approximately 41,000 employees of 1,300 employers in southern California and paid a weekly benefit which with unemployment insurance equals 65 percent of wages. (This percentage is applied to the average straight-time earnings of *classes* of employees, and there is no maximum limit other than that established by the average earnings of the class; the arrangement is

9. Local 770 has come close to this goal. In recent years it has added dental care and psychiatric care to an already long list of benefits available to union members.

thus essentially that used in the early plans of the Continental Can Company to be discussed in Chapter 5.) The supplemental benefit is payable for as long as the applicant receives an unemployment insurance benefit. The plan is financed by the very low employer contribution of 2 cents per man-hour, out of which is paid, not only supplemental unemployment benefits, but also supplemental disability and supplemental workmen's compensation. (The last two types of benefits are paid at a higher rate than are unemployment benefits, 80 percent instead of 65 percent of wages.)

Brewery Workers (BFCSD). In 1960, a SUB plan was negotiated by some New Orleans locals of the International Union of Brewery, Flour, Cereal, Soft Drink and Distillery Workers of America (BFCSD). At that time there were four breweries in New Orleans. Two, Falstaff and Jax, were large; the other two, Riegel and Dixie, were small. The unions in the small breweries were not interested in SUB. Their wages were somewhat lower, so that there was less latitude for the negotiation of fringe benefits; also they experienced less unemployment — probably because their companies were less automated and could exercise greater flexibility in the use of manpower — and hence felt less need for unemployment benefits.

In each of the large breweries there were four local unions: the bottlers (Local 161), the brewers (Local 158), the engineers (Local 178), and the drivers (Local 215). The bottlers' local was the largest, having about 700 members out of the total workforce of 1,100, and was also the most exposed to unemployment.

In the negotiations of 1960, Local 161 wanted the union to demand some kind of unemployment-benefit plan, but the other three locals, which had experienced relatively little unemployment, were reluctant to sacrifice a wage gain for this fringe benefit. When the bottlers insisted, a compromise was reached whereby the employers contributed to two separate funds — a pooled fund for the bottlers and an individual-account fund for the other three locals. The employers contributed 5 cents per man-hour to each fund, and each fund paid a flat weekly benefit of $20 ($25 from 1963 on). The pooled (SUB) fund paid benefits for a maximum of 16 weeks, which was the maximum duration of the Louisiana UI program at that time. The individual-account plan paid benefits until an employee's account was exhausted.

In the years that immediately followed the establishment of the SUB plan, employment in the industry improved to the point where most of the bottlers were getting nothing from the SUB fund, while their counterparts in the other three locals were building up substantial individual bank accounts. In 1964, to satisfy the growing discontent in Local 161, another compromise was effected. The SUB fund of the bottlers was divided into two funds — one of the pooled type, the other of the individual-account type — and the employers' nickel was divided between the two. The vested fund received 4 cents and the pooled fund only 1 cent. (This change was equivalent to the negotiation, at about this time, of the "hard nickel" in the auto SUB plans, as described in Chapter 6.)

There are a few additional multi-employer plans, such as that of the photoengravers of New York City,[10] which operate very much like some of the SUB plans — for example, like those of the plumbers and pipefitters of New York—but they are not included in this review because they do not have a direct relationship to the public unemployment insurance program. There may also be a few true multi-employer SUB plans which have been missed by the present search.

General View of SUB Growth

It is not possible from data readily available to present a complete record of the chronological growth in the number of SUB plans.[11] Since 1959, data on private unemployment-benefit plans have been accumulating in the files of the Department of Labor under the reporting requirements of the Welfare and Pension Disclosure Act, but it would require a major research effort to identify in these data each new SUB plan and the year in which it was negotiated. Of more immediate use is a series, *Current Wage Developments*, in which the Bureau of Labor Statistics has kept track of most negotiations affecting SUB plans.

For the purposes of this study, the series has many limitations: it includes plans that do not conform to the definition of SUB used here; it excludes settlements affecting smaller firms (under 1,000 employees); it excludes settlements in which benefits were increased without corresponding

10. An unemployed union member covered by the New York Commercial Photoengravers' Unemployment Fund may receive three unemployment benefits: an unemployment insurance benefit from the state and two benefits from the union. The union had its own unemployment-benefit fund, supported by a tax on its membership, before there was a public program. Then, in 1957, the union negotiated an additional fund—for the commercial photoengravers only—which is supported by employer contributions. As of 1965, an unemployed commercial photoengraver could draw as much as $55 from the state fund, $37 from the union fund, and $20 from the employer SUB fund. Since the average wage of the union members was about $195, the average unemployed member could count on an unemployment benefit equal to about 57 percent of his wage.

11. Of the unions, only the Rubber Workers were able to supply such a record for the SUB plans covering their own members.

increases in employer contributions; it excludes all settlements in which wages were not at issue, even though supplementary benefits may have been affected; it does not reflect the new groups of workers brought into previously existing plans by acquisition of one firm by another; and finally, for the years 1955 through 1960, settlements are not distinguished according to whether they established a new SUB plan or modified a pre-existing plan, nor is there any information on the number of employees affected. Hence these data, shown in Table 2–3, can be used to gain only a general impression of the growth of SUB.

For the first three years, almost all the settlements shown in the table represent the establishment of new SUB plans; during the next three years, an unknown number of the settlements represent modifications of previ-

TABLE 2–3a

Number of Contract Settlements Affecting SUB Plans,[a] in Manufacturing
and Nonmanufacturing, by Year, 1955–1960[b]

Year	Number of settlements in		
	Total	Manufacturing industries	Nonmanufacturing industries
1955	9	8	1
1956	96	n.a.	n.a.
1957	9	8	1
1958	5	5	0
1959	25	20	5
1960	5	5	0

TABLE 2–3b

Number of Contract Settlements in Which SUB Plans[a] Were Established or
Modified, and Number of Workers Affected, by Year, 1961–1965

Year	SUB plans established		SUB plans modified	
	No. of settlements	No. of workers affected	No. of settlements	No. of workers affected
1961	7	29,000	57	734,000
1962	9	27,600	108	670,000
1963	2	3,400	24	137,000
1964	8	19,000	42	730,000
1965	—[c]	45,000	—[c]	215,000

Source: U.S., Department of Labor, Bureau of Labor Statistics Annual Supplements to Current Wage Developments, with additional unpublished data furnished by the Bureau of Labor Statistics.

[a] See text for limitations affecting these data.

[b] For these years the available data do not distinguish between settlements that established SUB plans and those that modified previously existing plans.

[c] The total number of settlements in 1965 is estimated at 63, but the data for that year do not indicate how many of them established a new SUB plan and how many modified a previously existing plan.

ously existing plans; after 1960, the data show clearly that most settlements represent modifications of old plans rather than the establishment of new ones.

It would be a mistake to conclude that, because there were 96 settlements in 1956 and only 9 in 1955, 1956 was ten times as important for SUB. If the settlements were weighted by the number of employees affected, the year 1955 — in which SUB plans were established in the very large firms of the auto, can, and agricultural implement industries — would be seen to be about the equal of 1956.

The large number of settlements in 1959 mostly effected modifications and reflect the three-year cycle of the original SUB contracts negotiated in 1956. This same wave is perceptible in 1962 and 1965. In the same way, the wave set up in 1955 is still visible in the data of 1961 and 1964, and less so in 1958. Included in Table 2–3 are the multi-employer plans established in 1959 (RCIA), 1960 (ILGW, CJA, BFCSD), 1961 (UAW), and 1962 (PPF, IBEW).

As far as this writer knows, California is the only state which has recorded the growth in union agreements containing SUB provisions [24]. The available data are shown in the tabulation below, which reflects the situation in California as it existed on each of the indicated dates. Although the data contain some plans which do not meet the definition of SUB as used in this study, they probably reflect the general trend in SUB plans fairly accurately.

California: Union Agreements Providing SUB

Date	All agreements		Agreements providing SUB		
	No.	Workers covered	No.	Workers covered	
				No.	% of all workers
June 1956	1,331	1,268,600	12	28,000	2.2
June 1957	1,447	1,335,100	28	56,850	4.3
December 1959	1,420	1,352,560	47	79,170	5.9
June 1963	1,545	1,389,270	81	105,670	7.6

Between 1956 and 1963, SUB agreements increased from 12 to 81 and the number of covered workers from 28,000 to 105,670. That this represents relative as well as absolute growth is shown in column 5. The proportion of all workers covered by SUB more than tripled, increasing from 2.2 percent to 7.6 percent. Even more significant, this growth continued through the entire period. The rate of growth of SUB in California is undoubtedly much greater than the rate in the country as a whole.

The historian of SUB, standing in 1965 and looking back over a decade of development, might find the following categories useful in his attempt to visualize the main lines of growth. (1) The plans negotiated by the Auto Workers and the Steelworkers in 1955 and 1956 with the auto companies and the basic steel companies, respectively. (2) The plans negotiated by these same unions with the agricultural implement companies, on the one hand, and with the can and aluminum companies on the other. (3) The plans negotiated by these same unions with the makers of auto parts and with other fabricators of metal products. (4) The plans negotiated by the Brick and Clay Workers with the refractories; the plans negotiated by the Rubber Workers with the Big Four rubber companies and with the numerous other fabricators of rubber products; and the plans negotiated by the Cement Workers with the companies in their industry. (5) The plans offered to a variety of unions (for example, IAM, IBEW, IUE, OCAW) by companies which had already negotiated SUB plans with the major union in the industry — for example, in the auto, steel, rubber, and cement industries. (6) The multi-employer plans. (7) A miscellaneous collection of plans, mostly small, that do not fit exactly into any of the other categories, including a few plans recently established in the railroad and aerospace industries.

The historian might also find useful a summary view of all the possible union-company relations which can mark the birth of SUB plans. Most SUB plans involve a single company and a single fund. But there are seven other possible combinations of singular or plural unions, companies, and funds. SUB plans have been generated in all eight ways. The following is a list of the possible combinations with an example of each.

Union	Company	Fund	Example
One	One	One	UAW with Ford
One	Many	Many	UAW with Ford, General Motors, et al.
One	One	Many	USWA (two locals) with International Harvester
One	Many	One	ILGWU with garment companies
Many	Many	One	ILGWU and Teamsters with four companies
Many	One	One	IUOE, Teamsters, and HCL with Hudson Cement Corp.
Many	One	Many	Eight different unions with Allis-Chalmers
Many	Many	Many	All plans combined

Present Extent of SUB Plans

The most detailed tabulation of SUB plans is contained in a report published by the Bureau of Labor Statistics in 1965 [25]. This report was based on an analysis of 1,773 collective bargaining agreements, each covering one thousand workers or more — exclusive of government, railroad, and airline agreements — which were in effect during 1962–1963. The report does not cover the numerous small SUB plans, but does include practically all the large ones. It does not attempt to chronicle changes in the provisions of the plans, but is a picture taken at one point in time.

According to the report, of the 1,773 agreements analyzed, 247 (14 percent) contained SUB provisions. Of the agreements providing for SUB 95 percent were in manufacturing industries, chiefly in the durable-goods sector and within that sector chiefly in primary and fabricated metals, transportation equipment, and nonelectrical machinery. In the nondurable-goods manufacturing sector, SUB was most prevalent in the apparel and rubber industries.

Table 2–4, which is derived from the report, shows the industrial distribu-

TABLE 2–4

Industrial Distribution of Workers Covered under Major Collective Bargaining Agreements Containing SUB Plans as Percent of All Workers Covered under Major Agreements, 1962–1963[a]

| Industry division or group | Workers covered by agreements providing for SUB[b] | | |
	Total	% distribution	% covered in industry
Manufacturing	(000's)		
Transportation equipment	593.6	31.9	60.9
Primary metal industries	553.7	29.7	92.4
Apparel and other finished textile products	249.1	13.4	58.2
Machinery, except electrical	144.4	7.7	55.0
Rubber and miscellaneous plastic products	94.3	5.1	84.9
Fabricated metal industries	77.1	4.1	54.5
Stone, clay, and glass products	22.6	1.2	19.8
Textile mill products	18.9	1.0	23.7
Electric machinery, equipment, and supplies	13.1	0.7	3.3
Instruments and related products	2.1	0.1	4.6
Printing, publishing, and allied industries	2.0	0.1	2.7
Miscellaneous manufacturing industries	1.5	0.1	8.5
Food and kindred products	1.2	0.1	0.3
Furniture and fixtures	1.1	0.1	4.2
Chemicals and allied products	1.0	0.1	0.9
Nonmanufacturing			
Retail trade	43.6	2.3	14.3
Transportation	30.0	1.6	4.4
Mining, crude petroleum and natural gas production	7.9	0.4	1.2
Construction	6.3	0.3	0.7
Total, all industries	1,863.5	100.0	25.0

SOURCE: [25, p. 78].

[a] The major agreements analyzed each covered 1,000 or more workers. They represented almost all agreements of this size in the United States, exclusive of government, railroad, and airline agreements.

[b] Figures represent the number of workers covered by the basic collective bargaining agreements and not necessarily those covered by the SUB plan.

tion of SUB agreements according to the number of covered employees. In these large plans, 75 percent of all employees covered by SUB were in the three industries of transportation equipment, primary metals, and apparel. Another 17 percent were in machinery, rubber, and fabricated metals. The remaining 8 percent were scattered among thirteen industries.

Of the 7.4 million employees represented in the 1,773 contracts analyzed, 1.9 million (25 percent) were covered by SUB plans. By industry, this percentage varied from 92.4 percent in primary metals, where large firms predominate, to less than 1 percent in the food, chemical, and construction industries. There were also many industries represented in the 1,773 contracts which had no SUB plans in effect at all.

The 247 agreements which contained SUB provisions established 174 "plans," that is, 174 separate funds. There can be fewer plans than agreements because the signatories to separate agreements may contribute to a single fund, as happens in all multi-employer plans. Of the 174 plans analyzed in the report, 167 were single-employer plans and 7 were multi-employer plans. Of the 1.9 million employees covered by the 174 plans, only 34,300, or 2 percent, were in individual-account plans; the other 98 percent were in plans with pooled funds. The 174 plans were distributed by union as follows:[12]

Aluminum Workers (AWU)	2
Auto Workers (UAW)	58
Carpenters (CJA)	1
Cement Workers (CLGW)	1
Chemical Workers (ICW)	1
Glass Workers (UGCW)	3
Garment Workers (ILGW)	1
Electrical Workers (IUE)	2
Machinists (IAM)	3
Maritime Workers (NMU)	1
Meatcutters (MCBW)	1
Oil Workers (OCAW)	1
Photoengravers (LPIU)	1
Plumbers (PPF)	1
Retail Clerks (RCIA)	2
Rubber Workers (URW)	10
Seafarers (SIU)	1
Steelworkers (USWA)	74
Independent and company unions	10
Total	174

12. This tabulation was derived from unpublished data furnished to the author by the Bureau of Labor Statistics. The plans of the Glass Workers, the Photoengravers, and those of a few of the independent unions are not SUB plans as defined in the present study.

A measure of the importance of SUB to a union is the proportion of union membership covered by SUB plans. According to the best estimates from available data, supplied by the unions most active in the SUB field, the following proportions were covered as of 1965:

Union	Percent of total membership
Auto Workers (UAW)	86
Brick and Clay Workers (UBCW)	18
Cement Workers (CLGW)	66
Electrical Workers (IUE)	10 full SUB, plus 38 limited SUB
Garment Workers (ILGWU)	95 limited SUB
Machinists (IAM)	8
Rubber Workers (URW)	72
Retail Clerks (RCIA)	7
Steelworkers (USWA)	85

Table 2–5, which shows the distribution by union of employees covered by SUB plans, is perhaps the best single picture of what the baby born in 1955 has become. Taken together with the text table above, which shows the proportion of union members covered by SUB plans, it is also the best indicator of possible future trends. Understandably, the unions have been the dynamic factor in the past growth of SUB. The firm may be the mother of SUB, but the union is its father. Depending on how the unions rate SUB as an objective in their scale of values, the future growth of SUB will be fast, slow, or nonexistent. The possible future growth of SUB as seen in the light of Table 2–5 is discussed in Part IV.

TABLE 2–5a

Estimated Coverage of SUB Plans Negotiated by Unions with 2,000 or More Members under SUB Plans, as of 1965

Union	Estimated no. of members covered
Auto Workers (UAW)	908,000
Steelworkers (USWA)	747,000
Garment Workers (ILGWU)	438,000
Electrical Workers (IUE)	171,000[a]
Rubber Workers (URW)	121,000
Machinists (IAM)	73,000
Maritime Workers (NMU)	33,000
Aluminum Workers (AWU)	24,000
Retail Clerks (RCIA)	22,000
Cement Workers (CLGW)	21,000
Operating Engineers (IUOE)	10,000
Plumbers and Pipefitters (PPF)	10,000
Allied Industrial Workers (AIW)	6,900
Brick and Clay Workers (UBCW)	4,400
Progressive Steelworkers	4,400
Electrical Workers (IBEW)	12,000
Carpenters (CJA)	3,000
Office Employees (OEIU)	2,000
Photoengravers (IPEU)	2,000
Total	2,612,700

TABLE 2–5b

Unions with SUB Plans Covering Fewer Than 2,000 Members or Covering
Unknown Number of Members, as of 1965

Armco Independent Union
Boilermakers, Iron Shipbuilders, Blacksmiths, Forgers and Helpers, International
  Brotherhood of
Bookbinders, International Brotherhood of
Brewery, Flour, Cereal, Soft Drink and Distillery Workers of America
Bricklayers, Masons and Plasterers International Union of America
Chemical Workers Union, International
Die Sinkers' Conference, International
Coopers' International Union of North America
Distillery, Rectifying, Wine and Allied Workers' International Union of America
Engineers, American Federation of Technical
Federal Labor Union
Federated Aluminum Council
Firemen and Oilers, International Brotherhood of
Hatters, Cap and Millinery Workers, International Union of
Hod Carriers, Building and Common Laborers' Union, International
Longshoremen's and Warehousemen's Union, International
Meatcutters and Butcher Workmen of North America, Amalgamated
Mine, Mill and Smelter Workers, International Union of
Molders and Foundry Workers Union of North America, International
Oil, Chemical and Atomic Workers International Union
Packinghouse Workers, National Brotherhood of
Papermakers and Paperworkers, United
Pattern Makers League of North America
Plant Guard Workers of America, United
Printing Pressmen and Assistants' Union of North America
Stone and Allied Products Workers of America, United
Teamsters, Chauffeurs, Warehousemen and Helpers of America, International
  Brotherhood of
Textile Workers Union of America

SOURCE: Interviews and correspondence with unions, supplemented by various published materials.
  a Of these, 141,000 were covered under plans supplementing only the duration of UI
benefits.

3

THE CAUSES OF SUB

Why does SUB appear in some situations and why does it not appear in others? This is the twofold question to be answered in the present chapter. The answers are largely drawn from the details of the history just recounted and at the same time they complete that history, as roots are part of the complete tree. Knowledge of SUB's causes is essential to an understanding of its nature.

In the spring of 1955, when the auto-UAW negotiations were impending, Daniel Bell wrote: "Reuther, the one-time Socialist, is seeking to make the American worker genuinely a middle-class individual. And this is the historic import of the negotiations this spring" [26]. At about the same time, Chernick and Berkowitz were developing the proposition that a vigorous, democratic union movement creates a "market" for the novel, the striking. The union, in adjusting to this market, needs proposals with which to appeal to its membership and to the community at large. The guaranteed annual wage was such a proposal. Attractive in itself, it fitted the pattern of collective bargaining at its modern "stage of opulence" [27].

There is truth in these and similar generalizations on the nature of SUB, but they need to be complemented by a more detailed analysis of the specific roots of the phenomenon under study. At the outset of such analysis it must be emphasized that the roots of SUB are complex and interwoven. Although ten separate causal factors are distinguished here, the ten do not represent categories that are either necessary or entirely consistent; that is, it would be possible to use other categories, and the ones used here are to some extent overlapping.

It should also be pointed out that each factor has a twofold aspect, positive and negative. As the presence of a given factor helps to explain why SUB exists, so its absence is part of the explanation for the absence of SUB. Since SUB is comparatively rare, the negative aspect of the factors is obviously important. This fact needs to be kept in mind during the following analysis, which understandably stresses the positive causality of all the factors except the last. The last factor is entirely negative in its causality.

1. Unemployment: The Employee's View

In the order of importance, the causal factor to be discussed first is undoubtedly experience with unemployment. Only those workers who have been or who expect to be unemployed are seriously interested in programs of unemployment benefits. In the middle 1940's the CIO unions made the guaranteed annual wage their prime objective because they expected heavy unemployment during the reconversion period following the war. This was especially true of the unions whose members had been most in demand during the war, such as those in the steel, maritime, and transportation equipment industries.

In the 1950's, the resurgence of interest in GAW (later SUB) had a different source. In this period, there developed a widespread fear of technological change and its impact on jobs. This fear was fed by an unemployment rate that even during prosperous times remained relatively high. In the two years preceding the negotiation of SUB, several CIO unions held national meetings to study the threat of unemployment posed by "automation," and it was this threat that Walter Reuther used to win his skilled members to at least a passive support of SUB.

The relationship between SUB and unemployment is illustrated very clearly in the case of those employees of the auto companies who belong to the Pattern Makers of North America. In 1955, after negotiating SUB plans with the UAW, the auto companies offered the same kind of plan to the Pattern Makers, but these workers declined the offer on the ground that they rarely experienced unemployment. Later, in the early 1960's, they began to encounter some unemployment as the result of technological changes. Fearing that more of the same might be in store for them, they began to demand the benefits they had spurned before and succeeded in negotiating a number of SUB plans. (As of the end of 1966, a booming economy had so dried up unemployment in their occupation that some of them were again questioning the wisdom of having established SUB plans.)

In the same way, the tool and die workers of Detroit, who in 1955 had let pass the opportunity to establish a SUB plan, negotiated a multi-employer SUB plan in 1960. The reason for their change of attitude was a sharp increase in unemployment in their occupation.

When the Cement Workers finally achieved a SUB plan in 1959, the force behind their belated drive was their experience with the unemployment that accompanied the industry's modernization program. Likewise, in 1965, when the Cement Workers and the Rubber Workers negotiated unusually liberal amendments to their SUB plans (see Part II), they were motivated by the threat of unemployment accompanying technological change.

The American Can Company manufactures metal, paper, glass, and plastic containers, and negotiates with many different unions. There are no SUB programs outside the metal container industry, and relatively few plans have been negotiated with unions other than the Steelworkers.

According to the company, this situation is largely attributable to the steadier employment pattern in the production of other types of containers than in the metal container industry.

Within the metal container industry, the Machinists are somewhat less interested in SUB than are the Steelworkers because machinists are less exposed to unemployment. Even during the slow periods in the can industry there is work for machinists in servicing equipment. This accounts for the developments in 1965, when the Steelworkers negotiated a marked liberalization of the existing SUB plans while the Machinists decided to retain the old provisions of their SUB plan and to take their gains in the form of higher wages and a higher pension.

The following tabulation reflects the degree of interest in SUB manifested by the various unions with which American Can negotiates.

Employee group	No. of locations for which agreements have been negotiated	
	Total	No. providing for SUB
Steelworkers	44	44
Machinists	21	18
Lithographers and photoengravers	15	1
Teamsters	9	2
Electrical workers (IBEW)	7	1
Can workers	3	3
Office employees	2	2
Sheet metal workers	1	1

In the case of 12 other unions negotiating with this company, none of the agreements provided for SUB. (It will be realized that at a given location there may be more than one union involved, each of which negotiates for those members who work there.)

Although the Machinists as a group are not especially interested in SUB (the ratio indicated in the table above is not representative of the Machinists' contracts generally), a particular local union may rate SUB very high in its list of objectives. For example, in 1965, a Machinists' local in Scranton, Pennsylvania, negotiated a SUB plan plus a severance-pay plan with Capitol Records, in exchange for which the union gave up a wage increase during the first year of a five-year contract. The union was greatly influenced in its choice by the threat of unemployment. According to the union, demand for the product of this company fluctuated greatly from week to week, and employment fluctuated correspondingly. Further, the opening of a new automated factory in the midwest seemed to the union to threaten a very serious employment loss in the long run. A measure of the union's concern is the negotiation of a relatively high employer contribution to the employment security fund — 10 cents per hour worked.

The Hanna Mining Company has eight contracts with the Steelworkers, of which seven provide for a SUB plan. The principal reason for the single exception seems to be the unemployment pattern of the eighth plant. According to the company, "there has not been a single instance of a layoff during the ten years this operation has been in production." It will be recalled that the multi-employer SUB plan of the New Orleans Brewery Workers required three separate funds to satisfy all the workers in a union of less than 1,000 members. Different experience with unemployment was the reason for the three funds. Many other examples of how unemployment leads to a demand for SUB could be cited, but the foregoing suffices for the purpose of illustration.

While unemployment can stimulate a demand for unemployment benefits, it can also limit the benefits payable. For example, the SUB plan which the ILGWU negotiated in 1960 was limited to unemployment caused by the closing of a business, and the primary reason for the limitation was the very heavy seasonal unemployment characteristic of the ladies' garment industry. Foundries provide another example. Higher than average unemployment is one of the main reasons that Steelworkers in foundries, although they need SUB more than their brethren in the basic steel industry, frequently do not have a SUB plan at all; when they do have one, it usually contains less liberal provisions than those in basic steel. A foundry usually has a few main customers who have to be supplied with made-to-order products, and orders are irregular. As a result, employment in the individual foundry fluctuates considerably more than employment in the average basic steel plant. (Because the irregular fluctuations in individual plants tend to offset each other statistically, the real variations in employment are much obscured in the overall statistics for the industry.)

Unemployment is discussed so much that a misleading impression is easily created that the fear of unemployment is a constant, overriding concern of the average employee. Actually, substantial numbers of employees go through their working life without ever experiencing serious unemployment. Even when unemployment rises to 8 percent and public concern over the situation dominates the editorials, those who are still working constitute 92 percent of the labor force. Granted that twice or thrice 8 percent of the labor force will experience some unemployment in the course of the entire year, granted also that the threat of unemployment hangs over everyone in the labor force, yet for the average employee and his union the threat is not imminent enough to lead them to take out insurance against it. The unions are not much more inclined than other people to repair the roof while the sun is shining. It takes the threat of darkening rain clouds to galvanize negotiators into action.

Whatever the explanation, one fact is clear: the average employee ranks many other objectives higher than a program of unemployment benefits. Just as fear of unemployment is the main explanation of why SUB has appeared where it has, so the absence of that fear, felt as an immediate threat, is the main explanation of the lack of SUB in most labor contracts. The fact that the threat of unemployment at any one time and place is limited is probably the chief reason why SUB plans ten years after birth still cover less than 4 percent of the industrial workforce.

In August of 1955, the Opinion Research Corporation surveyed the employees of five mass-production industries which did not yet have a SUB plan. These were basic steel, rubber, electrical machinery, building materials, and petroleum refining. Employees in these industries were asked what improvements they would like most in their forthcoming labor agreements. Only 8 percent put "the guaranteed annual wage" in first place. Somewhat later, in the spring of 1956, Harold Stieglitz reported on the results of a poll of 51 union leaders [28]. He asked these men, who represented about seven million members, how they evaluated SUB as an objective. He found that few of them planned to seek SUB in their own industry and concluded that SUB did not attract the universal interest in 1956 that pensions had in 1949 and 1950.

Nearly ten years later, in 1965, a survey was conducted by this writer among 75 of the larger unions which were considered the most likely to be interested in SUB. This later survey found the picture unchanged. The great majority of the unions rated SUB low on their scale of values; many other objectives came before this one. The most usual reason given for SUB's low ranking was the absence of a serious threat of unemployment to the bulk of their membership. Typical is this response of the Office and Professional Employees Union (OEIU): "Our bargaining agreements do not contain provisions for SUB benefits because the overwhelming majority of our members are not in need of such protection. Layoffs in the office and professional field are usually quite short or else are permanent. Local negotiators say: 'It is hard enough to get what you need; so why bargain for something you don't?' " [29]. Many unions replied that it would be nice to have SUB, but that there were too many other things they wanted more.

The paper industry illustrates both the current lack of union interest in SUB and the possibility of a change in that attitude. During the SUB decade, the demand for paper products rose continuously, and the number of production workers in the pulp and paper industry increased from about 450,000 to almost 500,000. As a result, there was not much long-term unemployment. Neither was there any significant amount of seasonal unemployment: on a month-to-month basis, the employment pattern in the paper industry has not varied by much more than 5 percent throughout any year. Furthermore, general turnover rates in employment have tended to be less than in the average manufacturing industry. In the four-year period 1960–1963, when the monthly accession and separation rates for all manufacturing averaged about 4.0 percent each, the accession rate in the pulp and paper industry averaged 2.6 percent and the separation rate 2.8 percent. A factor contributing to this relative stability has been the location of many mills and primary plants in sparsely populated areas where the mill is the dominant industry and there is less opportunity for a change of employers.

Given the circumstances, it is not surprising that the Pulp, Sulphite and Paper Mill Workers (PSPMW) have shown relatively little interest in unemployment benefit plans. As of 1964, only about a quarter of the union's membership was covered by severance-pay plans and none was covered by a SUB plan. However, in 1964 the union reported that technological change in the industry was beginning to be felt in a serious way and that the interest of the union's membership in protection against the threat of unemployment was increasing. In the same year, the union published a 450-page study entitled *Automation: Its Impact upon Collective Bargaining*, which included a detailed explanation of the auto-type SUB plan.

There are entire industries in which unemployment is relatively rare for most firms and SUB is consequently ruled out as a serious possibility. No further explanation need be sought for the absence of SUB in these situations. Factors 3 through 10 are therefore relevant chiefly — though not only — to firms in which unemployment is felt as a significant threat. Why do some of these firms have SUB, while others do not?

2. Unemployment: The Employer's View

To account for the birth of SUB plans, it is not enough to explain why employees demand such plans; it is also necessary to explain why employers grant the demand. In addition to the general reasons why an employer grants any demand of his employees, he has three reasons that are specific to SUB. Throughout the industrial era, employees have resisted changes in technology or organization that threaten their jobs. Such resistance is still a factor to be reckoned with, for although in the abstract there may be a recognition of the desirability of change, in the concrete those adversely affected by the proposed change understandably object. A program like SUB helps to lessen worker resistance to such changes.

It was this consideration which motivated the Alan Wood Steel Company to agree, in 1965, to a dramatic liberalization of its SUB plan (originally negotiated in 1956). Although unemployment was less of a problem for this company than for the average steel firm (Alan Wood is one of the very few steel companies which has never had to reduce SUB payments because of drains on the SUB fund), its profits had fallen off, and it had reached the conclusion that, in order to survive, it would have to modernize.

However, as soon as it embarked on an ambitious program of modernization, it encountered serious employee resistance. For example, performance on a new 110-inch plate mill proved to be so poor that the innovation represented a loss rather than a gain. There seemed to be two reasons for the poor performance on the part of the employees. (1) They were afraid of working themselves out of a job. (2) They were playing the usual cat-and-mouse game that precedes the setting of an incentive standard for a new job — the lower the standard, the higher the incentive earnings that may be earned later.

To enlist fuller cooperation of its workforce, the company had first proposed a profit-sharing plan and then, when this was refused by the union, a cost-savings-sharing plan combined with a liberalized SUB plan. The SUB plan as amended pays 85 percent of gross wages for extended periods — in some cases, for as long as unemployment lasts.

As mentioned above, the provisions of SUB in the rubber and cement industries were greatly liberalized by the negotiations of 1965. After this date, the rubber and cement industries led instead of following the auto and steel industries. Both parties to the 1965 negotiations were influenced by the threat of unemployment associated with technological change. The unions wanted protection from it, and the companies provided the protection as the price for introducing needed changes at a faster rate.

Another possible use of SUB is closely allied to its function of facilitating technological change. After SUB plans were established in the steel industry in 1956, two companies closed some plants that had become obsolete. The union is convinced, though positive proof is lacking, that the companies acted more swiftly and more drastically than they otherwise would have because the SUB fund was available to cushion the shock of the closings. As this possible use of SUB becomes widely recognized, it may influence the negotiation of SUB plans in the future.

There is another possible use of SUB which may appeal to an employer. SUB helps to maintain an employer's labor force intact during temporary layoffs. The addition of SUB to his weekly income while unemployed may be the factor that induces a worker to wait a while longer on the chance that he will be recalled to his former job. Employees with low seniority tend to drift away during layoffs, even the short ones that characterize the auto model changeover. According to one of the major can companies, almost half of its employees who are laid off fail to return when recalled. In basic steel, it is particularly important that former employees answer recalls because a longer training period is required than for the average job on a production line.

The operation of the seniority system may, in some situations, provide a third reason why an employer finds SUB useful. In many seniority systems, a displaced worker has the right to "bump" another worker with less seniority and take over the job the latter is currently holding. The latter in turn can then bump someone else. In some circumstances this domino-like effect is very disruptive of plant efficiency; accordingly, the employer would prefer that the first worker take a layoff instead of initiating the series of job changes involved in the bumping process. The existence of SUB is a significant inducement for workers to accept a layoff and refrain from exercising their bumping rights. Of course, in situations where the employer prefers that the worker exercise his option to bump, this possible effect of SUB will be seen as a reason for *not* negotiating a SUB plan. Both situations occur and are discussed in Part III.

Another reason which may influence employers to negotiate a SUB plan was voiced by an official who had represented the Ford Motor Company in the 1955 negotiations. Speaking in 1957 on some of the reasons why SUB was desirable from the viewpoint of employers, Richard L. Johnson stressed the need to take care of workers at the low end of the seniority list: "It may well be that industry has gone too far in many of its other employee benefits, including not only pensions and group insurance, but vacations, transfer and recall rights, even wages themselves, in favoring seniority. Perhaps from the viewpoint of attracting and retaining young and eager personnel the time has arrived to balance off some of our existing emphasis on seniority" [30].

If a firm decides, as Ford did in 1955 [12], that its employees need larger unemployment benefits than those provided by the public program, it can choose either to liberalize the public program or to institute a private supplemental program. The political philosophy of some employers may incline them to prefer SUB as an alternative to the further extension of governmental activity. Additional reasons that an employer might have for negotiating a SUB plan are developed in the following sections dealing with the causal factors of wage levels and taxes.

3. Level of Wages

The next factor in order of importance is wages, or, more specifically, high wages. A high wage encourages a demand for unemployment benefits in several ways. First, the high-wage earner is the most dissatisfied with the regular UI benefit because he is the one most affected by the limitation on the maximum benefit, which in many cases prevents him from receiving a UI benefit equal to 50 percent of wages, a goal frequently proposed as the minimum level of adequacy. An analysis of the data on benefit adequacy in UI collected by the Bureau of Employment Security in 1960–1962 shows this limitation to be a major defect of the UI system [31, pp. 93–96].

Second, the high-wage earner is not only most in need of SUB; he is also best able to purchase it. As a worker's income rises and he has money left over after satisfying basic needs, he feels he can afford to buy more of other goods and services — for example, more insurance. The great increase in the demand for life insurance at the turn of the century was a direct result of the growth in the national income. Likewise, the growth in real wages is probably the principal explanation of the strong trend since the early 1950's toward wage supplements of all kinds, especially pensions and health insurance.

Third, the high-wage earner, feeling the impact of the income tax, is the one most inclined to take some of his earnings in the form of fringe benefits rather than in wages. The tax advantage to him is less in the case of SUB than in the case of some other wage supplements because income taxes must be paid on SUB payments when received, but there is still some advantage, as explained below in the discussion of the fourth factor.

Finally, unions are sensitive to their public image and sometimes feel that after a certain point a wage gain is better taken in a form that has lower visibility than an outright increase in hourly rates.

Practically all SUB plans are found among employees who have higher-than-average wages. The operation of this factor is seen most clearly in cases where high-wage members of a union have SUB while lower-wage members of the same union do not. Thus members of the United Steel-workers of America who work in basic steel generally have a SUB plan, while most of those who work in foundries or fabricating plants do not. Members of the United Auto Workers who work for the automotive companies generally have a SUB plan, while most of those who work for other companies do not. Members of the Rubber Workers who work for the Big Four have a SUB plan, while those who work in other rubber fabricating plants generally do not. Of the members of the Cement, Lime and Gypsum Workers, those who work in cement have a SUB plan, while those who work in lime and gypsum do not. Of the Brick and Clay Workers, members who work in refractories generally have SUB plans, while those in work in the face-brick industry generally do not. In each of the above examples, the members who have the SUB plan are the higher-paid workers. Moreover, where a SUB plan does exist among the lower-paid branches of a union the provisions of the plan are often less liberal. For example, in the multi-employer plan of the Buffalo District Carpenters, one division consists of members who work on floor coverings; these members have a lower wage scale, and their SUB plan pays lower benefits than the SUB plan of the other members.

The wages which are income for the employee are a cost for the employer and influence the birth of SUB under this aspect also. When the author polled the 75 unions mentioned above, he found that one of two reasons was usually given for rating SUB low in the scale of union objectives. As mentioned above, the reason most frequently given was that unemployment posed little threat for the majority of the union's membership. The next most frequently mentioned reason was that the industry could not afford SUB.

In this context, "afford" could have two meanings. The first and most likely is that, with only a given amount of money available for employee remuneration, the employees preferred to take it in forms other than SUB. This meaning was discussed above.

The other meaning is that SUB represents, in some sense, additional, or extra, cost. Is this true? As a generalization subject to modification, it may be said that usually SUB does not represent an increase in labor costs over that which would have been incurred in the absence of a SUB plan. Although not always so crystal clear as when the Ford Motor Company and the Auto Workers negotiated the first SUB plan, it is nevertheless generally true that the money which the employer agrees to contribute to the SUB fund would have gone to the employees in any case — if not in the form of SUB, then in some other form.

As between two unions negotiating with the same company, it is not so clear that the union not demanding SUB always gets the exact equivalent in some other form. The practice varies with companies and with situations. For example, when the Pattern Makers of North America declined SUB in 1955, they received an equivalent raise in their wage rates from Ford but not from Allis-Chalmers.

The generalization advanced above, that SUB does not add to the total labor cost that would be incurred by the employer in the absence of SUB, is true only as a first approximation. The total labor cost is not entirely independent of the form of the cost. A different total bargain may be reached if part of the bargain includes SUB. An employer may be willing to put 5 cents an hour, for example, into a SUB plan where he would have been willing to put only 4 cents into wages because he sees some additional advantages to be derived from SUB. Besides the four advantages mentioned in the discussion of the second factor above, and the tax advantage mentioned below, the employer may see an advantage to putting the 5 cents into a SUB fund rather than into the base wage rate, which is used for calculating other wage costs, such as pensions, insurance, and incentive payments.

On its part, a union may be willing to accept 5 cents in the form of SUB where it would demand more in some other form. In addition to the advantages noted in the first factor above, and other advantages noted in factors 4, 5, and 6 below, a union may consider that the employer's acceptance of the *principle* of SUB represents a long-run gain for which it is worthwhile to sacrifice some other gain currently attainable. This is probably the way Walter Reuther reasoned in 1955 when he rejected the stock savings plan of General Motors in favor of SUB.

4. Taxes

It has been standard procedure, in negotiating a new SUB plan, to specify that acceptance of the plan is contingent upon the issuance of certain rulings by the taxing authorities as to the status of transactions under the plan. The rulings thus specified are four: that the employer's contributions are a business expense; that the contributions are not wages for the purpose of determining liability for social security taxes under FICA and FUTA; that the contributions are not income to the employees at the time they are paid into the fund; and that the fund is a nonprofit organization and hence its income (interest) is tax exempt. In addition, it is usually specified that the agreement is contingent upon rulings to be obtained from other governmental authorities to the effect that contributions to the fund are not wages for purposes of the Fair Labor Standards Act, and that benefits received from the fund are not wages for the purpose of determining eligibility for UI benefits. (This last is crucial; without it UI benefits could not be paid and SUB could not be truly "supplemental.")

The tax-exempt status of the earnings of the fund constitutes the chief tax advantage of a SUB plan. Other tax advantages are minor. As of 1965, the employer's exemption from social security taxes is more nominal than real because FUTA is limited to the first $3,000 of wages and FICA is limited to the first $6,600 of wages — limits normally exceeded by the regular wages of the high-wage employees covered by SUB plans.

The benefits paid from pooled SUB funds are taxable as income at the time of receipt. Under such an arrangement, the government receives somewhat less and the employees keep somewhat more of the employer's contributions than if the contributions had been considered wages and taxed as such at the time of payment into the fund. This is because (a) the payment of taxes is delayed and (b) the persons who receive these unemployment benefits (the unemployed) are probably in a lower tax bracket than the persons (the employed) who would have received the money in the form of wages. But the difference is small.

(The Internal Revenue Service has had a significant influence on the development of SUB. The reader may recall how the rulings of the IRS entered into the decision of the ILGWU. In 1956 the Detroit Tooling Association constructed an unemployment benefit plan that was acceptable to the union, but because it could not obtain favorable rulings from the IRS, the plan was eventually transformed into the supplemental pension plan mentioned above. In 1960, the Brewery Workers of New Orleans negotiated a modified SUB plan which was also ruled upon unfavorably by the IRS, and the negotiating parties had to start over again. Many other instances of this sort have occurred.)

5. Other Wage Supplements

Another factor is the degree to which other wage supplements, the so-called "fringes," have already been achieved. If other, more highly rated, benefits like pensions, health insurance, and vacations have already been attained, the union is more likely to be seriously interested in negotiating a plan of unemployment benefits. In some instances an unemployment plan has been negotiated ahead of a pension or health plan, but such instances are rare. Of the nearly 2,500 contracts negotiated by the Steelworkers, approximately 95 percent provided insurance and 54 percent provided pensions, but only 20 percent provided SUB. The respective percentages for the Auto Workers were approximately 90 percent, 54 percent, and 24 percent. In 1963, of the 163,000 welfare and pension benefit plans on file with the U.S. Department of Labor, less than 1 percent provided unemployment benefits, and the employers had contributed twenty times as much to health funds as they had to unemployment funds.

The Industrial Union of Marine and Shipbuilding Workers of America (IUMSW) rates all the following above SUB in its list of immediate objectives: wages, pensions, insurance, vacations, working conditions, holidays with pay, severance pay. The United Hatters, Cap and Millinery Workers (HCMW) once cultivated a lively interest in the guaranteed annual wage. A. D. H. Kaplan says of this union: "Its union literature has revealed more systematic thought on the problem of the annual wage than is to be found in the labor press generally, not excepting that of the CIO unions" [32, p. 35]. But as of 1965 the union reported: "We have no systematic policy regarding SUB. Other economic requirements for our members take priority over SUB" [33].

A significant determinant in a union's evaluation of various benefit programs can be the age distribution of its membership. The union is less likely to demand unemployment benefits if older workers are in the majority. Older workers are better protected from unemployment by seniority and are likely to be more interested in additional health or pension benefits than in unemployment benefits. Age and seniority also affect the kind of SUB plan chosen. The older workers want the plan to contain provisions which will protect the fund from being drained by those members — presumably the younger and the more recently hired — who are laid off earlier. The Ford Motor Company made a major issue of this danger during the original SUB negotiations in 1955 and devised a benefit formula which canceled credit units faster as the fund shrank, and thus saved more of the fund for later layoffs. The UAW not only agreed, but negotiated a further strengthening of the protective mechanism: as the fund shrank, credit units were charged off faster for the unemployed with low seniority than for those with high seniority.

The current tendency of unions to negotiate wage supplements began to show itself strongly during World War II and continued during the postwar period. Especially in the last decade, wage supplements have grown both absolutely and as a percentage of total labor costs. During the period 1951–1965, according to the Bureau of Labor Statistics, wage supplements had been rising about 6 percent annually, nearly twice the 3.2 percent average annual union-negotiated gain in wages. Since the upward trend shows no signs of slackening, as time goes on and goals are substantially achieved in pensions, health benefits, and vacations, a significant increase is likely to occur in the demand for unemployment benefits. However, as indicated below in the discussion of alternatives, this increased demand for unemployment benefits will not necessarily take the form of a demand for SUB.

6. Unionization

While there is close correlation between this factor and factors 3, 7, 8, and 9, it has sufficient significance in itself to merit separate treatment. Understandably, SUB is found predominantly — almost entirely — among employees who are unionized. SUB is essentially group insurance, and group action usually requires group organization, which is supplied by a union. The leadership factor discussed below operates more effectively in the context of a union. Where the leader thinks he knows better than the average worker what is best for the worker, the union organization enables the leader to put this judgment into practice.

As compared with an equivalent wage gain, SUB may have advantages for the union as an institution. A wage increase is negotiated once and for all, but SUB payments offer the opportunity for continued union activity. The union is represented on the board of administration and supplies its members with continuing information regarding the fund. Union activity is especially visible in the multi-employer plans, which may be housed in the same building as the union headquarters and are often administered by former union members. The union may also like SUB because the program is of particular help to union members with low seniority. The dissatisfaction of these members with union policy, which tends to favor the high-seniority employees, at times threatens union harmony. The negotiation of a SUB plan proves to these low-seniority members that the union is concerned about them. Furthermore, SUB is a complex program requiring a degree of expertise which only large groups of workers can afford to hire. As a matter of fact, nearly all of the preliminary technical work connected with SUB was carried out by a small number of persons, chiefly in the Steelworkers' and Auto Workers' unions.

The presence and activity of unions has also made a difference in the nature of SUB. Early plans of guaranteed income were generally established on the initiative of the employer. For the most part, they took the form of a guarantee of employment to the most stable part of the employer's workforce, in exchange for which the employee agreed to work overtime at regular rates during peak periods and to do work at other than his regular occupation during slack periods. Both these forms of cooperation are disliked by the unions and are conspicuously absent from the SUB plans.

It may safely be said that SUB plans would be next to nonexistent today if it had not been for the unions.

7. Size of Firm

Unemployment-benefit plans are much more common among larger firms, principally because programs that have the character of insurance, such as SUB, are better suited to large firms, where the risk insured against can be spread over a wide base. An additional reason is that in large plans administrative costs are spread over a greater number of units and hence are lower per unit. In small plans, administrative costs can absorb a disproportionate part of the available funds. For these reasons, the single-employer SUB plan is not particularly well suited to companies with less than several hundred employees.

Another reason for the relative absence of SUB among small firms is that small firms tend to have either no unemployment or too much unemployment. When the firm is operating normally, the entire labor force is needed and works; when the firm's business slows down, almost the entire force may be laid off. If such a firm has a SUB plan, either the fund is not used at all or the demands made upon it are so great that it proves inadequate.

The device of the multi-employer SUB plan overcomes most of the difficulties posed by firms of small size. If it could be widely used, it would almost eliminate size of firm as a decisive factor in the explanation of the birth of SUB plans. The further use of this device is probably limited to situations in which multi-employer bargaining on wage contracts occurs. As of 1965, about one quarter of all union members bargained collectively with an association of employers. Where a union does not bargain with an association, it will find great difficulty in negotiating a multi-employer plan. However, at their 1966 convention, the Auto Workers announced plans to use the multi-employer device to extend SUB to the firms, most of them small, that supply parts to the automotive industry.

Data are available to illustrate the relationship between SUB and size of firm in the contracts of the Steelworkers and Auto Workers. As of 1963, the Steelworkers had 2,483 contracts covering 883,459 employees. Of these contracts, 77 percent were small (less than 200 employees), but they accounted for only 51 percent of all SUB contracts and only 3 percent of all employees covered by SUB. By contrast, major contracts (those covering more than 1,000 employees), although they were only 5 percent of all contracts, accounted for 16 percent of all SUB contracts and 56 percent of all employees covered by SUB. Among the 112 major contracts, there were only 32 which did not provide SUB. However, size and SUB do not invariably go together even in the Steelworkers' contracts. Of the 487 contracts which provided SUB, 80 covered 1,000 or more employees, while 162 covered less than 100, with a few of them covering less than 10.

Roughly similar relationships characterize the contracts of the Auto Workers. For example, as of 1963, major contracts represented only 8 percent of all contracts but accounted for 21 percent of all contracts with SUB. On the other hand, small contracts represented 70 percent of the total, but they accounted for only 36 percent of SUB contracts. Of all SUB contracts 12 percent covered less than 50 employees. For the most part these very small plans are explained by the following factor.

8. Institutionalism

The next factor may be called for lack of a better term institutional uniformity — the tendency of an institution (union or firm) to set up an employment benefit plan as part of its general policy. The Auto Workers and the Steelworkers, for example, have a tendency to negotiate a SUB plan wherever they have members, no matter how few the members and no matter how slight the hazard of unemployment. This tendency explains the existence of plans that have never paid a benefit or that cover only a handful of employees.

Sometimes the demand for institutional uniformity is only a gesture. One rubber fabricating company reported:

> We have 17 plants, 12 of which are organized. In these 12 there are 22 unions. Six plants are organized by the United Rubber Workers, and these are the only plants in which any demands have been made for supplemental unemployment compensation benefits. We have been given a copy of the tire plan as a proposal periodically for the last several years as a formal sort of gesture. However, the tire company bargaining pattern has no effect on us since it is not competitive. Little interest has been shown by the local memberships in any expenditure of money for this purpose, possibly because we have had relatively stable employment for years in these particular plants. The demand has never been seriously pushed [34].

Geography makes a difference. In negotiations with the Auto Workers, for example, the nearer a company is to Detroit the more pressure it comes under to have a SUB plan. In the case of the Steelworkers, the vicinity of Pittsburgh is the magic region in which SUB must appear in a contract, no matter what the circumstances of a particular firm. Sometimes the determining factor is proximity to another firm which has SUB, whatever the region. Both influences are illustrated in the following comment of a company which explained why, out of eight contracts with the Steelworkers, two — rather than eight or none — provided for a SUB plan:

> The reason for having only two such plans with the Steelworkers union instead of eight or none is largely a result of geography. The plan in Pittsburgh was brought about largely because of the insistence of the Union. Their plea was that regardless of the size of the plant they could not think of agreeing to a contract in the Pitttsburgh area without following the steel union policy which included SUB. The other plan, at our plant [in the South] resulted largely because our plant is located directly across the street from the —— steel company, a rather sizeable operation which followed the steel pattern, and the local District Director insisted that because of the proximity of our operation it was necessary to do likewise [35].

One company with a SUB plan covering 35 Steelworkers reported it had been reluctant to establish such a plan: "We felt the administrative costs for a SUB plan for a small group of employees would be excessively high, and the only reason we had a SUB plan in this location was because the United Steelworkers made strong and repeated demands for it, and our management was convinced the union was prepared to strike the plant indefinitely if we refused" [36].

Management sometimes objects to pattern bargaining because it imposes on all firms provisions like SUB that bear more heavily on "bystander" firms, especially small ones, than on the "target" firms which negotiated the provision in the first place. Foundries, for example, find the identical SUB provisions more expensive than do the basic steel companies which first negotiated them because work in foundries is more labor-intensive and because the foundries have more unemployment. After the 1965 steel negotiations, R. Conrad Cooper of the United States Steel Corporation publicly voiced management's objection to pattern bargaining.

It is true that strong unions seek to impose the contract with the best terms on the whole industry, but it is also true that unions are not uniformly successful in this strategy. The 1963 statistic quoted above is relevant here: of the roughly 2,500 contracts negotiated by the Steelworkers, less than 500 provide for a SUB plan. Most of the metal-fabricating firms escaped this obligation entirely; of those which did have SUB programs, some were liable only for the 5 cents negotiated originally (1956) rather than for the 9.5 cents negotiated later (1962) with the basic steel companies. On the other hand, in the cement industry, the very liberal SUB provisions negotiated in 1965 with the target companies of southern California — which experience relatively little unemployment — have become the obligation of all companies, even those in the east, which have been experiencing considerable unemployment.

Firms, too, manifest institutional uniformity. After negotiating a SUB contract with Union A, perhaps a large industrial union, a firm may extend SUB readily to its other employees, whether or not they have ever demanded it. This is the general policy, for example, of Deere and Company in the agricultural implement industry. This institutional policy is the chief explanation of why SUB plans appear in some few locals of international unions that have never shown any interest in them.

This institutional policy also explains the existence of most SUB plans for office employees. Some companies, such as the Kaiser Aluminum and Chemical Corporation and the Bethlehem Steel Corporation, extended the identical SUB plan to their office employees. Other companies, such as those in the auto industry, provided an equivalent but different benefit for their office employees. Still other companies have refused on principle to supply any substitute for SUB to any group of employees.

Institutional policy can also affect the form that a SUB plan takes. Large corporations that engage in many different operations find themselves negotiating a single type of SUB plan if they deal with a single union but more than one type if they deal with many unions. The Ford Motor Company, for example, engages in many different productive activities such as coal mining, steelmaking, and glassmaking, in addition to manufacturing automobiles and a large array of other finished products. But all the UAW members engaged in these various activities are under one SUB plan. Thus there are employees engaged in glassmaking who have the individual-account type of plan if they work for a glass company, but have the auto-type SUB plan if they work for Ford. Likewise there are employees engaged in steelmaking who have the steel-type SUB plan if they work for a steel company but the auto-type plan if they work for Ford. And so with workers in other economic activities included in the wide scope of the Ford Motor Company.

On the other hand, Kaiser Industries Corporation, which is a collection of highly independent divisions, has negotiated five different types of SUB plans with eight different unions. Kaiser Aluminum and Chemical Corporation has negotiated an aluminum-type plan (generally, but not completely, similar to the steel-type plan) with the Auto Workers, a cement-type plan with the United Brick and Clay Workers, and an auto-type plan with the Rubber Workers. The Kaiser Steel Corporation has negotiated a steel-type plan with about 8,000 of the Steelworkers, while the Kaiser Aluminum and Chemical Corporation has negotiated an aluminum-type plan with about 9,000 other members of the Steelworkers. Finally, the Kaiser Jeep Corporation has negotiated an auto-type plan with the Auto Workers.

9. Leadership and Personal Values

In all affairs involving groups of people, the personality and the values of the leader can be decisive in the choice of group objectives. He is one of the more elusive factors in evaluating group decisions, and here especially the would-be historian should keep in mind the observation of Arthur Schlesinger regarding past decisions — that some of the factors involved may have been obscure even to the man making the decisions and that the historian must beware of "ascribing to premeditation what belongs to fortuity and to purpose what belongs to chance."

In explaining the long-sustained drive of the Steelworkers for the guaranteed annual wage (later SUB), one should probably put high in the list of causal factors the personal dedication to this goal of the union's president, Philip Murray, and the union's general counsel, Arthur J. Goldberg. The latter in particular waged a vigorous campaign within the union to establish as a prime objective the negotiation of some form of guaranteed income.

Walter Reuther was personally convinced of the value of unemployment benefits and used all his leadership skills to persuade first his own membership and then the automotive companies to set up the original SUB program. Without Reuther, there would have been no SUB program in 1955. The same Reutherian fervor was evident 12 years later, when the UAW's president obtained this pledge from the union's twentieth constitutional convention (May 1966): "In 1967 we will not sign a basic agreement except as it contains the guaranteed annual salary for the production and maintenance workers of this union" [37, p. 733]. It was like an echo of the original GAW campaign (see also Appendix B to this volume).

The late Burl Phares was president of the Glass Workers in 1955 and shared Reuther's enthusiasm for what was still being called GAW but had clearly become SUB. Since the Glass Workers negotiated earlier than the Auto Workers that year, Phares planned to be the first to negotiate a SUB plan. However, he was not able to bring his membership along with him. The companies went over his head to the employees and succeeded in persuading them that an individual-account plan would be preferable to the UAW-type plan which their president favored. Finding that the membership would not support a strike for SUB, Phares settled for the alternative.

The multi-employer SUB plan of the Carpenters in Buffalo is attributable almost entirely to the leadership of one man, the district director of the union, whose principal problem originally (i.e., in 1960) was to sell the plan to his own membership. The multi-employer plan of the Retail Clerks in Los Angeles is likewise attributable to the personal leadership of one man, the local union's secretary. The form which the multi-employer plan of the Electrical Workers in Detroit took (pooled, rather than individual-account) was due directly to the union leaders and their actuarial consultants. The research director of one large union reported: "Our union considers SUB most important in its collective bargaining program. However, in spite of all-out efforts we have been successful in convincing only a few locals of its importance" [38]. Several other research directors reported almost exactly the same situation — the union's leaders had not been able to convince the membership.

One union staff member who is acquainted with both the International Ladies' Garment Workers' Union and the Amalgamated Clothing Workers of America was asked why the ILGWU has stressed SUB, while the ACWA has ignored it. His reply emphasized the role of subjective factors:

On the basis of everything I know about the way in which the order of priorities emerges in our collective bargaining, I am persuaded that subjective factors are largely responsible for the difference, to date, between the ACWA and ILGW as to the relative place of SUB among union collective bargaining objectives. Even when all other things are equal, choosing between improving an existing program and starting a new one can be a difficult one for union officials. In this case there is not only the difference in personality of the union officials, but differences in the history and style of the two organizations, and undoubtedly differences in judgement with regard to the ultimate preferences of a majority of members among the options available to the negotiators. Also . . . sometimes the success of a program originally adopted by an innovating local may push it to the forefront in national negotiations [39].

The differences between the two multi-employer SUB plans negotiated by the Detroit locals of the Plumbers and Pipefitters (one plan paid $35 for 26 weeks, while the other paid $25 for 52 weeks) stemmed from no ascertainable economic difference but were attributable, in the judgment of those who participated in the negotiations, to differences in the subjective values of the respective union leaders.

10. Alternatives

Even in situations where the union and the employer have agreed to establish some form of unemployment benefits, SUB is not the inevitable choice. There are alternative unemployment-benefit plans, and these contribute to answering the second part of our central question: why does SUB appear in some situations but not in others?

One alternative is the individual-account plan which has no connection with the state UI program. This is the type of plan that the Glass Workers chose and that the Cement Workers would have preferred. It is the type of plan that the Machinists in the Douglas Aircraft Company chose in 1965, when the Auto Workers in the same company chose SUB. There are many other instances of this kind of divided choice within one company. In addition to cases already cited — such as the diverse plans of the New Orleans Brewery Workers — the Granite City Steel Company, which has a regular SUB plan with the Steelworkers, has negotiated an individual-account plan with Local 50 of the International Chemical Workers (ICW). (This plan has cost the company more than a SUB plan would have.)

For many unions, a severance-pay plan ranks higher than SUB in the scale of union preferences. Severance pay is the first choice, for example, of the Packing House Workers (UPWA), the Stereotypers and Electrotypers (ISEU), the Lithographers and Photoengravers (LPIU), the Bakery and Confectionery Workers (ABCW), and many others. According to a report from the Amalgamated Clothing Workers of America (ACWA), that union would probably try to negotiate a severance-pay plan before it seriously demanded a SUB plan. Since 1956, the Mine, Mill and Smelter Workers (MMSW) have regularly demanded SUB in negotiations but thus far have always been willing to settle for some alternative gain. In 1964 the union probably could have won a SUB plan but preferred to establish a plan of severance pay instead. The Southern California Rapid Transit District has negotiated three unemployment-benefit plans with its employees; one of these is SUB but the other two are severance-pay plans.

Severance-pay provisions appear in about one third of all major contracts (contracts covering 1,000 or more employees) and are negotiated most frequently by five unions — the Auto Workers, Steelworkers, Communications Workers, Garment Workers, and Electrical Workers (IBEW). The proportion of major contracts containing a severance-pay provision has doubled in the last decade, and such contracts currently cover something more than three million employees.

In industries characterized by large seasonal fluctuations, a vacation-pay plan may be used as an unemployment-benefit plan. The Carpenters (CJA) have negotiated many vacation-pay plans. Carpenters are reluctant to take a vacation during the summer because this is the time when work is most readily available. In the winter an extended vacation does not appeal to many of them unless they can go to a place like Florida. So they take their vacation pay in a series of short periods during the winter, whenever they are unemployed.

One of the reasons why the Seafarers (SIU) have not followed the Maritime Workers (NMU) in negotiating a SUB plan is that in 1951 the Seafarers negotiated a "vacation fund" to which all employers covered by the agreement contribute. This fund is of the individual-account type and, despite its name, may be used for any purpose; in practice it is frequently used to tide a man over between jobs. As of 1965, the average Seafarer could expect to accumulate about $800 per year in his "vacation" fund.

On the west coast, the Longshoremen (ILWU) went far beyond SUB when, in October of 1960, they signed a Mechanization and Modernization Agreement with the Pacific Maritime Association. By this agreement, employers committed themselves to contribute 4.5 percent of their payroll to a fund to be used to protect union members against the threat of unemployment stemming from the industry's projected program of mechanization and modernization. The parties agreed to freeze registrations as of

1958 and to make registration coastwide, so as to facilitate shifts of workers from area to area. The agreement guaranteed weekly earnings up to the equivalent of 35 hours per week, contained a flat guarantee against layoffs, and made numerous arrangements for early retirement, both voluntary and compulsory.

In the case of some of the alternatives to SUB, especially in the case of severance-pay plans and individual-account plans, a weighty argument in favor of the alternative is its relative simplicity as contrasted with the complexity of SUB. The simpler plan is easier for the parties to negotiate; also, it uses up less of the available money in administration. Both considerations weigh heavily in the scales of the smaller unions and firms.

An Example: International Harvester Company

It may be helpful to see in more detail the pattern of SUB plans in one large corporation, such as the International Harvester Company, that negotiates with a variety of unions. This corporation is presented not as typical but merely as exemplifying a number of the causal factors discussed above. Looking at one company in all its relations to SUB may serve to unify factors which were divided for purposes of discussion.

As shown in Table 3-1, in 1965 the International Harvester Company had 25 SUB plans in operation at its manufacturing and engineering operations in the United States. Of these plans 9 were negotiated in 1955 and 9 in 1959; 3 plans were negotiated in 1956, 2 in 1960, and 1 in each of the years 1957 and 1961.

The International Harvester Company has a general policy of extending SUB to most, though not to all, of its hourly employees at its manufacturing and engineering operations. This policy explains the two SUB plans established for nonrepresented employees. The company makes many different products and in its negotiations is usually guided by the general conditions of the industry manufacturing each product. For example, the company has a facility that manufactures twine. Since SUB plans are not usually found in the twine industry, the company does not make SUB available in these plants.

There are two chief reasons for the burst of new plans in 1959. First, at that time the threat of unemployment loomed large for some International Harvester workers. During World War II, the company had been forced by production needs to keep open a number of old plants which had been in existence at the time that the International Harvester Company was incorporated in 1902. Some of these plants had become obsolete and no longer were suitable for modern production. After the war, the company

TABLE 3-1

International Harvester Company Agreements Establishing SUB Plans in the
Years 1955–1965 Which Were Still in Operation in 1965

Year plan negotiated	Employee group	No. of employees covered	No. of agreements	Type of plan
1955	Steelworkers (USWA)	400	1	Auto
1956	Steelworkers (USWA)	25	1	Steel
1959	Steelworkers (USWA)	26	1	Auto
1955 (1959)	Electrical Workers (IBEW)	280	6	Auto
1955	Production and Maintenance Workers (UAW)	34,000	1	Auto
1955	Clerical and Technical Workers (UAW)	2,650	1	Auto
1955	Technical Engineers (AFTE)	220	1	Auto
1955	Printing employees	180	1	Auto
1955	Harvester Federal Labor Union	750	1	Auto
1955 (1959)	Firemen and Oilers (IBFO)	60	3	Auto
1955	Society of Engineering Employees	700	1	Auto
1956	Progressive Steel Workers	4,000	1	Steel
1956	Mates and Pilots (MMP)	4	1	Steel
1957	Bricklayers, Masons and Plasterers (BMP)	30	1	Steel
1959	Machinists (IAM)	425	3	Auto
1959 (1964, 1965)	Teamsters (TCWH)	250	3	Auto
1959	Operating Engineers (IUOE)	70	2	Auto
1959	Nonrepresented employees exclusive of sales operations	5,200	a	Auto
1959	Technical engineers, architects, and draftsmen	60	1	Auto
1959	Plumbers and Steamfitters (PPF)	90	1	Auto
1959	Carpenters and Joiners (CJA)	130	3	Auto
1959	Office Employees (OEIU)	100	1	Auto
1960	Nonrepresented employees—Wisconsin Steel	150	a	Steel
1960	Pattern Makers (PML)	183	1	Auto
1961	Die Sinkers (DSC)b	69	1	Auto
1963	Plant Guards (PGW)	178	1	c

a No agreement; plan maintained in accordance with company policy.
b Plan excludes journeymen die sinkers, who rejected SUB.
c Nonfunded plan providing separation pay only.

began a program of modernization of its production facilities. This
included building or purchasing several new plants in the early years after
the war and, in the late 1950's, the phasing-out of some of the older plants,
including the giant McCormick Works, which had been in operation for
nearly 90 years. Second, International Harvester, unlike some other companies, had not offered a compensating benefit to unions which had not

negotiated a SUB plan in 1955. When the unions that had declined SUB realized that they would not get any other benefit in its place, they decided that they might as well have SUB. Under the threat of unemployment this generalized desire for SUB became focused sharply enough for action.

The company has a general rule, adopted for the sake of simplicity in administration, that there is to be only one SUB fund for each international union. One exception to this rule occurs in the case of the Steelworkers, who have three separate funds, established at three different times. The 1955 plan, which covers warehouse workers organized by the Steelworkers, is of the auto type. The 1956 plan, which covers workers in a steel mill, is of the steel type and hence could not be integrated with the preceding plan. The 1959 plan is of the auto type and according to general policy should have been integrated with the 1955 plan; its separate status seems to have been simply an oversight. The other exception occurs in the case of the Auto Workers, who have one fund for UAW production workers and another for UAW clerical-technical workers. The difference in unemployment experience is so great between these two groups that separate funds seemed desirable. The clerical-technical workers have much less unemployment.

With the exception of five plans which are based on the steel pattern, the International Harvester Company accepts the SUB plan as negotiated between the auto companies and the UAW and applies it unchanged to other employees, no matter what their particular line of work. The advantage of administrative simplicity outweighs any advantages that might come from trying to adapt the automotive-UAW plan to the various industries in which International Harvester is involved or to the other unions with which it negotiates.

The Pattern Makers in the company rejected SUB back in 1955, both on principle and because they expected to negotiate an equivalent gain in basic wage rates. When they became convinced that they were not going to receive any equivalent, they asked for SUB, and the regular auto SUB plan was negotiated in 1960. Similarly, the Die Sinkers declined SUB in 1955. In all probability this was for the same reason that the Pattern Makers had declined it. However, when the Die Sinkers finally negotiated for SUB in 1961, the plan was restricted to nonjourneymen because the journeymen's wage rates by that time reflected settlements elsewhere in the industry which the company held included additional amounts in place of SUB. This has caused no problem, probably because the Die Sinkers have a long tradition of sharing available work and SUB runs counter to that tradition.

The plan negotiated with the United Plant Guards in 1963 pays only separation benefits and not supplemental unemployment benefits. Some years earlier, the union had been offered the full package of severance pay and SUB but had decided that it would take only severance pay. Although this is not a SUB plan, it has been included in the list to illustrate the individual differences that can determine workers' decisions with respect to SUB. Like the journeymen Die Sinkers, the Plant Guards simply declined SUB without getting any additional benefits by way of compensation. The separation pay that the members of this union receive is identical with the separation pay they would have received had they also accepted a full SUB plan. The reason for the union's decision has not been ascertained. International Harvester had only four employees in the Mates and Pilots Union but had established a separate plan for them.

Summary

In the industries where SUB exists, the major factor in its initiation has been experience with unemployment sufficient in duration and depth to arouse the interest of both labor and management in private supplementation of UI benefits. Where the other factors have come into play, they have acted in a supporting role. All these factors have also played a part in the growth of SUB, as described in Part II.

PART II
ANATOMY OF SUB

INTRODUCTION TO PART II

What is the nature of the SUB program whose emergence has been chronicled in the preceding pages? This is the question which the remainder of the study attempts to answer. Since the nature of anything is manifested both in its structure and in its operation, the question must be answered in two stages — by describing SUB's structure (Part II) and by narrating its activities (Part III).

The most comprehensive description of the structure of current SUB plans is contained in a Bureau of Labor Statistics study of 174 major SUB plans functioning in the winter of 1963 [25]. It is assumed throughout Part II that this basic document is available to the reader. To the data contained there the present study adds a chronological analysis of the changes in provisions that occurred during the decade 1955–1965, a discussion of the issues raised by alternative provisions, and a description of some additonal plans that are especially interesting.

The task of Part II is complicated by the great variety of SUB plans. In Part I, the term "SUB" was used as though it referred to something simple and stable; in fact, SUB is neither. SUB is the family name of some very different cousins who have developed in widely diverging ways. Since it is not practicable to describe in detail the evolution of all such plans, it is necessary to be selective. Accordingly, four basic plans have been selected for consistently detailed treatment. Other plans are discussed on an irregular basis and only to the extent that this can be done without unduly complicating the analysis.

The four core plans, which appear in all the tables, are those negotiated by the following unions and companies: the Auto Workers (UAW) with the auto companies; the Steelworkers (USWA) with the basic steel companies; the Rubber Workers (URW) with the basic rubber companies; and the Cement Workers (CLGW) with the cement companies. Although minor differences occur within each of these four groups, the major provisions are sufficiently similar for each group to be treated as a homogeneous unit. (Around each core plan are grouped many plans that derive their main characteristics from the core plan but differ from it and from each other in varying degrees.) The other plans most frequently included in the tables or mentioned in the text are those negotiated by the Auto Workers with several companies in the agricultural implement industry (Allis-

Chalmers, John Deere, International Harvester) and by the Steelworkers with the major can companies (American Can and Continental Can). Finally, special attention is accorded a heterogeneous group of multi-employer plans which are little known, have considerable potentiality, and contain some unusual provisions. The core plans take in about three fourths of all employees covered by SUB, and they exemplify all the more significant choices that have been made in the construction and development of SUB plans. Anyone who is familiar with these SUB plans can say without serious qualification that he is fairly well acquainted with the SUB family.

Since SUB plans provide for the supplementation of state unemployment insurance benefits, it is convenient to describe their provisions in the familiar unemployment insurance terms of eligibility and disqualification (Chapter 4); amount and duration of benefits (Chapter 5); financing (Chapter 6); and administration (Chapter 7). Changes in the plans are presented in approximate chronological order, according to the dates of the contracts in which the changes were negotiated.

As remarked above, SUB exhibits a multiplicity of provisions. Anyone who attempts to describe the development of SUB plans, even the core plans, runs the danger of being so blinded by the dust of details as to lose sight of the major features in the landscape and thus fail to achieve perspective and balance. To lessen this danger, Part II takes certain liberties with its sources.

SUB provisions are contained in collectively bargained contracts which are necessarily expressed in legal language abounding in technicalities. Since this study is not intended as a technical handbook for the SUB practitioner but is written for the ordinary reader who is primarily interested in ascertaining the general impact of a provision, the description given here eschews the exact legal language of the provisions, omits many details, groups some provisions otherwise than as they appear in the contracts, and in general sacrifices minute exactitude for the sake, it is hoped, of a better general understanding of the major features of SUB.

The reader may find it helpful to keep in mind a general picture of the number of significantly different SUB plans negotiated by the various companies and unions represented in the core plans during the decade 1955–1965. In the steel industry there have been only two different plans: the first plan (1956) remained unchanged through the negotiations of 1960, and the 1962 plan remained unchanged through the negotiations of 1965. There have been three plans in the cement industry; four in the industries of auto, agricultural implement, and canmaking; five in the rubber industry. (See Appendix B for the 1967 changes negotiated in the plans of the rubber, auto, and agricultural implement industries. These changes rank among the most significant in the history of SUB.)

4

ELIGIBILITY AND DISQUALIFICATION PROVISIONS

Logically, the first decision to be made in constructing a SUB plan is to determine who is to be eligible for the benefits provided by the plan and under what conditions. Decisions on the amount and duration of benefits depend very much on who is to receive the benefits, while decisions on contributions and administrative procedures are merely the means to achieve goals already established. In practice, of course, all these decisions are interdependent. Considerations of cost and administrative feasibility, for example, exert a significant and sometimes decisive influence on the selection of eligibility criteria and benefit formulas.

The eligibility and disqualification provisions of SUB plans are the area in which controversies arise most frequently. Benefits and contributions become key issues only when a new contract is being negotiated; once agreed upon, they remain settled through the life of that contract. But issues affecting eligibility and disqualifications can arise at any time in the course of the day-to-day administration of the plan.

Controversy over eligibility and disqualification provisions tends to be not only the most frequent but also the most intense. These provisions bear directly on the sensitive spot of the relative bargaining strength of labor and management. They touch directly on management's desire to maintain control over its workforce, on the one hand, and on labor's desire to increase its freedom from such control, on the other.

In the following description, eligibility and disqualification provisions are grouped under three headings, according to the specifications of the provisions: (1) the required quantity and quality of employment; (2) the required quantity and quality of unemployment; (3) the required relationship to UI.

Required Quantity and Quality of Employment

It is generally accepted that in any plan of guaranteed income, the guarantee extends only to those who are "regularly attached" to the workforce. The usual test of regular attachment is the employment history of the employee. Only those who have worked a specified length of time under specified conditions are considered regular members of the workforce and thus covered by the guarantee.

The lower this first requirement is set, the greater will be the cost of the plan, not only because a greater number of employees will be covered, but also, and especially, because the added workers — those less strongly attached to the workforce — are the ones most liable to experience unemployment. In setting the requirement, two extremes are to be avoided. If so much employment with the firm is required that the guarantee applies only to those who probably will never experience any layoff, it becomes meaningless. On the other hand, if too little employment is required, the cost of the guarantee becomes too great. Generally speaking, the practical norm adopted is that a substantial proportion, although not all, of those who experience unemployment must be protected by the plan.

Single-Employer Plans

In SUB plans, attachment to the workforce is defined either in terms of seniority (the length of time in which the worker has had some sort of connection with the company) or in terms of the length of time actually worked. In all the single-employer plans, seniority is the common measure of attachment. ("Seniority" is used loosely here to include "continuous service" and "accredited service," which may be accumulated somewhat more easily than seniority as strictly defined.)

Generally an employee acquires seniority status after a certain number of months at work — at the Ford Motor Company, for example, when he has worked 3 months within the 12-month period following the date of hiring. Thereafter, his seniority accumulates so long as there is no break in his attachment to the establishment. Seniority may therefore accumulate even during layoffs. (Seniority is broken by a quit, discharge, failure to report to work when recalled, or a continuous layoff equal in time to some designated period, generally the length of the accumulated seniority.)

Table 4–1 shows the eligibility requirements for selected SUB plans as they stood at the end of 1965. Of the plans that used seniority as the measure of attachment to the employer's workforce, all required at least one year. The plans of the Steelworkers generally required two years. The steel companies had originally proposed three years, the union had proposed one year, and a compromise on two years had been reached. Although this was a stricter requirement than that which had already been negotiated by the Auto Workers, the Steelworkers had achieved an offsetting gain in the duration of benefits — 52 weeks instead of the 26 weeks in the auto plan. The three and five years required by the plans in the electrical manufacturing industry are the more noteworthy because the benefits for which eligibility is thus restricted are themselves more limited than in the usual SUB plan. The provisions shown in Table 4–1 are substantially the same

TABLE 4-1

Minimum Seniority and Minimum Actual Working Time Required for Eligibility under Selected SUB Plans, as of December 1965

Plan	Seniority required	Actual working time required
	(years)	
UAW and auto companies	1	
UAW and agricultural implement companies	1	
URW and rubber companies	1	
USWA and steel companies	2	a
USWA and can companies	2b	50 percent of the work days in each of 4 consecutive months
CLGW and cement companies	1c	
IBEW, IUE, UE, and General Electric, Westinghouse	3	
IBEW and Radio Corporation of America	5	
Multi-employer plans		Various requirements in addition to UI requirementd

a Originally (1956) the steel plan contained a working-time requirement in addition to seniority; this requirement was dropped in 1962.

b Originally (1955) the requirement was 3 years; later (1958) it was reduced to 2 years.

c Originally (1959) the requirement was 2 years; later (1962) it was reduced to 1 year.

d Examples are cited in the text.

as in the original plans. As indicated, only a few changes have been made.

The original steel plan had combined a seniority provision with a time-worked requirement.[1] The latter was eliminated after June 30, 1962, because "This test barred some employees from benefits even though they had credit units. It became especially troublesome because of the long layoffs and spotty employment which many employees have experienced since the Plan went into effect" [40].

The can companies also used time worked as well as seniority. The additional requirement stemmed from the seasonal nature of employment in the canmaking industry. These companies have always employed many more workers during the summer season than during the winter, and the time-worked requirement was added in order to exclude most of the temporary workers. The seasonal workers in the can industry are of two types. Some are college students; they may or may not return in the spring

1. In addition to 2 years of continuous connection with the employer, some actual work was required in at least 6 of the previous 12 months, or in 12 of the previous 24 months, or in 18 of the previous 36 months, or 1,100 hours in the 12 months preceding layoff.

after the fall layoffs, but in any case they are not considered permanent members of the workforce. The others are "regular" seasonal workers, who return year after year and not infrequently take advantage of openings to become full-year workers. The plan aims to exclude the first, but not necessarily the second, type of seasonal worker. For purposes of seniority status, an employee who returns in the spring is credited with continuous service during the winter layoff. Hence, seasonal workers would not have been excluded from SUB by the simple seniority requirement; to achieve this end, a time-worked requirement was necessary.

This work requirement has been lessened in successive steps, as the result of union pressure and a more stable employment pattern. The union wanted to include the "regular" seasonal workers, although apparently willing to exclude the college students. The company yielded to the union pressure partly because seasonal unemployment had decreased in many of its divisions. Among other causes of the more stable employment pattern, the provision for sabbatical leave introduced in 1962, under which employees in the top half of the seniority list receive a 13-week vacation every five years, resulted in the granting of vacations during the slack season and the hiring of seasonal workers as replacements. Since this development, the plants have been offering steadier work to some employees who used to experience regular seasonal unemployment.

On the whole, SUB plans use a stricter standard of attachment to the employer's workforce than do the UI programs, and there seems no immediate likelihood that the standard will be relaxed. In the past, some unions have requested such a change but have not made a major issue of it. Union members tend to be somewhat less concerned than union leaders. The bulk of the union membership believes that it would not gain, and might even lose, by a liberalization of existing eligibility requirements. Union leadership, on the other hand, tends to be impressed by the advantage flowing to the union as an institution from making SUB more available to the entire membership.

Some management representatives favor an easing of eligibility requirements because they believe that by making SUB available to the low-seniority employees they can more easily maintain the company's labor force. This consideration appeals especially to managers in plants that are subject to regular, short-period layoffs, such as occur in the auto industry in connection with model changes.

Multi-Employer Plans

In some industries, workers change employers so frequently that seniority as a method of rationing jobs is not feasible. Most of the multi-employer SUB plans are in industries of this sort and hence cannot use seniority as a measure of labor-force attachment. Such plans make use of the alternative standard, time worked.

The following examples are all as of 1965. In the plan of the Buffalo Carpenters, an eligible applicant for SUB must have worked at least 32 hours in covered employment in each of 5 months during the 12-month period preceding his application; or, in the 24-month period preceding his application he must have worked at least 32 hours in covered employment in each of 6 months in the first year and at least 32 hours in each of 4 months during the more recent year. The plan of the Plumbers' Local 98 (Detroit) requires that an applicant must have acquired at least 12 credits within 12 consecutive months. The plan allots one credit for each month in which the employee works 8 to 15 hours and two credits for each month in which he works 16 or more hours.

The plan of the Retail Clerks in southern California has three alternative eligibility standards: 400 hours in the 6 months preceding layoff; 700 hours in the 12 months preceding layoff; and 1,000 hours in the 18 months preceding layoff. The plan of the Detroit tool-and-die workers (UAW Locals 155 and 157) also has alternative eligibility standards: if the applicant's most recent employer is a participating member of the Detroit Tooling Association (the contracting organization) no additional eligibility standard is specified beyond the requirement that the applicant be eligible for UI. If his most recent employer is not a member, the applicant is required to have worked for a participating employer in at least three payroll periods in the previous 104 weeks.

The plan of the Garment Workers requires that the applicant have worked for a participating employer in not less than four calendar quarters in the eight consecutive quarters immediately preceding the quarter in which the employee was terminated. In addition, the employee must have been a "permanent employee" of the company as determined by the board of trustees. The plan of the Maritime Workers also requires that the applicant be entitled to "permanent" employment, in the sense that he have a regular berth and not be a relief man. In addition, the applicant is required to have worked 200 days in the last three consecutive years. (The original provision required the applicant to have worked 500 days in the preceding three years, of which 200 days had to have been worked in the immediately preceding year.)

Required Quantity and Quality of Unemployment

Quantity of Unemployment

Having specified, by means of employment requirements, those employees whose unemployment may be compensable, a SUB plan must go on to specify the unemployment situation which the plan undertakes to cover. The first specification concerns the quantity of unemployment that is required and is expressed in the provisions that pertain to the waiting period and to periods of partial unemployment.

Waiting period. As a rule all plans require that the waiting week in the state UI program be served before SUB becomes payable. As explained below, an exception occurs in most of the plans negotiated by the Auto Workers in the case of those employees who are temporarily laid off out of the line of seniority. On the other hand, the SUB plans in the electrical industry have a very long waiting period: benefits are not payable until state UI benefits have been exhausted. (See Appendix B.)

In the original plans of the Continental Can and American Can companies there was an eligibility clause which prevented a person from receiving pay for more than 2,080 hours in any 12-month period. (This kind of provision, known as "banked overtime," is common in GAW plans.) The clause specified that, in addition to the usual waiting week, an employee must wait additional weeks, their number based on the number of hours in excess of 2,080 for which he had received wages or SUB — counting 22 hours for each week he received SUB — in the immediately preceding 52 weeks. This provision was never actually put into practice. Several union staff members were opposed to it, and the company had discovered the complexity of the records required to implement it; as a result, it was dropped from the contract in 1956, before SUB payments began.

Partial unemployment. Should a SUB plan undertake to compensate a worker for partial (part-week) unemployment, or should it concern itself only with those who experience one full week of unemployment? Put in this way, the problem of partial unemployment is an eligibility problem, which is properly treated in this chapter. But, since partial unemployment must also be discussed when dealing with the benefit amount (Chapter 5), in order to avoid repetition the entire discussion of partial unemployment is postponed to the following chapter.

Quality of Unemployment

The provisions that define compensable unemployment are of two sorts, those that relate to personal causes of unemployment and those that relate to impersonal, or environmental, causes. The first category includes two principal requirements — that the applicant be able to work and that he be willing to work. Of these two, the second is the more complex, comprising provisions that regulate four situations: the quit, the strike, availability for work, and refusal of work. It is also the more controversial. When the core plans were being negotiated, both labor and management made disqualification provisions a key issue. In cases where seniority was not broken, labor wanted easier disqualifications than those in most state UI programs, while management insisted that disqualifications in SUB should be stricter than those in UI. On the whole, though with some exceptions as explained below, the views of management prevailed in the core plans.

Ability to work. This requirement appears as an explicit and separate provision in only the steel and can plans. In the other plans, it is implied in the definition of "layoff," that is, the employee who is unable to work is usually considered not to be on layoff and is therefore not eligible for SUB.

The requirement can operate indirectly through the provision that an applicant must be eligible for UI. Since UI usually requires an applicant to be able to work, the UI standard on ability is thus automatically introduced into the SUB plan. In some plans there are exceptions to the general requirement that UI be received; such exceptions are treated as a group in a later section. Here we are concerned only with SUB provisions which directly require that the applicant be able to work.

The direct SUB requirement covers two quite different situations. In Situation No. 1, the employee is unable to do *any* work normally provided by the company. In Situation No. 2, the employee is unable to perform his regular work but could perform other work to which seniority would entitle him if such work were available. These two situations must be considered separately. In Situation No. 1 a further distinction is needed for clarity. If the employee was in this situation when he stopped work, and his inability to work was thus the cause of his stopping work, he is disqualified for SUB under all plans. But if he becomes unable to work after having been laid off and while drawing SUB, he may continue to draw SUB under the can and steel plans, which were amended to this effect in 1959 and 1962, respectively. Indeed, in the steel plan, SUB payments are continued even if suitable work becomes available to the disabled applicant. Any benefits paid in Situation No. 1 are not, of course, unemployment benefits. They are disability benefits paid out of a SUB fund. Such benefits are not paid by the SUB plans of the Auto Workers and Rubber Workers, partly because they are less needed. For these union members, the protection of sickness and accident insurance is continued for from 2 to 12 months after layoff.

Situation No. 2 is less clear-cut and more controversial. Before 1961, none of the plans had a specific provision which spelled out the status of an applicant whose ability to work was limited. The situation was clarified to some extent, though not entirely, in several cases that went to arbitration. In a 1958 case involving the rubber plan, a disabled employee was given light work until the company ran out of such work, when he was laid off. The arbitrator denied SUB in this case [41].

Two cases involving the steel plan turn on this issue. In a 1961 case [42], the arbitrator awarded SUB to the applicant on the grounds that there was a janitor's job in the man's seniority unit which he could have performed, even though the job was not open to him at the time. In a 1962 case [43], another arbitrator found the applicant ineligible because there were no light jobs available to which his seniority entitled him; the arbitrator added, however, that if the man had returned to a light job and had later been laid off he would have been eligible for SUB. In all three of these cases the applicant had been granted a UI benefit by the state. In protesting the payment of SUB, the employers evidently believed that a stricter norm of eligibility should hold for the private supplemental program than for the basic public program.

In 1961, the Auto Workers and Rubber Workers clarified the situation for their industries by negotiating an amendment which provided specifically that an employee fulfills the "able" requirement of SUB if he is able to do other work in the plant "to which he would have been entitled if he had sufficient seniority" [44].

Quit. It is not sufficient that an applicant for SUB be able to work; he must also be willing to work. This willingness is tested by three provisions relating to the actions, respectively, of quitting work, being on strike from work, and failing to seek work or refusing an offer of suitable work.[2] The first two issues relate to the applicant's current, or immediately past, job; the remaining issue relates to a possible future job.

All the core plans disqualify for unemployment caused by a quit, whether or not the quit was for a good cause. This provision has not been changed since the original plans were written. Here is probably the most important difference in disqualification provisions between SUB and UI programs; many of the latter pay benefits immediately to claimants if they quit with good cause and pay benefits after a delay if the quit was without good cause.

In this respect, the multi-employer plans differ from the core plans. Most

---

2. All SUB plans disqualify the employee who is discharged "for cause." This provision is generally accepted without dispute and is not under discussion here. Likewise, all plans disqualify an employee on disciplinary layoff, even though such an employee might be eligible for UI [45].

of the multi-employer plans have no specific provision of their own pertaining to quits but merely require that the applicant be eligible for UI; they thus in effect adopt the UI provisions covering quits. This is the only kind of provision relating to quits in the plans, for example, of the California Retail Clerks with the Food Employers Council, of the IBEW with the Electrical Contractors of Detroit, of the Plumbers and Pipefitters with the General Contractors of the same city, and of the Buffalo Carpenters with the Associated Contractors of that area.

The multi-employer plans were negotiated with little, if any, discussion of this issue, and one can only speculate on the reasons for this departure from the pattern of the single-employer plans. One reason probably is related to seniority provisions. In the single-employer plans, which use seniority, a worker who quits loses his seniority and thereby is automatically excluded from SUB. Since the multi-employer plans typically do not use seniority, there is not this automatic exclusion. Another reason is probably administrative convenience. The parties involved took the easiest course and settled for disqualification provisions that were identical with those in UI. The typical procedure in establishing a multi-employer plan is for the negotiators to agree on an amount of money to be contributed by the covered employers and then to appoint a board of trustees to whom is committed the whole of the remaining task, including the determination of the plan's provisions. The trustees were undoubtedly attracted by the simplicity of the arrangement whereby the SUB plan utilized the UI administrative machinery, paying SUB to whoever was able to present a valid UI check.

This easy solution of the voluntary quit issue may have been facilitated by conditions which make that issue in the multi-employer plans less of a problem than it is either in other SUB plans or in UI generally. In the multi-employer plans, first of all, most of the transient employees, among whom the quit rate is higher, are excluded by time-worked requirements. Second, except in the plan of the Retail Clerks in California, the multi-employer plans include few, if any, women employees, who tend to have a higher quit rate than men. Third, in these plans, the union holds almost complete control of the available jobs, and is in a position to ascertain the circumstances of any quits that occur and to take appropriate action to the extent that union politics permit. Finally, three of these plans are in Michigan, and the Michigan UI disqualification for quitting was relatively strict at the time the SUB plans were established. For all these reasons, the usual employer resistance to the payment of unemployment benefits to voluntary quits may have been blunted in the case of the multi-employer plans.

Strike. The strike might be considered a special case of the voluntary quit. The employees cease to work, but the employment relationship is not immediately terminated. The strike disqualification is, on the whole, stricter in SUB plans than in the UI program, and no substantial change has been made in this SUB provision since the original plans were negotiated. It is not surprising that the strike disqualification is stricter in SUB than in UI. SUB is the product of agreement, and any employer is likely to be reluctant to subsidize the unemployment resulting from an act of industrial warfare.

Although the strike provision is stricter in all SUB plans than in the UI program, it is less strict in some SUB plans than in others. It is less strict in the auto, agricultural implement, rubber, and cement industries than in the can and steel industries. In the first group of plans the typical strike disqualification states that an employee is eligible for SUB if his "layoff was not a consequence of any strike, slowdown, work stoppage, picketing (whether or not by employees), or concerted action, at a Company plant or plants, or any dispute of any kind involving employees whether at a Company plant or plants."

The extension of the SUB disqualification to include strikes by the contracting union at *any* plant of the employer resolved a long-standing dispute between management and labor in favor of the former. In the UI program, a classic dispute was carried on for years between the auto companies and the UAW as to whether benefits should be paid to union members employed by a company at one location who are on layoff because of a strike by members of the same union employed by the same company at another location. Management has always claimed that the payment of benefits in such a situation would enable the union to whipsaw the company by striking a small but essential company operation, whose shutdown would lead to the discontinuance of other operations and thus have the effect of a general strike without imposing on the union the cost of such a strike. The issue went to the Michigan Supreme Court, which ruled in favor of the union; thereafter, however, the legislature amended the law to prevent such UI payments.

The cement plan, which began late (1959), has a somewhat less restrictive provision. To the above language the cement plan adds the following clause: "but this provision shall not disqualify an employee from receiving a layoff benefit if he nevertheless is found eligible for a state system unemployment benefit for the same week of layoff "[46]. While the union has not succeeded in making the SUB provision less restrictive than the UI provision, it has prevented management from making the SUB provision more restrictive. In this respect, the cement plan differs from all the other core plans, although it resembles the multi-employer plans.[3]

The interpretation of the strike disqualification is complex and difficult. (In the UI program, many states which permit local offices to make decisions on all other UI disqualification issues reserve decisions on strike issues to the state central office.) A number of hypothetical strike situations were proposed to the representatives of the unions and companies in the first group of plans (auto, agricultural implement, rubber, and cement). Although the language of the strike provision is practically identical in these auto-type plans, the solutions to the hypothetical situations varied widely. This variation is perhaps to be expected in view of the very limited experience which the plans have had with the strike provision. Interpretation of the provision will become more definite only as actual cases arise and are decided. However, from a close reading of the provision, from the various opinions expressed by the parties in interviews, and from the occasional instances in which the provision has been applied, the following would seem to be a reasonable interpretation of the scope of the strike disqualification in the auto-type plan.

SUB is clearly *prohibited* if the strike is by employees who are members of the union which has the SUB contract and who are employed by the company at any plant or installation of the company.

SUB is *uncertain* if the strike is by employees other than members of the contracting union and if, as a result, the company lays off members of the contracting union; SUB would probably be paid in this situation, especially if the strike is not at a company plant. If members of the contracting union are not laid off but are without work because they refused to cross a picket line, they probably would be considered "not on layoff" and would not be eligible for SUB. However, if the union could convince the company that there was danger of physical violence in crossing the picket line, SUB might be paid, especially if UI benefits were paid. Finally, if, when Company A is struck, companies B and C close down in support of A, the employees of B and C might or might not be eligible for UI and SUB. (The answer is obviously critical to the often-discussed possibility of the auto companies' use of this defensive technique.)

SUB is clearly *payable* if the layoff is due to a strike of employees not members of the contracting union and not employees of the contracting

3. The acceptance of UI strike norms by the cement industry is not quite complete. The UI norm is not accepted by companies which have plans in New York and Rhode Island, where UI benefits are paid to strikers after the strike has lasted for seven and six weeks, respectively.

company; it is also payable if the layoff is due to a strike by the contracting union at a company other than the contracting company, for example, at a supplier of the contracting company.

The steel-type plan has stricter strike provisions than has the auto-type plan. In the steel and can plans, SUB would not be paid in any of the situations cited above except that of a layoff due to a strike of another union at another company. Specifically disqualifying are layoffs which are the consequences of a strike in the following situations. (1) A strike by members of the Steelworkers employed by any company. Thus SUB was denied to the Steelworkers in the can industry who were unemployed during the steel strike of 1959. (2) A strike which prevents the ingress or egress of necessary materials, if the strike is by (a) any employees of the company or (b) employees of transportation or utility companies.

Availability for work. The relationship of the SUB applicant to his current or previous job is not the only test of his willingness to work. Almost as important, and much more complicated, is his attitude toward other available jobs.

The explicit requirement that a SUB claimant be available for work is found only in the steel, can, and rubber plans. In the other core plans this requirement is implicit in the requirement that the claimant be eligible for UI. As the latter requirement has been gradually modified by the negotiation of various exceptions (Table 4–3), some plans — for example, the plans negotiated by the UAW with the auto and agricultural implement companies — have been left with no requirement that a claimant be available for work. There seems to be nothing in the plan of American Motors, for example, to prevent an employee, after he has exhausted UI, from going on a hunting trip, so informing the company, and requesting that his SUB checks be forwarded to his vacation headquarters. The employer's only means of testing the employee's availability is to offer him a job with the company. A company which had experienced heavy layoffs, as American Motors did in 1966–1967, would not be able to use this test.

The possible size of the problem of availability is increased in the cement, rubber, and can plans by their provision of very long-term benefits — up to three, four, and five years, respectively. In the can plan, the 1965 provision of full benefits after the exhaustion of UI benefits increases the potential size of the problem even more. When a can company closes a plant in an isolated community, the relation of SUB to labor mobility and availability will be given its most severe test. (And see Appendix B.)

Refusal of suitable work. All SUB plans require the applicant to accept an offer of suitable work or be disqualified completely. The issue of job refusal usually turns on the definition of "suitable" and is the object of a constant tug-of-war. The employee would like to have the right to bid on open jobs within a wide area (preferably the entire area) of the company's operations, but would not like to be required to take any specific job. The employer would like the right to put the employee into any one of a large number of jobs (preferably into any job), but would not like to be required to offer any specific job to any individual employee.

Neither labor nor management ever gets its way completely; through bargaining they have established positions which reflect every possible degree of compromise and which are expressed chiefly in terms of seniority provisions. Such provisions are relevant to the present discussion because the most usual application of the suitable work disqualification occurs when the applicant for SUB exercises an option given him by the seniority provisions to take a layoff rather than an offered job.[4] When the employee does not have this option, no problem arises with respect to SUB: if he refuses the offer of a job which he has no option to refuse, he is discharged and therefore is not eligible for SUB. The problem arises when he refuses a job he has an option to refuse: is he then eligible for SUB?

Disqualification for refusal of suitable work may be controlled directly by a specific provision or indirectly by the general provision that the applicant for SUB must be eligible for UI. Thus the applicant may be required to surmount a "double hurdle," as the unions describe it: after satisfying the direct SUB requirement, the applicant may still be disqualified for SUB by the indirect UI requirement.

Some unions have striven to eliminate this double hurdle by negotiating an exception to the general rule that eligibility for SUB presupposes eligibility for UI. An exception covering refusal of suitable work has been negotiated in some SUB plans and is described in a later section of this chapter, where all exceptions to the rule are treated together. Although not discussed here, Exception 7 in Table 4–3 should be recognized as an essential part of the way in which SUB plans handle the refusal of work.

In the older guaranteed-wage plans a bargain was frequently struck whereby in exchange for greater security the employees granted the employer more flexibility in the utilization of their services. They agreed to work, temporarily, at jobs other than their usual ones and to work overtime at regular rates to offset the full pay received during the slack periods. In the years of preparation for SUB, the leading unions stated

4. Because seniority provisions differ so much—not only between firms, but even between departments within a firm—the discussion here can proceed only in very general terms.

repeatedly that they would not negotiate such concessions in exchange for any SUB plans.

This was one of the issues in the 1962 steel negotiations. The steel companies, having a suitable-work provision that was from the beginning somewhat less strict than that in other plans, asked the Steelworkers to reciprocate by giving them an added degree of freedom in the utilization of manpower. The union emphatically refused:

> The union members take strong exception to the Company members' proposal on the grounds that it would destroy the present seniority and job assignment rights which have been established in the Basic Agreement to protect the economic and the job status of the employee. The company members' proposal would substitute for the union's hard-won seniority rights to determine job security, the pre-union system of favoritism and discrimination. It would serve to merge all employees into one undiscriminated labor pool. . . . The Union members state that from the beginning it was clearly understood by the parties that the establishment of the SUB Plan would not enlarge management's rights under the Labor Agreement. The Company's proposal runs contrary to this understanding [47].

This instance of a successful union defense of labor standards is typical. Almost without exception the unions have been able to avoid making any such concession. Any job that the members could refuse before SUB, they continued to be able to refuse after the establishment of SUB. This does not necessarily mean that having refused such a job they are still eligible for SUB. They may or they may not be, depending on the wording of the suitable-work provision in their plan. Still more depends on the interpretation given that provision. It is unsafe to think one knows the significance of such a provision in any plan unless one has investigated actual experience under that plan. However, a few general guidelines may be indicated.

Table 4-2 shows the various forms this provision took in the core plans. From the beginning, the steel plan had the more liberal provision, which most of the other plans eventually adopted. In the steel plan, if an employee had an option to refuse a job (very few had this right), he could exercise the option without losing his eligibility for SUB. However, the steel plan, as of 1965, was less liberal than some of the others with respect to the "second hurdle," eligibility for UI. If an employee was disqualified by the UI agency for refusing work which was suitable by UI standards, he was automatically ineligible for SUB. The steel plan has never contained an excepting provision to cover this situation (see Table 4-3).

As shown in Tables 4-2 and 4-3, the auto plan underwent a significant modification of this eligibility condition in 1961. Before the 1961 amendments, most employees who refused "other work" were disqualified for

TABLE 4–2

Disqualification for SUB Because of Refusal of Other Than Regular Work
with Company: Selected SUB Plans, 1955–1965, by Type
of Work Refused, Plan, and Date

Plan and date	Any work	Any other work	Any suitable work	Any work which company may properly assign or employee may be required to accept	Work employee has no right to refuse under collective bargaining contract
UAW and auto companies					
1955		X[a]			
1958		X[a]			
1961					X
1964					X
UAW and Allis-Chalmers					
1955				X	
1959					X
1962					X
1964					X
UAW and John Deere					
1955		X			
1958		X			
1962		X			
1964		X			
URW and rubber companies					
1956				X	
1959				X	
1961				X	
1963				X	
1965					X
USWA and steel companies					
1956					X
1960					X
1962					X
1965					X
USWA and American Can					
1955	X				
1959			X		
1962					X
1965					X
UCLGW and cement companies					
1959	X[b]				
1962	X[b]				
1965	X[b]				

[a] This disqualification did not apply to skilled tool-and-die, maintenance and construction, or powerhouse employees, who could refuse work outside their respective departments and still receive SUB if eligible for UI.

[b] There is no provision in the SUB plan itself regarding disqualification for benefits if other work is refused. However, the practice in the industry is to allow little or no option to refuse work.

SUB even though the general labor contract allowed them to refuse such work. Only three specified classes of skilled workers could exercise their option to refuse a job and still remain eligible for SUB. After the 1961 amendments, any employee who had such an option under the general labor contract could exercise it without thereby disqualifying himself for SUB. This change made the auto plan like the steel plan, which had had this language from the beginning. The 1961 amendments to the auto plan also removed the "second hurdle," the UI requirement. If the exercise of his option disqualified an employee for UI, then eligibility for UI ceased to be a prerequisite for SUB (see Table 4–3, Exception 7).

The rubber plan has always used the language of the first Allis-Chalmers plan, which was the last major SUB plan negotiated by the Auto Workers in 1955 and contained a few liberalized provisions not found in the earlier plans. The provisions of the rubber plan were not determined until 1956 and, not unnaturally, reflected the latest and — from the union standpoint — most improved plan. The language of the rubber plan is broad and can be applied to a variety of situations, but it would seem that employees with the option to refuse work could generally exercise their option without losing eligibility for SUB. Prior to 1963, these employees could, however, be stopped by the second hurdle, the UI requirement. An amendment negotiated in 1963 (see Table 4–3, Exception 7) removed this dependence on the UI program.

The two can companies originally (1955) disqualified an applicant who refused "any work," but in 1962 both companies adopted the language of the steel and — by this time — auto plans. A 1965 amendment provided that a laid-off employee may refuse two job offers without penalty. If he refuses three offers, he is limited to two years of SUB payments.

Among the agricultural implement companies, Deere & Co. has never changed the original wording of its strict provision, under which an employee is disqualified for the refusal of "other work." The way in which this provision has been interpreted and administered would need to be investigated before one could judge its actual impact. This plan has the second hurdle also: in all cases, the applicant for SUB who has refused an offer of work is held to the requirement that he must be eligible for UI. In all these provisions, the Deere & Co. plan is similar to the plans in the cement industry.

As indicated in Table 4–2, the cement plan has never had a specific provision covering the refusal of work. The absence of this provision probably reflects the prevailing practice in the industry, which does not recognize any employee option in this matter. As pointed out earlier, if there is no option there is no problem. For the same reason, the cement plan does not need an exception to the requirement that an applicant be eligible for UI (see Table 4–3).

Unemployment due to "acts of God." In addition to the personal factors that determine whether unemployment is compensable — such as the ability and willingness to work — there are two groups of impersonal, or environmental, factors. Of these, one group operates to exclude unemployment due to an "act of God," that is, to a cause completely beyond the control of the employer, such as a flood or an earthquake. All the core plans and nearly all other SUB plans have this provision.

Disputes easily arise as to whether the event that caused the unemployment should be classed as an "act of God." For example, in 1958 a layoff occurred in a plant of the United States Steel Corporation because of a lack of fuel, which in turn was the result of a severe cold spell. When the company refused to pay benefits under this provision, the union took the case to arbitration. The arbitrator upheld the company.

In recent years, the provision has been amended so as to apply only to unemployment of more than two weeks' duration. The amendment was adopted by the steel and can plans in 1962, by the auto and agricultural implement plans in 1964, and by the rubber plan in 1965. Since few "acts of God" shut down an operation for as long as two weeks, the provision now has little application outside of major disasters.

Unemployment resulting from a permanent layoff. The other group of impersonal factors operates to exclude any but the most severe form of unemployment, namely, that which follows upon a permanent layoff. The provision is not phrased in these terms, but usually specifies that the plan is limited to layoffs incurred for such reasons as technological change, abolition of a job, or the closing of the business. Plans with such a provision resemble both severance and SUB plans and combine the limitations of both. Like severance plans, and unlike the usual SUB plan, they are limited to permanent layoffs; like the usual SUB plan, and unlike severance plans, the person laid off must be unemployed.

An example is provided by the Garment Workers' (ILGWU) plan, which is limited to unemployment resulting from the termination of business by the employer (see Part I). Another example is the Technological Adjustment Pay plan negotiated between Armour and Company and the Packinghouse Workers (UPWA) in 1961. If a plant or department closes permanently, a man may either accept severance pay or request transfer to another Armour plant. If he chooses the latter, the company will supplement his unemployment benefits while he is waiting for the transfer, which is made as openings in other plants occur.

A plan negotiated between the United States Borax Company and the Chemical Workers (ICWU) attempted to distinguish two types of layoffs and to treat the resulting unemployment differently. According to the original plan (1957), an employee laid off because of technological change was entitled to a lump-sum payment, while an employee laid off because of a general curtailment of operations and unemployed for 90 days was entitled to a SUB payment, which, with unemployment insurance, equaled 75 percent of his former wage. Problems arose in distinguishing between the two kinds of layoffs, and amendments were negotiated in 1960 and 1962 which resulted in a different kind of distinction. Employees with eight or fewer years of seniority were made eligible for SUB payments when laid off. Longer-service employees were given an option: no matter what the reason for their layoff, they may choose a lump-sum benefit and forfeit recall rights, or choose weekly payments equal to the normal straight-time pay for 1 to 52 weeks, depending on age and length of service.

In contrast to plans which limit benefits to unemployment caused by technological change is the Kaiser Steel-USWA plan, which covers only "workers on layoffs due to causes other than changes in technology or work methods." The reason for the limitation seems to be that the company has a separate long-range plan which protects workers against loss of employment, and even against reduction of income, resulting from changes in technology or work methods.

Required Relationship of SUB to UI

As explained in Chapter 1, the dependence of SUB on UI in the matter of eligibility conditions has been a controversial issue from the beginning (see also Chapters 5 and 11). The unions, especially the Auto Workers, hoped to use SUB as a lever to move UI in the direction of greater liberality and to this end wanted to make SUB entirely independent of UI. Management was insistent that the private program should not "undercut" the standards of the public program and wanted to make UI standards a minimum upon which to erect higher SUB standards. The resolution of this early dispute clearly favored management's position, and practically all plans require UI eligibility as a condition for SUB eligibility.

With the passage of time, however, the unions, especially the Auto Workers, have succeeded in negotiating a growing list of exceptions to the requirement that the SUB applicant be eligible for UI. Whereas the original SUB plans had contained only three or four exceptions, and none of these very controversial, by 1965 the number had grown to a dozen in the plans of the Auto Workers and Rubber Workers, and several of them touched on very controversial areas. These exceptions had early acquired the name of "little Romans" because they were listed in the contract by small Roman numerals. In some of the later, revised, contracts they appeared in the form of Arabic numerals within parentheses and were called "tented Arabs." In this study, the term "Arab" is used indiscriminately, regardless of the particular contract, to refer to one of these exceptions.

Table 4-3 lists the chief "Arabs" and shows the changes that have occurred in them. The first four exceptions, which appeared in most of the original plans, have never been the subject of much controversy. The next three (5, 6, and 7) came into the plans later and were the fruit of struggle. The next four (8 through 11) also came into the plans later, but they occasioned little controversy. The last item in the list is the most recent one and is a kind of catchall. As is clear from the table, the auto-type plans provide for more exceptions than do the steel-type plans.

The first exception listed is first, also, in importance. Without it there would be no possibility of the private program's supplementing the duration of the public program. This exception meant much more originally in the steel plan, which provided up to 52 weeks of benefits, than in the original auto plan, which was limited to 26 weeks. Since at that time 26 weeks was, with one exception, the maximum provided by any state UI program, the steel plan had to provide this exception or see its duration provision stultified.

The second exception, referring to a second waiting week in UI, appeared in all the original plans. It was directed at the few states which then required two waiting weeks before UI benefits could be drawn. Although no state now requires 2 waiting weeks, there is another requirement against which this exception may prove useful. A number of states (28 as of the end of 1965) require a second waiting week if a second spell of unemployment begins in a benefit year and continues into a new benefit year. The exception was widened to cover this situation in the auto and agricultural implement plans in 1964. Quantitatively, this second exception is no longer important. (See Appendix B for elimination of waiting week in the plans of the agricultural implement industry.)

In the auto and agricultural implement industries, when a reduction in force is made (this excludes layoffs resulting from model change, inventory taking, and plant rearrangement) the companies sometimes find it necessary to temporarily lay off employees out of line of seniority. For workers thus laid off, it frequently happens that this is their first layoff in a year and they are therefore required to serve a waiting period in the UI program. Without UI, they would not get SUB either. To make these workers more

TABLE 4-3

Exceptions to Receipt of UI Benefits as Requirement for Eligibility for SUB,
by Reason for Nonreceipt of UI Benefits: Selected Plans, 1955–1965

Reason for nonreceipt of UI benefits, by plan	Inclusion (X) or exclusion (0) of exception, by date				
	First plan[a] (1955 or 1956)	Second plan[a] (1958, 1959, or 1960)	Third plan (1961 or 1962)	Fourth rubber plan (1963)	Other fourth plans and fifth rubber plan (1964 or 1965)
1. Exhaustion of UI benefits					
UAW and auto companies	X	X	X		X
UAW and Allis-Chalmers	X	X	X		X
URW and rubber companies	X	X	X	X	X
USWA and basic steel	X	X	X		X
USWA and American Can	X	X	X		X
UCLGW and cement companies		X	X		X
2. Second waiting week					
UAW and auto companies	X	X	X		X
UAW and Allis-Chalmers	X	X	X		X
URW and rubber companies	X	X	X	X	X
USWA and basic steel	X	X	X		X
USWA and American Can	X	X	X		X
UCLGW and cement companies		X	X		X
3. Insufficient earnings					
UAW and auto companies	X	X	X		X
UAW and Allis-Chalmers	X	X	X		X
URW and rubber companies	X	X	X	X	X
USWA and basic steel	X	X	X		X
USWA and American Can	X	X	X		X
UCLGW and cement companies		X	X		X
4. Earnings above state limit					
UAW and auto companies	0	X	X		X
UAW and Allis-Chalmers	X	X	X		X
URW and rubber companies	X	X	X	X	X
USWA and basic steel	X	X	X		X
USWA and American Can	X	X	X		X
UCLGW and cement companies		0	0		0
5. Totally disabled while on layoff					
UAW and auto companies	0	0	0		0
UAW and Allis-Chalmers	0	0	0		0
URW and rubber companies	0	0	0	0	0
USWA and basic steel	0	0	X		X
USWA and American Can	0	0	X		X
UCLGW and cement companies		0	0		b
6. Partially disabled[c]					
UAW and auto companies	0	0	X		X
UAW and Allis-Chalmers	0	0	X		X
URW and rubber companies	0	0	0	X	X
USWA and basic steel	0	0	0		0
USWA and American Can	0	0	0		0
UCLGW and cement companies		0	0		0

TABLE 4–3 (*Continued*)

Reason for nonreceipt of UI benefits, by plan	Inclusion (X) or exclusion (0) of exception, by date				
	First plan[a] (1955 or 1956)	Second plan[a] (1958, 1959, or 1960)	Third plan (1961 or 1962)	Fourth rubber plan (1963)	Other fourth plans and fifth rubber plan (1964 or 1965)
7. Refusal of work with company which claimant has a right to refuse under collective agreement					
UAW and auto companies	0	0	X		X
UAW and Allis-Chalmers	0	0	X		X
URW and rubber companies	0	0	0	X	X
USWA and basic steel	0	0	0		0
USWA and American Can	0	0	0		0
UCLGW and cement companies		0	0		0
8. Receipt of military terminal pay					
UAW and auto companies	0	0	X		X
UAW and Allis-Chalmers	0	0	X		X
URW and rubber companies	0	0	0	X	X
USWA and basic steel	0	0	0		0
USWA and American Can	0	0	0		0
UCLGW and cement companies		0	0		0
9. Receipt of statutory retirement or disability benefits which claimant could receive while working					
UAW and auto companies	0	0	X		X
UAW and Allis-Chalmers	0	0	X		X
URW and rubber companies	0	0	0	X	0
USWA and basic steel	0	0	0		0
USWA and American Can	0	0	0		0
UCLGW and cement companies		0	0		0
10. Receipt of retraining allowances from federal or state program					
UAW and auto companies	0	0	X		0[d]
UAW and Allis-Chalmers	0	0	X		0[d]
URW and rubber companies	0	0	0	X	0[d]
USWA and basic steel	0	0	X		X
USWA and American Can	0	0	X		X
UCLGW and cement companies		0	0		0
11. Automatic retirement without company pension					
UAW and auto companies	0	0	X		0[e]
UAW and Allis-Chalmers	0	0	X		0[e]
URW and rubber companies	0	0	0	X	0[e]
USWA and basic steel	0	0	0		0
USWA and American Can	0	0	0		0
UCLGW and cement companies		0	0		0

TABLE 4–3 (*Continued*)

Reason for nonreceipt of UI benefits, by plan	Inclusion (X) or exclusion (0) of exception, by date				
	First plan[a] (1955 or 1956)	Second plan[a] (1958, 1959, or 1960)	Third plan (1961 or 1962)	Fourth rubber plan (1963)	Other fourth plans and fifth rubber plan (1964 or 1965)
12. *Other reasons, if denial of SUB is contrary to intent of plan*					
UAW and auto companies	0	0	0		X
UAW and Allis-Chalmers	0	0	0	.	X
URW and rubber companies	0	0	0	0	X
USWA and basic steel	0	0	0		0
USWA and American Can	0	0	0		0
UCLGW and cement companies		0	0		0

[a] The 1959 plan was the first plan in the cement industry.

[b] The exception is broader in the cement plan than in the steel plan insofar as the benefit is payable in the cement plan whether the disability was the cause of layoff or occurred after layoff.

[c] The exception is applicable where the claimant is unable to do work offered by the company but is able to do other work to which he would have a right if he had sufficient seniority.

[d] The exception was dropped from these plans for technical reasons. The payment of SUB in this situation is provided for elsewhere in the agreements.

[e] The exception was dropped from the SUB plan after the Internal Revenue Service had ruled unfavorably on this type of payment from an unemployment fund.

willing to accept such layoffs, an exception has been negotiated in the plans of the Auto Workers allowing these employees to be paid a benefit which even without UI equals 62 percent of gross wages.

The third exception covers the case where an employee has not had sufficient earnings to qualify for UI benefits but has some credit units under the SUB plan. This is probably a rare situation, but it can occur once an employee has attained SUB eligibility because of the way in which SUB credits are accumulated, as is explained in the next chapter. (A related additional exception appears in the plans of the Auto Workers: if an employee's UI benefit would amount to less than $2, the employee need not apply for it; the SUB plan will consider him as having received it.)

The fourth exception was introduced to maintain a differential favoring the employee who did some work over the employee who did not work at all. An employee who is partially employed may earn more than the allowable state limit and thus become ineligible for UI. If such a worker is also denied SUB — because he is ineligible for UI — it could happen that he would receive less income than one who did no work. This undesirable effect, which was discussed earlier in connection with the requirement that stipulated the quantity of unemployment, is guarded against by the fourth exception. This "Arab" was in the original basic steel, can, and rubber plans; it was added to the auto plans in 1958–1959;[5] it has never been adopted by the cement plan.

Although Exceptions 5 and 6 both relate to a condition of disability, they are essentially different. The fifth exception applies only to an employee who at the time of layoff was able to do his regular work and who became disabled (unable to do his regular work or any work) while on a compensable layoff. Since an employee in this situation is usually disqualified for UI,[6] without this exception he would also be disqualified for SUB. The exception was introduced into the plans of the Steelworkers in 1962 but is not needed in the plans of the Auto Workers or Rubber Workers because these plans do not pay SUB in this situation. It is arguable whether the provision in the cement plan should be looked upon as an exception or as an addition; the plan has a separate provision for the payment of sickness and disability benefits from the SUB fund.

The sixth exception, which appears only in the plans of the Auto Workers and Rubber Workers, and only as a late emendation, differs essentially from the fifth exception. It is not a disability benefit but a true unemployment benefit. An applicant must not be completely disabled but must be capable of performing some job to which his seniority would entitle him if such a job were open. This exception is very close in nature to the following one.

The seventh exception, governing the refusal of suitable work, was added to the plans of the Auto Workers in 1961 and to the plans of the Rubber Workers in 1963. It has never been a part of the plans in the steel, can, or cement industries. This exception was discussed above, when treating of the direct SUB disqualification for the refusal of suitable work. Considering the amount of controversy that has surrounded this provision, it has given rise to a disproportionately small number of cases, as is noted in Part III.

One of the long-time objectives of the Auto Workers has been to use the SUB program to liberalize the disqualification provisions in the UI program, and to make them uniform among the states. The union took a step in this direction in 1962 when it was able to add to the American Motors plan a provision limiting to six weeks the effect of any UI dis-

5. The Allis-Chalmers plan had this exception from the beginning. In this as in several other provisions, the Allis-Chalmers plan, which was the last major plan to be negotiated by the UAW in 1955, was more liberal than the other plans in the auto and agricultural implement industries negotiated earlier that year.

6. As of 1965, there were nine states which paid UI benefits in this situation.

qualification in any state. If after six weeks an employee is still disqualified for UI benefits, eligibility for UI is no longer a prerequisite for eligibility for SUB. This exception appears in no other plan. As of the end of 1965, no case had arisen and no benefit had been paid under this provision.

The next three exceptions — 8, 9, and 10 — cover situations in which the applicant for SUB is concurrently in receipt of benefits from certain state or federal programs. Since most states disqualify applicants for UI if they are receiving such benefits, the exceptions are necessary if a SUB plan wishes to pay such employees. The plans of the Auto Workers include all three exceptions; the plans of the Rubber Workers include the eighth and tenth exceptions; the plans of the Cement Workers include none of these exceptions. As can be seen from Table 4–3, all of these exceptions are of more recent origin.

The eleventh exception governs the situation in which an employee has been compelled to retire but is not eligible for a company pension. It sometimes happens that such a person is ruled ineligible for UI on the score of not being able and available for work. This exception makes possible the payment of SUB even though UI is denied. Although paid from the SUB fund, the benefit is more like a retirement than an unemployment payment. This exception was added to the plans of the Auto Workers in 1961 and to those of the Rubber Workers in 1963. It was dropped from both plans in 1964–1965 because the Internal Revenue Service ruled that, for tax purposes, it was improper to charge this type of payment against an unemployment-benefit fund.[7]

The last exception was added in 1964–1965. Found only in the plans of the Auto Workers and Rubber Workers, it is intended to introduce a maximum of flexibility into a SUB plan. If both parties agree that an exception to the requirements should be made in a particular case or in a particular class of cases, the board of administration may authorize the payment of SUB benefits even though there is no explicit provision in the plan to cover the situation. Since the consent of both parties is required, it is not likely to be applied widely; it will probably continue to be restricted to very clear, and rather infrequent, situations.

Summary

On the whole, the eligibility and disqualification provisions of SUB plans are stricter than the corresponding provisions of UI. Such changes as have

---

7. Actually, the benefit is still paid; the money comes initially from the general funds of the company, but the amount of the payment is then offset against future contributions to the SUB fund.

been made in the SUB provisions have been mostly in the direction of liberalization. The SUB plans specify the quantity and quality of employment required in order to limit SUB payments to employees who are members of the "regular" workforce. In nearly all plans, the requirements are stricter in SUB than in UI. SUB plans of the steel type require two years of seniority, while those of the auto type require one year. Only a few changes have been made in this requirement, the most significant being the 1962 change in the cement plan, by which the seniority requirement was reduced from two years to one. In addition to the seniority requirement, the plans in the can industry include a time-worked requirement in order to exclude certain seasonal workers. The multi-employer plans, since they cannot express the requirement in terms of seniority, use only time worked.

Quantity and Quality of Unemployment Required

Except in some narrowly defined situations, all SUB plans require that a waiting week be served before payments begin if the UI law specifies a waiting week. Few changes have been made in this requirement. The treatment of unemployment for part of a week is discussed in Chapter 5. In general, SUB plans require that an applicant be able and willing to work. In the core plans, most of the provisions which spell out these requirements are stricter than the corresponding provisions in UI; but there are a few provisions in a few plans which are less strict than those in UI. Many changes have been made in these provisions. In most of the multi-employer SUB plans, the requirements are the same as those in UI.

Ability to work. An applicant for SUB who is completely disabled is eligible for SUB only in the steel plan and then only if he became disabled while on a compensable layoff. The situation with regard to the applicant who is unable to do his regular work but is able to do some other work in the company was obscure in all the core plans before 1961 but was clarified in the plans of the auto and rubber industries after that date by an amendment which specified that an employee fulfills the "able" requirement if he is able to do some work "to which he would have been entitled if he had had sufficient seniority." It would seem that, on the whole, the SUB requirement in this area is stricter than the corresponding UI requirement in most states.

Quits. All the core plans disqualify an applicant whose unemployment results from a quit, whether or not the quit was for "good cause." This provision, which is stricter than the usual UI requirement, has not been changed since the original plans were written. The multi-employer plans merely require that the applicant for SUB be eligible for UI; they thus in effect adopt the UI provisions relating to quits.

Strikes. In this area, as in that of the voluntary quit, the SUB provisions have undergone no substantial changes and are stricter than the corresponding UI provisions. The strike disqualification is somewhat stricter in the steel type of SUB plan than in the auto type. Of the core plans, the cement plan has the least restrictive provision. The precise meaning of the strike provisions in the various plans will not be clear until they have been applied to more actual cases.

Availability for work. In the development of SUB, some plans have been left without an explicit provision that the SUB applicant must be available for or actively seeking work. This lack could pose a problem after a claimant has exhausted his UI benefits and can no longer be required to report to the public employment office. The problem is most likely to be important in the plans that provide very long duration and/or full benefits after the exhaustion of UI. (See Appendix B.)

Refusal of suitable work. The most usual application of the suitable-work disqualification occurs when an applicant for SUB exercises an option given him by the general labor contract to take a layoff rather than an offered job: is such an applicant eligible for SUB? The steel plan and the rubber plan have always recognized the eligibility of such an applicant, and the auto plan did so after the amendments of 1961. In the cement plan the problem does not arise. The original and subsequent provisions of various plans are shown in Table 4–2. In the definition of "suitable" work, a given SUB plan may be more liberal or less liberal than a given UI law.

Acts of God. Practically all the core plans have always excluded unemployment attributable to an "act of God," but in recent years the provision has been amended so as to apply only to unemployment of more than two weeks' duration.

"Permanent" unemployment. None of the core plans and only a few of the other plans limit payments to unemployment that follows permanent separation from a job. These plans combine the limitations of both severance and SUB plans.

Relationship of SUB to UI Required

In general, eligibility for SUB requires eligibility for UI. Thus the typical SUB plan makes UI standards a base upon which to erect higher SUB standards. However, the unions, especially the Auto Workers, have succeeded in negotiating a growing list of exceptions to the requirement that the SUB applicant be eligible for UI. As of the end of 1965, there were a dozen such exceptions, as shown in Table 4-3. The multi-employer plans permit very few exceptions to the requirement that the applicant for SUB be eligible for UI; on the other hand, these plans add very few requirements to those imposed by UI. Three plans in Detroit, those of the Plumbers, the Pipefitters, and the Electrical Workers (see Chapter 2), come closest to achieving the independence from UI that the UAW has always aimed at.

5

THE BENEFIT FORMULA

The benefit formula is the heart of a SUB plan. On the realistic assumption that all employees regularly attached to the establishment will be covered by the plan and that few of these will be disqualified, the crucial question is, "How much will the plan pay and for how long?" This chapter examines the benefit formula in SUB, considering first the amount and then the duration of the benefits provided.[1]

Benefit Amount

Five elements of the benefit formula enter into the determination of the benefit amount: (1) the basic benefit-wage ratio, (2) dependents' benefits, (3) the limitation represented by the maximum benefit, (4) the benefit for partial unemployment, and (5) the reduction of benefits when the fund is below a certain level.

Benefit-Wage Ratio

The first and most important element is the basic benefit-wage ratio. By "basic" is meant the ratio before adjustment for any of the other four elements. Table 5–1 shows the basic benefit-wage ratios that have been used in six plans — the four core plans and the plans of Allis-Chalmers and Continental Can.

For the base of the ratio, the core plans have always used straight-time wages, exclusive of overtime and similar premium payments. Any difference among plans in the definition of straight-time wages would, of course, affect the value of a given percentage as applied to the base.

Nearly all the early plans used net wages (straight-time weekly wages, as defined in the respective contracts, minus income and social security taxes). Although the use of net wages automatically resulted in a kind of dependents' benefit,[2] this result was apparently not the primary objective. Net, rather than gross, wages seem to have been the preference of employers, who wanted to leave at least as great a work incentive (the percentage difference between take-home pay and unemployment benefits) for the

---

1. Payments other than SUB are sometimes made from SUB funds. Precisely because they are not SUB payments, they are treated not in this chapter but in Chapter 6, which deals with SUB funds.
2. The uniform ratio applied to net wages resulted in a higher benefit for the claimant with dependents because of less income tax withheld.

TABLE 5-1

Ratio of Regular Unemployment Benefits[a] (UI plus SUB) to Wages,[b] Selected SUB Plans, by Date of Plan, 1955–1965

Union and company	First plan (1955 or 1956)	Second plan[c] (1958, 1959, or 1960)	Third plan (1961 or 1962)	Fourth rubber plan (1963)	Other fourth plans and fifth rubber plan (1964 and 1965)
UAW and auto companies	65%[d] net wages 60%[d] net wages	65% net wages	62% gross wages+		62% gross wages+
UAW and Allis-Chalmers	65% net wages	65%–70% net wages[e]	62% gross wages+		62% gross wages+
URW and rubber companies	65% net wages	65% net wages	65% net wages	62% gross wages	65% gross wages+
USWA and basic steel	65% net wages	65% net wages	60% gross wages+		60% gross wages+
USWA and Continental Can	53.5%–64.4%[f] gross wages+	53.5%–64.4%[f] gross wages+	57.5%–63.5%[g] gross wages+		70% gross wages[h]
UCLGW and cement companies		55%, 57.5%, 60%[i] gross wages+	60%, 62.5%, 65% gross wages[j]+; or 30%, 32.5%, 35% gross wages[k]+		70% gross wages[h]+ or 50% gross wages[l]+

"+" indicates that dependents' benefits are added.

[a] Benefit for a week in which no work is performed and (except in the case of the latest cement plan) for which UI is received.

[b] Gross wages are straight-time weekly wages as defined in the respective contracts; net wages are gross wages minus estimated taxes.

[c] The plan negotiated in 1959 was the first cement plan.

[d] The 65% applied to the first 4 full weeks of any continuous layoff; the 60% applied to weeks of layoff thereafter.

[e] The applicable ratio, 65, 66, 67, 68, 69, or 70%, varied with the number of dependents (from 0 to 5).

[f] These percentages represent the range of the benefit-wage ratio which resulted from the earnings-benefit schedule set up in the plan. The schedule contained five earnings-class intervals and five different benefit amounts.

[g] Same as n. f, except that in this plan there were six earnings classes and six different benefit amounts.

[h] Twenty-eight times average straight-time hourly earnings.

[i] If 0 dependents, 22 times regular straight-time hourly rate; if 1 dependent, 23 times; if 2 or more dependents, 24 times.

[j] If state UI benefits were received: 24 times straight-time hourly rate if 0 dependents, 25 times if 1 dependent, 26 times if 2 or more dependents.

[k] If state UI benefits had been exhausted or denied because of disability while on layoff: 12 times straight-time hourly rate if 0 dependents; 13 times if 1 dependent; 14 times if 2 or more dependents.

[l] If state UI benefits had been exhausted or denied because of disability while on layoff, 20 times straight-time hourly rate.

single employee as for the employee with dependents. When the base of the ratio was changed to gross wages a few years later (1961–1962), the previously established equality of incentive was maintained by the addition of dependents' benefits.[3]

The change to gross wages was a union proposal stemming from three considerations: simplified administration, ease of understanding for the claimant, and the elimination of the geographic differentials and chronological changes in the dollar amount of SUB produced by variations in tax provisions. Under the previous formula, variations in state and local income taxes meant unequal benefits — because net wages were different — for workers of the same company earning identical gross wages but employed at different locations. Furthermore, any increase in taxes — federal, state, or local — caused an automatic reduction in SUB (but see Appendix B).

The choice of 65 percent in the original (1955) Ford-UAW negotiations was influenced by a study which the Ford Company had made of the living expenses of its employees. The choice was influenced also, of course, by employer concern over the maintenance of an adequate work incentive and by the desire of both the employer and the union to keep costs within reason. The Ford-UAW choice was subsequently incorporated in the other auto plans as well as in the early agricultural implement, steel, and rubber plans.

The few changes that have been made in the benefit-wage ratio have been in the direction of liberalization. All the plans have, at one time or another, increased the benefit-wage ratio.[4] The 1965 increases in the rubber, can, and cement plans gave these industries higher benefit-wage ratios than those used in the auto and steel industries, the originators of SUB. The increases were part of the price paid by companies in these industries for greater freedom to introduce technological changes. These settlements were also influenced by the liberality of the SUB agreement reached earlier in 1965 between the Steelworkers and the Alan Wood Steel Company. In that agreement, the benefit had been set at 85 percent of gross wages.

Although gross wages have been generally adopted as the base for the benefit-wage ratio, the relation of benefits to net wages (take-home pay) still retains significance as a measure of both work incentive and benefit adequacy. Table 5–2 shows some illustrative ratios of combined benefits

3. In the fourth rubber plan the change to gross wages was made without including a dependents' benefit, but the omission seems to have been merely an oversight, which was repaired in the fifth plan (but see Appendix B).

4. The steady rise in wage rates over the decade had the effect, of course, of increasing the absolute amount of the combined unemployment benefit (UI plus SUB), apart from any increase in the benefit-wage ratio.

TABLE 5–2

Estimated Ratios of Regular Unemployment Benefits[a] (UI plus SUB) to Net Wages[b] for Selected SUB Plans, for Typical Beneficiaries with No Dependents and with Four Dependents, January 1, 1966

Union and company	Gross wages	Unemployment benefits[c] (UI plus SUB)		Net wages		Unemployment benefits as a percent of net wages	
		No dependents	Four dependents	No dependents	Four dependents	No dependents	Four dependents
UAW and auto companies							
Example No. 1	$100	$62.00	$68.00	$83.62	$90.90	74.1	74.8
Example No. 2	130	80.60	86.60	108.16	115.44	74.5	75.0
URW and rubber companies							
Example No. 1	100	65.00	73.00	83.62	90.90	77.7	80.3
Example No. 2	130	84.50	92.50	108.16	115.44	78.1	80.1
USWA and basic steel							
Example No. 1	100	60.00	66.00	83.62	90.90	71.8	72.6
Example No. 2	130	78.00	84.00	108.16	115.44	72.1	72.8
USWA and can companies							
Example No. 1	100	70.00	70.00	83.62	90.90	83.7	77.0
Example No. 2	130	91.00	91.00	108.16	115.44	84.1	78.8
UCLGW and cement companies							
Example No. 1	100	70.00	76.00	83.62	90.90	83.7	83.6
Example No. 2	130	91.00	97.00	108.16	115.44	84.2	84.7

[a] Benefit for a week in which no work is performed and for which UI is received.

[b] Gross wages minus estimated deductions for income and social security taxes.

[c] It is assumed that the amount of SUB is not limited by the UI or the SUB maximum.

to net wages as of the end of 1965. Even the lowest figure, in the steel plan, was over 70 percent, while the highest figures approached 85 percent. As between low-wage and high-wage claimants the ratios were about equal. As between claimants with and without dependents, the ratios for claimants with dependents were somewhat higher in the rubber and steel plans, about equal in the auto and cement plans, and actually lower in the can plan, which no longer provides a dependents' benefit. The percentage differentials are small because the absolute amount of the dependents' benefit is small relative to the earnings of these high-wage employees. (In the Alan Wood Steel plan, benefits equaled about 95 percent of take-home pay for claimants without dependents and a slightly lower percentage for those with dependents.)

The early can plans used a benefit formula different from that found in any of the core plans (Table 5-1). The can formula set up wage classes and assigned a flat benefit to each class. Within each class, therefore, the benefit-wage ratio varied according to the actual wage received. The variation was larger the fewer the wage classes and the larger the resultant wage interval represented by a class. In the plan of Continental Can there were only 5 — later 6 — wage classes; in the plan of American Can there were 24.

The benefit-wage ratio of the 1958 Allis-Chalmers plan is worthy of special comment which is more appropriately included with the discussion of dependents' benefits that follows.

Dependents' Benefits

Unlike labor unions in other countries, unions in the United States have been apathetic to the inclusion of dependents' benefits in programs of unemployment benefits. The existence of such benefits in the typical SUB program (see Table 5-3) seems to be attributable primarily to the employer motivation mentioned above. This origin probably explains why all but one of the dependents' benefits provided by the plans have been of the "neutral" variety.

Whereas the positive type of dependents' benefits aims at replacing a greater proportion of net income loss for claimants with dependents, the neutral type aims merely at replacing the same proportion of net income loss for all classes of claimants. Such a benefit does not favor the claimant with dependents; it merely avoids paying him a smaller percentage of his take-home pay than is paid to the claimant without dependents. All but one of the plans that have provided dependents' benefits have aimed at providing this neutral type of benefit. (As noted above, in the discussion of Table 5-2, the intended effect is achieved somewhat more closely in the auto and cement plans than in the steel and rubber plans, which have a slight positive effect. The can plans have an actual negative effect.)

The only plan which intended to achieve a positive effect was the 1959 Allis-Chalmers plan. Under this formula, a larger percentage of *net* wages was paid to the claimant with dependents. Since the net wage of such a claimant was already larger than that of other claimants with the same gross wage, the larger percentage applied to a larger base resulted in a positive differential in favor of the claimant with dependents. (This kind of provision was favored at one time by the CIO for the state UI programs.) The Allis-Chalmers provision was lost in the general shift of the base from net to gross wages.

The relationship of SUB to UI with respect to dependents' benefits is worth noting. Since SUB is superimposed on UI, it is SUB which prevails. Thus in states which have no dependents' benefits, SUB creates a neutral differential which equalizes the proportion of take-home pay replaced for the two groups of workers — those with and without dependents. And in states which have dependents' benefits, SUB in effect substitutes its own differential for whatever the UI differential was.

Dependents' benefits were dropped from the 1965 can plan because the basic benefit-wage ratio of 70 percent was considered to be already rather high. The same reasoning may explain the omission of dependents' benefits when the UAW succeeded in negotiating a SUB plan with the Douglas Aircraft Company in 1965; the Douglas plan pays 65 percent of gross wages. The cement plan, however, retained its dependents' benefit even after the basic benefit-wage ratio had been increased to 70 percent. (And see Appendix B.)

SUB without UI

Claimants for SUB sometimes receive less than the benefit-wage ratios shown in Tables 5–1 and 5–2. When this happens, it is usually for one of two reasons. The first reason is that the UI component of the total benefit (UI plus SUB) is sometimes missing. When SUB is paid in the absence of UI (the situations in which this can happen are listed in Table 4–3), the question arises as to whether the SUB payment should be (1) the same amount as though UI were received; (2) a smaller amount, because any payment in the absence of UI is outside the proper scope of a "supplemental" program and represents an "extra" drain on the SUB fund; or (3) a larger amount (up to the SUB maximum), because the recipient needs more SUB when he does not have UI. The SUB plans have given all three answers at various times, but the trend has been toward the third answer, that is, the payment of a larger SUB amount when UI is not received.

During most of their existence, the auto and agricultural implement

TABLE 5-3

Ways in Which Selected SUB Plans Have Provided a Larger Unemployment Benefit to Claimants with Dependents, 1955–1965

Plan	Benefits based on net wages[a]		Benefits based on gross wages[b]		Variable maximum[c]
	Uniform fraction	Varying fraction	Uniform fraction plus flat allowance per dependent[b]	Varying fraction according to number of dependents	
UAW and auto companies					
First plan (1955)	X				
Second plan (1958)	X				
Third plan (1961)			$1.50 × 1–4 dependents		
Fourth plan (1964)			$1.50 × 1–4 dependents		X
UAW and Allis-Chalmers					
First plan (1955)	X				
Second plan (1959)		66⅔%–70% of net wages; 1–5 dependent children[d]			X
Third plan (1962)			$1.50 × 1–4 dependents		
Fourth plan (1964)			$1.50 × 1–4 dependents		X
URW and rubber companies					
First plan (1956)	X				X
Second plan (1959)	X				X
Third plan (1961)	X				X
Fourth plan (1963)					X
Fifth plan (1965)			$2.00 × 1–4 dependents		X

Plan			
USWA and basic steel			
First plan (1956)	X		X
Second plan (1960)	X		X
Third plan (1962)		$1.50 × 1–4 dependents	X
Fourth plan (1965)		$1.50 × 1–4 dependents	X
USWA and can companies			
First plan (1955)		$2.00 × 1–4 dependents	X
Second plan (1959)		$2.00 × 1–4 dependents	X
Third plan (1962)		$1.50 × 1–4 dependents	X
Fourth plan (1965)[e]			
UCLGW and cement companies			
First plan (1959)		55%, 57.5%, 60%; 0–2 dependents	
Second plan (1962)		60%, 62.5%, 65%; 0–2 dependents	
Third plan (1965)		$1.50 × 1–4 dependents	X

[a] Gross wages minus estimated taxes.
[b] This results in a fraction which varies (1) directly with the number of dependents and (2) inversely with wage level.
[c] Claimants with dependents qualify for a higher maximum benefit amount.
[d] The applicable ratio—66, 67, 68, 69, or 70 percent—varies with the number (1 to 5) of dependent children.
[e] This plan dropped all provisions relating to dependents' benefits.

plans gave the first answer: they subtracted from the total benefit that would have been produced by the ratios of Table 5–1 the estimated amount of UI that the claimant would have received if he had been eligible. The Allis-Chalmers plan was an exception from the beginning; it never subtracted estimated UI benefits, no matter why UI was not received. In 1961, when the duration of SUB was increased to 52 weeks and the possibility of the payment of SUB after the exhaustion of UI became a more serious issue, the Ford plan and the agricultural implement plans were amended to provide that when UI was not received because benefits had been exhausted (Table 4–3, No. 1), the estimated UI benefit would not be subtracted. Finally, in 1964, the subtraction of estimated UI benefits was abandoned by all the auto and agricultural implement plans in all circumstances; that is, no matter what the reason for the nonreceipt of UI. In these situations, SUB could be paid up to the SUB maximum, which in some plans was greater than the maximum when UI was received (and see Appendix B).

The first (1959) cement plan subtracted the estimated UI benefit in all (three) situations in which SUB was paid without UI (Table 4–3). This provision was never changed; but in 1962, when duration was extended to 52 weeks, the plan was amended to provide a separate benefit-wage ratio for the period of SUB that followed the exhaustion of UI benefits and also for the period during which UI benefits were denied because of disability while on layoff. This ratio was smaller than the one that prevailed during the period that UI was being received.[5]

Almost without exception,[6] the steel, can, and rubber plans gave the third answer. They did not subtract the estimated UI benefit but let the stated benefit-wage ratio govern the SUB payment up to the SUB maximum. Of course, these plans have never included as many "Arabs" (Table 4–3) as the auto plan.

Maximum SUB Payment

The second factor that can cause the SUB claimant to receive less than the stated benefit-wage ratio is the operation of the maximum benefit (SUB) as a separate limitation on the amount actually received. In the typical benefit formula, the amount of the SUB payment is: (1) the difference between the UI payment and the stated benefit-wage ratio, or (2) the

5. As of 1965, if UI benefits were received, the ratio was 28 times the average straight-time hourly wage; if UI benefits were not received, the ratio was 20.

6. In the American Can plan of 1955 the estimated UI benefit was subtracted in the case of the third "Arab" (Table 4-3); this provision was dropped from the 1959 plan. For a time, the rubber plan provided for the subtraction of the estimated UI benefit in the case of the first "Arab" if the claimant had already drawn UI benefits for 26 weeks (1959 and 1961 plans) or for 39 weeks (1963 plan).

stipulated maximum, whichever is less. No one receives more than that amount, no matter how high his wage. It is thus possible for the actual benefit-wage ratio of a particular claimant to be less than the ratio set down in the benefit formula. The limiting impact of the maximum on the effective benefit-wage ratio will be greater as the wage level is higher, as the UI benefit is lower, and as the SUB maximum itself is lower. These relationships are obvious.

The maximum payment needs to be seen in relation to three kinds of SUB payments: "regular" SUB, when UI is received; SUB when UI is not received; and SUB when augmented by dependents' benefits. These situations give rise, respectively, to the regular maximum, the dual maximum, and the variable maximum. Table 5-4 shows the maximum SUB payment in these three situations. (Also see Appendix B.)

Regular maximum. There are two considerations which underlie the decision to establish a maximum benefit amount. One consideration directly concerns the employer — with a maximum benefit, total costs are more easily controlled and calculated. The other directly concerns the employee — a maximum benefit limits the extent to which workers in states that pay low UI benefits may drain the fund at the expense of workers in states that pay high UI benefits. Both considerations work to hold down the maximum SUB payment.

Two other considerations work to raise the maximum. The typical worker covered by SUB is a high-wage worker and needs a high maximum SUB benefit if his combined benefit is to equal the desired percentage of wages. Also, a higher maximum is a step in the direction of the union's goal — that of paying all claimants the same proportion of their wages, no matter how small the UI component supplied by the program of a particular state. The latter considerations have exerted the stronger influence and have moved the regular maximum SUB benefit upward in the ten-year period. The increase in the maximum (it has doubled in most cases) has been more than enough to match the increases in wages and benefit-wage ratios. The available data on the extent to which SUB payments have been limited in amount by the SUB maximum are analyzed in Part III.

Not all the plans limited all claimants to a maximum benefit. The fourth (1964) Allis-Chalmers plan imposed no maximum on certain claimants who were without UI benefits within the period of normal UI duration (about 26 weeks in most states). The Continental Can plan operated without a maximum SUB payment throughout nearly all of its existence.[7] This

7. In the third (1962) plan, a maximum SUB payment was established for claimants who received no UI benefits at all. This provision was dropped from the fourth (1965) plan.

TABLE 5–4

Type and Amount of Benefit Maximums in Selected SUB Plans, 1959–1965

Union and company	Regular maximum	Special maximums	
		Dual maximum[a]	Variable maximum[b]
UAW and auto companies			
First plan (1955)	$25.00		
Second plan (1958)	30.00		
Third plan (1961)	40.00		
Fourth plan (1964)	50.00[c]		X
UAW and Allis-Chalmers			
First plan (1955)	25.00	(1–4): $48.30	X
Second plan (1959)	50.00	(1–4): $75.00	
Third plan (1962)	50.00	(1–4): $75.00 or $40.00[d]	
Fourth plan (1964)	60.00	(1–4, 6–9, 12): No maximum or $50.00[d]	X
URW and rubber companies			
First plan (1956)	25.00	(1–4): $48.30	X
Second plan (1959)	30.00	(1–4): $52.00 or $30.00[d]	X
Third plan (1961)	35.00	(1–4): $57.00 or $35.00[d]	X
Fourth plan (1963)	40.00	(1–4, 6–11): $62.00 or $40.00[d]	X
Fifth plan (1965)	50.00	(1–4, 6–11): $62.00 or $50.00[d]	X
USWA and basic steel			
First plan (1956)	25.00	(1–3): $47.50	X
Second plan (1960)	25.00	(1–3): $47.50	X
Third plan (1962)	37.50	(1–3, 5, 10): $60.00	X
Fourth plan (1965)	37.50	(1–3, 5, 10): $60.00	X
UCLGW and cement companies			
First plan (1959)	30.00		
Second plan (1962)	40.00		
Third plan (1965)	60.00		X

[a] A separate maximum, usually larger, is provided when UI is not received. Numbers in parentheses refer to exceptions ("Arabs") listed in Table 4–3 and indicate situations to which dual maximum applies.

[b] The regular or dual maximum is augmented by the amount of dependents' allowances; e.g., the fourth steel plan provided a maximum of $37.50 + ($1.50 × 1 to 4 dependents) or $60.00+ ($1.50 × 1 to 4 dependents). See Table 5–3.

[c] Estimated UI is no longer subtracted from the total unemployment benefit; hence this maximum benefit will be paid more frequently than previously when UI is not received.

[d] The smaller amount is applicable during a period of continuous unemployment in excess of the UI maximum potential duration period, e.g., 26 weeks. The larger maximum is payable only within the period of UI maximum potential duration.

plan, as shown in Table 5–1, established wage classes and assigned a flat total benefit (UI plus SUB) to each class. This total amount was paid no matter how small the UI component; that is, there was no maximum imposed on the SUB payment as a separate factor.

The absence of a limiting maximum benefit did not necessarily make the Continental Can plan more liberal than the plan which the Steelworkers had negotiated with the basic steel companies. In fact, throughout most of its existence this can plan was less liberal than the steel plan. Because the flat benefits assigned to the respective wage classes were low, the UI component of the total benefit bore most of the weight and left relatively little to be made up by the SUB payment. After 1964, however, when wage classes were abandoned and the benefit-wage ratio was set at 70 percent, still without a maximum on the SUB component, the can plan led all Steelworker plans in liberality. In 1965 the can plan eliminated the maximum even for the period following the exhaustion of UI benefits. This provision, taken together with benefits more liberal than average, makes the can plan the most instructive testing ground for the relationship of SUB to labor mobility and availability (but see Appendix B).

Dual maximum. The regular SUB maximum becomes especially limiting when SUB alone is paid without the UI component, as happens in the case of all the "Arabs" (Table 4–3). Some plans provide a special, usually higher, maximum in these cases. Such plans are said to have a "dual" maximum. The basic steel and can plans have always had a dual maximum. The rubber plan has always had a dual maximum. The cement plan has never had a dual maximum, and the UAW has negotiated one only exceptionally, as in the Allis-Chalmers plan. (The absence of any limitation on the maximum is, of course, the equivalent of a dual maximum.)

Some plans have had a triple maximum. The last two plans of Allis-Chalmers and the last four rubber plans had, in addition to the regular maximum paid while UI was received, two special maximums for the period when UI was not received: a higher than regular maximum during the period encompassed by a state's potential UI duration, and a lower than regular maximum beyond this period. The choice of a lower maximum for those who claimed benefits for the longer period was evidently dictated, not by the claimant's need, but by the desire to conserve the fund and/or the desire to sharpen the claimant's work incentive.

Variable maximum. As shown in Table 5–3, the typical SUB plan augments the regular benefit with a dependents' benefit. Obviously, the augmentation would be ineffective for those claimants whose SUB payment was already at the maximum. To avoid this limitation, the SUB maximum must be "variable," that is, it must vary upwards with the amount of dependents' benefit. In effect, this allows such claimants with dependents to carry the stated benefit-wage ratio up to a higher figure.

The steel, can, and rubber plans provided a variable maximum from the beginning. The auto and cement plans did not provide one until 1964 and 1965, respectively. The Allis-Chalmers plan provided a variable maximum originally (1955), dropped it from the 1959 and 1962 plans — probably because at this time the Allis-Chalmers regular maximum was higher than that in the other core plans — but restored it in 1964.

Partial Unemployment Benefit

The payment of SUB for partial (part-week) unemployment has more significance than may be evident at first glance. Starting as a simple provision to assure that the claimant who worked part of a week received no less income than the claimant who was completely unemployed, the partial benefit grew into a complex technique closely related to labor's long-time goal of transforming the hourly-rated employee into a salaried employee. The history of the partial benefit falls into two periods, marking the two phases of its development. The first phase occupied the period from 1955 to 1961; the second and more important phase began in 1961 with the inauguration of the "short-week benefit."

1955–1961. In the early SUB plans it was possible for the income (wages plus unemployment benefits) of the partially employed claimant to be less than, the same as, or greater than the income of the totally unemployed claimant. The difference in income was chiefly determined by two provisions: the provision represented by the fourth exception ("Arab") in Table 4–3 and the provision regulating the amount of earnings to be subtracted in calculating a partial unemployment benefit.

Without "Arab" No. 4, it was possible for the claimant who worked part of the week to receive less total income than the claimant who did not work at all; that is, it was possible for earnings to be enough to disqualify the claimant for UI, and therefore for SUB, and yet be less than the sum of UI and SUB. This "Arab" was not in the original auto and cement plans nor in most of the original agricultural implement plans, but by 1958 it had been incorporated in all the plans but one. The cement plan still lacked this provision as of 1965.

The other relevant provision regulated the amount of earnings to be subtracted in the calculation of the total income due the partially employed claimant. Some plans subtracted all earnings, with the result that income for partial employment was, at best, the same as for total unemployment. Other plans disregarded some earnings — usually the amount disregarded by the state in its calculation of the UI benefit — with the result that income for partial employment was greater than for complete unemployment by the amount of earnings disregarded.

Of the original plans, only steel (1956) and cement (1959) had disregarded some earnings in calculating the benefit of the partially employed claimant. The American Can plan adopted this provision in 1959, but none of the other plans had provided any differential in favor of the partially employed worker up to the time when the short-week development began.

1961–1965. The first short-week benefit was negotiated in the auto plan of 1961,[8] followed in 1962 by the agricultural implement plan and in 1963 by the rubber plan. A somewhat different type of short-week benefit was included in the steel, can, and cement plans of 1962. In the discussion of short-week benefits that follows, the "auto-type plan" includes the agricultural implement and rubber plans; similarly, the "steel-type plan" includes the can and cement plans.

The auto-type plan distinguished between scheduled and unscheduled short weeks. A scheduled short week was one used to adjust production to declining customer demand; an unscheduled short week was one used for any other reason. In the 1961 plan, a claimant working a *scheduled* short week was paid a benefit (UI plus SUB) equal to 65 percent of the missing hours (40 hours minus hours worked or paid for). In the 1964 plan, this figure was increased to 75 percent. In the 1961 plan, a claimant working an *unscheduled* short week received a benefit equal to only 50 percent of the missing hours. In 1965, this benefit was increased to 60 percent in the rubber plan, but it remained at 50 percent for the other auto-type plans. (Also see Appendix B.)

The Auto Workers seem to have had at least four objectives in view when they negotiated the short-week benefit (the order in which they are listed here is not necessarily the order of their importance to the union).

1. The union intended to assure the claimant a substantial difference in income as between working a part of the week and not working at all. As of 1965 the partially employed worker was sure of receiving 100 percent of his wages for the days he worked plus a benefit equal to 50 percent or 75 percent of his wages for the days lost. This sum will always be substantially greater than the unemployment benefits received by the claimant who is unemployed the entire week.

2. The union intended to deter the employer from adjusting production to demand by cutting the number of hours worked rather than the number

8. This was the year of major changes in the SUB plans of the Auto Workers. The attainment of the union's goals was facilitated by the selection of American Motors as the target company. For various reasons, American Motors was less opposed to some of the union's demands than were the other auto companies. For example, the scheduled short-week benefit, a crucial demand, represented less of a cost item to American Motors because that company, with its integrated operations, had rarely scheduled a short week.

of workers. From the viewpoint of the employer, cutting hours (work sharing) has several advantages: he can maintain his workforce; he can cut his unemployment costs, both UI and SUB; and he can avoid the operating costs attendant upon the practice of alternating layoffs with recalls. Included in operating costs are the temporary inefficiencies that result from the reorganization of production and from the "bumping" that ensues when employees threatened with layoff exercise their seniority rights to move to other jobs.

From the viewpoint of the long-service employee, the system of work sharing was a system of "sharing the misery." In seeking to discourage the practice of work sharing, the union was responding to complaints arising from its core members. That deterrence was one of the union's objectives is reflected in the relatively high benefit-wage ratio (75 percent) attached to the scheduled short week as contrasted with the regular ratio of 62 percent. Since the higher benefit is obviously not required to meet a greater individual need (the claimant who has worked part of the week is presumably in no more need than the claimant who has not worked at all), it could only have been intended as a deterrent to the use of the short week. This conclusion is strengthened by the relatively low benefit paid for the *unscheduled* short week; this benefit is less than even the regular benefit. Moreover, the union stated that deterrence was one of its objectives.

The distinction between scheduled and unscheduled short weeks seems to have evolved in the course of the negotiations between the UAW and the American Motors Company, the target company in 1961. In its original proposals, the union had made no distinction between kinds of short weeks, had asked for 100 percent of lost wages, and had demanded that the company pay this benefit directly out of pocket, not out of the SUB fund. American Motors said it was not greatly concerned about the cost of benefits for scheduled short weeks because, with its integrated operations, it rarely used these. The company was very much concerned, however, about the uncontrollable and unpredictable costs of unscheduled short weeks, such as resulted from breakdowns, lack of materials, errors in planning, etc. To meet the company's objection, and as part of the price of getting a new principle accepted, the union agreed that a lower benefit should be paid for unscheduled short weeks and that all short-week benefits should be paid out of the SUB fund.

The scheduled short-week benefit did change the cost situation as between cutting hours of work and cutting the number of workers. Before the short-week benefit, the employer could save more in direct labor costs, other things being equal, by sharing the work (putting everybody on short hours) than by any alternative way of reducing total man-hours. The short-week benefit of 65 percent removed the differential in favor of work sharing and made the costs of the various alternatives about equal. The short-week benefit of 75 percent made it more expensive for the employer, in terms of direct labor costs, to adopt work sharing than to resort to some system of layoffs.

3. The union intended to obtain for the hourly-rated employee the kind of income continuity enjoyed by the salaried employee. It will be recalled that this goal was included in the UAW's original six principles (Chapter 1). The short-week benefit represents an appreciable advance toward a weekly salary. Anyone who works at all during a week can normally count on receiving 80 to 90 percent of his regular wage.

4. The union intended to increase the employer's incentive to stabilize employment, especially within the week. Since the cost of irregular employment has been increased, this objective has obviously been attained to some extent. Perhaps the greater significance of the short-week benefit for employment stability lies in its quality of "visibility." Since there is an immediate and direct cost associated with irregular employment in a particular plant in a particular week, management is enabled to pinpoint the trouble area and is alerted to inquire into the causes. Thus the short-week benefit becomes a management tool.

The incentive to use this tool was decreased with the negotiation of the "hard nickel" in 1964 (see Chapter 6) and the consequent dilution of the employer's interest in preventing drains on the fund. Indeed, when the fund level is high, the availability of money for short-week benefits — money that can never be recaptured by the employer — may have the opposite effect and may actually diminish the employer's interest in preventing unemployment. Only when the fund is low is there much incentive left. (But see Appendix B.)

The objectives of the short-week benefit in the steel plan seem to have been very similar to those in the auto plan, though with some differences in emphasis related to differences in the nature of the plans. The short-week benefit in the steel, can, and cement plans makes no distinction between scheduled and unscheduled short weeks. For a week in which an employee performs any work, he is guaranteed the equivalent of 32 hours of wages in some combination of earnings, UI benefits, and SUB. The provision amounts to a guaranteed 32-hour week.

The steel plan needed the short-week benefit slightly less than did the auto plan to achieve the first objective, the establishment of a differential in favor of working over not working. As explained above, even before the adoption of the short-week benefit, the steel plan provided some differential in favor of the claimant who worked part of a week. Nevertheless, an important objective of the short-week benefit in the steel plan was to increase this differential substantially. Thus, while the totally unemployed claimant is guaranteed 60 percent of his wages, the partially employed claimant is — apparently — guaranteed 80 percent.

Actually, the guarantee has been substantially less than the 80 percent the union thought it was negotiating in 1962. The wage base for the regular SUB payment was the average straight-time hourly earnings, and the union presumed that the same base would be used for the short-week benefit. But the 1962 agreement did not specify the wage base for the short-week benefit, and the companies have been using the standard hourly wage rate, which is substantially lower, primarily because it does not include incentives. As a result, the short-week benefit has averaged closer to 60 percent than to 80 percent of average straight-time hourly earnings. This problem will no doubt come up for consideration in the 1968 negotiations in the steel industry.

Lacking a differentiation between benefits paid for scheduled and for unscheduled short weeks, the steel plan does not emphasize the second objective — deterrence — to the same extent as does the auto plan. The distinction is less important for steel than for autos. The productive processes in steel are such that usually it is not economical to shut down or start operations for brief periods of time. Most of the adjustments to declining demand are made by means of full weeks of layoff for a considerable period. Hence "scheduled" short weeks are less likely in steel than in auto production. However, deterrence was also a significant objective for the Steelworkers, who had been experiencing some part-week employment. Prior to World War II, work sharing had been practiced in the steel industry down to 24 hours per week; after the war, the minimum was raised to 32 hours.[9] However, this limitation on work sharing did not prevent individuals from having less than 32 hours in a week: the limitation meant merely that the average hours of work in a seniority unit could not be less than 32 for a long, planned period. Hence, short weeks of two or three days, usually of the unscheduled variety, could and did occur for individuals. In negotiating the short-week benefit, the union was responding to complaints of its members who had had this experience. One of the demands of the union during the 1959 strike was phrased as follows: "Reconstruct the benefit formula so as to discourage less than 32-hour weeks of employment at the Company." For the previous general and uncertain protection against short weeks, the union succeeded in substitut-

9. Two characteristics of the steel industry tend to limit labor mobility and induce work sharing. Steel production tends to be concentrated in certain localities, and fluctuations in output tend to be industrywide.

ing a very precise form of protection applicable to the individual worker.

The third and fourth objectives of the Auto Workers seem not to have been stressed in the steel negotiations of 1962. In the later amendments as in the original SUB negotiations, these objectives were more characteristic of the Auto Workers. However, the short-week benefit that was negotiated in steel did advance the worker closer to a salaried status and did increase — in some circumstances — the employer's incentive to stabilize employment. To the extent that these results were anticipated, they presumably represented some part of the union's objectives.

The qualification "in some circumstances" is necessary because of the dilution of experience rating. In the same negotiations in which the short-week benefit was established (1962), the experience-rating character of the steel plan was weakened (see Chapter 6), though not to the same extent as it was in the 1964 auto plan. Since 1962, it has been possible for situations to occur in which the availability of money for unemployment benefits — money that cannot be used for any other purpose — may induce rather than deter loose employment practices. This possibility is discussed in Chapter 11.

Reduction of Benefits

In all plans it was provided that, when the fund fell below a specified level, there would be a reduction in either the benefit amount or the benefit duration or in both. Table 5–5 shows the reduction provisions of the core plans as they were originally and as they were at the end of 1965.[10] As is clear, substantial changes were made in these provisions and, as a result, their impact was greatly diminished.

The steel plan placed its principal reliance upon a reduction of the benefit amount and was originally quite conservative, providing for a reduction in benefits when the fund dropped below 75 percent (in the American Can plan, 90 percent) of maximum funding. When this provision led to extensive reductions in benefits during the recessions of 1958 and 1961, the union insisted (1962) on lowering the trigger point to 35 percent of maximum funding.

The other SUB plans have never relied to any significant degree on a reduction in the benefit amount. The original auto plan used a very low trigger point, 13 percent, and later (1961) lowered this to approximately 8 percent. The cement and rubber plans, and also the Allis-Chalmers plan,

10. The table is used chiefly for comparisons over time within a given plan. It is less useful for comparisons between plans because the plans use different bases to which the percentages shown in the table apply. That is, maximum financing is defined differently in the various plans.

TABLE 5–5

Provisions To Reduce Amount and Duration of Benefits, Selected SUB Plans,
1965 Plan Compared with First Plan

Plan	Level of fund below which benefit amount is reduced	Level of fund below which potential duration is reduced
UAW and auto companies		
First plan	13% of maximum	85% of maximum
Plan in 1965	Approximately 8% of maximum	Approximately 50% of maximum
UAW and Allis-Chalmers		
First plan	No reduction	85% of maximum
Plan in 1965	No reduction	Approximately 40% of maximum
URW and rubber companies		
First plan	No reduction	80% of maximum
Plan in 1965	No reduction	Same
USWA and steel companies		
First plan	75% of maximum	52.5% of maximum
Plan in 1965	35% of maximum	No reduction
USWA and American Can		
First plan	90% of maximum	50% of maximum
Plan in 1965	35% of maximum	No reduction
USWA and Continental Can		
First plan	75% of maximum	No reduction
Plan in 1965	35% of maximum	No reduction
UCLGW and cement companies		
First plan	No reduction	50% of maximum
Plan in 1965	No reduction	33% of maximum

have never provided for any reduction in the benefit amount. The chief reliance of all these plans has been on a reduction of benefit duration, which is discussed in the next section. As of 1965, nearly all SUB claimants who were eligible to receive any benefit would have received the full benefit amount.

Benefit Duration

The benefit duration formula consists of two parts: the accumulation and the cancellation of credit units. The accumulation of credit units also has two parts: the rate at which credits are accumulated and the maximum number which may be accumulated at any one time. In the most usual combination of these three elements, one week of work earns one half a credit unit, up to a maximum of 52 units, and a unit is cancelled for each week of benefits. The chief variations from this typical formula occur in the maximum, some of the recent plans permitting an accumulation of credits up to 260 units and more. The evolution of the duration formula for the core plans is shown in Table 5-6.

Accumulation of Credits

Rate of accumulation. Before 1965 the provisions regulating the rate of accumulation of credits were generally similar in all the plans and had undergone only minor changes since their inception. Among the minor changes were provisions granting credits for partial weeks worked. These provisions were gradually liberalized until by 1962 all plans provided one half a credit for each week in which any work was performed or any pay received. An employee is not considered to have any credit units until he has been with the company long enough to satisfy the eligibility requirement of 1 or 2 years. At that point he is credited with the full year's (or years') credit units.

In 1965, changes in the can and cement plans made it easier for the worker to earn credits. The can plan, in connection with a substantial increase in maximum duration for long-service employees, allowed employees with 10 years or more of seniority to accumulate credits at the rate of 4 per week of work. The cement plan made the only major change affecting all employees when it increased the rate of accumulation from the customary one half to three fourths of a credit unit per week of work.

Maximum accumulation. Originally only the plans negotiated by the Steelworkers went beyond the 26 weeks of benefits normally provided by state UI programs. Thus most of the early SUB plans supplemented only the benefit amount and not the benefit duration of the public programs. In 1958–1959, the auto, rubber, and cement plans lengthened their maximum duration to 39 weeks to match the temporary extension of UI benefits provided by some of the state programs during that recession. A major change occurred in 1961–1962, when the auto and cement plans joined the steel plan in providing a maximum duration of 52 weeks, leaving only rubber among the core plans with a maximum duration of less than 1 year.

The year 1965 marked a major breakthrough when several plans went beyond, indeed far beyond, the previous limit of 1 year. In the cement plan, maximum duration became 2 years for those with 2 to 8 years of seniority and 3 years for those with more seniority. In the rubber plan, maximum duration varied among five seniority groups from 1 year of benefits for those with less than 5 years of seniority to 4 years for those

TABLE 5-6
Duration Formula in Selected SUB Plans, 1955–1965

Plan and date	Accumulation of credits		Cancellation of credits	
	Rate	Maximum accrual of benefit weeks	Normal rate	Rates applicable at lower levels of fund
UAW and auto companies First plan (1955)	0.5 credit per week for which 32 hours' pay is received[a]	26	1 credit per benefit week if fund is 85% or more of maximum	1.1 to 10 credits per benefit week, depending on seniority, if fund is at various levels below 85% of maximum
Second plan (1958)	0.5 credit per week for which any pay is received	Maximum number of state-system weeks, not to exceed 39	Same	Same
Third plan (1961)	Same	52	Same, except reduction point is approximately 50%[b] of maximum[c]	Same, except reduction point is 50%[b] of maximum
Fourth plan (1964)	Same	Same	Same	Same
URW and rubber companies First plan (1956)	0.5 credit per week in which 18 or 20 credit hours are worked[d]	26	1 credit per benefit week if fund is 80% or more of maximum	1.15 to 7.5 credits per benefit week, depending on seniority, if fund is at various levels below 80% of maximum
Second plan (1959)	0.5 credit per week in which any pay is received	Maximum number of state-system weeks, not to exceed 39	Same	Same
Third plan (1961)	Same	Same	Same	Same
Fourth plan (1963)	Same	Maximum number of state-system weeks, not to exceed 39	Same	Same
Fifth plan (1965)	Same	52 to 208 weeks, depending on seniority[e]	Same	Same

USWA and basic steel			
First plan (1956)	0.1 credit per 8 hours worked or paid[f]	52	1 credit per benefit week if fund is 53% or more of maximum	1.25 to 5 credits per benefit week, depending on seniority if fund is at various levels below 53% of maximum
Second plan (1960)	Same	Same	Same	Same
Third plan (1962)	0.5 credit per week of any work or pay[f]	Same	1 credit per benefit week	No provision
Fourth plan (1965)	Same	Same	Same	No provision
USWA and Continental Can				
First plan (1956)	0.1 credit per 8 hours worked or paid[f]	52	1 credit per benefit week	No provision
Second plan (1959)	Same	Same	Same, except see n. g	No provision
Third plan (1962)	0.5 credit per week of any work or pay[f]	Same	Same, except see n. c	No provision
Fourth plan (1965)	Same, if less than 10 years' seniority; 4 credits per week if more than 10 years' seniority[h]	Less than 10 years' seniority, 104; more than 10 years' seniority, 260	Same	No provision
UCLGW and cement companies				
First plan (1959)	0.5 credit per week for which any pay is received	Maximum number of state-system weeks, not to exceed 39	1 credit per benefit week if fund is 50% or more of maximum	1.2 to 5 credits per benefit week, depending on seniority if fund is at various levels below 50% of maximum
Second plan (1962)	Same	52	1 credit per benefit week if fund is 33% or more of maximum	1.2 to 5 credits per benefit week, depending on seniority, if fund is at various levels below 33% of maximum

TABLE 5-6 (*Continued*)

Plan and date	Accumulation of credits		Cancellation of credits	
	Rate	Maximum accrual of benefit weeks	Normal rate	Rates applicable at lower levels of fund
Third plan (1965)	0.75 credit per week for which any pay is received	1 to 2 years' seniority, 52; 2 to 8 years' seniority, 104; 8 or more years' seniority, 156	1 credit per benefit week if fund is 33 % or more of maximum	1.5 to 2.5 credits per benefit week if seniority is one but less than 8 years and fund is less than 33 % of maximum; 1.5 to 2 credits per benefit week if seniority is more than 8 years and fund is less than 20 % of maximum

a Between June 1, 1955, and May 31, 1957, only 0.25 credit per week was accrued by employees with less than 10 years' seniority.

b In the Chrysler plan, reduction point was at approximately 60 % of maximum funding.

c If benefit is reduced because of receipt of compensation (other than from company), 0.5 credit is canceled for each week of benefit.

d Eighteen applies to employees whose normal workweek is 36 hours; 20, to those whose workweek is 40 hours.

e In the fifth rubber plan, maximums varied according to seniority: less than 5 years, 52 weeks; 5 to 10 years, 78 weeks; 10 to 15 years, 104 weeks; 15 to 25 years, 130 weeks; 25 and over, 208 weeks.

f Hours paid included time lost by certain union officials and by disabled employees receiving workmen's compensation.

g If weekly benefit is reduced by one half or less because of the receipt of earnings, 75 % of credit is canceled for one week of benefit, 25 % if benefit is reduced by more than one half.

h Employees with more than 10 years' seniority on layoff prior to or after December 1, 1965, who had performed some work after December 1, 1964, are entitled to a maximum number of 260 weeks of benefits, even if they have no credits. If such an employee is returned to work for 52 weeks, 260 credits are restored.

with 25 or more years of seniority. In the can plans, maximum duration became 2 years for those with less than 10 years' seniority and 5 years for those with 10 years or more of seniority. In 1965 also, one basic steel company, Alan Wood Steel, amended its SUB plan to provide a maximum duration of 2 years for those with less than 10 years' seniority and unlimited duration for those with 10 years or more of seniority. The Alan Wood settlement, which was announced by David McDonald, president of the Steelworkers, on January 11, 1965, preceded by several months the negotiations in the can, cement, and rubber industries and had a considerable impact on them.

A precedent for such long duration of unemployment benefits was to be found in the railroad industry. The Washington Job Protection Agreement of 1936, as amended and extended, provided income protection against job displacement for periods as long as 5 years. This extended protection was available only in the event that a job was abolished because of a merger or (later) because of technological change.

Similarly, the 1965 long-duration provisions of the SUB plans were negotiated to meet possible job losses resulting from technological change. The background of the Alan Wood Steel plan has been briefly described in Chapter 3. The extended duration of the cement plan was a compromise negotiated in response to a union demand for complete security from the layoffs that were anticipated in view of changes taking place in the industry. The rubber and can plans were affected by similar considerations in their adoption of extended duration.

The probability that claimants will actually draw benefits for such extended periods was somewhat lessened because the plans which provided extended duration also provided opportunities for separated employees to find other jobs with the company. For example, in the Alan Wood plan, a laid-off employee is encouraged to join a labor reserve from which the company may draw to fill temporary openings. In the cement industry an employee whose job has been abolished may bump to another job and receive 95 percent of his former wage rate. The can plan gives employees laid off from one plant certain job preferences in other plants of the company.[11]

Nonetheless, the potential liability represented by these extended benefits is real, the more so because the applicant is not under strict obligation

11. The plan gives the employee with 2 or more years of seniority, laid off for any reason, a preference over new hires in other plants within the region; it gives the employee with 10 or more years' seniority, laid off without expectation of recall, preference over new hires in plants outside the region as well, if the jobs cannot be filled from plants within the region where the vacancy exists.

to accept the alternative jobs. For example, a laid-off employee of Alan Wood Steel may refuse assignment to the labor reserve for 12 consecutive months and still receive SUB, even if he has been denied UI by the state on grounds of having refused suitable work. In the can plan, an employee with 10 years' seniority (eligible for 5 years of benefits) may be disqualified if he refuses transfer to another plant — but only if the offered job could not be filled by a laid-off employee of that plant, or by a voluntary transferee, or by an employee of lesser seniority, to all of whom the job must be offered first.

In the cement plan, if a job is abolished, alternative jobs are limited to the employee's own plant, and the affected employee has the option to bump another employee or take the layoff. However, since he is guaranteed 95 percent of his former wage in the new job, it is expected that he will usually not opt for the layoff. Moreover, in the event of a plant closing, which represents the greatest potential liability, the company may require separated employees to take Termination Benefits (severance pay), which are less than SUB, in place of SUB. The rubber plan contains a similar provision; where a plant has been closed, the separated employees may be required to accept severance payments rather than SUB.

Cancellation of Credits

In the original Ford-UAW negotiations, a key issue was the conservation of the fund for the sake of employees who might be laid off toward the end of a serious decline in employment. The company insisted that the fund be protected against early depletion by those who would be laid off first. Otherwise, the company feared, it would come under great pressure to continue the payment of benefits, even though the fund was exhausted, when the long-service employees began to be laid off; these would be the employees most firmly attached to the company and for whom the company would feel the greatest responsibility. Without some mechanism to guard against early depletion of the fund, the company argued, no conscientious employer would feel that he had, in reality, a limited-liability plan, regardless of the language of the plan. The company finally devised a system for shortening potential duration by increasing the number of credit units canceled per week of benefits as the fund level sank.[12] With the exception of Continental Can, all the core plans initially adopted this system.

12. To this device, the invention of Richard L. Johnson, a member of the 1955 Ford team of negotiators, the union added a provision to cancel credits at a faster rate for claimants with less seniority. The long-service employees were thus doubly protected. The union worked up the schedule finally adopted.

There has been no major change in any of the plans in the rate of cancellation of credits when the fund is above the "danger" line. The original cancellation rate of one credit for one week of benefits has remained unchanged. There have been numerous changes, however — except in the rubber plan — in the stipulated danger line and in the rate of exchange below that line.

As Table 5-5 shows in capsule form and Table 5-6 shows in more detail, the changes have all been in the direction of postponing the time when a more rapid rate of cancellation becomes effective. Two developments account for this process of liberalization: more adequate financing and actual experience under the plans. The first is described in Chapter 6, the second in Part III. By these changes the value of the insurance policy represented by SUB has been somewhat increased for those laid off early in any long decline in employment and correspondingly decreased for those laid off later. However, the latter group is assured by the stronger financing provisions that depletion of the fund will be less liable to occur.

A reduction of potential duration may be used in conjunction with or in place of a reduction of the benefit amount as a method of protecting the fund. As may be seen in Table 5-5, the auto, agricultural implement, rubber, and cement plans have relied wholly, or almost wholly, upon reduction of duration to protect the fund, while the steel and can plans at first relied principally, and subsequently depended wholly, upon reduction of the benefit amount.

These two methods are similar in their effect on the distribution of a given amount of money over time, in that the fund is made to last longer. The methods differ in that the steel-type plan protects the potential duration of all employees at the expense of a lower weekly benefit for all, while the auto-type plan protects the potential duration of high-seniority employees at a possible cost to lower-seniority employees. If the parties to a plan are chiefly concerned with preserving the high-seniority worker's share of the fund, the auto-type plan will accomplish that result. It is understandable that the auto industry would stress the maintenance of the benefit *amount*, since most of its unemployment is of the recurring, short-run variety.

Multi-Employer Plans

In these plans, administrative convenience was a major consideration in the choice of a benefit formula. Just as this consideration usually dictated the simplest form of eligibility condition (the claimant for SUB must be eligible for UI), so it usually dictated the simplest of benefit formulas: a flat SUB amount — to be added to whatever the UI benefit was — and a duration identical with that of UI.

Of the eight multi-employer plans described in Chapter 2, all but one used a flat benefit amount, all in the $25–$35 range. Two of these plans, that of the Maritime Workers and that of the Buffalo Carpenters, had dual benefit amounts; they provided a higher SUB (flat) when it was received without UI than when it was received with UI. The only plan which did not use the flat benefit formula was the Los Angeles Retail Clerks' plan, which set its combined benefit at 65 percent of average straight-time earnings.[13]

Duration of benefits varied among these eight plans. Three provided a duration of 26 weeks, the most common duration of state UI programs. (The 16 weeks provided in the plan of the New Orleans Brewery Workers reflected the maximum duration provided by the Louisiana UI program when the SUB plan was established.) One of these plans provided a duration much shorter, and three a duration much longer, than the usual 26 weeks. The plan of the Maritime Workers provided 8 weeks; the plan of the Garment Workers provided up to 48 weeks; while the plans of the Detroit Pipefitters and the Buffalo Carpenters each provided a full year of benefits.

The multi-employer plans have, on the whole, undergone fewer changes in their benefit structure than have the single-employer plans. Such changes as have occurred have all been in the direction of liberalization of both benefit amount and benefit duration.

Summary

Over the ten-year period all of the core plans showed some increase in the benefit-wage ratio. The auto and steel plans experienced only one such increase. The rubber, cement, and can companies experienced unusual increases in 1965, when the ratio rose to 65 percent of gross wages in the rubber plan and to 70 percent in the cement and can plans. As of 1965, the total benefit (UI plus SUB) as a proportion of take-home pay varied from about 72 percent to 84 percent. The dependents' benefits that had been added in most plans increased the percentages very little; these benefits were too small to be significant. The second (1959) plan of Allis-Chalmers was the only one to provide a positive dependents' benefit, and this provision was dropped a few years later (1962).

13. The administrative task of computing the earnings of claimants was greatly simplified by calculating an average weekly wage for each class of workers (40 times the straight-time hourly rate of the class) and considering everyone in a given class to have earned that wage.

Some claimants receive less than these stated percentages either because the UI component of the total benefit is lacking or because the SUB maximum limits the dollar amount that may be paid. Both of these limitations have been lessened during the life of the plans. When UI was not received, the steel, can, and rubber plans always allowed the SUB benefit to be paid up to the maximum (they did not subtract the estimated UI in calculating such a claimant's benefit); the auto and agricultural implement plans were handling the situation similarly by 1965, with only the cement plan continuing to subtract the estimated UI benefit.

To cover the situation when UI is not received, the Steelworkers negotiated a special (higher) SUB maximum. As of 1965, this so-called "dual" maximum was operative in the plans of can, rubber, and Allis-Chalmers, as well as in basic steel. It was not a part of the other agricultural implement plans nor of the auto or cement plans.

The regular maximum SUB payment, applicable when UI is received, has been increased substantially in all the plans over the ten-year span. As of 1965, the can plan did not impose any limit on the maximum SUB payment (a critical provision). The "variable" maximum benefit is one that varies with the number of dependents; without it, the provision of dependents' benefits becomes ineffectual for high-wage claimants. The steel, can, and rubber plans provided a variable maximum from the beginning. The auto and cement plans first provided one in 1965.

One of the more significant later developments in the benefit formula was the negotiation of the short-week benefit in 1961–1963, when it became a standard provision of all the core plans. By means of this benefit, paid out of the SUB fund, the unions have approached one of their long-cherished goals, a guaranteed weekly income.

What was originally a key issue, the conservation of the fund for the sake of those who might be laid off later, has become much less significant through the liberalization of provisions regulating the reduction of benefits in the event of a declining fund. As of 1965, no plan reduced the benefit amount except in extreme circumstances, and only the rubber plan began the reduction of duration at an early stage in the decline of the fund.

The increase in the maximum duration of benefits has been one of the more significant developments in the SUB plans. Whereas originally only the plans negotiated by the Steelworkers went beyond the 26 weeks of benefits provided in most state UI programs, by 1965 all the core plans provided at least 52 weeks. The rubber, cement, and can plans had gone beyond 1 year, in some cases up to 5 years. Moreover, the Alan Wood Steel Company had introduced (in 1965) unlimited duration for employees with ten years or more of seniority.

The multi-employer plans present a much simpler picture. All but one of these plans used a flat benefit amount, and the usual duration of benefits was the same as that of the state UI programs. By way of exceptions to this general description, the plan of the Los Angeles Retail Clerks set its benefit as a percentage of wages, and the plans of the Detroit Pipefitters and the Buffalo Carpenters paid benefits for as long as a year.

A final development has been the payment of other than unemployment benefits from the SUB fund. A summary of these additional benefits is provided at the end of the following chapter (Table 6–5).

(Post-1965 developments are sketched in Appendix B.)

6
FINANCING PROVISIONS

The financing provisions of a SUB plan are like the engine room of a ship — vital, but complicated and on the dull side. For the sake of the general reader, the description of these provisions is considerably abbreviated; as a result the cautions voiced in the Introduction to Part II are especially applicable to this chapter.

Logically, decisions with respect to financing are consequent on decisions regulating eligibility and benefits; actually, a preliminary tentative estimate of the amount of money available for unemployment benefits is a significant factor in the choice of eligibility and benefit provisions. This mutual causality is recognized wherever it is particularly pertinent, but, for the most part, the description of financing provisions proceeds on the simplifying assumption that the decisions described in Chapters 4 and 5 have already been made.

The financial structure of a SUB plan consists essentially of two parts: the faucet regulating the flow of money into a tank and the size of the tank itself — that is, the contribution rate and the reserve fund. The chapter discusses these two elements in terms of, first, the principles and provisions of the original plans and, second, the subsequent development of the provisions.

Principles and Original Provisions

Contribution Rate

Principles. The selection of the original contribution rates was guided by three main principles. The contribution rate was to be adequate, limited, and variable.

It was to be adequate to build up a reserve fund in a reasonable period of time and to maintain or replenish the fund as benefits were paid. This requirement is most conveniently discussed in connection with the reserve fund.

It was to be limited in order to define the employer's maximum liability. The lack of such a limit was the main obstacle to the attainment of the original union goal — the guaranteed annual wage. The transformation of GAW into SUB began with the proposals made in the Latimer Report

[3, p. 83] and the Latimer Brief to limit the employer's liability. After stating that "the most important financial problem in connection with unemployment supplements has to do with the liability of the employer," the Latimer Brief listed as one of six basic principles: "Limit the liability of the employer to the amount contributed by him to the trust fund" [7, pp. 32, 33].

In some quarters skepticism was voiced about how limited the liability really would be. If the fund were dissipated, would not the employer be "morally obligated" to pay the promised benefits to his laid-off employees? What actually occurred in the event of inadequate reserve funds is noted in Part III, but the expectation of such "moral" pressure was the reason why the Ford Motor Company insisted on the benefit reduction table incorporated in the original UAW-Ford SUB plan (see Chapter 5).

Thirdly, the contribution rate was to vary directly, within the limit set by the maximum rate, in accordance with the employer's experience with unemployment. The employer's contribution was thus experience-rated to provide him with an additional incentive to prevent unemployment. Both the Auto Workers and the Steelworkers had emphasized this objective of SUB. Speaking for the Auto Workers, Nat Weinberg said: "As we developed our program it became clear to us that the proper description for our objective was 'guaranteed employment.' We made it clear from the outset that it is steady work we wanted, not pay for idleness" [48, p. 32]. W. A. Lacke, Continental Can's general manager of industrial relations, wrote of the 1955 negotiations: "The officials of the Steelworkers said on numerous occasions during our negotiations of the plan that one of their basic objectives in seeking such a plan was to induce management to bring about greater stability of employment. Further, that they would be happiest when no SUB benefits would be paid out" [49, p. 421].

Original provisions. Table 6–1 shows, among other things, the contribution rates originally established in the core plans. The first three columns of the table show the amount and the form of the maximum monthly contribution required by each plan. The UAW-Ford negotiations established a pattern of 5 cents in cash to be contributed to the fund for each paid hour. The Ford Company was willing to contribute more than 5 cents, but the union preferred that the available money be used elsewhere. The other auto plans provided for the same 5-cent contribution in cash, as did the agricultural implement plans.

The can companies were the first to negotiate a SUB plan with the Steelworkers. The Continental Can company believed that it could carry the plan with a 3-cent contribution, but, recognizing that the auto settlement had established a precedent which could not easily be ignored, agreed to be liable for an additional 2 cents if that should prove necessary [49, pp. 417–21]. Thus was born the form of contribution called "contingent liability."

The liability may be contingent in the sense of "whether" or "when," that is, whether the liability will ever have to be liquidated or merely when it will have to be liquidated. These two meanings of contingency have been combined in various ways in the different plans at different times. Even in those plans which made the liability ultimately inescapable (the "when" variety), the arrangement appealed to some employers because it permitted them to use the cash represented by the contingent liability until such time as the cash should be required for benefits.

The disadvantage of contingent liability is that the demand for cash may come at the time least convenient for the company to provide cash. Perhaps it was for this reason that the American Can Company followed Ford rather than Continental Can and negotiated a straight 5-cent cash contribution.

The Continental Can plan had a unique device for saving cash on even the "cash" contribution. The company had the option of discharging the 3-cent cash obligation by an actual cash payment or by crediting the amount to an "accrual account," which was just another form of "contingent liability." This option held for only a year at a time; at the end of the calendar year, the liability thus accrued had to be paid off in cash.

The steel plan, negotiated in 1956, a few months after the can plans, also made use of contingent liability. The steel plan established a 5-cent monthly obligation consisting of 3 cents in cash and 2 cents in contingent liability. The steel plan differed from that of Continental Can in its handling of contingent liability: the liability accumulated differently and had a different relationship to maximum funding.

Table 6–2 is merely illustrative. For three types of plans, it shows the amounts that would be contributed or saved at various levels of the reserve fund. For example, when 2 cents were required to bring the fund up to its maximum, under the auto plan 3 cents were saved in cash; under the steel plan 1 cent was saved in cash; under the Continental Can plan 3 cents were saved, 1 cent in cash and 2 cents in liability. In both the steel and can plans, contingent liability became an immediate liability to be paid off in cash when cash in the fund was insufficient to pay benefits. In the steel plan, because contingent liability accrued "in tandem" with the cash contribution, it produced a larger and more regular total monthly obligation than it did in the Continental Can plan.

The rubber plan broke with the 5-cent pattern and required the employer

TABLE 6-1

Financing Provisions of Selected SUB Plans, 1955–1965: Contributions

| Plan | Maximum monthly obligation | | Conditions under which contingent liability becomes payable in cash | Conditions under which further cash contributions are required | Disposition of amount by which actual contribution is less than maximum |
	Cash contribution[a]	Addition to contingent liability[b]			
UAW and auto companies[c]					
First plan (1955)*	5¢ per pd. hr.				Saved by company
Second plan (1958)**	Same				Same
Third plan (1961)**	Same			When fund is less than $300 per employee, company to reimburse fund for scheduled short-week benefits[d]	Same
Fourth plan (1964)**	Same			Same	Placed in Christmas bonus fund
URW and rubber companies					
First plan (1956)*	3¢ per pd. hr.				Saved by company
Second plan (1959)*	Same				Same
Third plan (1961)**	Same				Same
Fourth plan (1963)**	4¢ per pd. hr.				Same
Fifth plan (1965)**	5¢ per pd. hr.			When fund is less than 60% of maximum, company to reimburse fund for scheduled short-week benefits	Placed in annual bonus fund

USWA and basic steel				
First plan (1956)*	3¢ per hr. worked	2¢ per hr. worked	When fund assets are insufficient to pay benefits	Saved by company[b]
Second plan (1960)*	Same	Same	Same	Same[b]
Third plan (1962)*	4.5¢ per hr. worked[e]	9.5¢ per hr. worked[e]	Same	Up to 4.5¢ diverted to various funds (see text) then, up to 5¢ saved by company
Fourth plan (1965)*	Same	Same	Same	Same
USWA and Continental Can				
First plan (1955)**	3¢ per pd. hr.[f]	2¢ per pd. hr.	When fund assets are insufficient to pay benefits	Saved by company
Second plan (1959)**	Same	Same	Same	Same
Third plan (1962)**	Same	Same	Same	Same
Fourth plan (1965)***	15¢ per pd. hr.[f]	2¢ per pd. hr. if 15¢ does not raise fund to maximum level	Same	Up to 15¢ diverted to bonus fund;[f] up to 2¢ saved by company
UCLGW and cement companies				
First plan (1959)**	3¢ per pd. hr.		Until fund is initially at maximum financing—2¢ per pd. hr. Until fund reaches 50% of maximum financing—2¢ per pd. hr.; then 1¢ per pd. hr. until it reaches 66²/₃% of maximum financing	Saved by company
Second plan (1962)****	5¢ per pd. hr.			Same

TABLE 6-1 (*Continued*)

Plan	Maximum monthly obligation		Conditions under which contingent liability becomes payable in cash	Conditions under which further cash contributions are required	Disposition of amount by which actual contribution is less than maximum
	Cash contribution[a]	Addition to contingent liability[b]			
Third plan (1965)****	10¢ per pd. hr.	5¢ per pd. hr. if fund is below maximum financing; 7¢ per pd. hr. if fund is at maximum financing (see text)	When fund is below 32% of maximum financing	When fund is less than $150 per employee, company to reimburse fund for severance benefits paid	Same

* Fund pays unemployment benefits only.
** Fund pays unemployment and severance benefits. In the rubber plan, severance benefits are paid from the SUB fund only when that fund is 80% or more of maximum.
*** Fund pays unemployment, severance, sickness and disability benefits, and relocation allowances, and also supplements workmen's compensation.
**** Fund pays unemployment and severance benefits and also supplements workmen's compensation.

[a] Where the obligation is stated in terms of ¢ per hour, "paid hours" means hours worked plus certain hours not worked but paid for, e.g., vacations, paid holidays, etc.
[b] Contingent liability is a bookkeeping account which accumulates according to provisions of the plan. In the first and second steel plans, a portion of the when the reserve exceeded the required maximum, a portion of the contingent liability equal to such excess was canceled.
[c] Chrysler is not represented in the data relating to the third and fourth auto plans.
[d] An exception was American Motors, which makes reimbursement for such benefits without reference to the level of the fund.
[e] Not additive; combined maximum is 9.5¢.
[f] The company had the option of paying the cash contribution at the end of the year instead of on a monthly basis, accumulating the liability in an "accrual account" from month to month. In the fourth (1965) plan, it was provided that on every September 30 (after September 30, 1967), the company's payment to the fund is to be limited to the amount needed to raise it to the maximum financing level, and the balance not needed for that purpose is to be distributed as a bonus to employees in December unless the company and the union agree to some other disposition of the excess (for the welfare of the employees).

TABLE 6-2

Financing Methods of Three Types of SUB Plans: Form and Amount of Contribution Required at Various Levels of the Respective Funds

Contribution necessary to bring fund to its level of maximum financing[a] (cents per hr.)	Amount and form of contribution and amount saved, in cents per hr., by plan											
	5-cent cash plan (auto, all years)			3-cent cash, 2-cent contingent liability plan (steel, 1956–1961)				3-cent cash, 2-cent contingent liability plan (Continental Can, 1956–1964)				
			Amt. saved in cash			Amt. saved in		Cash or accrual account		Amt. saved in		
	Cash	C.L.[b]		Cash	C.L.	Cash	C.L.		C.L.	Cash	C.L.	
5 or more	5	0	0	3	2	0	0	3	2	0	0	
4	4	0	1	3	2	0	0	3	1	0	1	
3	3	0	2	3	2	0	0	3	0	0	2	
2	2	0	3	2	2	1	0	2	0	1	2	
1	1	0	4	1	1	2	1	1	0	2	2	
0	0	0	5	0	0	3	2	0	0	3	2	

[a] The amount of the maximum financing for each plan is not considered. Since it varied by plan, the table does not compare the actual cost of the plans to the companies involved.
[b] Contingent liability.

to contribute only 3 cents (cash) to the fund. The cement plan, negotiated several years after the other core plans, also provided only for a 3-cent cash contribution. (An extra contribution of 2 cents was to be made until the fund initially reached its maximum.)

Reserve Fund

Principles. A reserve is helpful to meet the seasonal, cyclical, and secular fluctuations in claims for benefits. Without a reserve fund, an employer's contribution rate would have to fluctuate violently and unpredictably, a mirror image of the changes in claims. With a reserve on which to draw for peak loads, the employer's contribution rate can remain steady within narrow limits. To avoid fluctuations in rates, some reserve would be needed even if all fluctuations in claims could be foreseen; a larger fund is needed because most fluctuations cannot be accurately forecast. Other things being equal, a firm that is sensitive to seasonal and cyclical changes requires a larger reserve than a firm whose employment pattern is more stable.

In those plans in which the employer contributes partly in the form of "contingent liability," his contribution rate may remain steady, but his payment of cash may fluctuate more or less violently, depending on how much of his obligation takes the form of regular cash payments to the fund. As noted in Part III, during the latter part of the long prosperity period that followed the 1961 recession, the basic steel companies were operating, for all practical purposes, on a pay-as-you-go basis.

In the core plans, the size of the reserve fund was dictated by three considerations, adequacy, economy, and employment stability. The first operated to keep the fund large enough; the other two, to limit its size. The terms "maximum funding" or "maximum financing" are used interchangeably to refer to the maximum size of the fund.

"Adequacy" is an elastic concept. No plan sought to provide complete protection, not even in the sense of guaranteeing the promised benefits to all who might be eligible for them. The provisions to reduce benefits when the fund declined (Chapter 5) are evidence that the plan did not seek to build funds large enough to handle all contingencies. Certainly, no plan provided a reserve large enough to cover the worst possible experience, the closing of the company. (The goal of the original UAW-Ford plan was to provide protection against 60 percent of the maximum risk exposure.) The norm of adequacy adopted by the core plans seems to have been that the fund should be large enough to pay full benefits to all eligible claimants when the firm's actual experience was not much worse than its average experience had been over an extended period.

The second consideration was simply that of economy, to avoid "wasting" any part of the money available for employee remuneration. There were other things to be done with the available money besides the purchase of additional employment security. Money committed to the SUB fund could not be used for any other purpose. After the SUB fund had become large enough to provide "reasonable" protection against "normal" experience with unemployment, the marginal utility of additional protection dropped rapidly, and other possible uses of the available money took precedence. The Internal Revenue Service also used the norm of "reasonableness" in determining the maximum size of the reserve fund to which tax-exempt status would be granted.

The third consideration was the desirability of providing the employer with an additional incentive to prevent unemployment. The measure of the incentive is the extent to which the employer can save on his contributions to the fund, and the only way to allow an employer thus to save is to set a limit on the size of the fund, and to permit the employer's contributions to diminish or cease while that level is maintained.[1] The importance accorded this third consideration by the Auto Workers is reflected in their original proposals, which would have relied much more on current financing (pay as you go) and much less on reserve financing than the plan finally negotiated with Ford. All the core plans established their reserve funds at a level which the employer could expect to reach in a few years, after which he could begin to save on his contributions. It was hoped that to some extent the operations of the reserve funds would be countercyclical; in the steel plan, the choice of hours worked as a method of calculating maximum funding was influenced by this consideration. However, the desire to make the plans countercyclical was never a major factor in their construction.

Original provisions. Table 6–3 shows the original provisions governing the size of the reserve fund. The methods of calculating "maximum funding," the level at which the reserve fund is considered adequate, are shown in column 1. In one way or another, all the methods involved estimates of the average benefit amount and the number of benefits. The latter factor depended, in turn, on the number of employees eligible for benefits and the estimated layoff rate among such employees.

1. This limit is not necessarily connected with the fundamental issue, mentioned earlier, of limited employer liability, which is solely a function of the contribution rate, not of the reserve fund. The employer who knows that this contribution rate will never go above a predetermined amount already has the limitation on liability that makes a SUB plan possible, regardless of the size of the fund.

TABLE 6-3

Financing Provisions of Selected SUB Plans, 1955–1965: Maximum Funding

Plan	Method of calculating monthly maximum funding	Amount of maximum funding per employee[a]	Adjustment of maximum funding with changes in average benefit amount	
			Benefit amount	Adjusted maximum funding as percent of normal maximum funding
	(1)	(2)	(3)	(4)
UAW and auto companies				
First plan (1955)*	$400 times (number of employees in active service plus those on layoff with credit units)	$400	$15.00–$19.99	80
			$10.00–$14.99	60
			$5.00– $9.99	40
			Less than $5.00	20
Second plan (1958)**	Same	Same	Same	
Third plan (1961)**	(Average benefit of preceding 12 months plus average weekly medical insurance premium) times (the number of employees on active service plus those on layoff with credit units for the month) times 16	Approximately $544[b]	Adjustment provided for in formula for maximum funding	
Fourth plan (1964)**	Same, except in the plan of General Motors[c]	Approximately $560[b]	Same	
URW and rubber companies				
First plan (1956)*	Initial funding (varying with company) times the ratio of (the sum of the number of employees in active service and the number on layoff with credits) to the number of employees in July 1956	Approximately $185	No adjustment	
Second plan (1959)*	Same	Same	Same	
Third plan (1961)**	Same	Same	Same	
Fourth plan (1963)**	Same	Same	Same	
Fifth plan (1965)**	Same, except initial funding increased	Approximately $250	Same	
USWA and basic steel				
First plan (1956)*	10.5¢ times hours worked in first 12 of preceding 14 months	Approximately $190[d] (cash plus contingent liability)	$12.00–$15.99	80
			$8.00–$11.99	60
			Less than $8.00	40
Second plan (1960)*	Same	Same	Same	

Plan	Formula	Approximately	Adjustment provided for in formula for maximum funding
Third plan (1962)*	12.5¢ times hours worked in first 12 of preceding 14 months or 100 times average monthly benefits paid in preceding 5 years	Approximately $225[d]	Same
Fourth plan (1965)*	Same	Same	Same
USWA and Continental Can			
First plan (1955)**	9¢ times hours paid[e] in 12-month period ending September 30 of last calendar year completed	Approximately $162[d]	$12.00–$16.00 80 $8.00–$12.00 60 Less than $8.00 40
Second plan (1959)**	Same	Same	Same
Third plan (1962)**	Same	Same	Same
Fourth plan (1965)***	21¢ times hours paid[e] in 12-month period ending September 30 of most recent calendar year	Approximately $378[d]	No adjustment
UCLGW and cement companies			
First plan (1959)**	$150 times "total number of employees" as of the third Monday of the month. excluding employees on layoff who have less than 2 years' seniority	$150	No adjustment
Second plan (1962)****	$225 times "total number of employees" as of the third Monday of the month, excluding employees on layoff who have less than 1 year's seniority	$225	Same
Third plan (1965)****	Cash fund: $225 times "total number of employees," as of the third Monday of the month, excluding employees on layoff who have less than 1 year's seniority Contingent fund: $175 times same number of employees as above	Cash fund: $225 Contingent fund: $175	Same

* Fund pays unemployment benefits only.
** Fund pays unemployment and severance benefits. In the rubber plan, severance benefits are paid from the SUB fund only when that fund is 80% or more of maximum.
*** Fund pays unemployment, severance, sickness and disability benefits and relocation allowances and also supplements workmen's compensation.
**** Fund pays unemployment and severance benefits and also supplements workmen's compensation.

a In some plans, maximum funding is calculated in terms of the number of hours worked; in other plans, it is calculated in terms of the number of employees. In order to facilitate comparisons among plans, the former has been converted into the latter.

b An average benefit of $30 plus health insurance premiums of $4 (in fourth plan, $5) is assumed.

c In the General Motors plan, the number of employees is the average number in active service plus the number on layoff with credits in the previous 52 weeks.

d It is assumed that on the average, 1,800 hours per employee are worked or paid.

e Hours worked plus certain hours not worked but paid, such as vacations, holidays, etc.

The auto and cement plans made the calculation directly in terms of dollars per employee. The steel plan made the calculation in terms of cents per hour worked in a previous 12-month period. The Continental Can plan was similar to steel; but the American Can plan (not shown) based its calculation on a total figure for all employees at the beginning of the plan, adjusted monthly by the ratio of the 12-month moving average of employment to the base-period average monthly employment. The rubber plan was like American Can in its use of the original number of employees as a base, but adjusted the monthly funding position by the ratio of the sum of the current number of employees and the number on layoff with credit units to the initial number of employees. The use of a moving average (steel and can plans) makes for less abrupt changes in maximum funding as employment rises and falls.

Column 2 of Table 6–3 shows the result produced by each funding formula. For convenient comparison, the maximum funding positions of the steel, can, and rubber plans have been converted into approximate dollars per employee. The reserve required in the auto plan ($400) was much larger than that in the steel ($190), rubber ($185), Continental Can ($162), or cement ($150) plans. The maximum funding position of the auto plan was not quite so large as it seems; during much of the plan's existence, an adjustment factor operated to keep the maximum funding level at about $300 per employee. The difference between the steel and Continental plans was not so great as it seems because contingent liability was counted as part of the reserve in the steel formula but not in the formula of Continental Can.

Adjustment factors were used in both the auto-type and steel-type plans, as shown in columns 3 and 4 of Table 6–3. Since the average SUB payment entered into the calculation of maximum funding, and since this payment could change without any change in the SUB plan — usually because the states had increased their UI benefits — an adjustment table to allow for such developments permitted finer "tuning" of the reserve fund to the potential demands on it. All increases in UI benefits had the effect of lowering the reserve required to reach maximum funding.

The use of the average SUB payment in the formula of maximum funding (auto-type plan) can have the effect of inhibiting contributions even when a fund is very low. If no benefits have been paid from a fund and if the average benefit is zero,[2] the reserve is at maximum funding, and no

2. In some plans, this effect was avoided by the following argument: "In a controversy as to whether, when no benefits are paid from a SUB fund, the average benefit is zero, I presented for the Steelworkers an affidavit from a former president of the Mathematics Association of America that zero divided by zero is not zero but an indeterminate

contribution is required. The operation of this factor in auto-type plans permitted the payment of Christmas bonuses from some small funds that were probably inadequately financed to pay unemployment benefits.

The picture of the provisions governing the reserve fund needs to be completed by reference to Table 6-1, column 5, which shows that originally all the core plans allowed the employer to save on his contributions after maximum funding was reached. As long as his contributions were thus experience-rated, the employer had an additional motive[3] to keep the level of maximum funding as low as possible. After experience rating was largely abandoned (by the steel plan in 1962 and by the auto and rubber and can plans in 1964–1965), it was to the employer's interest, other things being equal, to establish the level of maximum funding as high as possible.

Development of Provisions

All the core plans made some changes in their financing provisions in the course of the decade 1955–1965. The details of these changes, shown in Table 6-1 and Table 6-3, are discussed chronologically for each of the core plans in turn. The reader who is not concerned with details will find the principal changes summarized and explained at the end of this section. The reader who wishes to follow the details of the changes may be helped by first glancing at summary Table 6-4 and noting that these changes strengthened the financing of the plans in one or a combination of the following respects: an increase in the amount of the regular contribution (columns 1, 2, and 3); an increase in the level of maximum funding (column 4); or an additional contribution, in the form of cash or contingent liability, over and above the regular contribution (column 5).

Auto Plan

The auto-type plan alone did not increase its original monthly contribution rate (5 cents in cash). In 1961, however, when regular benefits were increased and the short-week benefit was introduced, the plan substantially increased maximum funding, from $400 per employee to approximately $544. Since most of the companies involved had been paying less than the

---

amount. Since maximum funding can be reduced only when the average weekly benefit is below a certain amount, the reduction cannot be made in the absence of an unqualified demonstration that the average is, in fact, below the critical amount. An indeterminate figure does not provide that unqualified demonstration. Harry Platt, the arbitrator, concurred" [50].

3. Additional, because the employer always has the motive stemming from the operation of the reduction table. The lower the level at which maximum funding is set, the sooner benefits begin to be reduced.

maximum contribution (because of their favorable experience with unemployment) this increase in maximum funding had the effect at that time of increasing the effective contribution rate. At the same time, an extra contribution to the fund was required equal to any scheduled short-week benefits paid when the fund level was less than $300 per employee. In 1964, a very significant change was made in the plan — with the negotiation of the "hard nickel." Thereafter, it was impossible for the employer to save any part of the 5-cent contribution. Any portion of the contribution not needed to raise the fund to its maximum level was to be paid into a Christmas bonus fund, to be distributed equally to all eligible employees at Christmastime.

The Chrysler and Allis-Chalmers plans differed somewhat from the other auto-type plans and for the same reason, that they were in financial difficulties. The 1951 Chrysler plan required the company to make substantial additional contributions to the SUB fund. In 1964, neither company adopted the "hard nickel" or provided a Christmas bonus fund. Neither company was expected to be able to save on its 5-cent contribution during the life of the contract, that is, through 1967. Also in 1964, a limited form of contingent liability was introduced into the Allis-Chalmers plan to permit the company to economize on cash.

Rubber Plan

The regular contribution was increased in 1963 from 3 cents to 4 cents when the benefit formula was liberalized and the short-week benefit was introduced. In 1965, the contribution was increased to 5 cents, in connection with a further liberalization of the benefit amount and benefit duration. In the same year maximum funding was increased for the first time — from the original $185 to $250 per employee. This change gave the rubber plan a maximum funding somewhat higher than that of the steel plan but stili much lower than that of the auto plan. In 1965, the rubber plan also provided an additional contribution to cover scheduled short-week benefits when the fund was less than 60 percent of its maximum. The rubber plan imitated autos in negotiating the "hard nickel" in 1965.

Steel Plan

All changes of any significance were made in the 1962 negotiations, so that in effect there have been only two different steel plans. In 1962, both the contribution rates and the level of maximum funding were markedly increased, partly because the benefit structure was liberalized and partly because the previous financing was considered to have been inadequate, for reasons noted in Part III. The contribution rate was increased from

3 cents in cash plus 2 cents in contingent liability to 4.5 cents in cash plus 5 cents in contingent liability. The experience-rating character of the plan was greatly diminished by two provisions. First, the maximum funding level was raised, so that it was more difficult to reach the point at which savings could begin. Second, some savings were diverted to other uses than SUB.

According to the new formula, the company was always required to bring the fund up to the new maximum funding, but the form of the contribution (cash or contingent liability) depended on whether the fund was below the old or the new maximum funding. If the fund was 4.5 cents or more below the old (lower) maximum, 4.5 cents in cash and 5 cents in contingent liability were required. If the fund was higher than this, some saving in cash was made; but the saving was picked up by contingent liability to maintain a total obligation of 9.5 cents (cash plus contingent liability).

At levels of the fund above the old maximum but below the new maximum, the entire contribution to the SUB fund was in the form of contingent liability.[4] When less than 9.5 cents was needed to bring the fund up to the higher maximum, the difference between the needed contribution and 9.5 cents, but not to exceed 4.5 cents, could be diverted to purposes other than SUB. The sum thus diverted was divided among the Savings and Vacation Fund, the Additional Contingent Liability Fund, and, in some companies, other welfare purposes agreed upon by the parties.

When the SUB fund reached the new maximum level, the employer was still committed to contribute (assume a liability of) 4.5 cents, to be divided among the above funds according to their changing needs.[5] Thus the employer could hope to save 5 cents, while he continued to accrue an obligation of 4.5 cents (3.5 cents in some companies). This obligation accumulated indefinitely and could never be canceled.[6] Complicated as the above description may seem, it is a simplified version of the actual financing formula. The maximum funding level of the reserve was increased from approximately $190 to $225 in cash plus contingent liability per

4. As long as the fund did not drop below the old maximum funding, the contribution continued to be made in the form of contingent liability even though there might be no cash in the fund. As a matter of fact, after 1964, many steel companies found themselves in this position.

5. When the Savings and Vacation Fund reached maximum funding, it "splashed back" the contributions that had "spilled over" from the SUB fund. This "splash-back" accrued to the Additional Contingent Liability Fund, which had no maximum funding, but could grow indefinitely.

6. Despite the irrevocable nature of this liability, the Internal Revenue Service has never recognized it as a business expense because the employer still has the use of the money.

employee. The adjustment factor was incorporated in the formula for maximum funding.

Continental Can Plan

This plan retained its original contribution rate of 3 cents in cash plus 2 cents in contingent liability until 1965, when a cash contribution of 15 cents was required, plus an additional 2 cents accrued to Contingent Contribution Liability if the 15 cents did not bring the fund up to the maximum level. As in previous plans, the "cash" contribution could be accrued for a year before becoming payable in cash. Any excess of the 15 cents not required to bring the fund up to maximum funding accrued to another fund, the Excess Welfare Account. Hence, after the 1965 changes, the plan was no longer experience-rated, except for the "additional" 2 cents of contingent liability. The new level of maximum funding was approximately $400 per employee, more than double the previous level. The large increases in the contribution rate and in the maximum funding level are explained by the notable increases negotiated in 1965 in SUB payments, in both amount and duration, and by the addition of three other types of benefits to be paid out of the SUB fund. (The three were relocation allowances provided in conjunction with a new system of transfer rights, under which laid-off employees received preferential rights over new hires in other plants; supplementation of sickness and disability benefits for which the basic payments were financed by an insurance company; and supplementation of workmen's compensation.)

In 1965 also, the adjustment factor was dropped from the plan, perhaps because with the loss of experience rating the employer was less concerned with keeping the fund small.

Cement Plan

The original cash contribution of 3 cents was changed to 5 cents in 1962 and to 10 cents in 1965 in order to support the increased benefits made available in those years. In 1965 also, contingent liability was introduced into the cement plan. In addition to the 10-cent cash contribution, the company assumed a 5-cent contingent liability.[7] This contingent liability became payable in cash under stricter conditions than prevailed in the other plans that used contingent liability. Instead of being payable only when the cash fund was insufficient to pay benefits, in the cement plan contingent liability was payable in cash when the cash fund fell below 32 percent of maximum funding. The 1965 plan further provided that the

7. The contingent liability accrued at the rate of 7 cents if the cash fund was at its maximum. In this situation, no cash was payable and contingent liability was therefore increased.

fund was to be reimbursed for any severance benefit paid from it if the fund level was below $150 per employee.

Maximum funding was increased for the cash fund — from $150 to $225 per employee — and a separate maximum level ($175 per employee) was established for the contingent liability fund. As of 1965, the cement plan was the only plan which still had an unrestricted experience rating; the employer's contributions were limited to the amounts necessary to achieve maximum funding in both funds.

Review of Financing Developments

In the decade 1955–1965, there were four major developments in the financing provisions of the core plans. (1) Financing of all plans was increased in terms of the contribution rate, or the reserve fund, or (usually) both. (2) Contingent liability was used more extensively and in new ways. (3) Experience rating was abandoned by most plans. (4) The SUB funds were called upon to pay a variety of benefits other than unemployment benefits. All of these changes are shown in chronological detail in Tables 6–1 and 6–3; the first three are summarized in Table 6–4.

Increased Financing

The auto and agricultural implement plans increased maximum funding alone. All the other plans increased both the regular contribution rate and maximum funding. The reasons for the increases differed somewhat among the plans. In the case of steel, it was necessary not only to finance increases in benefits but also to remedy the inadequacy of the fund for even the original benefits. The major thrust of the new (1962) financing provisions in steel seems to have been to get the fund up to the level of the *old* maximum funding. In what would appear to be a compromise, contributions to reach the level of the *new* maximum funding are made only in the form of contingent liability.

When the auto-type plans increased maximum funding in 1961, one reason was the liberalization in benefits negotiated at the same time. Another was the belief that the original maximum funding was inadequate. Still another reason may have been connected with the operation of experience rating. In the years immediately preceding 1961, most of the companies had been carrying the plan with a contribution of less than 5 cents. The union's demand for an increase in maximum funding may have been motivated by a desire to recover that portion of the 5 cents which was being saved by the employer and thus "lost" to the employees. The increase in the level of maximum funding had the effect of increasing actual contributions at that time, even though no change had been made in the contribution rate. Thus in 1961 the union may have already been reaching for

TABLE 6-4

Summary of Changes in Financing Provisions of Selected SUB Plans from First Plan (1955, 1956, or 1959) to Plan as of 1964 or 1965

Plan	Increase in maximum regular obligation		Contingent liability added to original plan	Increase in maximum funding	Addition to cash contribution or contingent liability other than regular obligation			Employer savings on SUB diverted to other purposes
	Cash contribution	Addition to contingent liability			For SUB	For scheduled short-week benefit[a]	For severance payments[a]	
	(1)	(2)	(3)	(4)	(5)	(6)	(7)	(8)
UAW and auto companies[b]	no	(never had)	no	yes	no	yes	no	yes
UAW and Chrysler	no	(never had)	no	yes	yes	yes	no	no
UAW and Allis-Chalmers	no	no	yes	yes	no	yes	yes	[c]
URW and rubber companies	yes	(never had)	no	yes	no	yes	yes	yes
USWA and basic steel	yes	yes	(always had)	yes	no	no	no	yes
USWA and American Can	yes	no	yes	yes	no	no	no	yes[d]
USWA and Continental Can	yes	no	(always had)	yes	no	no	no	yes[d]
UCLGW and cement companies	yes	no	yes	yes	[e]	no	yes	no

a Payments made from the fund for this purpose are replaced by additional contributions if the fund is below a specified level.

b Chrysler is not included.

c Amount of cash contributions saved is added to contingent liability.

d Savings to the employer are limited to the contingent liability.

e The first two plans required an extra contribution until maximum funding was initially reached.

the goal which it obtained in 1964 — the commitment of the full 5 cents. The increases in financing in the can, rubber, and cement plans seem to have been connected directly with increases in benefits, especially in 1965.

Contingent Liability

The core plans increased their use of contingent liability. Originally only the Continental Can and steel plans included this form of contribution. Later (1964–1965), contingent liability was included in the Allis-Chalmers, American Can, and cement plans. The plans using contingent liability varied in the way in which the liability accrued and in the conditions under which it was liquidated in cash. In the steel plan, contingent liability accrued with the cash contribution "in tandem" (Table 6–2); in the can and cement plans, it accrued only to the extent that the cash contribution was insufficient to reach maximum funding. (The Allis-Chalmers plan generally resembled the steel plan in its method of accrual.)

In the steel and can plans, contingent liability was not payable in cash unless the cash fund was insufficient to pay benefits; in the cement and Allis-Chalmers plans, payments in cash started much sooner, when the fund dropped below 32 percent of maximum funding (cement) or below 66 percent (Allis-Chalmers).

Experience Rating

As of 1965, experience rating had been abandoned or severely restricted in all the core plans except cement (Table 6–4). The Chrysler and Allis-Chalmers plans were only apparent exceptions to this generalization; in all probability, when their financial position has improved sufficiently, they will be brought into line with the other auto and agricultural implement plans. The abandonment of experience rating began in 1962 with the basic steel contract of that year; in 1964–1965 it spread to nearly all the auto, agricultural implement, and rubber plans.

The abandonment of experience rating seems to have been mainly due to a feeling on the part of the union members that what the employer saved they were losing. They felt that, because they had presumably foregone some wage increase as the price of getting the employer to contribute to a SUB fund, the money belonged to them. This feeling was strongest where the employer's savings were particularly high and among employees who expected to draw very little from the SUB fund.[8] An additional reason for

8. The funds of the SUB plans negotiated between the Electrical Workers (IUE) and the auto companies had been at high levels for some time prior to 1965, and the companies had been paying correspondingly little into the funds. As a result this union was particularly restless and its leaders had announced their intention to demand the elimination of experience rating. This announcement put considerable pressure on the UAW to do likewise.

restricting the operation of experience rating was the traditional union policy of seeking to equalize labor costs among competing firms.

In abandoning experience rating, the unions — especially the Auto Workers — were also abandoning one of the chief arguments they had originally advanced for negotiating a SUB plan, the incentive such a plan would provide employers to avoid unemployment. The original emphasis is reflected in two statements of Nat Weinberg, one of the chief spokesmen for the Auto Workers in the field of SUB. In late 1953, Mr. Weinberg said: "The UAW proposal is not supplemental unemployment compensation because its objective is primarily to stabilize employment and only secondarily to compensate workers for loss of income" [51]. Two years later he said: "No one can now say whether the 5 cent per hour company contributions will have to be continued indefinitely in order to replenish trust funds subjected to a steady drain of benefit withdrawals, or whether contributions will have to be resumed sporadically to replace occasional withdrawals, or whether contributions will cease entirely because there are no withdrawals to be replaced. We hope the last will prove to be the typical case, because stability of employment is our primary objective" [52].

In 1958, the Steelworkers were still[9] saying that "the Union is interested primarily in achieving continuous employment for its members, not in unemployment benefits. In setting up the SUB plans in the form which it did, the Union was offering the companies a definite financial incentive to stabilize production and employment. The Union would be satisfied if no benefits were paid out of the SUB funds, if that meant its members were continuously fully employed" [53, p. 55].

In justification for their change of position, the unions argued that experience rating had already accomplished nearly all that could be expected of it and that there was little danger that the companies would return to their former irregular employment practices.

The Cement Workers seem to have retained experience rating on grounds of principle. Union officials queried on the 1965 choice explained simply: "When an employer is at maximum funding, that means he is giving our people steady employment and we are satisfied. That is all we wanted in the first place." Whether the union will continue to see the issue in this light will depend partly on how much the membership of the Cement Workers is influenced by the example of other unions.

Other Kinds of Benefits

As the footnotes of Table 6–1 show, there has been a growth of benefits other than SUB paid out of the SUB fund. These other benefits include

9. See, earlier in the chapter, the comment of W. H. Lacke on the pre-SUB position of the Steelworkers [49, p. 421].

severance pay, sickness and disability benefits, supplements to workmen's compensation, and relocation allowances. Among the factors facilitating this growth was the availability of money produced by the SUB contributions and not immediately needed for SUB payments. The employees were reluctant to see the employer save on "their" 5 cents — or whatever the maximum SUB contribution was — and the employer, resigned to losing the entire contribution eventually, preferred to use part of the SUB contribution for these additional benefits rather than to set up separate programs, each with its own financing.

Of the additional benefits, severance payments are the closest in nature to SUB and also pose the greatest threat to the SUB fund. Since severance benefits are usually paid in lump sums, they can impose a sudden and very large drain on the fund. To protect the fund against this danger, the 1965 cement and Allis-Chalmers plans provided for an extra contribution reimbursing the fund for severance payments made when the fund was low. A similar provision was included in the American Can plan of 1962, but it was dropped in 1965 when the regular contribution was greatly increased. An equivalent provision was included in the rubber plan of 1961, which required the employer to pay severance benefits out of pocket while the SUB fund was below 80 percent of maximum.

As of 1965, in the auto, agricultural implement, and cement plans, any SUB payments that were made during the period of unemployment before the claimant was judged to be permanently separated and eligible for severance benefits were subtracted in determining the amount of the severance payment. In the rubber plan, severance benefits were not paid until a layoff had lasted a year; SUB paid during this period was *not* subtracted in determining the severance benefit. The steel industry has long had a modest severance-pay plan which has been financed separately from the SUB fund. For this reason it does not appear in Table 6–1; obviously it poses no threat to the SUB fund.

Comparison of Costs

Table 6–5 is a convenient summary of some of the larger aspects of SUB financing. For the core plans and for the multi-employer plans described in Chapter 2, the table shows the maximum contribution that may be demanded of the employer and the various benefits other than unemployment benefits that may be paid from the fund. Since the table omits many essential aspects of the total financing situation — for example, the division of the contribution between SUB and "other" benefits, the level of maximum funding, and the extent of experience rating — it can convey only a very general impression of the relative size of the financial burden borne by each SUB plan.

TABLE 6-5

Maximum Cost and Additional Benefits of Selected SUB Plans, March 1966

Plan	Maximum cost[a]	Benefits other than for unemployment paid from fund				
		Severance	Sickness and disability	Health insurance for unemployed	Relocation allowance	Supplementation of workmen's compensation
UAW and auto companies	5.0¢/man-hour[b]	X				
URW and rubber companies	5.0¢/man-hour[b]	X				
USWA and basic steel	9.5¢/man-hour	X	c	X		
USWA and can companies	17.0¢/man-hour[d]	X	X		X	X
UCLGW and cement companies	15.0¢/man-hour[d]				X	X
ILGWU and National Dress Manufacturers' Association	0.5% gross weekly wages	X				
NMU and East Coast shipping companies	25.0¢/man-day	X	X			X
PPF and New York City Contractors[e]	25.0¢/man-day		X			X
PPF and Detroit Contractors	10.0¢/man-hour					
IBEW and Detroit Electrical Contractors	5.0¢/man-hour					
CJA and Construction Industry Employers' Association (Buffalo)	42.0¢/man-hour		X	X		X
UAW and Detroit Tooling Association	6.0¢/man-hour					
RCIA and Los Angeles Food Employers' Council	2.0¢/man-hour		X			
BFCSD and New Orleans Brewers	1.0¢/man-hour					

a Inclusive of maximum addition to contingent liability, if any.
b Plan provides for extra contributions to fund under certain circumstances to replace scheduled short-week benefits paid.
c SUB is paid in lieu of disability benefits to a person disabled while on layoff if eligibility for such benefits has lapsed.

d Plan provides for extra contributions to fund under certain circumstances to replace severance payments.
e Plan also provides for emergency payments, which account for more than half of the disbursements from the fund.

The plans calling for the smallest rates of contribution were two multi-employer plans, that of the Garment Workers (ILGWU) and that of the Retail Clerks (RCIA), each of which required a contribution for SUB alone of about 1 cent per hour.

By far the most expensive plan was that of the Buffalo Carpenters (CJA), with its contribution of 42 cents per man-hour. Starting with a 5-cent contribution in 1961, this plan increased the required contribution as follows: 1962, 15 cents; 1963, 32 cents; 1964, 37 cents; 1965, 42 cents. More than half of this total contribution goes into SUB payments.

Of the core plans, the can and cement plans have become significantly more expensive than the others (autos, agricultural implement, rubber), but the former family also provides more kinds of benefits, and there is no way of estimating from the provisions of the plans themselves what proportion of the total contribution is to be allocated to SUB. Experience under the plans, discussed in Part III, throws some light on this question.

7

ADMINISTRATIVE PROVISIONS

Single-Employer Plans

In the original negotiations between the Auto Workers and the Ford Motor Company, the chief issue relating to administration was the union's demand for "independent administration." This demand was reflected in the fifth of the six basic principles with which the UAW entered into negotiation with Ford in the spring of 1955: "The plan should be administered by a Joint Board of Administration having equal representation from the Union and from management, with an impartial chairman to break deadlocks. Decisions of the Joint Board with respect to eligibility and disqualification would be made independently of decisions made by state agencies with regard to unemployment compensation" [10, p. 3].

In the fall of 1955, the UAW announced that, although it had failed to secure independent administration of the Ford plan, it had not abandoned this as a goal: "We have sought in recent negotiations and will continue to seek in future negotiations what we call independent administration of the guaranteed employment plans" [48, p. 34]. At the meeting at which this declaration was made, the Ford representative explained why the company had been and would continue to be unwilling to accept the union proposal for independent administration: "Its administration, as proposed, would be prohibitively expensive and would duplicate State unemployment compensation machinery. Its administration, as proposed, would put such questions as eligibility, disqualification, suitability of job offers, and similar issues under State unemployment compensation laws, into the area of day-to-day negotiations with the Union. Such administrative arrangements would have tended to break down State rules and State laws quickly" [48, p. 37].

The issue of administration was, of course, a derivative issue. The principal issue was whether the SUB plan was to have independent eligibility conditions (see Chapter 4). Only to the extent that the eligibility provisions of SUB were independent of UI would there be need for independent administrative machinery. The very limited degree of independence accorded to SUB (see Table 4–3) has meant that the administrative machinery of SUB could be simpler than the union had envisaged.

The following description of the administrative provisions of the core

SUB plans relates to the plans as they were in 1965. Where a provision had been changed from its original form, this change is noted.

Trustees

All plans provide for a trustee, usually a bank or other fiduciary institution. The trustee receives the employer's contributions and manages the fund. Some plans specify the type of investments in which the money may be placed; others do not. Generally, the money is invested in government bonds. Liquidity is an important requirement.

Applications

The immediate administrator of the plan is the employer, who receives applications for SUB, determines the applicant's eligibility and the amount of the benefit, and prepares the check. All the core plans originally had generally similar provisions regulating applications for benefits. The applicant registered in person each week at the company office, where he was required to exhibit his UI check as proof of his eligibility for state benefits. The latter requirement could delay the cashing of the state check when the claimant was unable to visit in one day the employment security office, the company office, and the bank. It could also result in the loss of SUB, if the claimant had already cashed his UI check.

There was apparently a good deal of dissatisfaction among claimants over this requirement, and the procedure was gradually changed in the auto and agricultural implement plans in 1958 and 1961, and in the steel, cement, and can plans in 1962. Under the changed procedure other proof of eligibility for UI was accepted. The other proof might be a document furnished by the state agency, or a receipt furnished by the bank which cashed the UI check, or even the notification eventually sent the employer by the state agency that the employer's account had been charged for benefits paid to claimant X.

In the same years — 1961 and 1962 — the core plans also modified the requirement that the claimant report in person. In the auto plan, all applicants were required to report in person only once in the entire period of layoff and otherwise were permitted to report weekly by mail. In many states during the layoffs consequent upon the model changeover, the claimant is not required to report in person every week for his UI check.[1] In such circumstances, the laid-off auto worker may delay filing for both

1. These state UI agencies do not require the claimant to report during his layoff because they recognize that he is almost certain to return to his original job in two or three weeks and it is usually not efficient to try to find him another job for the layoff period.

UI and SUB until he is called back to work. At that time he can fulfill the SUB personal reporting requirements and collect all the benefits owing to him for the weeks elapsed since he was laid off, without ever having been exposed to an offer of work.

In this provision, as in most others, the agricultural implement plans resembled the auto plans, but the Allis-Chalmers plan provided that the mail procedure could not be used after the exhaustion of state benefits. Since the claimant would not then be required to report to the public employment service, personal reporting to the company would be the only check on his availability for work.

The steel and can plans also permit reporting by mail but hedge the permission with further restrictions. The mail-reporting procedure is available only on request and is restricted to employees who are disabled, who have left the area to seek work, or who live a considerable distance from the plant.

Appeals

All plans provide for some form of appeal from the employer's determination. The steel, can, and cement plans provide that arbitrators are to be selected as cases arise. (During the period 1962–1965, the steel plan provided for a single arbitrator for the ten principal companies.) The auto and rubber plans provide for a board of administration to which disputes arising from the operation of the plan are submitted. The board consists of three members appointed by the company, three members appointed by the union, and an impartial chairman who is appointed by the other members and who votes only if the other members cannot reach a decision by majority vote.[2]

The auto and rubber plans provide a two-stage procedure: an appeal is filed in the first instance at the plant level, where it is handled by a local committee consisting of two persons appointed by the company and two appointed by the union. The few cases that cannot be settled at the plant level go to the board of administration just described. This procedure has the advantage of insuring uniform treatment throughout the company.

In some of the other plans, the original provisions allowed each plant to proceed directly to arbitration. In the steel industry, it was recognized early that this procedure was not desirable, and in 1958 the union and the companies agreed that "no dispute arising out of the SUB plan may be taken to arbitration by either party until discussion of such dispute has

2. The 1965 SUB plan negotiated by the UAW with Douglas Aircraft Company gives the board of administration somewhat broader powers. Under this plan, the board has general powers to resolve any issue involving interpretation or administration of the plan, rather than specifically enumerated powers restricted primarily to appeals.

been had between representatives of the company at the general office level and of the union at the international office level" [48a]. In 1962, this requirement was dropped in favor of a provision permitting disputes to be taken to arbitration by the district director of the union.

The cement plan underwent a similar change. The original provision established a local advisory committee consisting of two persons from the plant and two from the local union. If the committee could not settle the dispute, it called upon the director of the Federal Mediation and Conciliation Service to appoint an arbitrator. The 1962 cement plan introduced an intermediate step providing for discussion between the regional labor relations manager of the company and a representative of the international union.

The American Can plan of 1962 also added an intermediate step which is, however, optional. Either party may notify the other of its desire to have the grievance discussed between a representative of the company at the general office level and a representative of the union at the international union level. If this higher-level discussion fails to settle the dispute, the parties may proceed to arbitration.

Reports

All the core plans provide that the company and the trustee, as administrators, make certain reports on the operation of the plan. The original plans required only simple reports, limited for the most part to the finances of the plan. The reports included monthly statements on contributions and benefits and on the state of the fund.

Among the many changes made in the core plans in 1961–1962 were requirements for more detailed reports. The new reporting requirements aimed at eliciting information not merely on the state of the fund but also on the performance of the plan as a whole in relation to its objectives.

For example, since 1961 the auto plan has required a report on the number of beneficiaries who received the maximum benefit and presumably were limited by it. For another example, since 1962 the steel and cement plans have required a report on the number of different persons who have received benefits. This figure measures the beneficiary population and makes meaningful the number of exhaustees, which is also reported in the steel plan. The rubber and cement plans have increased their reporting requirements but in general have not required reports as detailed as those provided for in the auto and steel plans.

Cost of Administration

The core plans have always provided that the expenses of the trustee be paid from the fund. As of 1965, in all the core plans, the expenses incurred by the company in administering the plan were borne entirely by the company. This arrangement represented a change in the auto and rubber plans, which until 1961 had provided that the company be reimbursed by the fund for administrative expenses. There had been some disagreement over the amount which should properly be allowed for these expenses, and the companies resolved the dispute by absorbing them.

Multi-Employer Plans

The problem of administration is somewhat simpler in the multi-employer plans because these plans typically pay a uniform benefit and rely chiefly on a single eligibility condition, that the claimant be able to show a UI check. In the administration of these plans, the employer has a much less direct role to play. The task of administration is turned over to a central office equipped with a full-time staff. More often than not the office is located in the union headquarters and the staff consists of former union officials. The laid-off employees of all the employers covered by the plan come to this office to file their claims and receive their checks. The central office maintains all the records and submits regular reports to the board of trustees.

The board of trustees consists of equal numbers of employer and of union representatives, with provision for recourse to arbitration in the event of disagreement. Under these plans, the board of trustees participates in varying degrees in the details of administration. In some plans, for example, the board reviews the benefits paid in previous months and may raise questions regarding specific individuals or unusual situations. In some plans, also, the board's explicit approval must be obtained for the payment of benefits in certain situations. Finally, the board serves as an appeals tribunal.[3]

Expenses of administration, instead of being absorbed by the employer, are paid entirely out of the fund. For this reason, the record of administrative expenses is more complete for the multi-employer plans than for the single-employer plans (see Part III).

3. In the multi-employer plans the board of trustees frequently has more than administrative powers. It frequently has the broad power to change the substance of the plan as need arises. It may, for example, change eligibility conditions and the amount and duration of benefits.

PART III
EXPERIENCE OF SUB

INTRODUCTION TO PART III

By their fruits you shall know them. Since natures are known principally in their operations, the inner nature of SUB must be sought in the history of experience under the plans. The story of SUB's birth and development, as given in the preceding chapters, finds its real significance in the account of how the plans actually functioned. The remaining parts of this study provide an account of SUB experience — to the extent that such information is available. (At the time that this manuscript went to press, there had been no experience under the SUB amendments negotiated in 1967 — see Appendix B — in the rubber, auto, and agricultural implement industries.)

The more immediate and more measurable aspects of SUB experience are the concern of Chapters 8, 9, and 10, which seek answers to two questions: how much protection did the plans provide, and how much did this protection cost?

Statistical data relating to these questions were obtained from four sources: (a) regular reports supplied by a company to a union under the SUB agreement; (b) financial reports made to the U.S. Department of Labor under the Welfare and Pension Plans Disclosure Act; (c) special studies made by a few companies of the operation of their own plans; (d) replies received from companies and unions to specific questions addressed to them by the writer.

As plans matured, the unions felt the need for additional information regarding the operation of the plans and negotiated more detailed reporting requirements on the part of the employer. For example, for more recent years data are available on the number of different beneficiaries in a year, the number who drew the maximum benefit amount, and the number who exhausted their benefits. Hence the experience of the later years can be described more adequately than that of the earlier years. A more detailed account can be given of experience under the steel and auto plans than for any of the others. Some solid data were obtained for the rubber and agricultural implement plans, but the data presented for the can and cement plans are meager.

The combined data from all sources are sadly incomplete. Sometimes the information simply did not exist. Sometimes it existed, but the companies and the unions involved were reluctant to make it available. Sometimes the information existed and was available, but only on condition that the companies concerned not be identified. Sometimes the available data could not be exploited completely because of limited research resources. Since these limitations vary from period to period and from plan to plan, the history of SUB experience is very uneven and provides an uncertain basis for general conclusions. Often the best that can be done is to establish reasonable limits within which the answers probably fall. The warning voiced in the Preface is particularly pertinent here — this study is only a scouting expedition into the land of SUB.

Among the various plans, the data varied not only in quantity but also in form. It is therefore most convenient and least repetitive to present the available data by plan rather than by function. Accordingly, experience is surveyed first under the steel-type plan (Chapter 8), then under the auto-type plan (Chapter 9), then under a number of multi-employer plans (Chapter 10).

For each plan, the data are presented as far as possible according to the following simple arrangement:

    A. Extent of protection provided.
        1. Protection made available.
        2. Protection actually used.
            a. Number of benefits and beneficiaries.
            b. Amount of benefits.
            c. Duration of benefits.
    B. Cost of the protection provided.

There are some less measurable aspects of SUB experience. Two of these are discussed in Chapter 11: the effect of SUB on the allocation of labor and the relation of SUB to the public program of unemployment insurance.

8

EXPERIENCE UNDER THE STEEL PLAN

Protection Available

The chief measures of available protection are the proportion of employees who are insured (have the requisite seniority) and the number of weeks for which they are insured (the number of their credit units). Both measures may be related to the entire workforce (the employed plus the unemployed) or may be related only to those on layoff.

The proportion of the workforce that is insured usually varies inversely with changes in employment. The proportion insured declines as the company hires new employees with little seniority and eventually increases after the company has laid off employees. During the decade 1955–1965, employment in the steel industry exhibited its usual cyclical sensitivity, dropping sharply during the two recessions. It also experienced a mild secular decline. In 1965, although production had increased, the number of production workers in the basic steel industry was not so high as it had been ten years earlier,[1] substantiating the estimate of several companies that in 1965 about 90 percent of their covered employees had the requisite two years of seniority.

The proportion eligible for benefits would, of course, be smaller in the case of those on layoff than for the workforce as a whole. The Steelworkers have made estimates for two dates. The union estimated that on May 31, 1958, at the bottom of the 1958 recession, 67 percent of those on layoff were in the eligible group. The union also estimated that on May 31, 1960, at the beginning of the 1960–1961 recession and after heavy new hirings, 62 percent were eligible [54].

One of the can companies reported that in 1964 about 56 percent of its laid-off employees lacked the requisite two years of seniority. This high proportion probably reflects the heavy seasonal layoff which this industry experiences each fall. The layoffs are concentrated among college students who normally return to school at the end of the summer, terminating their seniority. Thus they never accumulate the necessary two years of seniority.

An important measure of the adequacy of supplemental unemployment

---

1. The membership total of the Steelworkers (USWA) dropped from 1,091,677 in 1958 to 878,770 in 1964.

benefits is the number of weeks of benefits for which workers are eligible, that is, the number of credit units they have. Exact information on this point is not available. There is no "benefit year" in SUB as there is in unemployment insurance; workers continuously take from and add to their stock of credit units as though it were a bank account. For the individual worker, a computation is made at the time he is laid off, but no data are available as to the aggregate number of credit units which have been accumulated by the workforce at any given time; accordingly, the total amount of what might be termed insurance in force is not known. However, any individual who has worked fairly steadily for two or three years, and thus has had some employment in each of at least 104 weeks, would have built up the maximum number of credit units (52), entitling him to 52 weeks of benefits.

Some indications of the extent of the protection available are contained in the actual experience of SUB beneficiaries described below. It may safely be assumed that the proportion insured and the number of their credit units were greater among the workforce, which includes the employed, than among only those who were laid off, since layoffs are usually made in inverse order of seniority.

Extent of Use

The actual use made of the SUB plan is reflected in the number of beneficiaries, along with the amount and duration of the benefits they drew. Information under these three headings is presented here for the seven basic steel companies for which continuous data were available. These seven companies employed slightly over one half of the employees covered by the SUB plans in the basic steel industry and included the three largest firms, three middle-sized firms, and one small firm. Unless otherwise specified, all the tables in this chapter refer to this group of seven companies. (Occasionally, when a hiatus occurs in the data of one of the seven companies, those figures are replaced in the table by data for a company of approximately equal size. The substitution is observable in the letters used to designate the different companies.)

Number of Beneficiaries and Benefits

Tables 8-1 through 8-3 make use of a "workforce" defined as the sum of the employees on the payroll at month-end and the employees on the layoff list. For purposes of SUB the steel companies carry seniority employees on the layoff list for two years. The employees on the layoff list are not necessarily unemployed; they may be working elsewhere or they may be out of the labor force. This extended concept of the workforce is the only one for which data are available, but it is also the appropriate concept for the present purpose. The employee "on layoff" remains attached to the employer's workforce not only in the sense that he retains recall rights but also in the sense that he is eligible to draw SUB for as long as he retains any unused credit units. For example, an employee could be laid off by a steel firm, go to work for some other firm, be laid off by the second employer much later, and then begin to draw SUB from the fund of the first employer, on whose layoff list he would still be carried.

The layoff figures are drawn from the quarterly reports which the companies make to the union and relate to the last working day of the months of February, May, August, and November. The figures for the number of beneficiaries (number of payments in a given week) are for the first calendar week which ended in the months of March, June, September, and December. (Although for most months the last working day is part of the first week which ends in the following month, the overlap of months requires the double-date designation used in Table 8–2.)

The number of beneficiaries at four points of time in each year are shown for the years 1958–1965 in Table 8–1. For the last six years of this period, the table also shows the proportion these beneficiaries were of the combined workforce of the seven companies. The steep rise during the period December 1960–March 1961 reflects the steel industry's cyclical sensitivity, which constitutes a reason for building a reserve fund.[2] The increases in unemployment in late 1962 and early 1963 were due to the layoffs that resulted from a drop in orders from customers who had stockpiled supplies earlier in 1962 in anticipation of a possible steel strike.

Table 8–2 presents three ratios for each of the seven companies. The first ratio, layoffs to workforce, is a kind of unemployment rate indicating the state of the economic climate. It establishes an upper limit to the number of SUB claimants and provides the chief explanation for the variations in the other two ratios. The companies tended to move together and to have high unemployment rates at approximately the same time. The companies differed more among themselves in periods of prosperity than in periods of recession, but in general the differences were less in this first ratio than in the other two.

The second ratio, recipients of SUB to number on layoff, generally varied directly with the first ratio. There are two plausible explanations for this direct relationship. First, as unemployment deepens, it cuts into

---

2. Not, however, a decisive reason. As shown later in the chapter, the steel companies have often preferred to operate on a pay-as-you-go basis.

TABLE 8–1

SUB Beneficiaries in Seven Basic Steel Companies as Percent of Workforce,
December 1958–December 1965

First calendar week ended in		No. of beneficiaries	% of workforce[a]
Year	Month		
1958	Dec.	22,508	n.a.
1959	Mar.	12,315	n.a.
	June	3,466	n.a.
	Sept.	64[b]	n.a.
	Dec.	5[b]	n.a.
1960	Mar.	2,546	0.6
	June	13,330	3.2
	Sept.	37,438	9.1
	Dec.	53,098	12.9
1961	Mar.	57,073	13.8
	June	28,123	6.8
	Sept.	13,567	3.3
	Dec.	12,182	3.0
1962	Mar.	8,161	2.1
	June	11,284	3.0
	Sept.	34,129	9.0
	Dec.	40,338	10.6
1963	Mar.	25,176	7.2
	June	3,704	1.0
	Sept.	11,864	3.4
	Dec.	15,066	4.3
1964	Mar.	9,814	2.9
	June	1,461	0.4
	Sept.	962	0.3
	Dec.	1,924	0.6
1965	Mar.	1,336	0.4
	June	504	0.1
	Sept.	658	0.2
	Dec.	15,007	4.2

SOURCE: Calculated from reports made by steel companies to United Steelworkers of America. For definitions, see text.

[a] For the years 1961 through 1965, the percentages are based upon work-force figures furnished by the seven companies; percentages for 1960 are based upon 1961 work-force figures.

[b] The steel strike was in progress during these periods.

the ranks of employees more likely to be eligible for SUB, those with higher seniority and more credit units. Second, in times of general unemployment, fewer of the laid-off employees find other jobs, and a greater proportion of them appear on the SUB rolls.

TABLE 8-2

Relationships[a] between Workforce, Employees on Layoff, and SUB Recipients, Seven Basic Steel Companies, Quarterly, 1961–1965

Date	Company A			Company B			Company C			Company D			Company E			Company F			Company G		
	LO/WF	SUB/LO	SUB/WF	LO/WF	SUB/LO	SUB/WF	LO/WF	SUB/LO	SUB/WF	LO/WF	SUB/LO	SUB/WF	LO/WF	SUB/LO	SUB/WF	LO/WF	SUB/LO	SUB/WF	LO/WF	SUB/LO	SUB/WF
1961																					
Feb.–Mar.	26	42	11	23	56	13	31	36	11	28	43	12	24	67	16	32	68	22	20	22	4
May–June	26	22	6	19	41	8	16	20	3	20	28	5	19	45	9	23	7	2	12	8	1
Aug.–Sept.	15	13	2	14	26	4	13	19	2	16	15	2	15	34	5	18	1	b	6	6	b
Nov.–Dec.	13	8	1	15	21	3	13	15	2	19	21	4	15	25	4	13	8	1	4	12	b
1962																					
Feb.–Mar.	5	3	b	12	20	2	9	19	2	10	25	3	10	25	3	10	1	b	3	32	1
May–June	15	36	5	14	20	3	17	41	7	14	23	3	15	17	3	17	4	1	4	24	1
Aug.–Sept.	13	38	5	17	56	10	28	40	11	18	54	10	19	46	9	20	49	10	12	36	4
Nov.–Dec.	18	36	7	10	53	5	27	68	18	22	57	13	22	49	11	18	21	4	15	49	7
1963																					
Feb.–Mar.	14	18	3	15	51	8	19	37	7	17	42	7	18	41	7	14	20	3	11	50	6
May–June	8	4	b	5	30	2	5	13	1	6	19	1	5	20	1	b	0	b	5	9	b
Aug.–Sept.	9	21	2	10	41	4	14	28	4	10	35	4	9	30	3	16	10	2	3	8	b
Nov.–Dec.	11	20	2	14	36	5	19	40	8	15	42	6	9	27	2	10	16	2	6	14	b
1964																					
Feb.–Mar.	11	47	5	11	36	4	10	22	2	11	32	4	5	38	2	b	28	b	4	27	1
May–June	9	30	3	3	21	1	4	7	b	4	14	1	1	13	b	b	0	b	2	4	b
Aug.–Sept.	5	13	1	15	2	b	14	6	1	2	17	b	1	16	b	1	6	b	1	5	b
Nov.–Dec.	7	16	1	3	4	b	5	9	b	4	36	1	1	33	b	6	9	b	1	7	b
1965																					
Feb.–Mar.	6	11	1	4	2	b	1	5	b	2	13	b	1	13	b	6	20	1	1	14	b
May–June	5	4	b	1	2	b	n.a.	n.a.	n.a.	2	6	b	1	27	b	2	b	b	b	27	b
Aug.–Sept.	4	3	b	1	1	b	n.a.	n.a.	n.a.	1	29	b	1	10	b	0	0	b	b	n.a.	n.a.
Nov.–Dec.	11	20	2	11	44	5	n.a.	n.a.	n.a.	15	48	7	9	36	3	20	36	7	3	37	1

SOURCE: Calculated from reports made by steel companies to United Steelworkers of America. For definitions, see text.

a LO/WF: Employees on layoff as percent of workforce.

SUB/LO: Recipients of SUB as percent of employees on layoff.
SUB/WF: Recipients of SUB as percent of workforce.
b Less than 0.5 percent.

As is to be expected, this general relationship shows numerous exceptions. Since the data represent a reading at a single point in time, they are easily distorted by temporary and unusual events. Moreover, the layoff figures of a single company often consist of layoffs in many of its individual plants, among which experience may vary widely. Thus, the total layoffs of a company may be small relative to its total workforce but, if they are concentrated in a single plant, they may include a sizable proportion of persons with sufficient seniority to be eligible for SUB.

For each of the companies, the proportion of those "on layoff" who received SUB was surprisingly low. It is evident that the SUB plan does not compensate every unemployed worker, nor does it compensate for all the unemployment experienced by those who have some unused SUB credits. In the five-year period, figures were available at 20 dates for seven companies. Of these 140 readings, only 10 showed 50 percent or more of the employees on layoff to be receiving SUB.

There are many possible reasons for the relatively large proportions not receiving SUB. Some of the nonrecipients may have found another job or may have temporarily left the labor force; some may have been serving their waiting week; some may have exhausted their credit units; some may have been disqualified for UI and hence for SUB; and, since layoffs are usually made in inverse order of seniority, many probably lacked the requisite two years. No information is available on the relative size of these different groups of nonrecipients; it no doubt varied from company to company and from period to period. The differences among the companies were noticeably larger in this second ratio than in the first. The reasons for the differences are no doubt to be found in the different categories of nonrecipients.

The third ratio, SUB recipients to workforce, is simply the product of the other two ratios. It conveys essentially the same information as does the last column in Table 8–1, except that it does so for the seven companies separately. Most of the comments made with regard to the first two ratios apply, with appropriate distinctions, to this ratio also. Table 8–2 is a rich table. An analyst well acquainted with the steel industry could derive much additional information from its relationships. But intensive analysis of experience under particular plans is beyond the scope of this scouting expedition.

Beginning with 1962, the steel companies reported the number of different persons who received some kind of SUB payment in the course of each year. These data, which are presented in Table 8–3, show the proportion of a company's workforce to whom the SUB plan had brought some tangible gain. This proportion largely determines the degree of support that

TABLE 8–3

Individuals Who Received One or More SUB Payments during the Year as Percent of Average Annual Workforce, by Type of Payment, Seven Basic Steel Companies, 1962–1965

Company	1962			1963			1964			1965		
	Regular SUB	Short-week	Either or both	Regular SUB	Short-week	Either or both	Regular SUB	Short-week	Either or both	Regular SUB	Short-week	Either or both
	(1)	(2)	(3)	(4)	(5)	(6)	(7)	(8)	(9)	(10)	(11)	(12)
A	19	11	26	17	12	25	n.a.	14	22	8	11	18
B	26	6	30	24	11	32	14	10	20	9	10	18
C	40	4	42	31	6	34	15	3	18	7	5	11
D	31	7	34	27	10	33	17	8	22	16	7	20
E	n.a.	n.a.	n.a.	20	5	24	7	3	10	6	4	10
F	22	10	29	14	12	24	2	11	13	11	n.a.	n.a.
H	7	1	7	3	2	4	2	1	2	1	1	2
Averages	25	5	29	22	9	28	11	7	16	9	7	14

SOURCE: Calculated from reports made by steel companies to United Steelworkers of America. For definitions, see text.

SUB can expect to attract from the union membership. In 1962 and 1963, years of considerable unemployment in steel, 29 percent and 28 percent, respectively, of the companies' workforce drew some benefits. In 1964 and 1965, prosperous years, the corresponding percentages were 16 and 14. The recession period, September 1960–June 1961, would have produced a much higher figure; for these same companies, the average was estimated at 33 percent.[3]

There was considerable variation among the companies. For the four years shown in the table, the percentages ranged from 7 to 42 in 1962, from 4 to 34 in 1963, from 2 to 22 in 1964, and from 2 to 20 in 1965. The company which had the lowest percentage consistently was Company H, a relatively small firm producing specialized steels. Very few of this company's employees ever drew a SUB payment.

The proportion of beneficiaries who drew a short-week benefit in the course of a year was nearly always smaller than the proportion who drew a regular benefit, but the difference between the two proportions tended to narrow as total unemployment declined. This was to be expected; as full employment is approached, a larger proportion of the unemployment that does occur is of the partial sort, caused by material shortages, machinery breakdowns, and similar work interruptions.

Table 8–4 fills out the picture of short-week benefits. Where Table 8–3 dealt with beneficiaries, Table 8–4 deals with the number of payments and shows the proportion of total payments that such payments represented. The proportion varied inversely with the level of unemployment. The average for companies A, B, D, E, F, and G for September 1962, when layoffs were relatively heavy (Table 8–2), was only 6 percent, while the corresponding figure for September 1965, when layoffs were light, was 38 percent. Evidently work sharing below 32 hours was not used to any great extent during periods of heavy unemployment as a way of adjusting the workforce to decreased demand for the product. Many companies did, however, make use of short weeks down to 32 hours; for this reason, as indicated earlier, the steel companies had been unwilling to adopt the short-week provisions of the auto-type plans. The larger proportion of short-week benefits in other years did not reflect a greater number of such benefits, and therefore a greater use of work sharing; it was the result simply of regular benefits shrinking faster than short-week benefits.

Of the seven companies, Company F consistently had the highest proportion of short-week benefits. This company had an unemployment rate

---

3. This estimate was made on the assumption that the number of different recipients in the course of a year is about 2.5 times the greatest number of recipients in any one week. (This relationship holds generally for data on all the unemployed.)

TABLE 8-4

Short-Week Benefits as Percent of Total Benefits, Eight Basic Steel Companies, Quarterly, 1962–1965

| First calendar week ended in | | Company A | Company B | Company C | Company D | Company E | Company F | Company G | Company J |
Year	Month	(1)	(2)	(3)	(4)	(5)	(6)	(7)	(8)
1962	Sept.	26	7	4	5	1	6	5	0
	Dec.	3	6	1	5	1	14	5	1
1963	Mar.	6	4	7	8	4	37	4	1
	June	14	12	8	16	8	100	11	0
	Sept.	18	12	6	13	14	43	48	0
	Dec.	7	11	7	5	8	31	28	0
1964	Mar.	11	10	12	13	10	56	3	0
	June	13	33	8	34	39	100	26	4
	Sept.	15	36	0	22	23	90	27	0
	Dec.	8	34	87	22	38	67	0	2
1965	Mar.	17	49	0	29	16	45	33	0
	June	41	42	n.a.	66	14	99	33	0
	Sept.	52	44	n.a.	24	11	100	6	n.a.
	Dec.	6	16	n.a.	8	12	10	47	0

SOURCE: Calculated from reports made by steel companies to United Steelworkers of America.

that, while not the lowest, was below the average. Company J, with an average unemployment rate, consistently had the lowest proportion of short-week benefits. The reason for this was not ascertained.

Amount of SUB Payments

Table 8–5 shows the average SUB payment with and without UI. During the period covered by the table, SUB supplied an average of 38 percent of the combined unemployment benefit. The low percentages in 1961 are explainable partly by increased UI benefits but chiefly by lower SUB payments, which, in turn, resulted from the operation of the reduction table. During most months of 1961, the majority of steel plans paid reduced benefits because their reserves were below 75 percent of maximum funding. The average SUB payment increased markedly after June 1962 because the maximum benefit was increased and because the impact of the reduction table was lessened (Chapter 5).

The high average SUB payment without UI (column 5) reflects the dual maximum in steel (Table 5–4) and also the absence of any provision in the steel plans to subtract the amount of "estimated UI." Most of these benefits were paid to claimants who had exhausted their UI benefits (Table 4–3, first exception).

The average SUB payment varied considerably from state to state. This is because the UI benefit, especially the maximum, varied from state to state and the SUB payment necessarily varied (inversely) to the same extent. Below are the average SUB payments made by one large steel company in June of the indicated years in each of three states.

State	1959	1960	1961	1962	1963	1964	1965
California	$13.47	$14.48	$ 8.83	$11.25	$21.12	$21.85	$16.33
Indiana	12.75	25.31	13.50	18.82	29.16	n.a.	31.00
Alabama	18.36	29.25	15.63	21.85	37.14	35.99	40.29

These three states were chosen because they illustrate the two extremes and the middle of the range of UI benefit amounts. (In 1965, the maximum UI benefit payable was $65 in California, $43 in Indiana, and $38 in Alabama.) The company's employees in Alabama regularly received SUB payments that averaged almost double those paid to its California employees.

Another view of the importance of state differentials is provided by can company B, which in 1965 had 34 plants located in various states. Of the total unemployment benefits received by its employees in all states in 1965, 54 percent came from UI and 46 percent from SUB. Employees in

TABLE 8–5

Average SUB Payment with UI as Percent of Total Benefit and Average SUB
Payment without UI, Seven Basic Steel Companies, Quarterly, 1958–1965

First calendar week ended in		SUB with UI				SUB without UI
Year	Month	UI	SUB	Total	SUB as % of total	
		(1)	(2)	(3)	(4)	(5)
1958	Dec.	$33.06	$18.56	$51.62	35	$33
1959	Mar.	33.02	15.46	48.48	31	30
	June	32.84	16.42	49.26	33	33
	Sept.	a	a	a	a	a
	Dec.	a	a	a	a	a
1960	Mar.	31.32	21.72	53.04	40	50
	June	37.58	21.57	59.16	36	50
	Sept.	39.57	22.37	61.94	36	52
	Dec.	39.10	22.35	61.45	36	33
1961	Mar.	39.42	12.91	52.33	24	26
	June	38.50	12.89	51.39	25	26
	Sept.	37.45	13.23	50.68	26	29
	Dec.	32.45	15.22	47.67	31	34
1962	Mar.	37.49	17.57	55.06	31	35
	June	40.35	17.51	57.86	30	39
	Sept.	40.20	29.19	69.39	42	62
	Dec.	39.89	30.63	70.52	43	62
1963	Mar.	39.23	30.52	69.75	43	62
	June	38.52	29.17	67.68	43	61
	Sept.	38.18	31.70	69.88	45	62
	Dec.	39.69	30.93	70.62	43	61
1964	Mar.	40.13	30.12	70.25	42	61
	June	40.31	30.01	70.32	42	61
	Sept.	41.40	29.27	70.67	41	62
	Dec.	39.33	29.37	68.70	42	61
1965	Mar.	42.39	25.69	68.08	37	60
	June[b]	42.49	25.87	68.36	37	62
	Sept.[c]	42.74	29.48	72.22	40	62
	Dec.[b]	45.47	32.10	77.57	41	63

SOURCE: Calculated from reports made by steel companies to United Steelworkers of America.

[a] A strike was in progress and no benefits were paid.

[b] Data for one company not available.

[c] Data for two companies not available.

Florida, who drew considerable SUB after exhausting UI, received 22 percent of their total benefits from UI and 78 percent from SUB. The comparable figures for employees in Wisconsin were the reverse; 80 percent and 20 percent.

Because of the limitation imposed by the maximum SUB amount payable under the plan, some benefits fail to equal the stipulated percentage of wages. Table 8–6 shows what proportion of all regular benefits were payable at one or other of the two maximums provided in the steel plans.

TABLE 8–6

Percentage of Regular Benefits Payable at Lower and Higher SUB Maximums, Seven Basic Steel Companies, Quarterly, 1958–1965

First calendar week ended in		At lower maximum (UI also received)	At higher maximum (UI not received)
Year	Month		
		(1)	(2)
1958	Dec.	35	93
1959	Mar.	35	89
	June	27	90
	Sept.	a	a
	Dec.	a	a
1960	Mar.	31	88
	June	26	91
	Sept.	30	91
	Dec.	34	95
1961	Mar.	34	98
	June	34	85
	Sept.	35	97
	Dec.	38	98
1962	Mar.	41	97
	June	30	98
	Sept.	25	70
	Dec.	25	68
1963	Mar.	22	80
	June	24	73
	Sept.	32	77
	Dec.	29	74
1964	Mar.	21	76
	June	26	97
	Sept.	25	84
	Dec.	22	90
1965	Mar.	9	75[b]
	June	15	76
	Sept.	27	72[c]
	Dec.	34	87[b]

SOURCE: Calculated from reports made by steel companies to United Steelworkers of America.

[a] The steel strike was in progress and no benefits were paid.

[b] Figures for one company were not available.

[c] Figures for two companies were not available.

Presumably most of the benefits paid at the maximum were limited by that maximum and therefore amounted to less than the stipulated benefit-wage ratio.

As was to be expected, the proportion of benefits paid at the maximum when UI was not received was very high. (The number of such benefits is shown in Table 8–7, column 2.) Indeed it is surprising only that any of these benefits were below the maximum. After June of 1962, when the stipulated benefit became 60 percent of gross wages and the maximum became $60, the only such claimants who would not have qualified for the maximum would be those whose gross wages were less than $100.

The increase in the maximum benefit negotiated in 1962 made a notable difference in the proportion of payments limited by the maximum. In the period up to June 1962, the proportion of payments at the lower maximum fell below 30 percent only twice, and the proportion at the higher maximum never fell below 85 percent. But in the period after June 1962, the proportion of payments at the lower maximum was always below 30 percent in every quarter except two, and the proportion at the higher maximum was always below 85 percent in every quarter except three. In this, as in most other characteristics, the history of SUB in the first decade of its existence has been one of increasing liberality.

In the discussions that have gone on for years in the UI program over what the maximum benefit should be, one norm that has been tentatively endorsed is the following: if no more than a quarter of the claimants are at (limited by) the maximum benefit, the maximum is satisfactory. By this norm, the steel SUB plan performed satisfactorily after the new maximum went into effect whenever the SUB payment was fully "supplemental," that is, when UI was received. In this situation, during the period September 1962 through 1965, the average proportion of benefits paid at the maximum was only 26 percent. By the same norm, the steel plan was far from satisfactory in the situation when SUB was the only benefit received. However, the latter situation was relatively infrequent: during the same period, SUB payments without UI constituted only 13 percent of all payments (average of column 3, Table 8–7).

Duration of SUB Payments

An adequate description of duration experience would require knowledge of the distribution of benefit payments according to duration intervals, the proportion of SUB beneficiaries who exhausted their benefits, and the length of unemployment represented by each exhaustion. There is little direct information on any of these three aspects of duration, but some inferences can be drawn from the data in Tables 8–7 and 8–8.

TABLE 8–7

SUB Payments with and without UI, Seven Basic Steel Companies,
Quarterly, 1958–1965

First calendar week ended in		With UI	Without UI	
				% of
Year	Month		No.	total
		(1)	(2)	(3)
1958	Dec.	20,166	2,853	12
1959	Mar.	11,548	1,030	8
	June	3,141	636	17
	Sept.	a	a	a
	Dec.	a	a	a
1960	Mar.	2,370	224	9
	June	12,868	175	1
	Sept.	36,333	786	2
	Dec.	48,950	3,052	6
1961	Mar.	43,139	12,276	22
	June	27,570	85	*
	Sept.	11,865	1,314	10
	Dec.	10,106	1,810	15
1962	Mar.	7,297	565	7
	June	9,398	428	6
	Sept.	31,467	1,678	5
	Dec.	34,957	3,212	9
1963	Mar.	19,644	4,948	22
	June	2,461	1,358	36
	Sept.	7,800	3,205	29
	Dec.	12,379	1,785	12
1964	Mar.	9,142	706	8
	June	1,362	457	25
	Sept.	804	400	33
	Dec.	1,744	269	13
1965	Mar.	1,270	123	10
	June	545	80	13
	Sept.	561	106	16
	Dec.	14,819	197	1

SOURCE: Reports made by steel companies to United Steelworkers of America.
* Less than 0.5 percent.
a A strike was in progress and no benefits were paid.

Table 8–7 shows the benefits paid with and without UI. If it is assumed
that nearly all of the SUB payments without UI were made to beneficiaries
who had exhausted their UI benefits and that most of these beneficiaries
had been eligible for the maximum duration in the state program — both

very reasonable assumptions, supported by direct evidence drawn from other plans — then column 2 represents payments made for periods beyond the UI maximum.

This maximum, and therefore the significance of column 2, varied during the period covered by the table. During most of the period the typical UI maximum duration was 26 weeks, and the payments in column 2 therefore represented unemployment that had lasted longer than 26 weeks. But during two periods of recession 13 additional weeks of UI benefits were generally available to SUB claimants: the Temporary Unemployment Compensation (TUC) program was in operation from June 1958 through June 1959, and the Temporary Extended Unemployment Compensation (TEUC) program was in operation from April 1961 through June 1962.[4] During these two periods SUB payments without UI (column 2) in general represented unemployment that had lasted longer than 39 weeks.

Interpreted in this light, the quantities in column 2 and the proportions in column 3 furnish some indication of the extent to which a SUB plan is likely to be needed to supplement the duration of UI benefits. The extent, while not negligible, is relatively small. During the period September 1962–December 1965 less than 11 percent of all SUB payments supplemented the duration of UI. (The long-term unemployed seem to represent about the same proportion of SUB claimants as they do of all the unemployed. For the three-year period 1963–1965, the long-term unemployed [27 weeks or more] in the nation's labor force averaged 12 percent of all the unemployed.)

The figures in columns 2 and 3 outline the general size of the problems that SUB may pose for labor mobility. The proportions in column 3 tend to vary inversely with the unemployment rate and probably reflect a changing composition of the unemployed. The higher proportions may include more of the unemployed who are the victims of structural change.

It is desirable to know the exhaustion ratio — the proportion of beneficiaries who exhausted their rights to SUB. This ratio is the most direct measure of the adequacy of a plan's duration provisions. However, it should not be thought of as a necessarily decisive measure. Exhaustions indicate that the program was inadequate for certain individuals but do not necessarily indicate that the program was inadequate in terms of its own objectives. The latter relationship is discussed in Chapter 12.

Data on the extent to which beneficiaries exhausted their benefits are available for two periods, 1960–1962 and 1963–1965. Two different meth-

4. The very sharp drop in the number of payments of SUB without UI (column 2) between March and June 1961 probably reflects the impact of the TEUC program, which began in April of that year.

ods of reporting exhaustions were used in the two periods, and neither was completely satisfactory. The early data are especially inadequate: they do not reveal the length of unemployment represented by each exhaustion (in the data an exhaustion after 1 week of unemployment is indistinguishable from an exhaustion after 52 weeks of unemployment); they do not reveal the number of different individuals who exhausted benefits (in the SUB program it is easy for the same individual to exhaust benefits repeatedly); and there is no way of identifying the relevant "beneficiary population" to which the number of exhaustees must be referred if an exhaustion rate is to be calculated.

Table 8–8 shows the number of beneficiaries and the number of exhaustions in nine basic steel companies during the years 1960 and 1961. Since this was the period of heaviest unemployment in the history of SUB, it constitutes an appropriate test of duration adequacy. Unfortunately, for the reason given above, a true exhaustion ratio cannot be derived from these data. Specifically, column 1 is a considerable understatement of the number of different beneficiaries who drew benefits in that quarter; moreover, most of the exhaustees in column 2 "come from" the beneficiaries not of the corresponding data in the first column, but of some earlier period.

In the 12-month period September 1960–August 1961, there were 24,027 exhaustions. The exhaustion ratio must be estimated by making use of the

TABLE 8–8

Ratios of Beneficiaries in First Week of Quarter to Weekly Averages
of Exhaustees during Quarter, Nine Basic Steel Companies,[a]
March 1960–February 1962

Date	Number of beneficiaries during first calendar week of quarter	Number of exhaustions		Ratio (col. 1:col. 3)
		Quarterly total	Weekly average	
	(1)	(2)	(3)	(4)
Mar.–May 1960	2,808	460	35	100:1.2
June–Aug. 1960	14,290	1,484	114	100:0.8
Sept.–Nov. 1960	40,271	3,862	297	100:0.7
Dec. 1960–Feb. 1961	59,300	6,188	476	100:0.8
Mar.–May 1961	61,789	6,793	523	100:0.8
June–Aug. 1961	29,605	7,184	553	100:1.9
Sept.–Nov. 1961	14,455	3,208	247	100:1.7
Dec. 1961–Feb. 1962	12,830	3,673	283	100:2.2

SOURCE: Reports made by steel companies to United Steelworkers of America.

[a] In 1961 the nine companies had an estimated workforce of 380,000, representing about 53 percent of all covered workers in basic steel.

relationship noted earlier: the number of different beneficiaries in the course of a year is usually two to three times as large as the greatest number in any week. The greatest number of beneficiaries in any one week during this period was 61,789, in the first week of March 1961. Applying a multiple of 2.0, 2.5, or 3.0 to this figure provides three alternative divisors of the number of exhaustions and produces alternative exhaustion ratios of 19 percent, 16 percent, or 13 percent, respectively. During this worst of periods, therefore, the exhaustion rate was probably something less than 20 percent.

Another way of looking at exhaustions is shown in column 4 of the table. Column 4 compares two weekly flows: the flow of beneficiaries in column 1 and the flow of exhaustees in column 3. They are to be thought of, not as coming one from the other, but as two streams flowing side by side, the former consisting of those beneficiaries for whom the program was still adequate,[5] the latter consisting of those for whom the program had just proved inadequate. Over a sufficiently long period of time their relative size provides some indication of the adequacy of the duration provisions of the program. In the period covered by the table, the stream of exhaustees averaged about one hundredth the size of the stream of beneficiaries. It must be remembered, of course, that the stream of exhaustees is flowing into a pool and that this pool is the most significant measure of the adequacy of duration. Unfortunately, we do not know the size of the pool because, although we know the flow into it, we do not know the flow out of it.

After additional reporting requirements were negotiated in 1962, data became available on the number of persons who exhausted their benefits in the course of a year, along with the number of persons who drew benefits in the course of a year. Hence, beginning in 1963 a fairly reliable exhaustion ratio became available. It is only "fairly" reliable because of certain technical limitations.[6] Moreover, the reports still did not contain any information on the number of benefits drawn before exhaustion.

---

5. It should be remembered that this stream is represented by only four weekly readings in the course of each year; accordingly, it supplies only a general indication of the average weekly flow of beneficiaries in the course of a year.

6. Beginning July 1, 1962, the companies reported quarterly on claimants who had exhausted benefits, distinguishing between two types, the claimant who had exhausted benefits for the first time and the claimant who had exhausted benefits more than once. For some unascertained reason, each type was reported as a cumulative total. When a beneficiary exhausted benefits for the second time, he was removed from the total of the first type and added to the total of the second type. The whole task was done visually and manually. Data reported in this way need to be interpreted carefully even when they are accurate, and the data of some companies were obviously not accurate.

Usable data obtained from five companies for three years are shown in Table 8–9. The average ratio of 18 percent for the year 1963 confirms the previous estimate that in a year of heavy unemployment the exhaustion ratio would probably be something less than 20 percent. Except for Company F, the deviations from this average were small. The average ratio of 2 percent for the year 1965 shows how low the exhaustion ratio can fall in a period of full employment. Evidently, the availability of liberal unemployment benefits does not automatically result in their utilization. Company F, which had the highest exhaustion ratio in 1963, had the lowest in 1965; the reasons have not been ascertained for either distinction.

The only available information on the average duration of SUB payments was furnished by one large basic steel company for the period 1962–1965. The average number of weeks of benefits drawn by laid-off employees of this company was as follows: 1962, 12.3 weeks; 1963, 10.5 weeks; 1964, 5.3 weeks; 1965, 7.7 weeks. No information was available on the distributions around these averages.

Costs of SUB

The costs of SUB may be reckoned in terms of contributions paid into or of benefits paid out of the SUB fund and may be expressed as a total dollar amount or as an amount per man-hour. The data are reported in the form of the total dollar amounts and are discussed first in this simpler

TABLE 8–9

Beneficiaries Who Exhausted SUB as Approximate Percent of Total Beneficiaries, Five Basic Steel Companies, Annual Figures, 1963–1965

Company	Exhaustees as approximate percent of beneficiaries		
	1963	1964	1965
B	17	13	2
D	17	10	1
E	21	18	4
F	38	4	a
H	6	16	4
Averages, 5 companies[b]	18	13	2

a Less than 0.5 percent.

b To avoid possible identification of the individual companies, only their exhaustion ratios have been shown. The average exhaustion ratios for the respective years have been based upon the following totals for the five companies combined: in 1963, 68,845 beneficiaries and 12,404 exhaustees; in 1964, 34,415 beneficiaries and 4,643 exhaustees; in 1965, 27,858 beneficiaries and 626 exhaustees.

form. Costs per man-hour, which represent the more significant measure of cost, are not reported directly but have been estimated.

Total Dollar Amount

In the steel industry, contributions to the SUB funds began in August 1956. Over the nine-year period ending in June 1965, total contributions[7] in the entire industry amounted to about half a billion dollars ($506.9 million). Benefits, which did not become payable until September 1957 (12 months after contributions began), totaled less than half of that figure ($225.8 million) as of June 1965.[8]

Tables 8–10 and 8–11 use the experience of four companies, which as of 1961 employed about 47 percent of all covered Steelworkers, to illustrate some of the variations in cost over time and among companies.[9] The effect of the new financing provisions can be seen in the doubled contributions (cash plus accrued contingent liability) after the negotiations of 1962. For three of the companies, benefits were a much smaller percentage of contributions in the later period than in the earlier one. The decrease was the result of both a lower unemployment rate and a higher contribution rate in the later period.

For the entire nine-year period, for the four companies combined, benefits paid amounted to 80 percent of contributions. It would be a mistake to conclude that the difference between contributions and benefits was represented by cash in the possession of the trustees and available for benefits. The difference is almost entirely represented by accrued contingent liability. The provision that allows "contributions" to be made in the form of contingent liability has, especially since 1962, practically put the steel plans on a pay-as-you-go basis. Consequently, the actual amount

7. In this discussion of the financing of steel SUB plans, "contributions" means the regular required cash payment and the accrual of contingent liability; "cash costs," when referring to contributions, means the cash contribution plus the amount of contingent liability paid off in cash; "cash outlay" includes all cash costs and any cash paid out of the reserve fund.

8. These figures are the sum of two subtotals separately estimated for the two periods into which steel experience naturally falls. The figures for the first period (August 1956–June 1962) are projections of data from 17 companies, which, as of 1961, employed 62 percent of covered Steelworkers. The figure for contributions is net, being total cash contributed and contingent liability accrued minus contingent liability canceled when funds were above maximum financing. Canceled liability amounted to $7.3 million. The figures for the second period, which began in July 1962, after the negotiation of the new plan, and extended through June 1965, are projections of data for 11 steel companies which, as of 1964–1966, employed almost 60 percent of all covered Steelworkers.

9. The companies are identified in these tables because the data have been reported to the U.S. Department of Labor under the Welfare and Pension Plans Disclosure Act and are a matter of public record.

TABLE 8-10

Contributions and Benefits, Four Basic Steel Companies,[a] by Fiscal Year, 1956-1965, in Thousands of Dollars

Period	U.S. Steel		Bethlehem Steel		Republic Steel		Jones & Laughlin Steel	
	Contributions	Benefits	Contributions	Benefits	Contributions	Benefits	Contributions	Benefits
	(1)	(2)	(3)	(4)	(5)	(6)	(7)	(8)
Aug. 1956-July 1957	$17,392	0	$9,427	0	$5,318	0	$3,327	0
Aug. 1957-July 1958	13,417	$14,411	7,595	$5,357	3,714	$2,601	2,570	$1,115
Aug. 1958-July 1959	13,812	10,247[b]	7,083	8,911[b]	4,549	5,381[b]	2,888	1,797[b]
Aug. 1959-July 1960	6,312	4,951	3,568	1,389	3,227	1,627	0	303
Aug. 1960-July 1961	10,546	20,422	5,386	9,930	3,086	6,844	1,980	2,659
Aug. 1961-June 1962	11,028	4,671	6,145	3,324	3,622	1,670	2,208	671
July 1962-June 1963	20,001	21,732	11,243	11,314	6,613	7,243	3,314	2,762
July 1963-June 1964	21,215	10,739	9,021	2,930	7,061	3,357	1,413	939
July 1964-June 1965	6,376	1,478	3,004	323	2,523	604	1,066	296

SOURCE: Reports made by steel companies to United Steelworkers of America.

[a] As of 1961, these four companies employed about 47 percent of all covered Steelworkers.

[b] Includes Ohio payments for prior periods, which had been held up until May 1959 awaiting clarification of their legal status (see Chapter 1).

TABLE 8–11

Average Annual Benefit Payments as Percent of Average Annual Contributions, Four Basic Steel Companies,
August 1956–June 1962 and July 1962–June 1965

Company	Two periods combined			August 1956 through June 1962			July 1962 through June 1965		
	Average annual contributions	Average annual benefit payments		Average annual contributions	Average annual benefit payments		Average annual contributions	Average annual benefit payments	
		Amount	% of contributions		Amount	% of contributions		Amount	% of contributions
	(*thousands*)			(*thousands*)			(*thousands*)		
U.S. Steel	$13,342	$11,081	83	$12,084	$10,940	90	$15,860	$11,316	71
Bethlehem Steel	6,941	5,434	78	6,534	5,782	88	7,756	4,855	63
Republic Steel	4,411	3,665	83	3,919	3,624	93	5,399	3,734	69
Jones & Laughlin Steel	2,085	1,317	63	2,162	1,309	60	1,931	1,332	69
Four companies combined	26,783	21,499	80	24,700	21,656	88	30,950	21,239	69

SOURCE: Derived from Table 8–10.

of cash that the company might have to find for SUB in a given period could be far larger than the sum represented by the maximum monthly contribution of 9.5 cents per man-hour.

In fiscal 1961, for example, the United States Steel Corporation paid $20.4 million in benefits to SUB claimants (Table 8–10). Required "contributions" that year amounted to $10.5 million. (The breakdown of this amount, which is not shown in the table, was $6.3 in cash and $4.2 million in contingent liability.) The additional $14.1 million in cash had to come from the reserve fund or — to the extent that the reserve was inadequate — from the company's working cash up to the amount which had accrued in "contingent liability" over the life of the plan. Since, as a matter of fact, about $13.2 million (not shown in the table), came from the latter source, the reserve fund must have contained very little cash — not more than $0.9 million — during the fiscal year. Thus, of the $20.4 million paid in benefits that year, about $19.5 million ($6.3 million regular cash contribution and $13.2 million of contingent liability paid off in cash) represented an out-of-pocket expense for the company in that year of heavy unemployment.

Obviously such a method of financing does not work countercyclically. For the steel companies the advantages of a reserve fund (Chapter 6) were evidently outweighed by the advantages of having the use of the cash in their business. This way of operating the SUB plan is very similar to the original proposal of the Auto Workers, who wanted to establish the auto companies on a partial pay-as-you-go basis in order to put the industry under greater pressure to stabilize employment (Chapter 1).

Costs per Man-Hour

This, the more significant measure of costs, must be discussed separately for Period I (August 1956 through June 1962) and Period II (July 1962 through June 1965) because the available data are much less complete for Period I than for the later period. For each period, the cost of contributions is discussed first, then the cost of benefits.

Period I. Since man-hours were not reported during this period, man-hour costs can only be estimated. During the first period contributions for most companies were usually at the maximum rate. Except during 1960, most companies made the full 5-cent contribution in nearly all the months of the period. However, since there were some months in which the companies contributed less than the full rate, the man-hour cost of contributions over the entire period must have been something less than 5 cents for practically all companies.

The year 1960 was unusual. During the first five to nine months of the year, all companies saved something in contributions, even those firms which had previously paid reduced benefits because of the low level of their funds. This anomaly is traceable to the steel strike of the preceding year (July 14 to November 5, 1959). The strike had the effect of reducing the base (man-hours worked) on which maximum financing was calculated and thus of decreasing the contributions required to reach maximum financing.

The data shown in Table 8–12 provide a base for some estimates of the man-hour cost of benefits. This table shows the experience of 17 companies, divided into two groups according to whether a company's cash contributions sufficed to pay all benefits or whether it had to pay off some of its contingent liability in cash. The first group contained 6 companies and the second, 11.

For the 6 companies which did not have to pay off any contingent liability in cash, the cost of benefits was obviously not greater than the 3-cent cash contribution. The estimated man-hour benefit costs for these 6 companies over the entire first period were, respectively, 0.5 cents, 1.8 cents, 2.0 cents, 2.1 cents, 2.3 cents, and 2.6 cents.[10]

The remaining 11 companies had to pay off some of their contingent liability in cash. For these companies, the amounts thus paid were estimated[11] to range from 0.2 to 0.9 cents per man-hour. Their regular cash contributions were estimated to range from 2.92 to 2.99 cents per man-hour, and their total costs were estimated to range from 3.12 to 3.89 cents per man-hour.

Although none of these 17 companies paid out in benefits the full 5 cents per hour that had been negotiated for the SUB plan, nearly all of them (all members of the 11-company group and even several of the 6-company group) reduced the amount of the weekly SUB payment during some months, especially in 1960, as mentioned above. In retrospect, it appears that full benefits could have been paid throughout this period, which included two recessions, at a cost of less than 5 cents per hour by

10. The method of estimation used was the following. If a company made the full contribution of 3 cents in cash and 2 cents in contingent liability, the ratio between the two totals at the end of any given period would be 3:2. To the extent that the actual ratio is less than this, it means that by contributing less than the full 3 cents on some man-hours, the company has saved some cash. This actual ratio may then be used to calculate the approximate number of man-hours on which contributions were based. Finally, total benefits divided by the number of man-hours gives the approximate benefit cost per man-hour. (Because this method of estimation does not allow for any canceled contingent liability, it slightly overstates the benefit costs per man-hour.)

11. The proportion paid in cash was taken as a percentage of total contingent liability, and this percentage was applied to the regular 2 cents per hour contribution rate.

TABLE 8-12

Benefit Payments, Cash Contributions, Accruals of Contingent Liability, and Reductions in Contingent Liability Account, Seventeen Basic Steel Companies,[a] August 1956–June 1962

	Benefit payments	Contributions		Reductions of contingent liability	
		3-cent cash contribution	Accrual of 2-cent contingent liability	Cancellations due to excess of fund over maximum financing	Amount of contingent liability paid off in cash[b]
	(1)	(2)	(3)	(4)	(5)
6 companies whose 3-cent cash contribution exceeded benefit payments	$ 11,098,700	$ 15,753,300	$11,059,985	$2,548,000	0
11 companies whose benefit payments exceeded the 3-cent cash contribution	130,130,200	105,840,600	71,532,500	1,973,300	$24,289,600
Totals, 17 companies	$141,228,900	$121,593,900	$82,592,485	$4,521,300	$24,289,600

SOURCE: Reports made by steel companies to United Steelworkers of America.

[a] In 1961, these 17 companies employed 62 percent of covered Steelworkers; 11 percent were employed in the first 6 companies, 51 percent in the other 11.

[b] Excess of benefit payments over 3-cent cash contributions (col. 1 minus col. 2).

the 6-company group and at about 5 cents per hour by the 11-company group.

Period II. For this later period, cost data are available in somewhat greater detail. Table 8–13 and Table 8–14 present data on the man-hour costs of contributions and benefits, respectively, for 12 companies, which included over half of all covered Steelworkers.

As shown in Table 8–13, during the first year of the new financing arrangements (Chapter 6), only 6 of the 12 companies (B, C, D, E, G, and L) had to make the full contribution of 4.5 cents in cash (column 1) and 5 cents in contingent liability (column 4). At the end of the first year, 4 of the 12 were still below the old level of maximum financing (B, C, D, E), 3 were above the old but below the new level (G, J, and L), and 5 (A, F, H, I, K) were at or above even the new level (columns 7 and 8). It is evident that the costs of a SUB plan can vary significantly between companies in the basic steel industry.

The following two years were prosperous years with relatively little unemployment. In fiscal 1964, only 4 companies (B, C, D, E) had to make any regular cash contribution; the rest of them made the entire contribution in the form of accrued contingent liability. In fiscal 1965, all companies made their entire contribution in the form of accrued contingent liability.

Column 6 shows the total eventual cost of the plan: the sum of cash contributions and the obligation to pay cash eventually. The average total cost of the 12 companies was 8.5 cents the first year, 7.7 cents the second year, and 2.6 cents the third year. The ranges of costs among the individual companies for these three years were, respectively, fiscal 1963, from 4.4 to 9.5 cents; fiscal 1964, from 3.7 to 9.5 cents; fiscal 1965, from 1.4 to 4.2 cents.

The actual cash costs (column 3) show a different pattern. For the first year, the average cash cost of the 12 companies (8.3 cents) was very close to the average total cost (8.5 cents), but in succeeding years the cash cost was much lower than the total cost. Also, cash cost differed among the companies more than did the total cost. The ranges of cash costs for the three years were, respectively, fiscal 1963, from 0 to 11.7 cents; fiscal 1964, from 0 to 7.8 cents; fiscal 1965, from 0 to 2.7 cents.

The man-hour costs of benefits by fiscal year are shown in Table 8–14 for 11 companies. For purposes of comparison, the estimated average costs of Period I are included (column 1). In any one year, benefits may be paid from one or more of three sources: regular required cash contributions, cash reserves in the fund, and contingent liability paid off in cash. Thus, in a particular period, benefit costs may be higher than total cash

TABLE 8-13

Contributions in Cents per Hour Worked and Condition of Fund, Twelve Basic Steel Companies,[a] by Fiscal Year, July 1962–June 1965

Company and fiscal year	Regular cash contribution (maximum, 4.5¢)	Contingent liability paid off in cash	Current cash costs[b] (col. 1 plus col. 2)	Contingent liability accrual (maximum, 9.5¢)[c]	Additional contingent liability accrual (maximum, 4.5¢ or 3.125¢)[d]	Total[e] contributions (sum of cols. 1, 4, and 5)	Reserve had reached maximum financing at end of period	
							Lower maximum financing	Higher maximum financing
	(1)	(2)	(3)	(4)	(5)	(6)	(7)	(8)
Company A								
July 1962–June 1963	1.1	1.0	2.1	5.0	1.7	7.8	yes	yes
July 1963–June 1964	0.0	3.7	3.7	3.7	3.1	6.8	yes	no
July 1964–June 1965	0.0	1.0	1.0	1.8	1.4	3.2	yes	no
Company B								
July 1962–June 1963	4.5	5.4	9.9	5.0	0.0	9.5	no	no
July 1963–June 1964	3.7	0.9	4.6	5.7	0.0	9.4	yes	no
July 1964–June 1965	0.0	0.1	0.1	2.5	[f]	2.6	yes	yes
Company C								
July 1962–June 1963	4.5	7.2	11.7	5.0	0.0	9.5	no	no
July 1963–June 1964	3.5	0.0	3.5	5.9	0.0	9.4	yes	yes
July 1964–June 1965	0.0	0.0	0.0	2.3	0.1	2.5	yes	yes
Company D								
July 1962–June 1963	4.5	5.9	10.4	5.0	0.0	9.5	no	no
July 1963–June 1964	4.0	3.8	7.8	5.5	0.0	9.5	yes	no
July 1964–June 1965	0.0	0.0	0.0	2.9	[f]	2.9	yes	yes
Company E								
July 1962–June 1963	4.5	5.5	10.0	5.0	0.0	9.5	no	no
July 1963–June 1964	1.2	1.0	2.2	5.5	0.2	6.9	yes	yes
July 1964–June 1965	0.0	0.2	0.2	1.9	0.4	2.3	yes	yes
Company F								
July 1962–June 1963	3.6	0.0	3.6	5.2	n.a.	n.a.	yes	yes
July 1963–June 1964	0.0	0.0	0.0	2.8	1.8	4.6	yes	yes
July 1964–June 1965	0.0	0.0	0.0	1.0	0.4	1.4	yes	yes

Company G								
July 1962–June 1963	4.5	3.4	7.9	5.0	0.0	9.5	yes	no
July 1963–June 1964	0.0	0.1	0.1	4.4	1.5	5.9	yes	yes
July 1964–June 1965	0.0	0.2	0.2	1.4	0.4	1.8	yes	yes
Company H								
July 1962–June 1963	0.0	0.0	0.0	0.0	4.4	4.4	yes[g]	yes[g]
July 1963–June 1964	0.0	0.0	0.0	2.4	1.3	3.7	yes[g]	yes[g]
July 1964–June 1965	0.0	0.0	0.0	0.0	1.5	1.5	yes[g]	yes[g]
Company I								
July 1962–June 1963	1.1	1.2	2.3	5.5	1.5	8.1	yes	yes
July 1963–June 1964	0.0	1.8	1.8	2.6	2.2	4.8	yes	yes
July 1964–June 1965	0.0	0.5	0.5	1.7	2.4	4.2	yes	yes
Company J								
July 1962–June 1963	1.6	5.1	6.7	7.1	0.4	9.1	yes	no
July 1963–June 1964	0.0	6.3	6.3	5.9	2.4	8.3	yes	no
July 1964–June 1965	0.0	2.7	2.7	2.3	0.4	2.7	yes	yes
Company K								
July 1962–June 1963	2.8	0.0	2.8	4.8	0.9	8.5	yes	yes
July 1963–June 1964	0.0	0.3	0.3	2.0	2.4	8.3	yes	yes
July 1964–June 1965	0.0	0.2	0.7	1.1	0.3	1.4	yes	yes
Company L								
July 1962–June 1963	4.5	4.6	9.1	5.0	0.0	9.5	yes	no
July 1963–June 1964	0.0	0.0	0.0	4.3	1.0	5.3	yes	yes
July 1964–June 1965	0.0	0.0	0.0	1.4	0.4	1.8	yes	yes
Averages, 12 companies								
July 1962–June 1963	3.8	4.5	8.3	4.8	0.5	8.5	—	—
July 1963–June 1964	2.2	0.8	3.0	4.9	0.6	7.7	—	—
July 1964–June 1965	0.0	0.2	0.2	2.1	0.5	2.6	—	—

SOURCE: Calculated from reports made by the steel companies to United Steelworkers of America.

a These companies accounted for over half of all covered Steelworkers.
b Benefits paid in period minus cash paid from reserve fund.
c Not additive. This maximum is reached only when cash contribution is zero.
d After January 1, 1964, the maximum accrual of additional contingent liability was 3.125¢.
e Total may not cross-foot, due to rounding.
f Less than 0.05 percent.
g A different method of financing is used by this firm.

TABLE 8–14

Benefit Costs in Cents per Hour Worked, Eleven Basic Steel Companies,[a]
August 1956–June 1965

Company	August 1956 through June 1962 (estimated)[b]	July 1962 through June 1965			
		July 1962 through June 1963	July 1963 through June 1964	July 1964 through June 1965	Average 3-year period
	(1)	(2)	(3)	(4)	(5)
A	3.4	4.2	3.7	0.9	2.9
B	3.8	10.3	4.8	0.6	4.9
C	3.4	11.7	3.9	0.1	4.8
D	3.9	10.4	4.5	0.7	4.8
E	3.6	9.6	2.2	0.2	3.6
F	3.5	n.a.	1.4	0.4	n.a.
G	3.0	9.1	1.4	0.2	3.2
H	2.0	0.8	0.5	0.2	0.5
I	2.3	5.5	1.8	0.5	2.5
J	2.1	9.8	6.3	0.2	7.6
K	3.5	3.9	0.9	0.2	1.6

SOURCE: Calculated from reports made by steel companies to United Steelworkers of America.

[a] In 1961, these 11 companies accounted for over half of all covered Steelworkers.

[b] For this period, contribution hours had to be estimated; for method of estimation, see fn. 8 to the text.

contributions. Over the long run, man-hour benefit costs are the most significant costs, to which contributions must ultimately be adjusted.

On the whole, Period II was more costly than Period I — partly because benefits had been liberalized in 1962 and partly because, in this three-year span, there were only two prosperous years to offset the high unemployment of fiscal 1963. When the data for fiscal 1966 and 1967 become available, Period II will probably average lower than Period I for many companies. Experience in fiscal 1965 shows how inexpensive a SUB plan can be for the steel industry in a nonrecession year.

The range of costs among the companies was widespread. In fiscal 1963, the range was 0.8 to 11.7; in fiscal 1964, from 0.5 to 6.3; and in fiscal 1965, from 0.1 to 0.9. It is noteworthy that the company which had the highest cost in fiscal 1963 (Company C) had the lowest cost in fiscal 1965.

Experience under the SUB plan of the Alan Wood Steel Company is particularly interesting because this company has had, since 1965, the most liberal of all the SUB plans (Chapter 5). During the first 20 months under the new provisions (July 1965 through February 1967), the plan paid out in benefits only 1.33 cents per man-hour (0.19 cents in regular benefits and 1.14 cents in short-week benefits). By way of comparison, in 1963, when the benefit provisions were less liberal but unemployment was much heavier, the plan paid out in benefits 4.72 cents per man-hour. The difference between the two periods illustrates once again that the chief determinant of costs in an unemployment-benefit program is the amount of unemployment. More important, the favorable experience under the new plan illustrates that when work is available, even a very liberal SUB plan does not necessarily result in higher SUB costs.

Review of Steel Experience

The decade 1956–1965 constituted a fair test for the steel SUB plans. The period included two mild recessions and a slight secular decline. These are the kind of nondisaster situations in which SUB is intended to function adequately.

The relatively small proportion of laid-off Steelworkers who received SUB payments (Table 8–2) was a major factor in keeping SUB costs low. Among the various companies individuals who received one or more SUB payments in the course of a year ranged from 7 to 42 percent of the work-force in a recession year like 1962, and from 2 to 20 percent in a prosperous year like 1965 (Table 8–3). The value placed on SUB by a company's employees probably varied directly with these percentages.

During recession periods, short-week benefits made up a relatively small proportion of all benefits (Table 8–4), an indication that work sharing below 32 hours was used relatively infrequently as a device for adjusting labor supply to demand.

SUB has augmented the UI benefit significantly; in recent years it averaged more than 40 percent of the total unemployment benefit (Table 8–5). At least since the 1962 amendments, the maximum benefit has been reasonably adequate: on the average, only about one quarter of SUB payments — when UI was also received — have been limited by the benefit maximum (Table 8–6).

The supplementation of UI duration has been a minor task of SUB: under the amended plan, only about 14 percent of all SUB payments had to fulfill this function (Table 8–7). SUB's own duration seemed reasonably adequate: the exhaustion ratio averaged less than 20 percent in the worst period and only 2 percent in the best period (Table 8–9).

The 1962 amendments increased the potential costs of the plan considerably, but actual costs have been mainly a reflection of economic conditions. In the first period (August 1956 through June 1962), the cost of contributions varied among companies but for most of them was close to the full 5 cents per hour worked, while benefit costs were estimated to range from 0.5 cents to 3.89 cents per hour worked. In the second period (July 1962 through June 1965), the cost of contributions ranged from 4.4 to 9.5 cents per hour in fiscal 1963 and from 0.3 to 4.2 cents in fiscal 1965, while the cost of benefits ranged from 0.8 to 11.7 cents per hour in fiscal 1963 and from 0.1 to 0.9 cents per hour in fiscal 1965 (Tables 8–13 and 8–14).

The steel SUB plan is characterized by its use of contingent liability in financing. This provision has placed operations very much on a pay-as-you-go basis. In most years, there has been very little cash in the reserve funds, and the companies have had to draw on their working cash to finance benefits in periods of heavy unemployment.

9

EXPERIENCE UNDER AUTO-TYPE PLANS

The SUB experience of other industries cannot be described in exactly the same way as experience in steel because the data available are somewhat different. The description of experience in other industries, however, follows the same general order: protection available, protection used, and cost of providing the protection. Experience under the auto plan takes up most of this chapter. Some additional scattered data are included for the agricultural implement and rubber industries, which have SUB plans generally similar to the auto plan.

Protection Available

The proportion of the workforce eligible for SUB usually varies inversely, as was noted in the preceding chapter, with increases and decreases in the total workforce. Although no continuous data are available on the proportion eligible, scattered evidence indicates that it is generally quite high. Among the workers of one auto company in 1960, when employment was relatively high and the proportion of the workforce eligible for benefits was presumably relatively low, 92 percent had the requisite one year of seniority. In the same company, in 1963, when again employment was relatively high, the proportion was 91 percent. In one agricultural implement company in 1964 the proportion was 92 percent.

The proportion of employees *on layoff* who were eligible for benefits would, of course, be smaller than the eligible proportion of the total workforce. Here again, only scattered data are available. Appendix Table 1 shows that during the recession of 1960–1961, 88.6 percent of auto company B's laid-off workers had the requisite one year of seniority.

Table 9–1 shows the experience of four major rubber companies over a period of years; for the reasons indicated in the table, these percentages are overstatements of the proportions not eligible for benefits. For the period shown, the proportion rarely exceeded one third and frequently was less than half this large. It would seem that generally the great majority of the laid-off employees had the necessary seniority. The unusually low figures in 1961 are a delayed reflection of the previous recession, during which the rubber companies had laid off large numbers of employees. In the following period of prosperity, the companies for the most part

TABLE 9–1

Laid-Off Employees without Requisite Seniority, as Percent[a] of All Those
Laid Off, Four Rubber Companies, 1961–1966

Year	Company A	Company B	Company C	Company D
	Percent	Percent	Percent	Percent
1961	2	n.a.	2	2
1962	16	n.a.	4	5
1963	30	45	30	3
1964	21	23	34	1
1965	17	37	33	3
1966	16	38	33	6

SOURCE: Calculated from data supplied by the companies.

[a] Laid-off employees having the requisite seniority who for one reason or another were *not* drawing SUB have been omitted from the base; these percents are therefore somewhat overstated.

recalled former workers rather than hired new ones. When the 1961 layoffs occurred, there were few new employees to be affected.

Company D's unusually low proportions of ineligible claimants reflect a decline in the company's workforce in the area in which it formerly had its chief operations. Most of the company's layoffs occurred in this area, and were therefore among employees with seniority; in other areas the company was expanding and experienced few layoffs.

Company C furnishes a good example of the variations that can occur even in one company's experience. The proportion without seniority was only 2 percent in 1961 as against 34 percent in 1964. Yet the number of layoffs in 1964 was much larger than in 1961 (about three times as large), and normally should have been associated with a smaller proportion of laid-off employees lacking seniority. The smaller layoff in 1961, which produced a smaller proportion of ineligible claimants, may have been concentrated in one plant and may therefore have cut more deeply into the ranks of those with high seniority, of whom a greater proportion would be eligible; or perhaps the company had taken on a substantial number of new employees a short time before the layoffs in 1964; or perhaps both factors were at work.

The extent of protection (number of credit units, or benefit weeks, available to laid-off employees) is not generally known, but there is at least one detailed study available. This is the study by auto company B of its SUB experience in the period April 1960–March 1961, referred to above.[1] Table 9–2 shows the number of credit units available at the time of layoff in relation to the length of the layoff. The table thus sheds light on the crucial

1. For a summary of the full study, see Appendix Table 1.

TABLE 9–2

Layoffs[a] at Auto Company B, April 1960–March 1961, Percent of Those Laid Off Having Adequate[a] Credit Units, and Percent Having 26 Credit Units

Length of layoff	% of total layoffs	Percent of layoffs involving employees with adequate[b] credit units	Percent of layoffs involving employees with 26 credit units
	(1)	(2)	(3)
1 week or less	57	[c]	[c]
More than 1 week	43	87	74
4 weeks or less	81	93	81
10 weeks or less	90	81	78
26 weeks or more	2	37	37

SOURCE: Calculated from data supplied by the company.

[a] Since the data are in terms of layoffs, not laid-off individuals, a given individual is represented more than once in the table if he was laid off more than once in the fiscal year.

[b] Credit units equal to or in excess of weeks of layoff.

[c] Inasmuch as these layoffs were too short to involve a SUB payment, the percents were not computed.

question of the extent to which benefits are available in proportion to the need for them.

Some 57 percent of the layoffs were for one week or less, and most of the affected employees were not eligible for benefits because they first had a waiting week to serve. Of the layoffs lasting more than one week, 87 percent affected workers who had at least enough credit units to match the length of their layoff, and 74 percent had 26 credit units, the maximum that could be accumulated at that time.

As would be expected, the proportion of the layoffs affecting employees who had credit units equal to the length of their layoff was large for short layoffs and progressively decreased as the length of the layoff increased. For example, in the case of layoffs for four weeks or fewer 93 percent of the workers affected had at least 4 credit units; but only 37 percent of the layoffs lasting 26 weeks or longer affected workers who had 26 credit units. This low proportion should be interpreted in the light of two considerations. First, the number of these long-term layoffs was relatively small — only 2 percent of the total number of layoffs. Second, these employees may not have been unemployed for 26 weeks. All that is known is that they were not recalled within 26 weeks by this company. They may have found other jobs or have left the labor force. Hence, the total number of layoffs involving employees who experienced extended unemployment but did not have sufficient credits was at most only 63 percent of 2 percent, or 1.3 percent.

Auto companies maintain a list of employees who are on layoff. Typically, a company carries an employee on the list for one or two years or for the length of his seniority, whichever is the longer. Occasionally an estimate is made of the proportion on the list who are eligible for SUB, namely, those who have been on layoff continuously for less than two years and who have some unused credit units. Data for one auto company (D) indicate that of those on the layoff list in the period 1960–1961 on the average more than half continued to be eligible for some SUB payments. The proportion varied, month by month, from 60 to 80 percent in 1960 and from 33 to 85 percent in 1961. In interpreting these figures, it should be recalled that not all on the "layoff list" are unemployed, and hence that the complements of these percentages are overestimates of the proportion of laid-off employees who needed but did not have the protection of the plan.

Potential duration in the auto plan is shortened (more than one credit unit is exchanged for one week's benefit) when the fund is at specified levels below the maximum. From the time the funds were well established until the end of 1961, this shortening of potential duration never occurred in the case of three companies, occurred during half the months in the case of a fourth company, and occurred during all the months in the case of the ill-fated Studebaker Company. Thereafter it occurred only in the case of American Motors and then only after 1965.

Extent of Use

Regular Benefits

Table 9–3 shows the experience of four auto companies and four agricultural implement companies in the payment of regular benefits from 1957 through 1965. Only combined totals are given for the auto companies since, in their case, individual firms could be identified by their respective magnitudes.

The cyclical sensitivity of the auto industry is reflected in the increased number of benefits marking the recessions of 1958 and 1961. The number of benefits paid in 1961 was almost four times the number paid in the following year and almost six times the number paid in 1965.

The experience of the agricultural implement companies also reflects some cyclical sensitivity but is particularly interesting because of the variations among companies. For example, Company C was untouched by the 1958 recession that is so evident in the experience of the other companies. On the other hand, from time to time one or another company has had to make extensive use of SUB in fairly prosperous periods — for example, Company D in 1959 and Company B in 1963. Company A paid relatively high benefits in 1965 (22,000) as well as in 1961 (30,000), while the other three paid substantially fewer benefits in 1965 than in 1961. This kind of

TABLE 9-3

Number of Regular Weekly Benefits Paid by Selected (UAW) SUB Plans in Auto and Agricultural Implement Companies, 1957–1965

Companies	Number of regular benefits, by year (thousands)								
	1957	1958	1959	1960	1961	1962	1963	1964	1965
Auto companies A, B, C, and D	526	2,728	2,087	1,129	2,341[a]	619[b]	505	542	420
Agricultural implement companies									
A	n.a.	n.a.	n.a.	n.a.	30	15	12	11	22
B	31	76	10	68	81	8	33	17	14
C	3	3	99	46	55	36	8	5	8
D	8	78	43	34	44	3	1	c	c

SOURCE: Some figures were obtained directly from the companies. Other figures were calculated by dividing the total amount of benefits paid by the average benefit.

[a] From the figure for 1961, the month of December is missing for two companies and the months of November and December for one company.

[b] The month of December is missing from the figure for 1962 for one company.

c Less than 500.

variation among companies in the same industry illustrates once again the fact that unemployment has many causes.

Short-Week Benefits

It will be recalled from Chapter 5 that, beginning in 1962, the auto-type SUB plans incorporated a short-week benefit, which brought the hourly-paid worker substantially closer to the status of the salaried employee. Tables 9–4 and 9–5 show the experience of major firms in the auto and agricultural implement industries with this benefit for the period 1962–1965. These tables aim chiefly at showing the proportion of all benefits paid that short-week benefits — scheduled and unscheduled — represented. (Note that the comparison is in terms of the number, not the amount, of benefits paid.) The absolute figures are not given because in some instances they would identify the companies. However, to assist in the interpretation of the data, they are expressed in terms of ratios to a base year.

Scheduled short-week benefits. Auto company A made some little use of the scheduled short-week benefit in three of the four years covered by the table, but made considerable use of it in 1963. Otherwise, none of the auto companies has paid any significant number of scheduled short-week benefits. The agricultural implement companies have made even less use of this benefit. Only one company (A) in one year (1965) made any significant use of it.

The limited use made of this benefit may have been due to a combination of three factors. First, since most of the period was fairly prosperous, there was no pressing need for these industries to curtail production by scheduling short weeks. Second, short-week benefits would have been particularly costly to most companies during this period because the fund levels were so low — consequent upon the increases in maximum financing negotiated in 1962 — and the companies would have had to reimburse the funds directly out of pocket for any scheduled short-week benefits paid. Third, since it was sometimes a matter of judgment as to whether a benefit should be labeled scheduled or unscheduled, the companies regularly settled the doubt in favor of the unscheduled benefit, which was less expensive.[2]

2. Newspaper reports indicate that in the early months of 1967 two of the auto companies scheduled a significant number of short weeks as a means of adjusting production to a decrease in demand. At this time, the funds were undoubtedly close to maximum financing and the "hard nickel" had been negotiated, so that short weeks may have seemed the most efficient and least expensive way of adjusting production to what it was hoped would be only a temporary decline in demand. (During the first six months of the year, one company paid scheduled short-week benefits at an average cost to the fund of more than 10 cents per hour.)

TABLE 9-4

Percent Distribution, by Type, of Total Number of SUB Payments and Their Relationship to Base Year 1962,[a] Four Auto Companies, by Year, 1962–1965

Company and benefit	1962 Ratio to 1962	1962 % distribution	1963 Ratio to 1962	1963 % distribution	1964 Ratio to 1962	1964 % distribution	1965 Ratio to 1962	1965 % distribution
Company A								
Regular benefits	100	36	133	27	69	26	51	17
Scheduled short-week benefits	100	10	486	30	52	7	123	13
Unscheduled short-week benefits	100	54	139	43	116	67	136	70
Company B								
Regular benefits	100	61	106	55	n.a.	27	92	40
Scheduled short-week benefits	100	2	200	3	n.a.	1	9	b
Unscheduled short-week benefits	100	37	134	42	n.a.	72	227	60
Company C								
Regular benefits	n.a.	n.a.	100[a]	4	1181	37	914	21
Scheduled short-week benefits	n.a.	n.a.	0	0		b		b
Unscheduled short-week benefits	n.a.	n.a.	100[a]	96	178	63	147	79
Company D								
Regular benefits	100	74	29	40	28	37	19	18
Scheduled short-week benefits	100	1	34	b	0	0	69	b
Unscheduled short-week benefits	100	25	125	60	141	63	254	82

SOURCE: Calculated from figures supplied by the companies.
[a] For auto company C, 1963 has been adopted as the base year because 1962 figures were not available.
[b] Less than 0.1 percent.

TABLE 9-5

Percent Distribution, by Type, of Total Number of SUB Payments and Their Relationship to Base Year 1963, Three Agricultural Implement Companies, by Year, 1962–1965

Company and benefit	1962 Ratio to base year 1963	1962 % distribution	1963 Ratio to base year 1963	1963 % distribution	1964 Ratio to base year 1963	1964 % distribution	1965 Ratio to base year 1963	1965 % distribution
Company A								
Regular benefits	123	98	100	48	86	58	178	62
Scheduled short-week benefits	a	b	a	b	a	b	a	11
Unscheduled short-week benefits	3	2	100	52	56	42	71	27
Company B								
Regular benefits	24	94	100	93	51	99	41	98
Scheduled short-week benefits	a	0	a	b	a	b }	9c	2
Unscheduled short-week benefits	22	6	100	7	10	1		
Company D								
Regular benefits	250	97	100	92	13	97	5	53
Scheduled short-week benefits	a	0	a	0	a	0	a	0
Unscheduled short-week benefits	88	3	100	8	4	3	61	47

a So few scheduled short-week benefits were paid by these companies that no useful basis exists for comparison of one year's experience with that of another.

b Less than 0.1 percent.

c In the data supplied by this company for 1965, no distinction was made between scheduled and unscheduled short-week benefits.

Unscheduled short-week benefits. For each auto company in this period unscheduled short-week benefits averaged over 50 percent of the total number of benefits. This high proportion is explainable chiefly by the favorable economic conditions existing during the period covered by the table. In such a period, most unemployment tends to be of the very short-run kind resulting from breakdowns, lack of materials, and so forth. The percentages were much higher here than in the steel industry, whose plan did not compensate for partial weeks of more than 32 hours.

Unscheduled short-week benefits as a proportion of total benefits among auto companies ranged from 43 to 70 percent for Company A, from 37 to 72 percent for Company B, from 63 to 96 percent for Company C, and from 25 to 82 percent for Company D. In the case of Company A the range principally reflected changes in the number of regular benefits; the absolute number of unscheduled short-week benefits did not fluctuate widely during the period, as may be seen by the ratios to the base year. By contrast, in the case of Company B, the wider ranges reflected fluctuations in the absolute number of unscheduled short-week benefits (the ratio to the base year rose to 227 in 1965) accompanied by relative stability in the number of regular benefits (the ratio ranged only from 92 to 106). For Company C and Company D, both of the above causes were operative, although in the case of Company D the very high figure (82 percent of total payments) in 1965 is primarily a reflection of the very small number of regular benefits paid in that year.

On the whole, the percentages for the agricultural implement companies, shown in Table 9–5, were significantly lower than for the auto companies. Only Company A had a comparable distribution. For the other two, short-week benefits as a proportion of total benefits varied between 1 and 8 percent. (The 47 percent figure for Company D in 1965 is not meaningful because the total number of benefits in that year was insignificant.)

Data with respect to short-week benefits paid by the rubber industry were available for only two companies and only for the years 1964 and 1965. Except for the year 1964 for one of these companies, no distinction has been made between scheduled and unscheduled short-week benefits.

In percentages, benefits paid by these two companies were distributed as follows:

Benefits	*1964*	*1965*	*Benefits*	*1964*	*1965*
Company C			*Company D*		
Regular	53	37	Regular	71	70
Scheduled short-week	1 ⎱	63	Short-week, scheduled		
Unscheduled short-week	46 ⎰		and unscheduled	29	30

The data for the two rubber companies are too fragmentary to reveal much of a pattern. If these fragments are typical, the rubber companies would seem to be closer to the auto companies than to the agricultural implement companies in their use of the short week, and Company C would seem to have made more use of it than Company D.

Beneficiaries

The SUB plans of the auto type require each company to report monthly to the union on the number of employees in active service and the number on layoff with credit units. Although this report is used principally to calculate maximum financing, it can also be used to calculate a kind of unemployment rate. These data are shown for the auto companies in Table 9-6 and for the agricultural implement and the rubber companies in Table 9-7. Except for auto company A, the rates represent all employees on layoff with credit units as a percentage of the approximate workforce of the company (number of the employed plus the unemployed with credit units).[3] In the case of auto company A, "employees on layoff" do not include those on temporary layoff, even when they have credit units.

The data in Tables 9-6 and 9-7 reveal the underlying economic forces — cyclical, seasonal, and secular — that are the chief explanations of SUB experience; hence they are useful in interpreting the other tables of the chapter. Also, because the data are in ratios, they may be used for comparisons among companies.

In Table 9-6, cyclical forces are largely responsible for the higher annual averages of all the auto companies in 1958 and 1961. Secular forces explain the lower-than-average annual rates of Company C in 1959 and 1960 and the same company's higher-than-average rates in 1964 and 1965.[4] They also explain Company D's relatively high rates in the years preceding 1963.

Company A seems to have lower rates than the others, but, as just explained, temporary layoffs are not included in these figures. It is significant that in 1958 its rate was about as high as the rates of the other companies, no doubt because during this recession year very short-term layoffs were a smaller part of the total.

---

3. Neither the numerator nor the denominator used in estimating the rate is exactly what would be desired. The numerator is understated because it does not include workers on layoff who lack credit units. The numerator is overstated because it includes the unemployed with credit units who were not eligible because they were serving a waiting week, were disqualified, or for some reason (for example, because they were employed) did not apply for SUB. The denominator is understated because it does not include the unemployed without credit units. The net result of these opposing influences is probably some slight overstatement of the rate.

4. Company C continued to have relatively high rates in 1966 and 1967.

TABLE 9-6

Laid-Off Employees with Credit Units as Percent[a] of Approximate Workforce,[b] SUB Programs of Auto Companies with UAW, by Year, 1956-1965

Company	Monthly percentages, by years									
	1956	1957	1958	1959	1960	1961	1962	1963	1964	1965
A[c]										
Range	2-7[d]	1-7	8-29	3-11	2-10	2-17[e]	1-5	1-4	[f]-1	[f]-[f]
Annual average	4[d]	3	19	7	5	8[e]	2	2	1	[f]
B										
Range	1-19[d]	1-23	4-41	2-46	1-26	2-38[e]	1-24	1-21	[f]-15	[f]
Annual average	9[d]	6	19	11	19	13[e]	4	3	2	3
C										
Range		14-30[g]	2-20	1-11	[f]-31	[f]-46[e]	[f]-51	[f]-8	1-44	1-24
Annual average		19[g]	12	3	4	11[e]	5	1	9	10
D										
Range	12-58[d]	5-34	31-67	8-48	12-52	11-65[h]	6-36	2-5	1-3	[f]-6
Annual average	32[d]	12	41	19	20	34	18	3	2	1

SOURCE: Calculated from data supplied by the companies.

[a] Rates represent laid-off employees with credit units as a percentage of the approximate workforce. Each monthly figure is for the last pay period (7 consecutive days beginning on Monday) of the month.

[b] For the auto companies, the "workforce" consists of the employed plus those on layoff with credit units.

[c] These rates are not directly comparable with rates for other companies because temporary layoffs (a layoff of less than 30 days for model change or of 12 days for any other reason) are not included in the figures for "laid-off employees with credit units."

[d] For 8 months.

[e] For 11 months.

[f] Less than 0.5 percent.

[g] For 5 months.

[h] For 10 months.

The ranges of the monthly rates reveal the auto industry's seasonal sensitivity; the upper end of the range of the ratios for all companies is high in all years, even good years. Employment fluctuates seasonally because of periodic retooling and because production of autos usually decreases during the last four or five months of the model year. Seasonal unemployment also explains the relatively narrower range of Company A's rates: the unemployment which was omitted from Company A's data was largely seasonal unemployment. For this reason, the annual averages of Company A may be taken as a measure of the more serious kinds of unemployment in the auto industry.

Table 9–7 presents similar data for the agricultural implement and rubber industries. The annual averages are lower in rubber than in agricultural implements, and are lower in both than in autos. The highest monthly rate among the four rubber companies in the years 1957 to 1965 was 22, whereas the highest among the auto companies was 67. The annual range of rates, a measure of the seasonal swing, was also narrower for both agricultural implements and rubber than it was for the auto industry. Among the agricultural implement companies, Company C had consistently lower ratios in most years. Among the rubber companies, there was no consistently lower pattern for any one company.

It would be desirable to know the number of different persons who received SUB payments. This figure is one measure of the degree of support that a SUB plan can expect to command from a company's workforce. It is also an indication of the type of unemployment for which SUB is being used. As compared with cyclical unemployment, for example, seasonal unemployment will result in a larger number of different individuals drawing benefits for a shorter time. Table 9–8 presents what little information is available in this area.

In 1960, when unemployment generally was not so heavy as in 1961, auto companies A and B made one or more regular SUB payments to over a third of their workforce. In 1963 for Company A this proportion was much smaller (21 percent). The continuous data which are available for agricultural implement company D show the proportion varying from about 10 percent in very good years like 1957 and 1964 to almost one third in the recession year of 1958 and almost one half in the recession year of 1961. In both good and bad years, the percentages of rubber company C were much lower than those shown for the companies in the other industries.

These figures, which are restricted to recipients of *regular* SUB payments, do not present a complete picture of all the employees who drew something from the SUB fund. In addition, there were the recipients of short-

TABLE 9-7

Laid-Off Employees with Credit Units as Percent of Approximate Workforce,[a] SUB Programs of Agricultural Implement Companies (with UAW) and Rubber Companies (with URW), by Year, 1956–1965

Company	Monthly percentages, by years									
	1956	1957	1958	1959	1960	1961	1962	1963	1964	1965
Agricultural implement										
A										
Range	11-32[b]	2-13	7-22	c-8	3-32	4-14	1-17	1-2	1-2	1-4
Annual average	19[b]	9	14	3	16	9	4	1	1	2
B										
Range	5-10	6-14	8-28	1-13	4-21	16-23	3-20	5-10	3-9	2-6
Annual average	7	10	19	6	15	20	8	8	6	3
C										
Range	3-17[d]	2-9	c-3	1-11	2-21	1-23	2-18	c-4	c-4	n.a.
Annual average	7[d]	4	1	3	9	13	8	1	1	
Rubber										
A										
Range		c-1[b]	c-15	1-4	2-9	6-15	c-6	1-2	1-3	n.a.
Annual average		c,b	7	2	5	10	4	2	2	
B										
Range		1-2[e]	4-22	2-6	3-6	3-14	2-5	4-6	2-6	n.a.
Annual average		1[e]	13	3	4	7	3	5	4	
C										
Range		c-2[b]	2-21	2-7[e]	3-7	4-16	2-5	2-5	3-8	n.a.
Annual average		1[b]	12	5[e]	5	9	3	4	5	
D										
Range		c-1[b]	1-15[e]	c-1[e]	1-10	2-12	2-4	2-7	5-9	2-5
Annual average		1[b]	6[e]	1[e]	4	7	3	5	7	3

SOURCE: Calculated from data supplied by the companies.
[a] The "workforce" consists of the employed plus those on layoff with credit units.
[b] For 5 months.
[c] Less than 0.5 percent.
[d] For 4 months.
[e] For 11 months.

TABLE 9–8

Percent of Workforce[a] Receiving One or More Regular SUB Payments
in the Course of a Year, Various SUB Plans and Years

Year	Auto companies			Agricultural implement Company D	Rubber companies	
	Company A	Company B	Company D		C	D
1957				13		
1958				31		
1959				18		
1960	38	34		30	8	16
1961				47	21	19
1962				15		8
1963	21		65[b]	23	6	11
1964				10	9	18

SOURCE: Calculated from data supplied by the companies.

[a] Workforce: annual average of figures for one week in each month for number of employees in active service plus those on layoff with credits.

[b] The figures for this company include individuals who received regular SUB and/or short-week benefits and/or separation payments.

week benefits and of separation payments. How numerous these payments can be is indicated by the experience of auto company D. In 1963, a prosperous year for this company (see Table 9–6), 65 percent of its workforce received one or more payments in the form of regular SUB, short-week benefits, or separation payments. To judge from the 1963 figure of 21 percent for auto company A (Table 9–8), and from Tables 9–4 and 9–5 above, the greater part of this 65 percent consisted of recipients of short-week benefits.

(The scope of Table 9–8 can be extended somewhat by reading it in connection with Tables 9–6 and 9–7. The top of the range of the monthly percentages may be regarded as an understatement of the number of different persons receiving one or more regular benefits in the year. Thus auto company B in 1960 had a top monthly rate of 26 percent, but Table 9–8 shows that 34 percent of its workforce received a regular benefit at some time or other during that year. Likewise rubber company C shows the following relationship for the four years (1960, 1961, 1963, 1964) in which data are available in both tables: 7 percent as against 8 percent, 16 percent as against 21 percent, 5 percent as against 6 percent, and 8 percent as against 9 percent.)

Appendix Table 1 is uniquely valuable as a complete picture of one company's total SUB experience in a year (April 1960–March 1961).

Several items in that experience are relevant to the discussion at this point. About two thirds (67.8 percent) of all laid-off employees received one or more SUB payments in the course of that year. Almost a third (30.7 percent) of all laid-off employees never filed an application for SUB. About two thirds of this second group (20 percent of the total) had the requisite one year of seniority but still did not file an application. The great majority of these nonfilers probably consisted of employees laid off for not more than one week, who would be serving a waiting period and therefore would not be eligible for benefits. Over half (56 percent) of all the layoffs were for no more than one full week.

Just a little over half (51 percent) of all full weeks of layoff during the year were compensated. No applications were submitted for 46 percent of these weeks of layoff, while for 3 percent the applications were denied. (For the bases on which these applications were denied, see Appendix Table 1.)

Seniority of Beneficiaries

It was argued against the negotiation of the first SUB plan that it would benefit only employees at the bottom of the seniority list. This alleged limitation is still a consideration in current discussions within the unions on the desirability of SUB. In evaluating this consideration it would help to know the actual distribution of payments by seniority in the SUB plans that have operated in the past decade. Unfortunately, only two fragments of such data are available, both reflecting the experience of one company in the auto industry.

In the auto industry, supplemental unemployment benefits have not been confined to short-service employees. Table 9–9, which shows the experience of Company A in two years, indicates that SUB beneficiaries among seniority groups have been much more proportional than might have been expected. This surprising result is partly explained by the marked seasonal pattern in auto employment: during the model change-over, even long-service employees are laid off at least a short period. To some extent also, the presence of high-seniority employees on the SUB rolls is explained by the option often exercised by such employees to be on layoff rather than accept other available jobs to which they have a right (see Chapter 11). Thus workers with 20 or more years of seniority were proportionately represented among the beneficiaries, although they drew a disproportionately small share of the benefits. These higher-seniority employees shared more widely in SUB in 1960 than in 1963 because in the earlier year cyclical influences had caused layoffs to cut more deeply into the workforce. Another factor influencing the lower percentage of

TABLE 9-9

Percent Distribution of SUB Beneficiaries by Years of Seniority,
Auto Company A, 1960 and 1963

Years of seniority[a]	Percent of workforce		Percent of total beneficiaries		Percent of total benefits	
	1960	1963	1960	1963	1960	1963
Less than 1	8	n.a.	0	0	0	0
1 to 4	21		22		25	
5 or less		n.a.		40		57
5 to 9	26		30		38	
6 to 10		n.a.		23		19
10 to 19	23		29		25	
11 to 20		n.a.		26		18
20 or more	22		19		11	
21 or more		n.a.		11		7

SOURCE: Calculation from data supplied by the company.

[a] The data are drawn from two separate studies in which different groupings are shown.

benefits drawn by the higher-seniority employees was a reduction in the time required for the model changeover.

Benefit Amount

Table 9-10 shows the average amount of the regular weekly SUB payment during the period 1957-1965 for four auto companies, four agricultural companies, and one rubber company. During this period the benefit formula was substantially the same for all of these companies. It provided 65 percent of *net* wages until late in 1961 (1963 in the rubber plan) and 62 percent of *gross* wages thereafter. The rubber plan began to pay 65 percent of gross wages as of June 1965.

Between 1957 and 1965, the average SUB payment for these companies approximately doubled, an increase that was much greater than the increase in either wages or UI benefits. The growth in the SUB amount seems to have been attributable primarily to the increases which occurred in the benefit-wage ratio and in the maximum benefit. The full impact of these changes in the benefit formula became evident in 1962 (1964 for rubber). For all the auto companies, for agricultural implement companies C and D, and for rubber company C, the average benefit rose by more than 50 percent in the year following the change. The increase was only about 30 percent for agricultural implement company B, while there was practically no change for agricultural implement company A.

TABLE 9–10

Average Annual Regular Weekly Benefit,[a] Auto and Agricultural Implement Plans with UAW and Rubber Plans with URW, 1957–1965

Company	Average weekly benefit, by year								
	1957	1958	1959	1960	1961	1962	1963	1964	1965
Auto									
A	$14.99	$15.28	$19.94	$19.95	$18.67	$28.45	$28.14	$31.42	$31.49
B	n.a.	n.a.	17.11	16.05	18.04	28.51	28.62	29.83	32.05
C	15.55	14.10	18.62	13.25	10.23	16.66	30.83	32.23	25.69[b]
D	13.00	13.17	18.40	18.60	20.07	32.21	31.40	32.21	33.12
Agricultural implement									
A	n.a.	n.a.	n.a.	n.a.	38.55	39.23	38.92	40.36[c]	47.77
B	15.94	15.88	22.50	20.24	17.69	23.11	27.99	29.94	34.34
C	19.70	19.49	22.81	22.59	22.33	41.87	42.00	47.57[c]	52.54
D	n.a.	10.11	10.93	15.83	13.04	22.26	23.18	26.43	25.78
Rubber company C	n.a.	n.a.	n.a.	16.27	22.12	22.20	13.75	29.04	35.07

SOURCE: Calculations by the company or by the author.
[a] With and without UI, exclusive of short-week benefits.
[b] Average for 11 months.
[c] Average of November and December of 1963 and first 10 months of 1964.

For rubber company C, the average benefit was notably lower in 1960 and 1963 than in other years. The difference may reflect a different distribution of payments by state. If in a given year most payments occur in states with relatively high UI benefits, the average SUB payment will be low, and vice versa.[5] The unusually high benefit for that company in 1965 also reflects the increase in the SUB formula (from 62 percent to 65 percent) which became effective in June of that year.

Other things being equal, the average benefit would be expected to rise somewhat in recession years, when layoffs affect the largest proportion of employees with high seniority and high wages. This factor is lost, however, among the many other factors affecting the average benefit and does not appear clearly in these annual data.

Generally speaking, the average benefit has been higher for the agricultural implement companies than for the auto companies. It is not known whether the low rates of rubber company C are characteristic of the rubber industry generally. The main factors accounting for these variations are probably differences in weekly earnings of the laid-off employees and in distributions of layoffs by state. Fairly accurate weights could be assigned to these and other causal factors by a more complete analysis of data that are in the possession of the companies. Agricultural implement company D has a consistently lower average benefit than any of the other companies in the industry. In all probability, this situation is chiefly the result of the company's layoffs being concentrated in states with relatively high UI benefits. Auto company C had a notably lower average benefit in the three years 1960, 1961, and 1962; the reason for this difference was not ascertained.

All the companies in the table paid full benefits throughout the period covered by the table. Although the auto-type plan provided for a reduction in the benefit amount when the reserve funds fell to a certain level, this level was set so low that it was never reached by any of these companies.

Table 9–11 throws some light on experience of six companies under the provisions setting the maximum benefit. The table shows the proportion of regular benefits that were paid at the maximum level. Since these data became available only after additional reporting requirements were negotiated in 1961, the table begins with the year 1962. Between 1962 and late 1964 these plans provided for a single (nonvariable) maximum of $40.00; in late 1964, becoming fully effective in 1965, the maximum was raised

5. To illustrate how large the state difference can be, the average SUB payment for rubber company C in 1963 ranged from $7.44 in Massachusetts to $42.10 in Tennessee. Company C had experienced a very heavy layoff in one of its plants in Massachusetts in 1963.

TABLE 9–11

Percent of Regular Benefits Paid at the Maximum Level, SUB Plans (UAW) in Four Auto Companies and Two Agricultural Implement Companies, 1962–1965

Company	Percent paid at maximum level			
	1962	1963	1964	1965
Auto				
A	12.0	13.0	12.0	4.0
B	14.0	13.0[a]	n.a.	7.0
C	n.a.	n.a.	n.a.	11.0
D	2.5	3.7	7.0	1.0
Agricultural implement				
B[a]	3.0	9.0	17.0	7.0
D	0.8	5.5	18.1	2.6

SOURCE: Calculated from data supplied by the companies.

[a] About 75 percent of these payments were made in combination with UI. For other years and other companies, the corresponding information is not available.

and made variable — $50.00 plus a dependents' allowance of $1.50 to $6.00. As a result of this increase in the maximum, a sharp drop in the percentages occurred in 1965. (Also in 1965 many states increased their UI benefits.) For all companies and for the entire period, the figures ranged from 1 percent to 18 percent, with half of the figures falling in the range of 7–14 percent.

On the whole, these proportions are lower than those experienced by companies under the steel plan. It will be recalled that the steel plan provided a maximum of $37.50 plus dependents' allowances if state benefits were received and $60.00 plus dependents' allowances if state benefits were not received. Since the great majority of benefits are paid in conjunction with UI, and since in this situation the auto plan provided a higher maximum benefit than the steel plan, the difference in experience between the two types of plans is probably attributable chiefly to this difference in their provisions. It may be attributable also to the provision in the auto plan whereby the estimated UI benefit was deducted even when UI was not actually received. The steel plan never had this provision. Finally, it may be attributable also to differences in the wages of the laid-off employees in the respective industries and to variations in the distribution of benefits according to the states in which they were paid. There are some scattered data which seem to indicate that in Michigan the proportion of auto workers limited by the maximum SUB payment was small. For example, at auto company B in 1960, only 4 percent of the benefits paid in Michigan were at the maximum, as compared with 27 percent of those paid in Texas.

SUB in relation to UI. It would be desirable to know what proportion of the combined unemployment benefit was provided by SUB and how close the combined benefit came to the proportion of wages specified in the plan (i.e., the target benefit amount). On this aspect of experience, data are available only for auto Company B in the year 1960. Appendix Table 1 shows that this company's average SUB payment ($17.12) provided 30 percent of the average combined unemployment benefit ($56.91). If every claimant had received 65 percent of his take-home pay (the benefit-wage ratio specified in the plan at that time), the average combined benefit would have been $58.06. The actual benefit ($56.91) was therefore very close in that year to the target benefit.

For this same auto company in 1960, similar data are available on a state-by-state basis. The text table below shows such data for six selected states: Connecticut, New York, and Wisconsin (high UI-benefit states), Missouri and Texas (low UI-benefit states), and Michigan (an in-between state).

State	Average SUB payment	Average UI payment	Average combined benefit (1 + 2)	SUB as % of combined benefit	Target benefit amount
	(1)	(2)	(3)	(4)	(5)
Connecticut	$ 8.83	$46.15	$54.98	16	$55.37
New York	9.92	46.47	56.39	18	57.15
Wisconsin	9.96	47.73	57.69	17	57.98
Missouri	23.29	29.51	52.80	44	57.53
Texas	28.82	27.35	56.17	51	59.23
Michigan	17.76	39.93	57.69	31	58.35

In the three high UI-benefit states, SUB averaged less than a fifth of the combined unemployment benefit; in Missouri and Texas, it averaged about half; in Michigan, about a third. The actual (combined) benefit was markedly below the target benefit only in Missouri and Texas, and even in those states the actual benefits were 92 percent and 94 percent, respectively, of the target benefit. Thus, even at this early date (1960), when the SUB maximum was only $30 (it had become $50 by 1965), the union had almost attained its announced goal of equalizing unemployment benefits for all its members, no matter in what state they worked.

Benefit Duration

The text table below presents a few data on benefit duration for two auto companies and two rubber companies in recent years. (The figures are simple averages, obtained by dividing the total number of payments by the number of different beneficiaries in a year.)

	Average number of payments per beneficiary					
	1960	1961	1962	1963	1964	1965
Auto company A				5.8		
Auto company B	3.9					
Rubber company C	8.5	13.8	n.a.	13.4	12.4	13.6
Rubber company D	7.1	13.3	8.3	12.0	11.7	12.2

For the rubber companies, average duration was about two months in two of the years (1960 and 1962) and about three months in the remaining years. Duration of benefits for the two auto companies for 1960 and 1963, respectively, was about half that of the rubber companies in the corresponding years.

The difference between the industries chiefly reflects the impact of the yearly model changeover in auto production. During the annual shutdown large numbers of auto employees experience a brief period of layoff. In the rubber industry there were fewer layoffs, but the ones that did occur were for fairly lengthy periods and may reflect the technological changes which have been occurring in that industry during recent years.

Some additional light on the duration of SUB is provided by data on SUB payments without UI. Since nearly all such payments are made to applicants who have exhausted their UI benefits, they are some indication of long-term unemployment. The text table below presents such data as are available for three companies and various years.

	Percent of regular SUB payments made without UI				
	1960	1962	1963	1964	1965
Auto company A		2	4	2	4
Auto company B	2				
Agricultural implement company B		9	11		

Even these low percentages are an overstatement of the extent to which SUB was used for long-term unemployment, not only because some of these payments were made to persons other than UI exhaustees, but also because some of the exhaustees were individuals who were entitled to only a few weeks of UI benefits.[6]

6. In addition to illuminating the area of benefit duration, this table throws some light on the highly controversial area of the "tented Arabs." The relation of the table to this problem is discussed below, at the end of the section on duration.

One measure of the adequacy of the benefit duration provided by a SUB plan is the plan's exhaustion ratio, that is, the proportion of beneficiaries who exhaust their SUB entitlement. The exhaustion ratio is a reflection of two provisions, the duration ratio, which determines the rate at which credit units are accumulated, and the maximum duration, which limits the total number of units that may be accumulated. Exhaustion of SUB after a few weeks of benefits reflects only the duration ratio, while exhaustion after a long period of unemployment may reflect also the maximum duration.

Some data on exhaustion experience were obtained for one auto company and two rubber companies. The text table below shows this data for auto company A for the years 1958, 1960, and 1963. The first year was one of severe recession, the next included part of a recession, and the third was a fairly prosperous year. During the first two years, the maximum duration provided by the plan was 26 weeks; during the third year, it was 52 weeks.

	1958	1960	1963
Beneficiaries as percent of workforce	50	38	20
Exhaustees as percent of beneficiaries	33	8	3
Exhaustees as percent of workforce	17	3	0.6

In 1958 exhaustions were very numerous, even more numerous than is indicated by the table, which reflects experience in that year only up to September. An unusual 50 percent of the entire workforce drew some SUB payments, and of these a third exhausted their credits. Thus 17 percent of the workforce needed more protection than the plan provided. The exhaustees differed considerably among themselves in the number of benefits drawn before exhaustion. As Table 9–12 shows (for auto company A), only 16 percent of the exhaustees were eligible for the maximum of 26 weeks. Thus even in this period when unemployment was heaviest and when the maximum duration was limited to 26 weeks, only 5 percent of the beneficiaries (16 percent of 33 percent) were limited by the maximum and could have taken advantage of a longer maximum duration. Here is an example of why extension of maximum duration is the least costly form of liberalization.

In 1958, exhaustees with fewer than the maximum number of credits (26) comprised 84 percent of all exhaustees and 28 percent of all beneficiaries (84 percent of 33 percent). As Table 9–12 shows, 7 percent ex-

TABLE 9–12
Percentage Distribution of Exhaustees by Number of Payments,
Auto Company A, 1957–1964

No. of payments	1957	1958[a]	1959	1960	1961	1962	1963	1964
1– 5	24	2	n.a.	14	22	17	29	24
6–10	52	5	n.a.	19	19	31	17	15
11–15	21	16	n.a.	23	17	19	15	20
16–20	2	21	n.a.	12	13	17	10	16
21–25	1	40	n.a.	7	9	9	10	9
26	[b]	16	n.a.	25	20			
26–40							7	17	9
41–52							2	7
Total	100	100		100	100	100	100	100

SOURCE: Calculated from data supplied by the company.
[a] Data for the year 1958 are limited to weeks prior to September 9.
[b] Less than 0.5 percent.

hausted within 10 weeks, while 40 percent drew benefits for 21–25 weeks; the average for all exhaustees was 20 weeks. The 84 percent who exhausted in less than 26 weeks would not have been helped by a longer maximum duration; they could have been helped only by a liberalization of the duration ratio, that is, the rate at which credits are accumulated.

The year 1960 provides a picture of the same duration provisions operating in a more favorable environment. Instead of 50 percent, only 38 percent of the workforce drew SUB and only 3 percent exhausted. These exhaustees constituted 8 percent of all beneficiaries. As shown in Table 9–12, a quarter of the exhaustees (2 percent of the beneficiaries and less than 1 percent of the workforce) drew the maximum number of benefits (26 weeks) and were probably limited by this maximum. A full third of the exhaustees were claimants eligible for 10 or fewer benefits, and over half were eligible for 15 or less. Obviously, in this year layoffs were concentrated among the more recently hired employees.

By 1963 the maximum duration had been increased to 52 weeks, so that this year reflects the operation of a higher maximum in a period of prosperity. In this year only 20 percent of the workforce drew SUB and only 0.6 percent exhausted their benefits. The exhaustees comprised 3 percent of the total number of beneficiaries. As shown in Table 9–12, 19 percent of the exhaustees (0.6 percent of the beneficiaries and 0.1 percent of the workforce) drew 26 or more benefits and were therefore helped by the longer maximum provided by the negotiations of 1961. In 1963, only 2 percent of the exhaustees drew benefits for 52 weeks and could thus attribute their benefit exhaustion to the limitation imposed by the maximum. The rest were limited by the duration ratio, that is, the rate at which credits are accumulated.

The text table below is a convenient summary of the main conclusions that have been drawn from the preceding text table and Table 9–12.

Exhaustees limited by	1958		1960		1963	
	Exhaustees as % of		Exhaustees as % of		Exhaustees as % of	
	Benefi-ciaries	Work-force	Benefi-ciaries	Work-force	Benefi-ciaries	Work-force
Maximum duration	5	2.3	2	0.8	0.06	0.01
Duration ratio	28	14.7	6	2.2	2.94	0.59
Total	33	17.0	8	3.0	3.00	0.60

Although derived from the experience of only one auto company, the data are probably representative of the experience of most of the other auto companies and of the agricultural implement companies.

Data on the exhaustion experience of rubber company C and rubber company D for the five years 1960 through 1964 are shown in the following text table. As compared with the workforce of auto company A, the employees of these two rubber companies seem to have experienced less unemployment (beneficiaries as a percent of the workforce), but a larger proportion of those who did become unemployed exhausted their benefits (exhaustions as a percent of beneficiaries).

	Year and company									
	1960		1961		1962		1963		1964	
	C	D	C	D	C	D	C	D	C	D
Beneficiaries as % of workforce	8	16	21	19	n.a.	8	6	11	9	18
Exhaustees as % of beneficiaries	n.a.	2	21	15	n.a.	16	24	34	19	14
Exhaustees as % of workforce	n.a.	0.3	4.2	2.9	n.a.	1.3	1.4	3.7	1.7	2.5

This difference in experience may be accounted for by either one of two factors, or both. Since the layoffs were somewhat lighter in rubber than in autos, they may have been concentrated to a greater extent among low-seniority employees, who would have fewer credit units and therefore would exhaust sooner. On the other hand, layoffs in rubber companies, as contrasted with the typical seasonal layoffs of the auto industry, may have reflected more long-term unemployment, and may thus have produced a higher exhaustion ratio. Lacking data on the length of unemployment prior to exhaustion, it is not possible to assign weights to these two factors. The low percentages in the last line of the table, exhaustees as a percent of the workforce, indicate that even before 1965, when the maximum duration was increased to 52 weeks, the duration provisions had proved reasonably adequate.

SUB without UI

It will be recalled from Chapter 4 that SUB's dependence on UI has been a controversial issue from the beginning and that the Auto Workers have gradually succeeded in negotiating some exceptions ("tented Arabs") to the requirement that eligibility for SUB presupposes eligibility for UI. Experience under these exceptions is reflected in the text table above (p. 217), which shows for three companies the percent of regular SUB payments made without UI. This table can be used to establish parameters for the controversy and to mark the outer limits of its significance.

The table reflects experience under all the exceptions combined. The percentages in the table are small, even for this combined experience. But further, these small percentages primarily reflect the least controversial of the exceptions, that which provides for payment of SUB after UI benefits have been exhausted. For example, of the figures in the table, exhaustion of UI benefits accounted for four fifths of the 2 percent of auto company B in 1960, four fifths of the 4 percent for auto company A in 1963, and three fourths of the 11 percent for agricultural implement company B in 1963. The remaining small proportions of these small percentages represent the outer limits of the number of benefits which involve the more controversial exceptions. If these available data are at all representative, it would seem that, quantitatively, the controversial "Arabs" have not been important.

It should not be assumed, however, that the incidence of cases involving the "Arabs" is a measure of the importance of the larger issue of SUB and its impact on labor relations. As Chapter 11 shows, this larger issue encompasses much more than the "Arabs."

Costs

As was remarked in the previous chapter, the costs of SUB may be reckoned in terms of contributions or of benefits and may be expressed as a total dollar amount or as an amount per man-hour. The data are reported in the form of total dollar amounts and are discussed first in this simpler form. Generally, cost data were available for four auto companies, four agricultural companies, and four rubber companies.

Total Dollar Amount

Appendix Table 2 shows the annual contributions and benefits under the plans of these 12 companies during the 10-year period 1956–1965. During this period, the auto companies contributed $488.4 million, of which 50 percent was paid in benefits. The agricultural implement companies contributed $62.4 million, of which 41 percent was paid in benefits. The rubber companies contributed $28.6 million, of which 68 percent was paid in benefits.

The auto-type plan operates with a clear countercyclical effect, as may be seen in the contrasting behavior of contributions and benefits in the recessions of 1957–1958 and 1960–1961. During these two periods, contributions fell markedly as benefit payments rose. They fell for two reasons. The first is obvious: there were fewer man-hours on which the employer had to make a contribution. The second reason is less obvious but equally important. In the auto-type plan, maximum financing is based on the size of the workforce (those employed plus those on layoff with credit units). As this base decreases, the level of maximum financing becomes lower and more easily attained.[7] When the level of maximum financing has been attained, all contributions are suspended. It is possible, therefore, that an employer will reach maximum financing and be free of the obligation to contribute to the fund just at the time when the flow out of the fund is greatest. For example, auto company A's fund fell by $1 million between April and May 1958, but its relationship to maximum financing rose from 71 percent to 116 percent, and contributions ceased.

Appendix Table 3 also shows this countercyclical characteristic of the funding formula. Three of the four auto companies reached maximum financing during the recession of 1958 and did not drop significantly below this level until late 1959. The agricultural implement companies reached maximum financing somewhat later, in various months of 1959, and the rubber companies reached it in various months of 1960. These companies reached maximum financing at a later date than did the auto companies because, since they had less unemployment, their maximum financing level did not drop so sharply. Most firms in all three industries reached maximum financing in a number of months during the recession of 1961.

In a period of decreasing employment, this countercyclical effect is clearly desirable: it helps the employer at no immediate cost to the employee. (The employees who are members of the workforce when the employer's contribution decreases are still protected, inasmuch as financing

7. For example, a decrease of 1 in the workforce, on which maximum financing is calculated, may reduce the amount needed to reach maximum financing by as much as $544, which is equivalent to a saving of the 5-cent contribution on more than 10,000 man-hours.

for them is still at the maximum level.) The effect of the financing formula in a time of increasing employment may be less desirable. It tends to act as a deterrent to new hiring because each added employee makes maximum financing the harder to attain. A method of financing based, as are most of the auto plans, on current employment is more cyclically sensitive during both the downswing and the upswing than one based on hours worked or on a moving average of the number employed in a past period (but see Appendix B, n. 9).

Appendix Tables 2 and 3 reflect not only fluctuations in unemployment but also changes in the financing formula itself. In 1961, in the auto and agricultural implement industries, the level of maximum financing was raised to support an increase in the regular benefit and the inauguration of short-week benefits. The higher level of maximum financing resulted in most companies making large contributions in the period 1962–1965, even though benefits in this period were low. The rubber plan increased benefits in 1963 but, instead of raising the level of maximum financing, the plan upped the maximum contribution from 3 cents to 4 cents. This alternative method of supporting the burden of additional benefits avoids the danger of overfunding which is inherent in the method of raising the maximum-financing level.

Costs per Man-Hour

Costs per man-hour, which represent the most significant measure of cost, were sometimes reported directly but more often had to be estimated.[8] Estimates for four auto and three agricultural implement plans during the first decade of their experience are shown in the text table below.

Estimated Costs in Cents per Man-Hour, 1956–1965

Plan	Contributions	Benefits
Auto co. A-UAW	4.3–4.5	2.1–2.2
Auto co. B-UAW	4.0–4.1	1.8–1.9
Auto co. C-UAW	4.1	2.7
Auto co. D-UAW	5.7	3.9
Agr. impl. co. A-UAW	4.5	1.7
Agr. impl. co. B-UAW	4.1	2.9
Agr. impl. co. C-UAW	4.7	1.8

Except for auto company D, the man-hour contribution cost of each of these companies was between 4 and 5 cents, with auto company B having

8. The major problem of estimation is to convert total contributions to contributions in cents per hour. Where the latter is known, the cost of benefits in cents per hour may easily be calculated by multiplying the ratio of total benefits to total contributions by the basic man-hour contribution cost. The estimates used here are largely based on the same reports from which Appendix Tables 2 and 3 are drawn.

the lowest cost. Costs in the earlier period, 1956–1961, were similar to those in the later period, 1962–1965. The effect of the heavier unemployment experienced in the earlier period was balanced in the later period by a higher benefit rate and a higher level of maximum financing. Also, as explained above, the increased employment of the later period made the maximum-financing level the harder to reach.

The cost of benefits in the 10-year period was considerably less than the cost of contributions and varied more among the companies. The estimated benefit cost in four of the seven plans was around 2 cents per man-hour. In two other plans it was close to 3 cents, and in one plan it was almost 4 cents. Although not shown in the table, there was considerable variation among companies in costs for different periods. Among the auto companies, the highest figure was 17.6 cents for Company D during 1961 and the lowest figure (after the plans became fully functioning) was 0.5 cents for Company C during the first four years of operation. Among the agricultural implement companies, the highest figure was 6.0 cents in 1960–1961 for Company B, and the lowest figure was 0.2 cents for Company C during the first year and a half of operation.

Because of the way in which maximum financing is calculated, as explained above, it is possible for a company with high benefit costs to pay contributions at a lower rate than one with low benefit costs. For example, over the 10-year period in the auto industry, Company C had benefit costs of 2.7 cents per man-hour as against Company A's cost of about 2.1 cents, yet Company C contributed at a rate of only 4.1 cents as against Company A's contribution of about 4.4 cents. For another example, agricultural implement company B had the highest benefit cost (2.9 cents) but the lowest contribution rate (4.1 cents) of the three companies in that industry; in contrast Company A's benefit cost was 1.8 cents, while its contribution rate was 4.7 cents.

In the rubber industry, the cost of contributions was considerably less than in the other two industries. During the period in which the maximum contribution was 3 cents (1956–1962) all of the rubber companies were at, or almost at, the maximum financing level and therefore paid less than 3 cents in a considerable number of months — 36 months in the case of Company A, 23 months in the case of Company B, 8 months in the case of Company C, 30 months in the case of Company D. Although the maximum contribution was increased to 4 cents in 1963, since maximum financing was not increased the 4 cents were not paid unless needed. For two of the four companies the full 4-cent contribution was needed, while for the other two it was not.

The man-hour costs of benefits in the rubber plans could not readily be estimated. However, because total benefits were significantly less than total contributions for each of the rubber companies, as indicated above, the man-hour costs of benefits must have been proportionately less than the man-hour costs of contributions. They were also less than similar costs in the auto and agricultural implement industries.

Fund Adequacy

As of 1965, all but 2 of the 12 plans whose experience is described in this chapter had been able to pay full benefits at all times. The two exceptions were auto companies — Chrysler and American Motors — which, at different times, had to reduce the potential duration of benefits. All the other funds maintained a strong position throughout the 10-year period, as may be seen in Appendix Table 3, which shows that the funds were usually above 50 percent of maximum funding. Not recorded here is the experience of the Studebaker Corporation, which, when it closed its South Bend plant in 1963, was able to pay only a small fraction of its SUB liabilities.

In 1961, despite the strong position of the funds, the UAW negotiated an increase in maximum funding in the auto and agricultural implement plans. There were probably three reasons for this increase. First, changes negotiated in 1961 had put new burdens on the funds in the form of a higher benefit amount and the addition of short-week benefits. Second, the increase in maximum funding helped to equalize the cost of the plan among the companies. Without any increase, one auto company would have been paying the full 5-cent contribution, while the others, which were already at maximum funding, would have been paying nothing.[9] Third, the union probably had its eye on the money that some companies (those at or near the maximum) were saving and that the union considered it was losing. By raising the level of maximum funding, the union could prevent any further such loss, at least for a time.[10]

By the end of 1965, the SUB funds of the core auto-type plans were certainly adequate and may have been overfinanced. Two auto companies had paid out in benefits less than 50 percent of their contributions in the 10-year period; three agricultural implement companies had paid out less than 40 percent. Several companies reported that in some states their SUB reserves were greater than their UI reserves. None of the plans is designed,

9. Among the agricultural implement companies, a different disparity existed: in 1961, Company B had paid out benefits equal to 73 percent of its contributions (Table 9-13) and yet was at maximum funding (Appendix Table 3), while the other companies with less unemployment were still liable for contributions.

10. In 1964, when maximum funding could not well be increased again because the reserves were already adequate, the union took the direct step of diverting to other employee-benefit funds any savings that might otherwise have accrued to the companies.

of course, to withstand a long-term major decline of the company. To achieve protection against such a risk, it would be necessary to devise some form of reinsurance. The UAW has proposed that the auto companies contribute to a common fund for this purpose, but its proposal has never been accepted. The alternative would be for the union to establish a rein-surance system of its own — a supplement to SUB.

The text table below presents, for the auto and agricultural implement industries, a useful measure of adequacy: the ability of the fund to carry the heaviest annual benefit load in the plan's history. For each plan, the figures show the value of the fund at the end of 1965 as a multiple of the product of the largest annual number of regular benefits paid in the 10-year period and the average benefit amount in 1965.

Auto co. A-UAW	3.0
Auto co. B-UAW	3.7
Auto co. C-UAW	1.7
Auto co. D-UAW	1.0
Agr. impl. co. A-UAW	12.0
Agr. impl. co. B-UAW	1.4
Agr. impl. co. C-UAW	1.5
Agr. impl. co. D-UAW	4.3

Even without further contributions, all of these funds could pay regular benefits equal to the heaviest yearly demand of the last decade. The multiple varied generally between 1 and 4, with one fund having a multiple of 12.

Maximum funding has always been lower in the rubber plan than in the auto plan. In the rubber plan before 1965, maximum funding was $185 per covered employee, as compared with the original maximum of $400 and the later (1961) maximum of $544 in the auto plan. The first increase in the rubber plan occurred in 1965, when maximum funding was raised to $250 per covered employee[11] (see also Appendix B).

During the 10-year period, the rubber plans were also adequately financed. Although contributions for the four companies amounted to less than 3 cents during this period, the cost of benefits was even less, and the ratio of benefits to contributions was moderate, even under the older and lower level of maximum funding (Appendix Table 3).

If unemployment for these companies during the next 10 years is no

11. The union had been asking for this increase in maximum funding since 1961, but the companies had resisted. In 1965, the companies themselves proposed that the level be raised. The companies' changed attitude may be traceable in part to the negotiation of the "hard nickel" in 1965. Since no part of the contribution could any longer be saved, the companies may have preferred to pay money into a SUB fund rather than to distribute it as a Christmas bonus.

heavier than it was during the 1955–1965 decade, they should have no difficulty in meeting all the claims that may be made upon their SUB plans while they continue operating under the 1965 provisions. Future liberalizations of eligibility and benefit provisions could, of course, change the picture somewhat but would never be so important a factor as the future pattern of unemployment itself.

10

EXPERIENCE UNDER MULTI-EMPLOYER SUB PLANS

As explained in Chapter 2, the multi-employer device has expanded the scope of SUB and made it a possibility in industries to which such a plan might at first sight seem unsuitable. Although the numbers currently covered by multi-employer plans are not great, interest in such plans has been growing in recent years, and they have penetrated new industries. The future may very well see a marked increase in their numbers. Hence particular interest attaches to experience under these plans.

Another reason for the interest in multi-employer plans is their similarity to UI. Because they resemble UI more than do the single-employer plans, their experience is more relevant to the issue discussed in Chapter 11 — whether experience under SUB establishes the feasibility of liberalizing UI benefits to the point where they equal the combined benefits provided by the typical SUB plan.

Although the data presented here are fragmentary, they suffice to indicate what a more complete investigation might yield. In the case of at least some of the multi-employer plans, the chief limitation on the presentation of SUB experience in this study was not so much lack of data as lack of resources (time and personnel) at the command of the researcher. Considerable information is available in this area, waiting to be gathered and analyzed by some future investigator. The reader will recall that the plans whose experience is narrated here are described in Chapter 2. He will usually find it necessary to review the description in order to understand this narration.

Maritime Workers (NMU)

The drop of 40 percent in seafaring employment in the four years preceding the inauguration of the Maritime Workers' Employment Security Plan was an important factor in bringing that plan into existence. In the course of the first decade of the plan's operation, seafaring jobs decreased by about another 20 percent. The plan, therefore, has undergone a substantial test, and the union's interest in it has remained strong.

Table 10–1 shows annual benefit payments; included are severance payments, which were added to the plan in 1961. As is clear, the maritime

TABLE 10-1

Claims Paid, All Types, Employment Security Plan of Maritime Workers (NMU), Number and Amount, by Year, 1957-1965

Year	Regular[a] employment security claims		Severance payments[b]
	No.	Amount	
1957	3,925	$ 182,685	—
1958	7,648	458,574	—
1959	9,206	668,171	—
1960	9,088	628,146	—
1961	8,126	581,174	$ 95,933
1962	10,380	1,076,852	645,750
1963	15,207	1,730,907	722,729
1964	11,587	1,058,292	787,838
1965	19,021	2,304,698	617,328
Totals	94,188	$8,689,499	$2,869,578

SOURCE: National Maritime Union.
[a] For the definition of "regular" claims, see text.
[b] Severance payments were added to the plan in 1961.

industry is not markedly sensitive to cyclical influences, which are over-shadowed by the forces of secular decline. The unusually large increase of 1963 over 1962 was attributable to two special events — the longshoremen's strike at the beginning of 1963 and, later, the lay-up of the S.S. "America." The sharp increase in payments in 1965 was also attributable, at least in part, to a strike of masters, mates, and pilots, which idled the seamen without affecting their eligibility for SUB or UI.

On the average, about 70 percent of payments from the fund have been in the form of "regular" payments and the remaining 30 percent in the form of severance. "Regular" payments are made to seamen in the following situations: laid off, waiting to reship after vacation, suffering disability preventing reshipment, waiting to reship after disability, engaged in legal proceedings, and taking care of a disabled spouse. Three of these six situations reflect genuine unemployment, while three do not. Payments for layoffs have accounted for over 70 percent of all the regular benefits, and at least two thirds of the remainder have consisted of payments to seamen waiting to reship after a vacation or waiting to reship after disability. Hence, over 90 percent of all benefits paid from the fund have been genuine unemployment benefits.

For the most recent year for which data are available (1965), Table 10-2 shows the distribution of claims, other than severance payments, according

TABLE 10–2

Number and Amount of Regular Claims Paid by Employment Security Plan
of Maritime Workers (NMU), 1965, by Duration of Claim

Duration of claim (in weeks)	No. of claims paid		Amount of claims paid	
	No.	% distribution	Amount	% distribution
Less than 1	441	2.3	$ 5,947.31	0.3
1 but less than 2	4,231	22.2	169,657.82	7.4
2 but less than 3	3,742	19.7	250,786.64	10.9
3 but less than 4	2,028	10.7	185,534.96	8.1
4 but less than 5	2,022	10.6	256,961.01	11.1
5 but less than 6	1,474	7.7	228,389.05	9.9
6 but less than 7	907	4.8	173,987.14	7.5
7 but less than 8	2,026	10.7	507,766.85	22.0
8 but less than 9	2,132	11.2	517,913.45	22.5
9 or more	18	0.1	7,753.91	0.3
Total	19,021	100.0	$2,304,698.14	100.0

SOURCE: National Maritime Union.

to duration. Claims of less than four weeks' duration made up over half of the total number of claims but accounted for only a fourth of the total benefit amount. At the other end of the distribution, claims of eight weeks' duration (the normal maximum) accounted for only about 11 percent of the total number of claims but represented 22 percent of the total benefit amount.

Administrative costs have been on the high side as compared with costs in some of the other plans. As a proportion of benefits paid, administrative costs amounted to 15 percent in 1963, 21 percent in 1964, and 17 percent in 1965.

Since the weekly SUB payment has been notably higher when UI is not payable ($40 instead of $25), it would be desirable to know the proportion of benefits paid without UI. The available data, however, do not show this distribution.

The stipulated contribution of 25 cents per man-day has been more than adequate to finance the program. Indeed, the fund grew so fast that contributions were discontinued for the two-year period June 1963–July 1965. During this period, covered employers contributed an additional 25 cents to the pension fund instead. Beginning in July 1965, the employers resumed their 25-cent contribution to the Employment Security Plan and began to make an additional 25-cent contribution to a newly established automation fund, from which benefits were to be paid to seamen laid off or demoted because of technological changes.

A contribution of 25 cents per day amounts to about 3 cents per man-hour. Since this amount was more than adequate to pay all the various types of benefits, and since layoff benefits amounted to about two thirds of total benefits, the cost of benefits for unemployment resulting from layoff could not have been more than about 2 cents per man-hour.

As usual in multi-employer plans, the financing arrangement did not provide employers with any additional incentive to avoid unemployment. (The contribution is uniform and there is no opportunity for employers, even as a group, to save on this contribution.) The issue of incentive has particular significance in this plan because the maritime industry operates with the aid of a substantial government subsidy. As of 1964, a federal "operating differential subsidy" accounted for 72 cents out of every dollar of wages received by seamen on subsidized ships. In July of 1965, the Maritime Subsidy Board disallowed subsidy reimbursement for certain wage and benefit increases negotiated under three collective bargaining agreements. The Board held that the wage increases exceeded the Presidential wage guidelines and that the pensions were considerably higher than those paid in other industries. Although the Secretary of Commerce reversed this decision of the Board, he recognized the need to exercise some control over collective bargaining in the maritime industry: "It has become increasingly evident during recent years that the Government...cannot continue, in good conscience, to give routine and automatic approval of substantial wage and employee benefit increases after collective bargaining agreements have been signed" [55].

Garment Workers (ILGWU)

This, the largest of the multi-employer plans, pays benefits only in the event of a company's going out of business. Table 10–3 shows the number of terminated shops (this is the language of the plan) each year and the payments of severance and unemployment benefits that resulted from the closings.[1] The two types of benefits are not alternatives but are additive, that is, every eligible separated employee receives a lump-sum severance payment; the employee who remains unemployed receives, in addition, weekly SUB payments. SUB payments have been the larger of the two, averaging about 60 percent of total payments.

The numbers of terminated shops and resulting applications each year are remarkably uniform and reflect little cyclical sensitivity. This situation probably mirrors the good business conditions that have prevailed in the

---

1. In 1967, the name of the plan was changed to Supplemental Unemployment Fund and the severance payments were renamed "lump-sum benefits."

TABLE 10-3

Terminated Shops, Applications, and Amount of Payments, SUB Plan of Garment Workers (ILGWU), by Year and Type of Payment, Inception through 1965

Year	Terminated shops		Applications[a] for benefits		Amount of payments		
	No.	% of all shops (estimated)	No.	% of all covered employees	Severance	SUB	Total
	(1)	(2)	(3)	(4)	(5)	(6)	(7)
Inception–1961	305	2.7	5,958	1.5	$ 666,328	$ 800,280	$ 1,466,608
1962	440	3.7	9,824	2.3	1,074,687	1,606,380	2,681,030
1963	482	4.1	9,547	2.2	1,004,558	1,671,240	2,675,835
1964	467	3.9	9,836	2.3	1,056,700	1,768,022	2,824,722
1965	426	3.5	9,449	2.2	1,035,859	1,490,996	2,526,855
Inception–1965	2,120	—	44,614	—	$4,838,132	$7,336,918	$12,175,050

SOURCE: International Ladies' Garment Workers' Union.

[a] This approximates closely the number of different applicants.

garment industry during the period in which the plan has been functioning. If the economic climate should become less favorable, the numbers of terminated shops and of applications would probably rise. Because the industry expects this to happen eventually, it has continuously strengthened the reserve of the fund.

As could be expected from such a limited plan, relatively few of the covered employees became beneficiaries. On the average, of the 425,000 to 450,000 covered employees, only about 2 percent drew one or more benefits in any given year.

This plan records the relationship between potential and actual duration in SUB — that is, between the maximum number of weeks of benefits which applicants are entitled to draw and the weeks they actually draw. On the average, applicants have used something over half of their potential duration. As occurs regularly in UI also, the ratio of utilization tends to decrease as potential duration increases. The average number of weeks utilized per applicant has been about 10.

In recent years, of all the applicants, more than four fifths have been women and about two thirds have been aged 45 or older. For the period 1960–1963, the percent distribution of applicants by length of employment with the terminating employer is shown below. As may be seen, in these years over 40 percent of the applicants had been employed by the terminating employer for less than 5 years and about a quarter had been employed for 10 years or longer.

Percent Distribution of Applicants by
Number of Years Employed in Terminated Shop

Year	1–4	5–9	10–15	16 or more	Total
1960	49	25	15	11	100
1961	48	29	14	9	100
1962	43	31	16	10	100
1963	44	29	17	10	100

As of the end of 1965, the appeals committee had heard about 150 appeals from firms and about 400 from individuals. The administrator's original decision was upheld in about two thirds of the cases in each category. Most appeals turned on the technical question of the eligibility of those workers who had been employed by firms which were considered "successor" organizations.

Annual receipts and disbursements, for SUB and severance payments combined, are listed below. As shown, receipts regularly exceeded disbursements, so that by the end of 1965 reserves in the fund totaled over $27 million.

Year	Receipts	Disbursements	Excess
1958	$ 415,935.00	$ 176,676.00	$ 239,259.00
1959	2,755,496.00	76,570.00	2,678,926.00
1960	4,961,047.00	152,946.00	4,808,101.00
1961	5,850,852.00	1,514,176.00	4,336,676.00
1962	5,962,879.00	2,733,078.00	3,229,801.00
1963	6,428,182.00	3,203,703.00	3,224,479.00
1964	6,847,607.00	3,331,357.00	3,516,250.00
1965	7,259,084.00	3,013,425.00	4,245,659.00

In recent years, administrative expenses have averaged about 6 percent of benefits paid. In comparison with the costs of other multi-employer plans, this is reasonably low. As would be expected, it is higher than the administrative cost of the union's pension fund, which in the same period averaged about 4 percent of benefits paid.

The following excerpt is taken from the administrator's 1965 report to the board of trustees. The reader may find it a welcome oasis in a dry desert of data. Entitled "A Case in Our Records," the excerpt reads:

Behind the statistics are people. Such were the almost 300 trained artisans who were employed in a rather small New England town near the Canadian border.

The owner of the firm, who was known as one of the deans of the industry, was able to provide employment opportunity to the town since the early 1940's. Within a short time, the shop became an important economic support of the community which had few small factories.

Recently, the college-trained sons of the original owner decided to liquidate the shop. As a result, during the Christmas season of 1963, the employees were told that the factory would be closed as of the New Year. Workers who had been employed up to 20 years with the firm were forced to search for new employment, if it could be found. As of the present [1965], efforts to interest employers in availing themselves of the reservoir of trained workers have proved futile.

Approximately $150,000 in benefits from the Fund were distributed to the workers involved, which together with state employment benefits helped ease the economic catastrophe. It is this kind of human situation which is reflected in the tables found in this report.

Detroit Electrical Workers (IBEW)

As of mid-1966, after two and a half years of operation, this plan had not made a single SUB payment. Although there is thus no "experience" to record, the lack itself is significant. The complete absence of payments is compelling evidence of administrative control of claims. This degree of control is the more significant because of the circumstances: the administrator of the plan was a former union member; and also, the plan provided for considerable freedom from UI (see Chapter 2).

In June of 1966, when the author was in Detroit examining this plan, there were 65 jobs on the union's open list. At the same time there were 20 unemployed union members who did not want any of the jobs on the open list. None of these unemployed members was receiving SUB. Most likely, they had not even applied for it. If they had applied, they would have been offered one of the open jobs on the list. According to the contract, they would have been allowed to refuse one such offer without loss of SUB. If they had refused a second job, which would have been offered to them immediately, they would have become ineligible for SUB and would have gone to the bottom of the employment list.

In all probability, most of them succeeded in drawing some UI benefits. In the UI program, a claimant is allowed some little time to find the kind of job he wants. If a particular job market is controlled by a union, as is almost universally true in the construction industry, the UI agency is especially likely to allow a union member some "canvassing time" before pressuring him to take a particular open job.

Three circumstances probably facilitated claims control in this plan at that time (June 1966). First, the job market was very tight. If the administrator had approved the payment of benefits, the contributing employers, who could not get enough workers at the time, would probably have entered a vigorous protest. Second, there was a kind of experience-rating feature of the plan which operated to prevent unnecessary payments. To illustrate: in the 1965 negotiations, the employer contribution of 15 cents per man-hour was cut to 5 cents, and the 10-cent saving was put into wages. Although from the employer's viewpoint there was no possibility of saving, and hence no experience rating, from the viewpoint of the union the fact that reductions in contributions could result in higher wages constituted a direct incentive to avoid unnecessary expenditures from the fund. In this sense, the plan was "experience-rated." Third, the total weekly benefit provided by the plan ($30 plus UI) equaled only about 50 percent of the average union member's take-home wage. An unemployed man had considerable incentive, therefore, to prefer work and wages to unemployment and benefits.

Plumbers and Pipefitters (PPF)

SUB plans have been negotiated by PPF locals in the New York and Detroit areas. Since the plans of the New York locals are of the individual-account type and have only a minimal relationship to UI, it would not be the best use of limited space to include here a detailed statistical account of their experience. However it is worthwhile to note one interesting aspect of their experience, using New York Plumbers' Local No. 2 as an example.

The Additional Security Benefit Fund (ASBF) of Local No. 2 pays four types of benefits. It supplements three New York State programs — unemployment, disability, workmen's compensation — and also supplies payments to meet "emergencies." In the first three situations there is available a proof of entitlement, a check from the state, and payment from the ASBF is almost automatic. In the fourth case, the ASBF administrator, a former union official, must judge whether the emergency warrants payment from the fund. "Emergency" payments have been increasing to the point where this category has become larger than the other three combined. For example, in the first nine months of 1965, payments under the four categories were as follows: supplemental unemployment, $476,000; supplemental disability, $61,000; supplemental workmen's compensation, $19,000; emergency withdrawals, $790,000.

To retain the fund's tax-exempt status, the plan must be selective in its definition of "emergency," and the administrator must deny many requests of union members for such payments. The members have grown restive under this enforced restraint, and a strong faction within the local has proposed giving up the advantage of tax exemption in exchange for greater freedom in drawing on the fund. Administrators of the fund are reluctant to see this development take place, not only because of the loss of tax-exempt status but also because they fear that the fund will quickly be dissipated. The issues involved in this choice are essentially those that face a union when it must decide whether to negotiate a SUB plan at all and, if so, whether the plan should be of the pooled or of the individual-account type.

It will be recalled that the Detroit locals — No. 98 of the Plumbers and No. 636 of the Pipefitters — established pooled-fund plans, which paid three types of benefits. The experience of Plumbers' Local 98 in paying these benefits during 1965 and 1966, as shown below, illustrates again how few unemployment benefits are paid when the demand for labor is strong and jobs are available.

Benefit	1965		1966	
	Weeks	*Amount*	*Weeks*	*Amount*
Unemployment (SUB)	0	0	411	$14,385.00
Workmen's compensation	274	$ 9,590.00	282	9,870.00
Nonoccupational disability	408	14,280.00	1,063	37,205.00
Totals	682	$23,870.00	1,756	$61,460.00

In 1965, no unemployment benefits at all were paid; in 1966 the insured unemployment rate (the number on layoff as a percentage of the covered workforce) averaged less than 0.1 percent over the course of the year. The evidence of this plan reinforces the conclusion reached in the review of the Electrical Workers' plan: even though administered by someone other than the employer himself, and even though not controlled by the UI definition of suitable work, such plans can operate without developing any significant amount of "abuse."

During the two years shown in the table, unemployment benefits comprised about 17 percent of the total benefits paid from the fund. The cause of the large increase in disability benefits in 1966 was not ascertained.

Carpenters (CJA)

Of the several carpenters' SUB plans noted in Chapter 2, some data on experience were obtained from the largest, the plan of the Buffalo District Carpenters. Established in 1960, the plan began to collect contributions in June of 1961. It began to pay benefits in January of 1962, without the usual preliminary year or two for the accumulation of funds. By May of 1962 the plan was overdrawn by $13,000. In this crisis two amendments were negotiated: the employers' contribution was tripled (from 5 cents to 15 cents per man-hour) and the benefit amount was doubled (from $10 to $20 per week). New forms of benefits and new contributions were added in succeeding years until by the end of fiscal 1965 the fund was paying, besides supplemental unemployment benefits, supplemental workmen's compensation benefits, supplemental disability benefits, and benefits for jury duty. The unemployment benefits had been increased to $35 per week for the first 26 weeks and $50 per week for the next 26 weeks. The employer's contribution had been increased to 42 cents per man-hour, of which 30 cents or more represented the liability of unemployment benefits.

In fiscal 1964 and 1965, which were average years for the construction industry in the Buffalo area, unemployment benefits comprised about 90 percent of all benefits paid from the fund. During these years, payments for the three principal reasons were as follows:

Year	Workmen's compensation	Disability	SUB
1964	$13,650	$16,750	$360,390
1965	20,080	35,330	421,190

This great preponderance of unemployment benefits is not found in the other plans that provide the same three types of payments. Although all the reasons for this preponderance have not been ascertained, one reason certainly is seasonal unemployment. In construction, especially in a northern city like Buffalo, unemployment has a marked seasonal pattern. In 1965, for example, 51 percent of all SUB payments were made in the four months January through April. Because of seasonal unemployment, a large proportion of all employees covered by the SUB plan draw some benefits in the course of a year. As may be seen below, there is a very wide sharing in the benefits of the program, wider than in any other SUB plan for which data are available.

Fiscal year	Individual beneficiaries		No. of benefits
	No.	As % of all covered employees	
1963	1,260	50	17,033
1964	1,103	44	12,013
1965	1,071	43	12,034
1966	967	35	n.a.

Although the proportion of employees drawing one or more benefits in the course of a year fell in 1966, a boom year for construction in the Buffalo area, it was still over one third, and the average for the four years was over 40 percent.

Administrative costs for this plan have been moderate. In recent years, they have been averaging about 2 percent of contributions and about 6 percent of benefits. Very little use has been made of the extended benefits which are available after the first 26 weeks. Of the 12,034 benefit checks paid in fiscal 1965, only 479 were $50 checks.

Bricklayers (BMP) Local 45

This local, also of Buffalo, New York, negotiated a SUB plan at about the same time as did the Carpenters. The Bricklayers' plan, which was mentioned but not described in Chapter 2, is essentially similar to the Carpenters' plan except that it pays only unemployment benefits. As of 1965, covered employers in the Construction Industry Employers Association of Buffalo were making a contribution of 10 cents per man-hour, and benefits were set at a flat rate of $15.00 per week up to a maximum duration of 26 weeks. As is usual in multi-employer plans, eligibility for UI was a prerequisite for eligibility for SUB.

The trustees of this plan have followed a conservative financing policy. At the end of fiscal 1965, the fund had over $200,000 in reserve, an amount sufficient — on the basis of experience — to pay two years of benefits without further contributions. Nevertheless, the 1965 report of the trustees warned: "In such times, when the Fund balance is substantial, it will be necessary for the Committee [Joint SUB Fund Committee] to resist the temptation to enlarge or extend the benefit payments, because it must be realized we are in the beginning of a building boom which can go on in the Buffalo area for a few years but not forever. When this boom has finally subsided and all the needed buildings and other facilities have been built, then will their SUB fund be called upon to help the participants during the years of lighter work until the next surge for work makes itself felt again."

As in the case of carpenters, unemployment among bricklayers has a marked seasonal pattern. In 1963, 1964, and 1965, unemployment benefits paid in the first three months of the year (January through March) were 69 percent, 53 percent, and 49 percent, respectively, of the total year's benefits.

Administrative expenses were similar in size to those of the Carpenters' plan. In relation to benefits paid, administrative expenses were 5.5 percent in fiscal 1963, 6.0 percent in fiscal 1964, and 10 percent in fiscal 1965. The increase in the percentage in 1965 mainly reflects the decrease in the amount of benefits paid that year.

Retail Clerks (RCIA) Local 770

The SUB plan negotiated by this union with the Food Employers Council of Southern California stands out, even among multi-employer plans, for its similarity to UI. Hence it has special relevance for the issue as to whether experience under SUB constitutes a valid argument for paying equally liberal benefits in the UI program (see Chapter 11). The eligibility conditions in this plan were, if anything, easier than those in UI. As in UI, open jobs in the industry were filled through the state employment service, and the plan's disqualifications were the same as in the California UI program, which allowed the payment of benefits under some conditions to employees who had voluntarily quit their jobs.

Here also, the available data on experience were not complete. Although this plan will be able to supply a wealth of information eventually — when the data have been put on tapes and computerized — only a fraction of the potential information was available at the time this study was being made.

The SUB fund is used to supplement three state programs, UI, workmen's compensation, and disability payments. The tabulation below shows SUB payments as a proportion of the total benefits paid from the fund.

Year	Total payments	SUB payments		Administrative expenses	
		Amount	% of total payments	Amount	% of total benefits
1961	$1,200,065	$673,722	56	$52,320	4.4
1962	1,039,039	561,430	54	54,082	5.2
1963	1,155,093	494,113	42	49,437	4.3
1964	1,117,409	456,748	41	52,514	4.7

In the recession year of 1961, SUB payments amounted to 56 percent of total payments from the fund, but they had declined to 41 percent by 1964, when employment was relatively high. These proportions are lower than in the Buffalo Carpenters' plan, but higher than in the Detroit Plumbers' plan.

Employers have contributed to the plan at the rate of 2 cents per man-hour. Since this contribution has proved adequate to finance the three types of benefits, and since SUB payments comprised only half of the total payments for the period, it follows that the cost of unemployment benefits has not been more than 1 cent per hour. This cost makes it one of the least expensive of the SUB plans.

The relatively low cost of SUB payments under this plan is partially explained by the relatively high California UI benefits, which accounted for a greater-than-average share of the combined unemployment benefit. Another explanation is the relatively low unemployment rate which characterizes retail trade as a whole. A comparison of the average insured rate[2] for all industries and for wholesale and retail trade during the recession year of 1961 and the prosperous year of 1965 shows that in both years trade had an unemployment rate well below that for all industries. The rates are national averages.

Year	All industries	Wholesale and retail trade
1961	5.6	3.4
1965	3.2	2.1

The low cost of unemployment benefits under the plan are the more noteworthy because of the high labor turnover rate that characterizes retail food stores. In the retail food industry of southern California, almost half the employees are separated from an employer each year. After 10 years, only about 15 percent are still in the industry. As of 1965, the industry needed an average workforce of about 38,000 employees, including both full-time and part-time workers. In the course of that year, about 60,000 different persons worked in the industry; about 22,000, therefore, were temporary workers. Since the retail food industry is not markedly seasonal, this large proportion of temporary workers is not to be ascribed primarily to seasonal factors. The nature of the labor turnover may be seen in the experience of one supermarket employing, on the average, about 700 workers. During the year 1965, of this store's workforce, 276 quit, 110 were discharged, and only 10 were laid off.

Among other factors of explanation for the low SUB cost in the face of

2. The number of UI-continued claimants as a percent of covered employment.

high turnover are the following. Of the temporary employees, many would not be eligible for SUB because they lacked sufficient employment. Of those discharged, many were let go because of dishonesty, and would not be eligible for SUB. Of those who quit, many would have quit without "good cause" as defined by the UI agency and hence would not have been eligible for UI or SUB.[3] Finally, many of those who quit or were laid off found employment almost immediately with other employers in the same industry. Others who quit may have left the labor force. Demand for labor in this industry has been strong in recent years, and the union has had the equivalent of a seniority agreement which requires employers to hire job-seeking union members before they take on new, nonunion, employees.

Administrative expenses have also been on the low side. During the four years 1961 to 1964, total administrative expenses as a percent of total benefits were 4.4 percent, 5.2 percent, 4.3 percent, and 4.7 percent. Since the other supplemental benefits (disability and workmen's compensation) paid from the fund are probably more costly to administer than unemployment benefits, these average percentages may safely be applied to the SUB plan as a conservative estimate.

Brewery Workers (BFCSD) of New Orleans

It will be recalled from Chapter 2 that four locals of the Brewery Workers of New Orleans negotiated two unemployment benefit plans with the brewers of that city, one a pooled plan, the other an individual-account plan. It will also be recalled that in 1965 the pooled fund was split into two parts, of which one remained pooled, while the other became an individual-account fund, both covering members of the same local. The original pooled fund is known as Fund No. 1, the original individual-account fund is known as Fund No. 2, and the newly established individual-account fund is known as Fund No. 3. This situation provides an unusual opportunity to see the two types of plans operating side by side.

Table 10–4 summarizes the experience of these three funds through 1966. On the average, Fund No. 1 covered about 700 employees and Fund No. 2 about 400. The man-hour contributory cost for each fund was the same, 5 cents per hour worked. Fund No. 1 regularly paid out a rela-

---

3. In the spring of 1964, the SUB plan was amended, on employer insistence, to disqualify employees who quit; nothing was specified regarding the cause of the quit. In the fall of 1965, California amended its UI law to disqualify for the duration of unemployment—instead of for five weeks, as previously—those who quit without good cause; the state continued to pay benefits immediately to those who quit with good cause. The SUB plan, partly for administrative simplicity, adopted the state UI distinction between quits with and without good cause.

tively larger amount of benefits and, as a result, accumulated a relatively smaller reserve. As of January 1, 1965, before the third fund was created, Fund No. 1 had only 56 percent of the combined reserves, although it covered 73 percent of the employees and therefore received 73 percent of the combined contributions.

If the expenditures of Fund No. 2 had been limited to unemployment connected with layoffs, as was the case with Fund No. 1, the difference in benefit expenditures between the two funds would have been much greater. Nearly all the expenditures from Fund No. 2 were for reasons other than layoff, as may be seen in Table 10–5, which shows benefits paid from Fund No. 2 according to the reason for payment. Through 1965, payments

TABLE 10–4

Contributions and Expenditures, SUB Funds of New Orleans Brewery Workers (BFCSD), by Year, 1961–1966

Year and fund	Contributions	Benefits		Administrative expenses	
		No.	Amount	Amount	% of benefits
	(1)	(2)	(3)	(4)	(5)
1961					
Fund No. 1	$99,786[a]	566	$11,335	$6,850	60
Fund No. 2	48,037	93	1,872	4,073	210
1962					
Fund No. 1	54,899	707	14,105	6,429	46
Fund No. 2	30,267	136	2,727	4,093	150
1963					
Fund No. 1	53,752	912	24,160[b]	6,871	28
Fund No. 2	30,739	109	2,747	3,807	138
1964					
Fund No. 1	53,650	789	21,345	6,771	32
Fund No. 2	31,423	210	5,267	4,491	85
1965					
Fund No. 1	10,843	170	4,670	7,902[c]	169[c]
Fund No. 2	33,145	273	6,836	4,096	59
Fund No. 3	43,361	38	950	[c]	[c]
1966					
Fund No. 1	10,309	328	8,200	1,590	19
Fund No. 2	32,500	244	6,109	4,113	67
Fund No. 3	41,079	88	2,198	6,324	288

SOURCE: Administrator, New Orleans Brewers and Brewery Workers Welfare Plan.

[a] Contributions for two years, 1960 and 1961.

[b] Benefit was increased from $20 to $25 in 1963.

[c] For the year 1965, all administrative expenses for Fund No. 3 were charged to Fund No. 1.

TABLE 10-5

Number and Amount of Claims Paid, SUB Fund No. 2, New Orleans Brewery Workers (BFCSD), by Reason for Payment and Year, 1961–1965

Reason	1961		1962		1963		1964		1965		Totals, all years	
	No.	Amount	No.	Amount	No.	Amount	No.	Amount	No.	Amount	No.	Amount
Resigned	8	$ 489	4	$ 846	5	$ 466	9	$1,549	16	$1,057	42	$4,407
Separated	11	573	14	1,196	7	700	17	1,206	7	92	56	3,767
Retired	5	506	4	685	5	1,277	2	633	11	4,582	27	7,683
Layoff	—	—	—	—	1	100	1	458	1	480	3	1,038
Death	5	304	—	—	1	204	4	1,402	2	514	12	2,424
Totals, all reasons	29	$1,872	22	$2,727	19	$2,747	33	$5,248	37	$6,725	140	$19,319

SOURCE: Administrator, New Orleans Brewers and Brewery Workers Welfare Plan.

to laid-off employees amounted to only 5 percent of total benefit payments. Obviously Fund No. 2 had not functioned primarily as an unemployment-benefit program.

The relatively high benefits paid out in 1963 and 1964 (Table 10–4) are explained by two factors. One was the increase in the weekly benefit amount from $20 to $25: this change was made in 1963. The other was the introduction, during this period, of much automated equipment, with many resulting layoffs and terminations. By the end of 1964, the transition had largely been accomplished; the relatively low benefits in 1965 and 1966 reflect the generally prosperous condition enjoyed by the brewery business in New Orleans in those years.

Although the SUB Fund No. 1 pays benefits for only 16 weeks, there has been no pressure for an extension of duration. From the inception of the plan through 1965, less than a dozen employees had drawn the full 16 weeks.

As of 1965, the $25 SUB payment plus the Louisiana UI maximum of $45, to which practically all brewery workers are entitled, provided a total unemployment benefit of $70. This amount represented a little over 50 percent of straight-time wages for most of the workers covered by Fund No. 1. Nevertheless, there has been no pressure to increase the size of the weekly benefit.

Beginning in January of 1963, a partial benefit of $10 was added. Thereafter, a man who worked one day usually got three payments: his wage, partial UI, and partial SUB. A man who worked two days normally received only his wage for those days because two days' earnings were usually high enough to disqualify him for UI, and without UI he could not receive SUB. This, it will be recalled, was the situation that led to the negotiation of the short-week benefit in the auto and steel SUB plans.

Administrative costs are shown in columns 4 and 5 of Table 10–4. These costs have amounted to almost $10 per man per year over the lifetime of the plan. In the case of Fund No. 2, this is the price paid for the fund's single advantage, that it forces the employee to save. As a percentage of benefits paid, administrative costs have been very high, higher than for any other multi-employer plan. The relatively small amount of unemployment benefits paid is certainly one explanation. Another is the small size of each fund, which provides only a narrow base over which to spread the inevitable overhead expenses.

11

OTHER ASPECTS OF SUB EXPERIENCE

This chapter discusses two important aspects of SUB experience that are less easily measured than those examined in the preceding chapters: first, the effect of SUB on the allocation of labor and, second, the significance of SUB for the development of UI.

Effect on Allocation of Labor

Demand for Labor

The utilization of the workforce is a function, in the first place, of the demand for labor. Any effect that SUB might have on the demand for labor through added "purchasing power" would be significant only in those local economies where SUB covers a substantial portion of the labor force. In Flint, Michigan, for example, where over 40 percent of the nonagricultural labor force is linked directly to the auto industry and is eligible for SUB during that industry's typical mass layoffs, it could happen, on occasion, that half of this covered workforce would be drawing SUB in a given period. In such a situation, when the SUB contribution to local spending is at its peak, SUB might be replacing about one fifth of the wages of one fifth of the local labor force. (In Michigan, in recent years, SUB has replaced about 20 percent of average straight-time earnings of the recipient.) SUB might have a similar impact in other situations, such as the closing down of a plant with a SUB plan in a small town in which it is the dominant employer. Except in these unusual situations, it is not likely that SUB has a measurable effect on the demand for labor by the community at large.

Does SUB have an effect on the demand for labor by the company with the SUB plan, that is, does SUB help to stabilize employment within the company? The unions, especially the Auto Workers, said it would; they advanced this anticipated effect as an important justification for the establishment of SUB plans. The probability that SUB has had the anticipated effect varies between the earlier period, when experience rating was in force, and the later period, when experience rating was practically inoperative (see Chapter 6).

In the earlier period, SUB probably had some influence on decisions affecting the workforce. Because of SUB, unemployment became more costly, and the cost was felt directly by the company experiencing the unemployment.[1] Plant managers have reported being under pressure from headquarters to reduce these costs, and industrial relations managers have reported that they watched these costs as one indication of possible mismanagement in particular plants. A few large corporations carried experience rating within the company down to the plant level and divided the company's total SUB costs among the individual plants according to each plant's experience. They did so because in their judgment SUB costs were a significant factor in planning plant procedures. Finally, at least one auto company, under the direct stimulus of SUB costs, established a system whereby the SUB claimants from one plant could be referred to open jobs at another plant.

One of the objectives of the unions which negotiated the short-week benefit (Chapter 5) was to discourage the use of short time (work sharing) by the employer. The exact extent to which the short-week benefit has had this effect is uncertain, but there is no doubt that it introduced a new factor which was explicitly considered by the employer in planning layoffs. Even in this brief review of SUB experience, instances were encountered where the pattern of layoffs was arranged to minimize the payment of short-week benefits. For example, in late 1965, when American Motors was laying off large numbers of employees, the company and the union differed strongly over the pattern to be followed in scheduling the layoffs. The difference stemmed chiefly from the company's endeavor to minimize, and the union's endeavor to maximize, the payment of short-week benefits. The pattern finally adopted included an agreement that, in that season, Christmas would be considered to fall on December 24, 1965, and New Year's Day would be considered to fall on January 3, 1966. The short-week benefit has also changed somewhat the relative costs of working a smaller group overtime and working a larger group short hours. In all probability, however, the effect of this change in costs has not been significant.

Abandonment of experience rating (in 1962 by the steel-type plans and in 1965 by the auto-type plans) has given SUB a relationship to employment stabilization the opposite of that originally intended. The change in financing provisions did more than merely remove a previous incentive to avoid layoffs; it provided a positive incentive to accept more unemployment than would otherwise be economical. The employer's contribution to the SUB fund has become a fixed cost, in that money not needed for unemployment benefits is used for other purposes — a bonus, in the case of the auto-type plans. As a result, unemployment benefits up to a level that can be sup-

---

1. The division of the added cost between employer, employee, and consumer is relevant here but is not ascertainable.

ported by the contributions are no longer a variable operating expense, and in some situations where the avoidance of unemployment would involve an additional cost, it may be cheaper for the employer to lay off employees and let the fund pay the unemployment benefits involved. He would thus "get something for his money."

Back in 1955, shortly after the Steelworkers had negotiated a SUB plan with the Continental Can Company, W. A. Lacke, industrial relations manager of the company, wrote an article in which he discussed the possible impact of SUB on employment stabilization. After illustrating what could be done to stabilize employment by citing the recent history of one of his company's plants, the author went on to discuss the impact SUB might have if it should become a fixed cost. In that case, said the author, the company would have to ask itself whether it was good business to incur certain costs and risks (he specified these in some detail) which were involved in the effort to stabilize employment: "Is it good business to do all these things if the end result is merely to make sterile a greater portion of the trust fund than will be the case if we do nothing to reduce the number of employees who are laid off?" [49]. There is some evidence that this reverse impact of SUB on employment stabilization is actually being felt. For example, a few SUB administrators have reported that they detect a change in attitude on the part of plant managers, who now tend to reply to a question regarding a possibly excessive number of SUB claims: "What's the difference? They don't cost anything."

The experience of one basic rubber company may illustrate the effect that SUB had originally, when it was experience-rated, and its effect after it had become a fixed cost. This company used to shut down on Fridays when inventory was too large but, after the initiation of the short-week benefit, stopped the practice because it had become too expensive. When interviewed in late 1965, after experience rating had been abandoned, an official of the company remarked that the company would probably resume the earlier practice. The union can, of course, protest, as it did before SUB, against "loose" employment practices, but it now has less incentive to do so. As the phenomenon of "reverse seniority" demonstrates, short-term layoffs no longer necessarily displease all the affected employees.

An employer who wishes to close a plant will be concerned about the fate of his workforce. If the company has a SUB plan, this concern may be lessened. The Steelworkers believe that several companies which closed plants shortly after the inauguration of SUB made the move more rapidly and more drastically than they otherwise would have. Whatever effect SUB had in this direction in the past may be magnified, now that SUB has become a fixed cost.

The multi-employer plans have never been experience-rated in the ordinary sense, since they do not give the individual employer a direct financial incentive to avoid unemployment. However, as noted in Chapter 10, these plans generally give the union a direct inducement to avoid unnecessary drains on the fund. Since the union participates closely in the administration of the plan, the effect on the payment of benefits is similar to that produced by the customary experience-rating system, that is, there is a direct financial incentive to avoid unnecessary benefit payments and to define "unnecessary" somewhat strictly.

Supply of Labor

The principal effects of SUB on the supply of labor are most conveniently discussed in relation to the problem of labor mobility. Mobility in this context is not limited to geographic movement but includes all types of job movement, including movement between occupations. It may be assumed at the outset that SUB confers an added degree of freedom and mobility on the unemployed person in his search for another job and, hence, that the effect of SUB on him is clearly favorable. It only remains to ask whether SUB may have other effects, favorable or unfavorable. It is convenient to discuss these possible effects in terms of whether they involve mobility between companies or within a company.

Mobility between companies. The significance of SUB for labor mobility between companies varies somewhat depending upon whether it is related to short-term layoffs, where there is a definite expectation of a recall, or to indefinite or permanent layoffs, which may for convenience be designated long-term layoffs. In short-term layoffs, SUB helps to maintain the employer's labor force intact until he is ready to resume operations. The longer the training process involved, the more an employer is likely to value the help of SUB in maintaining his labor force. Thus, this effect would have somewhat greater significance in steel, for example, than in the can industry.

The desire of companies to retain their workforce intact during brief layoffs is nowhere more striking than in the auto industry during its annual model change.[2] Some plant managers in the auto industry have expressed the wish that eligibility for SUB be extended to employees of, say, three months' seniority. They expected that more of these recently hired employees would be available on recall if they were made eligible for SUB while on layoff. In many states, the UI agencies and the auto companies

2. In the late 1930's, the model change took from two to six months; 20 years later, it could be done in a period ranging from a few days to a few weeks, depending on the amount of change in the new model and the state of the market. Most of this improvement had been achieved before the advent of SUB.

have worked out an arrangement whereby the laid-off employees not only are not required to take other jobs but are not even required to apply for their unemployment benefits (UI and SUB) until recalled to work. This leaves the laid-off employees entirely free of reporting requirements during the layoff; many of them use this period, during which they are drawing UI and SUB, as a vacation period. (They then take vacation pay later in lieu of a scheduled vacation.) Although, strictly speaking, this is an improper use of unemployment benefits, the arrangement serves the interests not only of the employees but of the state and the companies as well. Certainly, any attempt by the Employment Service to refer these temporarily displaced workers to other jobs would involve considerable administrative expense and would produce few placements.

In offering a plan tailored to meet a risk that affects the low-seniority employee more than the high, employers may find another advantage. Having such a plan, employers may find it easier to recruit young employees for industries characterized — as are the durable-goods industries — by more than average instability of employment.

The multi-employer plans tend to operate within a tight geographic area, especially in prosperous times. Employers generally prefer that their unemployed workers refuse available jobs outside their area, hoping to conserve their own geographic labor pool. Since the funds in these plans are not experience-rated, the individual employer sees no immediate reason to follow a different policy.[3]

There seemed to be general agreement among both employers and union officials that the availability of SUB in the construction industry had diminished the willingness of unemployed union members to travel out of the area for jobs. For example, in a large eastern city in March of 1966, construction was at a low ebb and there were many unemployed union members. The business agent had received numerous requests for such workers from two neighboring states, but he could find few takers among his men. The jobs offered were not inviting: they paid lower wages than those in the home city, and they involved higher living expenses if the worker kept his family at home while he migrated to the job. Should these workers have filled these jobs? Probably not, though the answer is debatable. The only point made here is that whereas such jobs used to be attractive to an unemployed worker, they were no longer being taken, and the reason for the change — in the judgment of the labor and management

3. The unions involved in these plans allow traveling members of the union to receive SUB so long as they stay within the area under the jurisdiction of the fund. But if they leave the area and then apply for benefits, the union is likely to send them a telegram offering them a job in its local area. The claimant who refuses such an offer is disqualified.

people closest to the situation — was the availability of more adequate unemployment benefits.

Even within the territory under the jurisdiction of a multi-employer fund, the availability of SUB has made a difference in the willingness of unemployed workers to take some open jobs, especially jobs of short duration. In 1965, in one multi-employer plan, employment was high and workers scarce. Those on temporary layoff were declining temporary jobs offered at other locations. The business agent, who alone was aware of the situation in any detail, informed the administrator of the SUB fund, who threatened the workers with loss of benefits. The workers then began to accept the available jobs. That this effect of SUB is limited, however, is illustrated by the experience of the multi-employer plan of the Detroit Electrical Workers. Although this plan paid no benefits for over two years because some jobs were unfilled, the unemployed workers still did not take the available jobs, which for various reasons were not desirable.

In long-term layoffs, SUB supports the employee during the extended period sometimes required to find another suitable job. But SUB can also delay adjustment to the realities of the situation when a drastic change is inevitable. This is especially likely to happen in a small town where the SUB employer has been a major employer and has paid wages well above the average of the local economy. In this situation, it is possible for the worker's unemployment benefits (UI plus SUB) to be greater than the wages offered in the available jobs.

When one of the steel companies closed its plant in Eddystone, Pennsylvania, in 1963, about half of the displaced employees chose severance pay (normally the more appropriate benefit when the separation is permanent) and the rest chose SUB. Of those who chose SUB, about three quarters exhausted their benefits. As usual, there was little geographic mobility: of 800 displaced employees, only 40 accepted jobs, which were offered to all, in one of the company's midwestern plants.

The text table below shows the experience of American Motors Corporation with SUB during 1965. Excluding short-week benefits, the table shows by month the number of regular benefits paid with and without UI.

Number of Regular Benefits Paid

Month	With UI	Without UI	Month	With UI	Without UI
January	181	352	July	3,012	1,592
February	3,525	11	August	10,845	1,299
March	7,321	230	September	9,875	1,314
April	6,811	88	October	3,237	899
May	4,959	57	November	565	221
June	3,028	682	December	478	327

Heavy layoffs occurred in the early months of the year, February through May. The employees laid off at this time were told that they would probably not be recalled to work until the start of the new model run in the fall. (The temporary layoffs accompanying the model change are evident in the months of August and September.) From the marked increase in the numbers of benefits paid without UI during the period July through September, it would seem that many of those laid off in the winter and early spring had stayed unemployed until exhaustion of their UI benefits and probably thereafter. During 1965, the labor market was very tight. The company would have preferred that these claimants take other jobs during this period, even at the risk of losing its employees to other employers. (During this period, some of the auto plants in Detroit had relaxed their usual hiring standards and would take on the laid-off employees of another company even though such employees were subject to recall by their former employer.)

As long as a claimant is drawing UI as well as SUB, his availability for work is subject to testing by both the UI agency and the company. However, when he is drawing SUB alone (usually after exhaustion of UI), only the company retains any control over his availability for work, and then only if it has a suitable job to offer him. As of 1965, the auto-type plan had no specific requirement that the claimant be available for work in general. After exhaustion of UI, if the company did not have a suitable job to offer, the claimant was completely free. He could go on a vacation trip, so inform the company, and request that his SUB checks be sent to his vacation headquarters (but see Appendix B). In the steel plan, the claimant could be required to continue to report to the employment service, but since the employment service could not be required to report job refusals to the company, this provision was of dubious efficacy.

The most effective pressure on the long-term claimant to accept another job is the drastic drop in total benefits that usually occurs when UI has been exhausted and only SUB is left. This pressure is not present in the most recent (1965) can plan, which undertakes to pay the full 70 percent of gross wages even after UI has been exhausted and which imposes no maximum limit on the amount of the SUB payment (and see Appendix B). In all plans, if a SUB claimant who is not drawing UI should find another job and continue to draw SUB, the employer would have difficulty discovering this fact.

During 1966, a midwest foundry operating at full capacity regularly advertised for employees. There was such a shortage of manpower that the foundry was willing to hire workers on layoff from other companies, despite the probability that they would return to their previous employer when recalled by him. The company found, however, that many applicants, former employees of other foundries, declined to accept the jobs, which were among the less desirable, on the ground that they were not worth the sacrifice of UI and SUB.

Most aircraft companies have thus far (1967) rejected SUB, contending that because most of their layoffs are permanent, SUB is not an appropriate program for them. These companies fear that a SUB plan would tend to delay the movement of former employees into other jobs. Instead of a SUB plan, some of these companies have negotiated an Extended Layoff Benefit plan, which pays employees laid off for as long as five weeks a lump sum proportionate to past service. Unlike the typical separation-pay plan, benefits in this plan are not conditional upon severance of seniority.

Unemployment benefits tend to lessen, even if they do not entirely remove, union opposition to technological changes that are expected to result in long-term layoffs. This consideration was certainly a factor in the negotiation, in 1965, of more liberal SUB programs by the rubber and cement industries and by the Alan Wood Steel Company. The same consideration has probably entered into the negotiation of other SUB plans as well, for this function of SUB had been stressed from the beginning. In their campaign for the original SUB plan, the Auto Workers recognized that "a guaranteed employment program should place no obstacles in the way of technological progress" and insisted that the union's "guaranteed employment program [would] reconcile the dual objectives of technological progress and security for workers" [10, p. 40].

Mobility within a company. The influence of SUB on job movement within a company is particularly interesting. It is here that SUB has had its most marked effects and has raised the most controversy. The chief issue is the right of an employee to SUB when he has exercised his contractual right to a preferential layoff, that is, when he has declined, as he is permitted to do by the labor contract, other available work offered him by the company and has taken a layoff instead. For the background of this issue and for the SUB provisions relating to it, the reader is referred to Chapter 4, particularly to the section dealing with refusal of suitable work.

As will be recalled, eligibility for SUB in this situation is affected by UI requirements and by seniority provisions, both of which are varied and changeable. The UI provisions differ from state to state and are open to change at every legislative session.[4] Seniority provisions also differ, not

---

4. The application of these provisions produces further variation, even under the same state law. Although local offices are provided with norms of interpretation, there remains some room for personal judgment in determining the meaning of "available" and "suitable" in concrete situations.

only from industry to industry, and within an industry from company to company, but even within a company, from department to department. Moreover they are subject to frequent changes. Since a complete picture of this complex area is beyond the resources of this report, the treatment here attempts only to illustrate the principal ways in which the issue has arisen and has been handled.

The preferential layoff is of concern to the state UI agency because it calls into question the involuntary nature of unemployment resulting from the employee's own election. The agency must decide whether in these circumstances the employee has refused suitable work and whether he is available for work according to the UI law. The preferential layoff is of concern to the employer because it further limits his freedom to allocate manpower according to the dictates of efficiency. In the traditional form of the guaranteed annual wage, the employer's promise of increased security was matched by the employee's promise of increased flexibility. Some employers complain that the increased security provided by SUB is accompanied by less, rather than greater, efficiency in their use of manpower.

There are two general situations in which the preferential layoff is likely to be felt as a significant problem. The first is the partial shutdown, usually seasonal, scheduled for various purposes, such as inventory-taking, maintenance work, or, in the auto industry, preparation for the model change. In this situation, the company must retain some employees to do the required work, while laying off the remainder.

The second type of situation occurs only in the case of a company that has multiple plants within an area or multiple processes within a plant. Such a company often finds that one plant or process is speeding up while another plant or process is slowing down. In accordance with seniority provisions, the company may be required to offer employees about to be laid off from one department or plant jobs that are available in other departments or plants, and the employee is free to accept the offered job, or to choose a layoff instead.

In both types of situations, the employee who has an option to take the layoff is more likely to exercise it if the offered job is less desirable than his customary job, if the likelihood is great that he will shortly be recalled to his customary job, and if he has other uses for his time.

He is also more likely to exercise his option to take a layoff if the SUB payment is large and is independent of UI. These two conditions are sometimes interrelated. Thus, a laid-off worker who refuses a job and is therefore disqualified for UI may or may not be eligible for SUB (see Table 4–3); if he is eligible, he may be limited by the regular SUB maximum, or he may draw a special (higher) maximum (see Table 5–4). On this score, the rubber industry would seem to offer the widest scope for the exercise of the preferential layoff. As of 1965 in the rubber industry, in which seniority provisions were generally very wide (especially in Akron, Ohio), the SUB plan had the necessary seventh "Arab," and the plan provided a higher benefit when UI was not received. In all these characteristics, the Allis-Chalmers plan was similar to the rubber plan, and in one respect surpassed it. When UI was not received, the Allis-Chalmers plan provided an unlimited SUB amount for at least a limited period. (For the 1967 changes in the rubber plan, see Appendix B.)

There is no doubt that SUB has made the preferential layoff a significant current issue, especially in relation to seniority provisions, upon which it is having a marked impact. Historically, seniority has been a device for allocating the available work so that the long-service employees are retained on the job while the short-service employees are laid off.[5] The advent of SUB made a layoff more desirable in some circumstances than work. As a result, some unions have become insistent that seniority provisions be changed so as to allow the long-service employees a choice between taking available work or taking a layoff.[6] (See Appendix B.)

The union argues that it costs an employer no more to lay off one man than another, and that therefore long-service employees ought to have the right to choose to be the ones laid off when they so desire. To this argument the employer replies that the preferential layoff does increase costs in two ways. First, such an option aggravates the extent to which seniority provisions already interfere with the most efficient allocation of manpower; it adds uncertainty to complexity. Second, the cost of benefits (both UI and SUB) is likely to be less if layoffs are concentrated among the short-service employees because (a) a smaller proportion of these employees are eligible for benefits and (b) the benefits of those who are eligible tend to be lower in amount and shorter in duration than the benefits payable to long-service employees.

The union retorts that this last employer argument is a very good "social" reason for not concentrating layoffs among the short-service employees — from the viewpoint of society, it is not preferable to lay off

5. After the passage of the Wagner Act, the practice of negotiating seniority provisions spread rapidly until, by the end of the 1950's, such provisions appeared in over 90 percent of all agreements in manufacturing industries and in about half of the agreements in non-manufacturing.

6. While SUB was still in the discussion stage, the IUE foresaw clearly the impact that SUB might have on seniority provisions. At its annual convention in 1953, the union declared that as a result of SUB "the layoff clause of the future might provide that an employee has the right to take a layoff in lieu of a transfer to a lower-rated or less desirable job without losing his seniority."

those who lack the protection of unemployment benefits. The employer replies that there is also a "social" reason for not encouraging the practice of preferential layoffs. Upon being laid off, short-service employees are more likely than others to seek other jobs immediately. This has the advantage of keeping the employer's labor force down to a proper size and preventing the maintenance of an unnecessarily large labor pool. The net effect of the preferential layoff, the employer argues, is to require a larger labor force than necessary for the production of a given amount of goods.

The characteristic issues involved in the preferential layoff may be illustrated in the case of Company X, a basic steel company in the midwest employing about 5,000 workers. Company X has traditionally paid wages that are above the average in the steel industry and during the lifetime of SUB has experienced less than average unemployment. This company also has had an unusually liberal set of seniority provisions, which had been negotiated in the early 1950's before the advent of SUB.

The introduction of SUB ushered in a period of conflict over the seniority provisions. In the first stage of the conflict, friction began to develop because SUB made layoffs less undesirable than they used to be, and more employees began to exercise their seniority right to elect a layoff. As preferential layoffs multiplied, the employer began to review personnel policies that had been accepted for many years.

The second stage began in the early 1960's, when a downturn in industrial activity resulted in a large number of layoffs alternated with recalls. The company sometimes found itself forced to hire new employees while employees on layoff were declining to accept work at the lower end of the job scale and were choosing, instead, to remain on layoff with the support of UI and SUB. Although the company could not deny SUB to employees who exercised the option given them by the contract, it could protest the payment of UI benefits, and this it began to do on a much expanded scale. It contested cases that it had never contested before and carried its fight, when necessary, into the courts. For the most part, these protests were successful and resulted in disqualifications. Whenever a claimant was disqualified for UI, he was automatically cut off from SUB also, for the steel plan has never had the seventh exception shown in Table 4–3. The company made it clear to the union that it was adopting this policy of strictness in UI as a way of controlling what it considered to be abuses connected with the preferential layoff.

The successful disqualification campaign of Company X prepared the way for the third stage. When the union recognized that it would have to yield some ground on the revision of seniority provisions in the light of the new factor introduced by SUB, union and company worked out a compromise agreement whereby SUB was denied to an employee taking a preferential layoff whenever the exercise of such a preference would require the company to hire an additional employee.

Although this agreement disposed of most of the issues involved, some points of controversy remained, one of which concerned the "registration list." When a laid-off employee wished to be considered for jobs outside his own seniority unit, he signed a registration list from which openings were filled in the order of seniority. If he did not sign the registration list, and if there were jobs available to which his seniority would entitle him if he had registered, should he be considered to have refused an offer of work? As of 1966, the company had reluctantly accepted the union's interpretation that such an employee had not been "offered" work and consequently had not "refused" work. The company therefore did not immediately protest the payment of UI in such a case. However, after three weeks of benefits had been paid to such a claimant, the company regularly protested the UI claim on grounds of nonavailability.

The company also regularly informed other companies of the availability of its SUB claimants. It was not afraid of losing its employees because its wage scale was notably higher than that of others in the area. When manpower was very short in late 1965 through 1966, this company found that other companies were willing to hire its laid-off employees despite the probability that they would quit upon recall by Company X. During its disqualification campaign, the company encountered some instances where employees, after they had been disqualified for UI and SUB, accepted jobs they had earlier refused.

This impact of unemployment benefits on availability for work shows up also in a 1964 arbitration case [56] involving another company's employees who had accepted assignment to lower-rated jobs upon being told that the exercise of their option to refuse assignment and take a layoff would affect their right to short-week benefits. When this information was later established to have been incorrect, the employees demanded the benefits they would have received if they had chosen the layoff instead of the job. Their demand for benefits was disallowed by the arbitrator, but the point here is that their availability for work evidently depended on the unavailability of benefits.

In 1966, another instructive case involving the preferential layoff under the steel-type SUB plan went to arbitration [57]. The company, a medium-sized foundry, had begun to deny SUB to anyone who chose a layoff instead of an offered job. In its protest, the union (USWA) charged that the company was unilaterally changing past practice. The company argued that it was adopting a new practice to fit a new situation: the liberalization of

UI and SUB had so increased the desirability of layoffs relative to available jobs that the company had to adopt a different policy. The company based its appeal on an earlier case involving the United States Steel Corporation [58] in which the arbitrator (Sylvester Garrett) had ruled: "Past practice ...may not be extended to an entirely new situation in which supplemental unemployment benefits provided by the recent contract and unemployment compensation benefits totalled more than pay for working."

In its brief the company also called attention to another aspect of the case: "The Union wants the Company to permit an employee to take a layoff when work is available for him in another classification in accordance with the Agreement, and then attest to the State UC Board that he was laid off because no work was available, thereby enabling the employee to collect both UC and SUB benefits. The Company is of the opinion, based upon consultation with UC officials and its legal counsel, that such procedure would be illegal, involving falsification of records."

The arbitrator (Calvin L. McCoy) recognized the merit of the company's plea that SUB had changed the situation, but ruled that since SUB had been in operation for some years and the company had had ample opportunity earlier — notably in the 1965 negotiations — to change its practice, the company must be considered to have condoned the practice "at least technically for an extended period of time." The arbitrator therefore ruled in favor of the employee and granted him SUB. However, McCoy went on to add a warning: "The Arbitrator is fully aware of the legal consequences of falsifying records. He would now make it unequivocally clear that the Company need not withhold or misrepresent the true facts in the administration of its SUB program. If any employee's election to seek benefits rather than work, is based upon any misapprehension that the Company is obliged to utter a false statement to accomplish his purpose, then that employee should immediately disabuse himself of that notion."

This latter issue arose in a slightly different form in the negotiations of one of the agricultural implement companies in 1959. The settlement of a costly strike was being held up until the company would agree not to protest the payment of UI benefits when an employee exercised his contractual right to take a preferential layoff. The company finally agreed, in writing, that it would only "notify" the UI agency of the facts and would not "protest" the employee's claim. In most states this distinction would be meaningless, but in Wisconsin, where most of the company's operations were located, the distinction meant that UI benefits would be paid. The Wisconsin UI law has the unique provision that in the case of a company which is paying its way in the UI program, the UI agency may, if the company wishes, ignore what might otherwise be pertinent data relating to a claimant's labor-force status.[7] Since this company has been a positive-account employer, the Wisconsin agency has been paying UI benefits in situations involving the preferential layoff without passing judgment on whether or not the job offered by the company and declined by the employee is suitable by UI standards.

Another clear example of how SUB affected the desirability of jobs relative to layoffs is provided by the experience of one of the can companies. In one of this company's plants, the male employees had been seeking for several years to acquire seniority rights to certain jobs traditionally limited to females. In 1963, the male employees finally acquired rights to these jobs. In 1965, the SUB plan of the company was liberalized to pay a weekly benefit equal to about 80 percent of take-home pay. Thereafter, the male employees reversed their position and began to protest their being assigned to these jobs while the women were being laid off.

One of the major auto companies reported the following experience. For reasons not connected with the model changeover, 238 employees were laid off from a large plant. All these employees had the right to displace lower-seniority employees anywhere in the plant. Of the 238, 173 declined to exercise their right and chose instead to be laid off. Of the 65 who chose a job in preference to a layoff, 36 were ineligible for SUB (they had less than one year of seniority) and 20 obtained higher-rated jobs by bumping. Only 9 out of 238, therefore, took a lower-paying job when the alternative was UI plus SUB.

In the case of Company Y, a large manufacturer, the preferential layoff was welcomed as the lesser of two evils. The company had negotiated a very liberal seniority system which gave its employees bumping rights over a wide area. The exercise of these bumping rights was so disruptive (one layoff could produce a domino-like effect resulting in a dozen job changes) that the company was glad to have employees threatened with possible layoff accept the layoff instead of bumping down into already occupied jobs. This company not only refrained from protesting UI claims in this situation but took the positive action of urging the UI agency to cease disqualifying such claimants. As of 1965, in the state in which this company had its chief operations, the UI agency had adopted the policy of accepting such claims during the first three months. At the expiration of that period the seniority provisions gave the laid-off employee the opportunity to change or reaffirm his choice of a layoff. If the employee reaffirmed his choice of a layoff, the UI agency might hold him unavailable for work in

---

7. This is no more than what other states do at the time of model change (see above), except that the other states do not restrict the privilege to positive-account employers.

the week in which he had made the choice, but would honor his claim thereafter. Since the company had generally been a positive-account employer, this agency was, in effect, following the practice of the Wisconsin agency described above.

The experience of Company Y is not uncommon among firms with liberal seniority systems. They often prefer that senior employees take the layoff rather than bump junior employees. The availability of SUB increases the likelihood that some agreement can be reached to diminish the extent of bumping.

As of the end of 1966, the most liberal SUB plan was that of the Alan Wood Steel Company, which paid benefits equal to 85 percent of gross wages. Under this plan, most workers would have a higher net income for the year if they were unemployed for one quarter than if they worked the full four quarters. (This estimate includes an assumption that the average worker has $10 per week of work-related expenses.) During the first full year (1966) of experience under the plan, the company did not encounter any problems of allocation of manpower within the company. This favorable experience must be interpreted in the context of the economic climate of the year (production was high and there were very few layoffs) and of the company's seniority system, which applied to narrow units and provided few options. Nevertheless, the experience suffices to show that very liberal benefits do not necessarily give rise to problems in the allocation of labor.

The multi-employer plans operate in industries that do not make use of a seniority system and hence do not have the problem of the preferential layoff in quite the same form. Some of these plans have its equivalent, however, in the right they accord an employee to turn down at least one job offer. (See, for example, the Detroit plan of the IBEW as described in Chapter 2.) Other plans, which do not have an express provision to this effect, nevertheless frequently allow the privilege in practice. As noted earlier in this chapter, some of the employers and unions who were parties to multi-employer SUB plans reported that the availability of SUB had made laid-off workers unavailable for some jobs they used to accept.

To sum up: the effect of SUB on the allocation of labor is not large on either the demand or the supply side. On the side of demand, SUB makes unemployment more costly for the employer, and hence tends to diminish the size of the company's under-utilized labor pool. On the side of supply, SUB has had the opposite effect. The operation of the preferential layoff has probably increased slightly the size of the employer's workforce. Whether the effect on the side of demand is greater or less than the effect on the side of supply is uncertain, but in either case the net effect of SUB on the size of the labor force is probably quite small.

It is clear that SUB has lessened somewhat the mobility of labor within a company and has opened the whole area of seniority provisions to reconsideration and renegotiation. Whether this effect of SUB is desirable or undesirable is beyond the scope of this report to determine. Involved are all the considerations that go into the determination of the "proper" level of wages and length of the workweek. The effect of SUB on mobility may be some slight increase in the per-unit labor cost of production, with the long-service employees taking the difference in the form of increased leisure. To the degree — but only to the degree — that it is desirable to raise wages and/or shorten the workweek, an extension of the preferential layoff, supported by SUB, is a way of achieving these goals.

It is clear also that unions have more control over SUB than they have over UI, and, conversely, that employers sometimes use the UI disqualifications established by the state legislatures to escape the consequences of seniority provisions they have negotiated. Finally, it is fairly clear that the effect of SUB on intracompany mobility is not of major proportions, since it becomes an issue only in the two situations described above. In most situations, the seniority provisions with their traditional emphasis on rights to a job are controlling. However, this issue is certain to arise more frequently in the future as SUB payments are liberalized and as seniority provisions are renegotiated to reflect the change made by SUB in the relative desirability of job and layoff (see Appendix B).

Relation of SUB to UI

One of the perennial issues facing our society is the proper relationship to be maintained between the private and public spheres. For over a decade a large private system of supplemental unemployment benefits has been operating alongside the public system of unemployment insurance. What significance does this SUB experience have for the development of UI? This general question is divisible into five particular questions, which are discussed in the ascending order of their importance.

Has SUB Changed the Attitudes of Employers and Unions toward UI?

It was hoped in some quarters, and feared in others, that SUB would cause employers to favor higher benefits and less stringent disqualifications in the UI program. The expectation was rooted in three considerations. Since most UI benefits are tax free, while SUB payments are not, an employer can put a given amount of (net) unemployment benefits into the hands of his employees through the UI program at less cost than through SUB. Moreover, where an employer with a SUB plan is already paying the maximum UI tax rate, he could have the cost of his SUB plan diminished by the amount of any increase in UI benefits, without any increase in his UI costs. Finally, the likelihood that his employees will demand SUB unless UI benefits are liberalized may diminish an employer's resistance to such liberalization, especially if his UI tax rate is already at, or nearly at, the maximum.

There seems to be no evidence that employers have undergone any significant change in their attitude toward the UI program as the result of SUB. While it is true that UI provisions have been liberalized in some respects (tightened in others) since the birth of SUB, this development was merely a continuation of the historical process characterizing UI in the twenty years preceding SUB. The writer's study of developments in a number of states whose major employers have SUB plans uncovered no evidence of any SUB-related change in employer attitudes.

For this absence of a result which had been widely predicted there are at least four plausible explanations, of which the first two are strictly in terms of costs, while the other two have a wider reference. It will be convenient to illustrate the four in the case of the auto and steel industries, which employ most of the workers covered by SUB plans.

First, most SUB employers do not pay the maximum UI tax rate and are not deficit employers. Although the auto and steel companies were deficit employers in some of the years following the establishment of their SUB plans, these leading corporations do not expect to remain deficit employers. Over the long run they expect to pay into the UI fund at least as much as their employees draw out and hence they expect to bear the costs of all unemployment benefits paid to their employees, whether in the form of UI or SUB. During the lifetime of SUB, this has generally been their actual experience.

Second, these large companies have employees who are not eligible for SUB but would be eligible for any increased UI benefits. Some of these employees are not currently covered by the SUB plan at all, while others have not yet attained the requisite seniority. Increased UI benefits paid to these employees would represent a new cost to the employer. Further, any increase in UI benefits would increase the size of the subsidy enjoyed by deficit employers at the expense of nondeficit employers, among whom the auto and steel corporations with the SUB plans are normally included.

Third, as leaders of the employer community, such corporations tend to be sensitive to the effect of their actions on their smaller fellow-employers. Frequently accused of the opposite behavior, they are inclined to lean over backwards to avoid that charge whenever the economic cost of so doing is not too great. Even if it were economically advantageous for the auto and steel companies to favor increased UI benefits (as indicated above, this is unlikely), these corporations would be concerned about the added cost imposed on non-SUB employers.

Fourth, in the auto and steel corporations, company policy with respect to UI depends principally on the advice of specialists, some of whom have been active in the program since its inception. Over the years, these specialists have established patterns of thought and a set of principles relating to UI which they are not likely to abandon for any reasons relating to SUB. Indeed, since employer policies are more completely expressed in SUB than in UI, these specialists would be reluctant to see UI take over any part of the task currently being performed by SUB. These UI specialists in the large corporations tend to have considerable influence on employer policy nationally.

It was also feared by some that SUB would effect a change in labor's attitude towards UI. It was expected that labor leaders who succeeded in negotiating SUB plans for their members would become less insistent on improving the public program. The anticipated result seems not to have materialized. On both state and national levels, labor's efforts to liberalize UI continued to be as vigorous after SUB plans were established as before. For example, in Michigan, the home of the Auto Workers and of SUB, UI provisions were liberalized to a greater extent in 1965, the tenth anniversary of SUB, than on any other occasion in the previous 20 years. These liberalizing amendments stemmed from the unanimous recommendation of the Labor-Management Advisory Council, on which representatives of the unions and companies with SUB plans predominated.

The reasons for labor's continued interest in UI are similar to the reasons for the unchanged attitude of employers: not all members of the Auto Workers or the Steelworkers, for example, are covered by SUB, and not all of those who are covered are currently eligible. Moreover, as leaders in the labor movement, unions such as these are conscious of an obligation to the unions whose members do not have the added protection of SUB but are entirely dependent on UI. Finally, these unions are large enough to afford to employ UI specialists, who operate according to long-established and not easily changed principles regulating the relationship of organized labor to UI.

Time changes most things. As SUB plans spread more widely, as the concurrent operation of SUB and UI becomes an accepted way of life, and as the UI professionals are succeeded by newcomers with less commitment to old principles, some of the attitude changes predicted in 1955 may emerge.

Has SUB Increased the Costs of UI?

SUB could increase the costs of UI in two ways. First, through its example, it could result in the further liberalization of UI provisions. There is no clear evidence that SUB has thus far had this effect. It may, however, have this effect in the future, as the scope of SUB expands and as the knowledge of SUB becomes more widespread.

Second, SUB could affect the supply of labor, as discussed in the first part of this chapter. SUB could weaken the incentive of laid-off employees to become re-employed promptly and could thus cause them to draw UI benefits longer. It could also cause some employees to choose a layoff when they might have chosen a job, thus increasing the number of claimants for unemployment benefits. In all probability SUB has increased the cost of UI in both ways, but only to a very small extent.

Whatever the size of the increase in cost, it would seem to have social significance chiefly in the case of the employer who is at the maximum UI tax rate and therefore probably not paying his way in the UI program. The increased costs of other employers, those below the maximum UI tax rate, are borne mainly by themselves and have neither more nor less social significance than other business costs.

In the plans that have abandoned experience rating and thus made SUB a fixed cost, SUB may have the effect occasionally of lowering the costs of UI. In these plans, when a given amount of layoff time must be arranged, there may be a tendency for employers to use the short-week benefits or severance payments, which come out of the SUB fund, rather than make labor-force adjustments that add to their UI costs.

Should Deficit Employers Be Permitted To Operate SUB Plans?

It is an anomalous situation when an employer who is not paying his way in the UI program but is being subsidized by other employers negotiates a private unemployment-benefit plan to pay his employees higher total unemployment benefits (UI plus SUB) than are received by the employees of the subsidizing employers. The anomaly is aggravated when the employees without SUB earn lower wages than the SUB-covered employees. Thus for several years during the lifetime of SUB, while the auto and basic steel companies were deficit employers, the employers in the retail industry were paying more into the UI fund than their employees were drawing out. At the same time, wages of the retail employees were on the whole lower than auto and steel wages. To the extent that payroll taxes come out of what would have otherwise been higher wages, the low-wage retail workers were, in effect, subsidizing the UI benefits of the high-wage auto and steel workers, who at the same time were getting additional unemployment benefits in the form of SUB.

The issue of the relationship of deficit employers to SUB was raised most pointedly in 1955 in Michigan, the birthplace of modern SUB. At that time a bill was presented to the Michigan legislature by Representative Van Peursem which would have established a number of conditions to be fulfilled before the state would permit UI benefits to be paid simultaneously with SUB. One of these conditions was that the employer with a SUB plan must be paying his own way in the public program. Opposed by the Auto Workers and lacking the support of the auto companies, the bill was defeated. Among the reasons for its rejection were the administrative difficulties anticipated and the fear lest a precedent be set for legislative intervention in private labor-management negotiations.

A more direct and perhaps simpler way of avoiding the anomaly would be to raise the UI tax ceiling (the *potential* maximum tax rate) for employers with a SUB plan. The reason for establishing a tax-rate ceiling is the presumed inability of some employers to carry a higher tax. But in the case of an employer who freely negotiates a SUB plan, there is available objective and obviously relevant proof of his ability to pay more for unemployment benefits than he is currently paying in the UI program.

While it would be undesirable to establish an indefinite liability in the UI program, there would seem to be no insurmountable obstacle to increasing significantly the maximum potential tax rate for employers with SUB plans. These employers would pay the higher tax only to the extent that they were not paying their own way in the UI program and were being subsidized by other employers. Such an increase in potential tax liability would have some tendency to discourage the negotiation of SUB plans, a result that would be viewed either as a further advantage or as an offsetting disadvantage of the arrangement.

Should SUB Function Independently of UI?

As early as 1954, when SUB was under discussion as a substitute for the guaranteed annual wage, Paul A. Raushenbush proposed an "alternative" approach which would have completely integrated SUB with UI [59]. He suggested that an employer who had an adequate reserve be permitted to elect to have the state pay UI benefits higher in amount, or longer in duration, or both, with higher contribution rates to be assessed against the employer to cover the resulting higher costs. In the light of subsequent experience this proposal looks very sensible; at the time, however, it attracted no effective support and was not adopted by any of the states.

SUB came into existence as a separate program, with its relationship to UI a debatable issue.

It will be recalled from Chapter 1 that the Auto Workers took a firm position on this issue and demanded complete independence for SUB: "The requirement that the Joint Board of Administration make its own determinations independently of decisions made under state unemployment compensation laws is of the utmost importance" [10, p. 37]. The principal objection raised against this union position turned on the issue of labor mobility.[8] The Latimer Report, in which SUB had its genesis, recommended that SUB claimants be required to report to the public employment service[9] and that "the disqualifications applicable to unemployment insurance might reasonably be applied to the guarantee of wages" [3, p. 179]. The report also presumed that in exchange for enhanced security the unions would be willing to "remove to a substantial degree the limitations on personnel transfers which might otherwise be thought essential to protect labor standards" [3, p. 171].

Speaking in the year preceding the negotiation of the first SUB plan, Sumner Slichter, who strongly favored more liberal unemployment benefits, definitely objected to a private system that was completely independent of the public system: "The proposal of the United Auto Workers that there be joint [labor and management] administration of supplementary unemployment compensation impresses me as quite undesirable. In fact, it is a more or less impertinent suggestion that private machinery be created to replace public machinery. The union proposes that if a state agency declines the claim of a worker to unemployment compensation, the joint machinery established under the supplementary unemployment compensation plan may pay the unemployment benefits to the worker. It would be unwise for employers to agree to such a proposal" [60].

Shortly after the first SUB plan was negotiated, John McConnell,

---

8. It was also objected that if SUB claimants had to meet only SUB qualifying conditions, and if these were less strict than the conditions imposed on UI claimants, the workers covered only by UI would become acutely dissatisfied and would bring pressure on the legislature to relax the UI provisions. On the assumption that the original UI provisions were proper and that the easier SUB provisions, whatever their applicability to the select group of employees covered by SUB, would be unsuitable for the general run of workers covered by the public program of UI, it was argued that the UI program would thus be "undermined." The only way to prevent the generation of such pressure was to require SUB recipients to meet the same disqualification conditions as governed UI claimants.

9. "The employment office facilities of unemployment insurance are valuable instruments for making sure that a system of guaranteed wages by separate employers does not result at times in the creation of unnecessary pools of unemployment or underemployment" [3, p. 16].

reviewing developments for the Industrial Relations Research Association, wrote: "The crucial development coming out of the [Ford-UAW] negotiation was the decision to tie the company benefits to the prior determination of eligibility for unemployment insurance by the state unemployment agency. This decision has given us supplementary unemployment benefits rather than a rival and conflicting private system of unemployment insurance" [61].

A year after the negotiation of the Ford-UAW SUB plan, John Bugas, one of the negotiators for Ford, wrote: "There are other objections which, in our opinion, are based upon misunderstanding of the plan and attempt to project what other future plans might be, rather than what the Ford plan is: Often they [the objectors] are not aware, for example, that denial of a State unemployment compensation benefit by the State agency will automatically operate as a denial of the supplemental benefit also" [62].

It is true that in all the early SUB plans the unions failed to achieve their objective of complete independence of UI. However, those who attempted "to project what other future plans might be" have been justified by actual developments. In 1955, the auto SUB plan contained only three exceptions, none of them controversial, to the general rule that eligibility for SUB required eligibility for UI. By 1965, the number of exceptions in the auto plan had grown to over a dozen[10] and included situations in which an employee had been disqualified for UI benefits after having refused a job that the labor contract allowed him to refuse. In such a situation, the employee can at least receive SUB (and see Appendix B).

In the plan of American Motors, the tie to UI was loosened further by a 1961 provision whereby any UI disqualification ceased to be an impediment to the payment of SUB after six weeks. This has been the union's first and only successful move in the direction of using SUB to achieve the long-sought objective of limiting the duration of UI disqualifications to six weeks.

As of early 1967, very few benefits have ever been paid under the provision in the auto plans that a worker may refuse a job, be disqualified by UI, and still receive SUB. No benefits at all have been paid under the American Motors provision permitting payment of SUB after six weeks of UI disqualification. Neither have there been any benefits paid under the provision of the Detroit Plumbers' plan permitting the plan's trustees to ignore a UI disqualification. For all the heat engendered by the debate over this issue, its quantitative importance has not been great. (This issue

10. As of the same date, the exceptions in the SUB plans of the rubber and agricultural implement industries were substantially similar to those in the auto plan. In the basic steel plan, however, the exceptions numbered only five and in the cement plan, only four.

should not be confused with the related but broader issue of whether SUB should be paid after a refusal of work even though UI is being paid.)

Most SUB plans now have a maximum duration that is much longer than the maximum duration in UI. Potential SUB duration is especially long in the rubber, can, and cement plans. Since, as pointed out above, the employer has little opportunity to test the availability of SUB claimants after they exhaust their UI benefits, questions arise as to whether such claimants should be required to continue to report to the public employment service and whether the employment service should be willing to certify to the employer that this requirement has been met.

Could UI Be as Liberal as SUB?

For over a decade the private system of SUB has been operating alongside the public system of UI. Has this experience under the SUB plans, with their higher benefits and longer duration, thrown any light on the feasibility of paying similar benefits under the UI program? Couched in terms simply of feasibility, the question prescinds from any issue of political philosophy. Hence the phrasing of the question, "could" rather than "should."

The programs of SUB and UI are too different for experience in the one to be applied directly and simply to the other. SUB is confined to a more homogeneous workforce with higher-than-average wages, has more demanding eligibility requirements, has generally stricter disqualifications, is under the closer surveillance and control of the employer, and is under the discipline of a stricter kind of experience-rating system. Assuming that all these differences would survive if the UI benefit amount and duration were raised to the levels of the average SUB plan, it is necessary to ask what differences in experience these differences in structure might produce in three crucial areas: costs, improper payments, and labor mobility.

In the following discussion, it is assumed that the UI program is to be modified as follows: the benefit-wage ratio aimed at is to be increased from the current 50 percent to about 65 percent of gross wages. Allowing for income taxes and work-related expenses, this leaves about a 20 percent differential between working and not working. The maximum benefit is to be increased sufficiently to allow most beneficiaries to receive this percent of wages. (By "most" is meant at least 75 percent, the level attained in the steel plan since the maximum benefit in that plan was increased in 1962.) The fraction of base-year wages that a claimant may receive as benefits in his benefit year is also to be increased sufficiently to allow all fully employed workers to draw 52 weeks of benefits.[11] All other UI

11. Some SUB plans are less liberal than the model plan described here and a few are more liberal. But the bulk of SUB experience has been in plans similar to this model.

provisions governing benefits, including the eligibility and disqualification provisions, are assumed to remain unchanged.

Costs. In assessing the feasibility of any proposed liberalization of UI, the first question usually asked by legislators is "How much will it cost?" Obviously, the cost will vary from state to state, depending on the pattern of unemployment and the benefit formula in each state. The task of preparing a realistic answer to this crucial question for even one state is far beyond the scope of this essay, as will be immediately appreciated by anyone acquainted with the complexities of UI. Here we must be content with a general discussion of the factors involved in making such estimates.

The costs of existing SUB plans offer an obvious starting point for estimating what the costs of a UI program paying the same benefits would be. In the typical steel plan, SUB payments were about half the size of UI benefits and were paid for a somewhat longer period. A very rough calculation indicates that, for the major steel plans, costs averaged in the neighborhood of 1 percent of total wages over the first decade of experience. This cost varied considerably for other industries, depending on such variables as the pattern of unemployment in the industry, the level of UI benefits provided by the state in which the company's main operations were located (the lower the level of UI benefits, the higher the level of SUB costs), and many others. It would be very difficult to choose the SUB plans whose experience could be considered the criterion of future UI costs.

Whichever plans were chosen, actual past SUB costs would, for several reasons, be an understatement of future UI costs. If the existing SUB plans had been operating under the easier eligibility and disqualification provisions of UI, their costs would have been appreciably higher.[12] In particular, the easier eligibility conditions would have raised costs; the low-seniority employees excluded by the SUB plans are the ones with the highest incidence of unemployment. The seasonal worker also, a perennial problem for UI, would have become a SUB problem as well and would have raised SUB costs. The easier disqualification provisions of UI would not have been so significant as the easier eligibility conditions, but they also would have increased SUB costs to some extent. The payment of benefits to those who quit their jobs voluntarily would have represented the most significant difference in disqualifications.

All of the above possible sources of increased costs relate to companies

12. In 1961, the Ford Motor Company closed its plant in Chester, Pennsylvania. Several years later the UAW reviewed the experience of the 1,250 laid-off employees. The union found, among other things, that about 900 employees had drawn UI benefits, while only about 300 had received SUB payments. There are many explanations of the discrepancy (the main one being that many employees had accepted pension or separation payments), but it illustrates the validity of the proposition developed in this paragraph.

that currently have SUB plans. Still further increases may accompany the extension of liberalized benefits to employees of companies that do not now have SUB plans. As compared with SUB employers, many of these companies employ a greater proportion of "fringe" workers — young workers, old workers, seasonal and secondary workers (chiefly women), and various types of problem workers — among whom the incidence of unemployment and its duration are above average. The added costs connected with the extension of increased benefits to such fringe workers would be particularly large in any state that maintained uniform potential duration while extending potential duration to 52 weeks.

Two factors that limit costs in SUB would not be operative in UI. First, in a SUB plan, when the fund of that particular plan has been used up, no more benefits are paid. Thus, when the Studebaker Corporation went out of business in the United States, only a fraction of the covenanted SUB payments were actually made before the fund was exhausted. But in the UI program, all eligible Studebaker employees received full benefits. Second, at the lower levels of the SUB fund, credit units are canceled at increasingly higher rates in exchange for benefits, and this also has the effect of reducing costs, as compared with UI, which does not have this arrangement. A liberalized UI program would also have higher costs depending upon how much the higher and longer benefits increased the number of improper payments or discouraged labor mobility — possible results that are discussed below.

Anything like an accurate estimate of the total increase in costs would be extremely difficult and is, as a matter of fact, entirely lacking. If one had to estimate such a cost, and if no one took the estimate too seriously, an educated guess would be that a UI program that kept all its provisions unchanged but provided benefits equal to those paid by the major SUB plans would cost double that of the current UI program.

Improper payments. By an improper payment is meant one that would not have been made if the payer had known all the relevant facts. The recipients of improper payments are known as "working violators" if they are employed while drawing benefits, and as "nonworking violators" if they do not make themselves sufficiently available for work to satisfy the prescriptions of the program. Of the two, the nonworking violator presents the greater problem.

It is reasonable to expect that improper payments would be somewhat more numerous in a liberalized UI program than in either the current SUB or the current UI program. Such payments would tend to be more numerous than in the current SUB plans, for two reasons. First, the UI program includes more of the "fringe" workers mentioned above. It is among these workers, who move in and out of the labor force and whose work motivation is often below average, that the incidence of improper payments has always been greatest. Second, administrative control over claims is usually not so tight in UI as it is in SUB, where the employer himself is the disbursing agent and directly determines the eligibility of the claimant. However, when over long periods the employer has few jobs to offer — as happened at various times, for example, to Chrysler, American Motors, and Studebaker, as well as to some steel companies which closed plants in isolated communities — the employer's policing is probably less effective than that of the UI agency, which has a broader spectrum of jobs to offer claimants.

Improper payments would also tend to be more numerous in the hypothetical liberalized UI program itself than in the current UI program. By far the most effective policing force is the automatic control exerted by the differential between benefits and wages. Since the differential would be smaller in the liberalized program, this automatic control would be less effective. Furthermore, the longer duration provided by the liberalized program would aggravate the problem posed by the dubious claimant who is sometimes carried on the benefit rolls until exhaustion of his credits washes him out.

How serious the increase in improper payments would be is difficult to predict, since the present extent of such payments is one of the more obscure areas of UI.[13] Some additional illumination might be gained from a thorough study of the operation of the multi-employer plans mentioned earlier. These plans differ less from the UI program than do the single-employer plans, and they may provide a better base for predicting what might happen if the UI program were liberalized to provide benefits equal to those paid in the SUB plans.[14] However, the multi-employer plans do differ from UI in being confined to a more select group of employees and in having tighter job control. The significance of the latter characteristic shows in the experience of the multi-employer plan of the Detroit Electrical Workers (IBEW), which for two years (1964–1966) paid no benefits at all.

Labor mobility. The possible effects of a liberalized UI program on the supply of labor are so complex as to be largely speculative. On the whole,

13. Not much information is available beyond this writer's study, published over a decade ago [63].

14. The stipulated employer contribution, and hence the possible costs, in these plans vary from 1 cent per hour worked in the plan of the Los Angeles Retail Food Clerks to about 30 cents per hour in the plan of the Buffalo (New York) Carpenters.

more liberal unemployment benefits are likely to result in a given labor force working somewhat less in the course of a year because of a slightly higher separation rate and a slightly lower re-employment rate.[15] This result would be offset to some unknown extent by a better allocation of labor.

In a liberalized UI program, the preferential layoff and its accompanying phenomenon, "reverse seniority," would see a marked development and would have different social implications in UI than in SUB. In SUB, each employer meets the full costs of the benefits paid to his employees, and if he wishes to pay unemployment benefits to employees who are on a preferential layoff, that is his own business. In UI, it is possible for a deficit employer to shift excess benefit costs to other employers. Since the deficit employers would be under no financial pressure to avoid uneconomical personnel procedures, society would have to be concerned with the question of whether the high unemployment benefits were fostering undesirable mobility (movement out of employment) by encouraging employees to substitute leisure for work. Moreover, this problem of voluntary unemployment would be greatly aggravated in UI as compared with SUB for two reasons: (1) greater control over claims would be needed because of the inclusion of more "fringe" workers in UI than in SUB, while (2) there would actually be less control than in SUB, where the individual employer has direct control over the claims filed by his employees.

To some extent, UI benefits are now used by seasonal employers (e.g., canneries and summer hotels) as a wage supplement. In advertising for help, these employers often mention the availability of unemployment benefits after the season closes, with the clear implication that the benefits will constitute an addition to wages earned. These employers are often deficit employers, and when they are, the wage supplement that UI provides is partially subsidized by other employers. Over the long run, this arrangement tends either to lower wages in the subsidized industry or to expand it beyond its economic optimum. Higher unemployment benefits would tend to aggravate these and other similar effects.

A liberalized UI program might have a slight impact on the demand for labor. The cost of unemployment for the employer may be raised so high that he becomes over-cautious, for the good of the total workforce and the entire economy, in hiring new employees. Employers are already inclined to meet early increases in demand for their product by working their present workforce longer hours — overtime, if necessary — before they

15. In this context, the terms "separation" and "re-employment" are used in their most general sense, so as to include even the temporary job movements involved in the preferential layoff and recall.

begin to take on additional employees. The natural result of this policy is to produce the anomaly of two groups existing side by side, one unemployed, the other working overtime. The tendency to follow this policy might be aggravated if unemployment benefits were raised. In evaluating this possibility, one must recognize that the relevant cost to the employer is not always limited to the SUB contribution to be paid on an employee's wages, but may represent the much larger sum that a short-term employee draws from the SUB and UI funds — that is, 65 percent of his wages for half as many weeks as he had been employed. Seen from the employer's side, the effective hourly wage of an employee who worked for two years and then drew benefits for a year would be 133 percent of his nominal rate. Although an employer would have to decide whether hiring an additional employee is worth incurring this risk, it would rarely happen that this consideration alone would control his decision.

There seems to be little immediate likelihood that UI will be liberalized to the point where it equals and therefore eliminates SUB. Any realistic assessment of the future must assume that the two programs will continue to function side by side for some time to come.

Two developments are likely to mark their continued relationship. First, as SUB continues to grow in liberality and as its experience becomes more widely known, it is likely to exert more influence on the development of UI. The effect produced by SUB's decade of generally favorable experience must be to strengthen somewhat the case for further liberalization of the public program. Second, SUB is likely to continue to grow more independent of UI. The chief reflection of the gradual trend in this direction has been the negotiation of successive "Arabs" (and see Appendix B).

PART IV
REVIEW AND APPRAISAL

12

REVIEW AND APPRAISAL OF SUB

Labor's long-felt interest in a guaranteed annual wage was given concrete expression toward the end of World War II, when a number of industrial unions, led by the Steelworkers, made definite demands on employers for this form of income security. The influential Latimer Report (January 1947) found these demands unrealistic — at least at that time — and suggested instead a plan to supplement the benefits provided by the public program of unemployment insurance. Thus was conceived SUB, one of the more striking examples of social inventiveness in our time.

Eight years later (May 1955) SUB was born, sired by the Auto Workers out of the Ford Motor Company. The new-born program owed its characteristics not only to the unusually intensive study and propaganda promoted by its immediate parent, the Auto Workers, but also to the early proposals of the Steelworkers and to the efforts of the Ford Motor Company, which had devoted thousands of hours to the subject during the two years preceding the 1955 negotiations. It is the result, very likely, of this remarkably thorough preparation that the new program's provisions have stood up so well during the first decade of its experience.

SUB plans quickly spread to the can, steel, agricultural implement, rubber, cement, and other industries.[1] By 1965, they had reached the stage of development shown in Table 2-5. The spread of SUB to the industries listed in the table and its failure to spread to others are explainable in terms of one or more of the nine factors discussed in Chapter 3. The general picture has been one of restrained external growth along with considerable internal vitality. The existing plans have undergone continual change, new varieties of SUB plans have been invented, and the SUB idea has shown an infectious quality. Given favoring circumstances, SUB could "break out" widely. The dramatic SUB amendments negotiated in 1967 (summarized in Appendix B) are proof of the dynamism still latent in the SUB idea. While possessing less glamour than the "guaranteed annual wage," SUB has demonstrated greater vitality.

Because in this limited study it was not possible to examine all SUB plans, four basic plans were selected for detailed treatment — those nego-

1. In this study, a SUB plan is defined as a private plan of unemployment benefits whose eligibility or benefit provisions are linked directly with UI. The study thus excludes some plans that go by the name of SUB but do not conform to this definition, such as the individual-account plan of the glass industry.

tiated by the dominant unions in the steel, auto, rubber, and cement industries. These core plans represent about 70 percent of all employees covered by SUB and they exemplify all the most significant issues that have arisen in SUB experience. Included for less detailed study are some plans negotiated by the Auto Workers in the agricultural implement industry and by the Steelworkers in the can industry. Because of their relevance in terms of comparison with UI and their differences from the usual single-employer plans, attention was also accorded the major multi-employer plans.

In the light of a decade of SUB experience, it should be possible now to answer the question posed by one of the early writers on SUB: "In 1965, will we look back at 1955 and wonder why such a sound principle as the 'guaranteed annual wage' was ever a source of heated discussion in labor-management relations? Or will we condemn the historic decision of the UAW-CIO and the Ford Motor Company for its 'damaging effects on the American economy, perhaps leading to the socialistic state and a controlled economy'?" [64].

SUB may be appraised on two levels, the one more immediate, the other more fundamental. We may ask simply whether the program has achieved its objectives, or we may go on further to question whether the objectives themselves were desirable. These are distinct inquiries. The first is an inquiry into an internal relationship — the relationship of SUB to its own objectives. The other is an inquiry into external relationships — the desirable or undesirable effects that SUB may have had on other social goals. Such inquiries amount to an appraisal of SUB by the application of internal and external norms.

Internal Relationships

If we accept SUB as an existing institution and prescind from the issue of whether it ought to exist, the task of appraisal consists in answering the question: has it worked — has it done what it set out to do? A condensed and general answer to this question can best be given by a review of the two principal parts of this study, the structure of SUB and its operations. The review is made from the standpoint of the end of 1965.

Structure: Single-Employer Plans

In general, the provisions of SUB plans have developed in the direction of increased liberality, complexity, and differentiation. The trend toward increased liberality was inevitable; one of the more dependable laws governing benefit programs is that they grow more liberal.[2]

2. At a press conference held shortly after the negotiation of the SUB plan with the Ford Motor Company, Walter Reuther said of the plan: "It provides the principle upon which we are going to build the guaranteed annual wage" [65].

The trend toward complexity defeated the early expectation of the Steelworkers that "as experience is gained...substantial simplification of the plan may be negotiated" [53, p. 57]. Growth in complexity is also one of the more common trends in new programs; under pressure of experience, the plans are adjusted to meet a variety of situations, many of them unforeseen at the time of negotiation of the original plan.

The trend toward increased differentiation had both a negative aspect and a positive one. Some plans did not liberalize so rapidly as others.[3] On the other hand, as SUB expertise became more widely available, a plan which originally had pretty much followed another plan's leadership, as the rubber plan had followed the auto plan, began to negotiate independent modifications to meet its own particular needs.

Eligibility and disqualification. The only significant change in eligibility requirements occurred in the cement plan, which in 1962 lowered the requirement from two years of seniority to one year. As of 1965, none of the core SUB plans except those in the steel and can industries required more than one year of seniority. Even the one-year requirement is stricter than the corresponding provision in UI, and this is one of the more important differences between SUB and UI.

All the core plans disqualified employees who quit their jobs. This is another of the more important differences between SUB and UI, which in many states imposes only a limited qualification. There have been no significant changes in this provision.

The provisions regulating payment of benefits to claimants unemployed because of a strike were, in general, stricter than corresponding provisions in UI and were especially strict in the steel plan. A few minor changes have been made in these provisions, whose exact scope is still somewhat obscure because they have been applied in relatively few situations.

The principal development in the area of disqualification has been the negotiation of a growing number of exceptions ("Arabs") to the requirement that a claimant must be eligible for UI in order to be eligible for SUB. Among these exceptions, which are most numerous in the auto-type plan, the most controversial has been that regulating the eligibility of a claimant who has refused an offer of work. As of 1965, the plans handled this situation variously: SUB may be denied even if UI is paid; SUB may be paid only if UI is paid; or SUB may be paid even if UI is denied.[4]

3. Apart from the core plans studied here, there were many with the same basic structure that did not adopt any of the liberalizations.
4. In the last situation, SUB may be limited to the amount which would have been paid if UI had also been received, may be the maximum SUB payable when UI is received, or may be a sum equal to UI plus SUB when both are received. As of 1965, the can companies and Allis-Chalmers had taken this last step (see also Appendix B).

The core plans do not compensate for unemployment traceable to an "act of God," but the definition of such an "act" has been gradually amended to apply only to catastrophic situations.

Benefit amount. All the core plans have increased the benefit-wage ratio over what it was originally. As of 1965, the lowest ratio was in steel (60 percent of gross wages) and the highest percentages were in rubber (65), cement (70), and can (70). The Alan Wood Steel plan was unique in paying 85 percent. (And see Appendix B.)

The core plans have generally included dependents' benefits. However, in recent years these benefits were dropped from some plans as the basic benefit formula was notably liberalized.

The maximum benefit has undergone considerable development. The basic maximum has been increased markedly in all the core plans, and there has been a growing adoption of the dual maximum and the variable maximum.[5] In recent years, two plans — can and rubber — have taken the major step of eliminating the maximum.

The introduction of the short-week benefit (in 1961 in the auto plan and in 1962 in the steel plan) has been one of the more interesting developments of SUB. The short-week benefit has proved to be a significant step towards that long-sought objective of the hourly-paid worker, salaried status. Another objective of the unions in negotiating the short-week benefit was to deter employers from using the short week, that is, from sharing the available work among the entire workforce. The unions preferred that the employer lay off some employees entirely and work the others full time.

Benefit duration. The duration ratio (the rate at which credit units are accumulated) has remained relatively unchanged in the core plans. The maximum duration, however, has been significantly lengthened in most of them. As of 1965, the cement plan paid benefits for as long as three years, the rubber plan up to four years, and the can plan up to five years, while the Alan Wood Steel Company plan paid long-seniority employees indefinitely. The union demand for an extension of duration chiefly reflected the workers' apprehension that technological change would result in long-term unemployment, even for high-seniority employees. The companies could the more easily grant this demand because extension of duration is about the least costly of all forms of benefit liberalization.

5. Under a plan providing for a "dual" maximum, a different maximum is applicable when UI is received than when it is not; under a plan providing for a "variable" maximum, different maximums are applicable to claimants with dependents, varying with the number of dependents.

To insure that some money would be left in the SUB fund for high-seniority employees in the event of a prolonged decline in employment, the core plans have always provided that the benefit amount and/or the benefit duration should be reduced as the fund shrank below specified levels. The steel-type plan relied chiefly on reduction in the benefit amount, while the auto-type plan relied chiefly on a reduction of duration. The reduction provisions in all plans have been considerably relaxed over the years and have lost much of their original significance.

Other types of benefits. There has been a growth in the practice of paying benefits other than SUB out of the SUB fund. These other benefits include severance pay, sickness and disability benefits, supplements to workmen's compensation, and relocation allowances. Among the factors contributing to this tendency has been the availability of money accumulated from SUB contributions and not immediately needed for SUB payments. The employees were reluctant to see the employer save on part of "their" 5 cents — or whatever the maximum SUB contribution was — and the employer, resigned to losing the entire contribution eventually, preferred to use part of it for these other benefits rather than to set up separate programs for them, each with its own financing.

Financing. One of the major obstacles to the attainment of the original goal of a "guaranteed annual wage" was the indefiniteness of the liability to be undertaken by any employer who made the guarantee. SUB avoided this obstacle by limiting the employer's liability to a fixed rate of contribution up to a fixed level of the reserve fund. The auto and the steel plans started with a maximum contribution of 5 cents per man-hour, while the rubber and cement plans started with a 3-cent contribution. Over the years, the maximum contribution rate has been increased in all but the auto plan. By 1965, the maximum contribution rate was 5 cents per man-hour in rubber, 9.5 cents in steel, 15 cents in cement, and 17 cents in the can plan. These amounts do not necessarily reflect the relative costs of SUB because they are maximum, not actual, rates and because the plans with higher contribution rates were paying other kinds of benefits as well as SUB (see above) out of the SUB fund.

Originally, the unions stressed the importance of making the employer's contribution vary directly with the amount of unemployment experienced by his employees, thus adding to his incentive to stabilize employment. This experience-rating feature was largely abandoned by the steel plan in 1962 and by the auto, agricultural implement, and rubber plans in 1964. As of 1965, only the cement plan still permitted the employer to save on his contribution in proportion to the amount of steady employment he provided.

The abandonment of experience rating seems to have been mainly due to a feeling on the part of the union members that what the employer saved they were losing. They felt that because they had presumably foregone a wage increase as the price of getting the employer to contribute to a SUB fund, the money saved belonged to them.[6] This feeling was strongest where the employer's savings were particularly large and among senior employees who expected to draw very little from the SUB fund. An additional reason for restricting the operation of experience rating was the traditional union policy of seeking to equalize wage costs among competing firms.

In some of the plans, the employer made part of his contribution by assuming a "contingent liability." The liability was contingent either in the sense that it might never be paid off, or in the sense that the time of payment was indefinite. To the extent that the employer's "contribution" was made in this form, he had the use of the cash until it was actually needed to pay benefits. Beginning in the can and steel plans, the practice of accruing contingent liability instead of contributing immediately in cash spread to the cement plan and to the Allis-Chalmers plan. As a result of its use of contingent liability, the steel plan has been almost entirely on a pay-as-you-go basis and consequently has lost most of its countercyclical quality.

Maximum-financing provisions have been amended in all the core plans to increase the size of their reserve funds. The abandonment of experience rating by most of the plans made a high level of maximum financing more acceptable to the employer. Once his contribution became fixed, he would prefer to see all of it go into the SUB reserve fund, where it would be available for already covenanted benefits, rather than have any portion of it spent for some new benefit, such as a Christmas bonus.

(For 1967 financing charges, see Appendix B.)

Administration. In all the core plans, the employer has administered the plan and has absorbed a large part of the expenses connected with administration. Because no record has been kept of these absorbed costs, the total administrative costs of the various plans are unknown.

Experience has led to a simplification of the administrative procedures used in handling applications for benefits. The claimant is usually no longer

---

6. The extent to which SUB was considered to be an alternative to a wage increase varied among the plans. This relationship is clearest in the Ford plan—both in the circumstances surrounding the negotiation of the original plan (see Chapter 1), and in the provision that, should the plan be abandoned, the employer's contribution is to be transformed into an equivalent wage increase.

required to show the actual UI check as proof of his eligibility for UI; various other proofs are now acceptable. In some plans, especially those of the auto type, the claimant need not present his claim in person but may mail it.

One of the employer's important administrative tasks has been to make reports to the union on the operation of the plan. These reports became much more detailed after 1961–1962. In addition to routine information on contributions and on the number and amount of benefits paid, the reports then began to include such significant data as the number of claimants who exhausted benefits and the number whose SUB payment had been limited by the maximum benefit.

Structure: Multi-Employer Plans

These plans usually have two main eligibility requirements: the claimant must have worked a specified amount of time for participating employers, and he must be eligible for UI. They usually have no special disqualification provisions of their own but accept those of UI. It is thus possible in some circumstances for SUB to be paid to employees who have quit their jobs.

For reasons of administrative simplicity, nearly all the multi-employer plans pay a flat benefit amount and generally make their benefits available for as long as the claimant is eligible for UI. The contribution rate is uniform for all employers participating in a given plan but varies widely between plans. In 1965, the rate varied from about 1 cent per man-hour (plans of the Brewery Workers, Garment Workers, and Retail Clerks) to about 30 cents per man-hour (plan of the Buffalo Carpenters).

Administration of the plan is committed to a full-time administrator who, more often than not, is a former union official. Thus the employer's control over a multi-employer plan is less direct than his control over a single-employer plan.

Operation: Single-Employer Plans

The decade of 1955–1965 constituted a fair test period for the core SUB plans. The period included two mild recessions, which affected all the plans. In steel, the number of production workers showed a mild secular decline in the earlier part of the period. During the middle and latter parts of the decade, both the rubber and cement industries underwent considerable modernization, with consequent disruption of their labor forces. The auto and can industries experienced their usual seasonal fluctuations. These are the kind of nondisaster situations in which SUB is intended to function adequately.

How successful was SUB in achieving its objectives? How much protection did SUB provide for the covered labor force? For the unemployed? How much of this protection was actually used? And by whom? Were benefits adequate in amount and duration? Finally, how much did the plans cost, and were the funds adequate? These are the chief questions to be answered in an appraisal of SUB operations.

Protection available. No adequate data were available on the proportions of the workforce — still less on the proportions of the unemployed — who were eligible for benefits. What scattered data there were indicated that the proportions were larger in the auto-type plan, with its one-year seniority requirement, than in the steel-type plan, with its two-year requirement. In all plans, the proportions were apparently high enough to be generally satisfactory, since no serious attempt had been made by the unions to lower the seniority requirement.

Beneficiaries. The proportion of the covered workforce who draw some benefits in the course of a year goes far to determine the degree of support that SUB can expect to attract from the union membership. In steel, employees who received one or more SUB payments in the course of a year varied by year from 15 percent of the workforce to 30 percent. In one steel company, during the entire period 1962–1965, beneficiaries drawing SUB in the course of a year averaged less than 5 percent of the workforce. Under the auto-type plans, the proportion varied among companies and over time from 10 percent to 50 percent of the workforce. The available data seem to indicate that the average proportion was higher in the auto industry than in any of the other industries, primarily because of the annual model change, which results in large numbers drawing SUB for a short time. Generally, the lowest average proportion was found in the rubber industry. In the auto industry, SUB recipients have included a significant number of high-seniority employees. Again, the annual model change is the primary explanation.

Recipients of short-week benefits as a proportion of all beneficiaries tended to vary inversely with unemployment. As full employment was approached, a larger proportion of the layoffs was for part-weeks, reflecting lack of materials, breakdown of machinery, and other similar "frictional" interruptions of production. During recession periods, short-week benefits made up a relatively small proportion of all benefits, an indication that work sharing was used relatively little as a device for adjusting production to demand.

All the core plans exhibited considerable cyclical sensitivity, as reflected in the monthly proportion of the workforce drawing benefits. This monthly proportion varied greatly over time, as periods of recession and prosperity succeeded one another. In steel, for example, the proportion varied from less than 1 percent to 22 percent. On the average, this proportion was higher in steel than in autos, and higher in autos than in rubber. Comparable data were not available for other plans.

From the few scattered data available, it would seem that the proportion of those *laid off* who drew benefits varied greatly from company to company and from time to time. In rubber, the proportion varied from 99 percent down to 55 percent. In steel the proportion was lower, varying from 68 percent to less than 1 percent. Data from one auto company for one year (Appendix Table 1) show that almost a third of the laid-off employees did not even file for SUB.

Several factors may explain the low proportion of SUB recipients. Some of the nonrecipients may have found other jobs; some may have temporarily left the labor force, for example, to take a vacation; some may have been serving their waiting week; some may have exhausted their credit units; some may have been disqualified for UI and hence for SUB; finally, since layoffs are usually made in inverse order of seniority, many probably lacked the requisite one or two years of seniority. No information is available on the relative sizes of these different groups of nonrecipients; their relative sizes no doubt varied from company to company and from period to period, but lack of seniority was probably the chief factor.

Benefit amount. In steel, SUB payments averaged about 35 to 40 percent of the combined unemployment benefit (UI plus SUB); for the one auto-type plan for which data were available, the percent was roughly the same. This proportion varied greatly by states. For example, in 1965, employees of one can company received, on the average, 46 percent of their total unemployment benefit in the form of a SUB payment. This proportion varied from 20 percent for the employees in Wisconsin to 78 percent for the employees in Florida. (Some of the Florida benefits represented SUB payments made after UI had been exhausted.) For another example, in 1963, the average SUB payment of one of the rubber companies ranged from $7.44 in Massachusetts to $42.10 in Tennessee. In this way, the unions have achieved their long-sought goal of equalizing unemployment benefits for their members in all states.[7]

The limitation imposed by the maximum SUB payment prevents some

---

7. As indicated below, equal unemployment benefits may have unequal effects on labor mobility.

claimants from actually receiving the proportion of wages nominally provided in the plan. In the steel plan, after its maximum had been increased in 1962, claimants receiving — and presumably limited by — the maximum SUB payment averaged about a fourth of all claimants. In the UI program, a frequently proposed norm of adequacy is that the great majority of beneficiaries should receive the stipulated proportion of their wages without being held down by the established maximum. If 75 percent is taken as a "great majority," experience under the steel plan would seem to have been satisfactory in this respect. The scattered data available for auto experience seem to indicate that the proportion of claimants limited by the maximum under that plan was much smaller than under the steel plan. It is likely that under the auto-type plans nearly all the beneficiaries received the stipulated 62 percent of wages.

Duration of benefits. Under the steel plan in recent years, somewhere between 10 and 20 percent of all SUB payments were made after UI had been exhausted. Under the auto plan, this proportion was even smaller. Evidently, the supplementation of UI duration has not been a major function of the SUB plans.

Some claimants exhausted their SUB eligibility. Of these, some did so because they had been unemployed for a very long time; many more, because at the time of layoff they had only a few credit units. Under the steel plan, the exhaustion ratio (exhaustees as a proportion of all beneficiaries) approached 20 percent of all beneficiaries during periods of heavy unemployment but in more prosperous periods was much smaller. In 1965, for example, the average exhaustion ratio in steel was only 2 percent. Data for one auto company showed that 33 percent of beneficiaries exhausted their SUB credits in 1958 but only 3 percent did so in 1963.

Although the rubber companies tended to have less unemployment than the auto companies, what unemployment they had lasted longer, and the exhaustion ratio under the rubber SUB plans was higher. Even under the rubber plan, however, exhaustions for the years 1960–1964 averaged less than 3 percent of the workforce.

Under the auto plan, the average duration of benefits tended to be shorter than under other plans, probably because a large proportion of the beneficiaries were employees laid off briefly at the time of the annual model change. Auto experience is characterized by a large number of workers drawing benefits for a short period.

Financing. During the first decade of experience, the steel plans collected about half a billion dollars in contributions and paid out about half this amount in benefits. (For several of the largest steel companies the benefit-contribution ratio was as high as 80 percent.) The auto plans also collected about half a billion dollars, of which they paid out about half. The agricultural implement plans paid out about 41 percent of contributions, and the rubber plans paid out about 68 percent.

The auto-type plan was clearly countercyclical in its operation, with contributions dropping sharply as benefits rose. Because of its use of contingent liability, the steel plan in recent years has not been countercyclical. As unemployment and benefits increased, contingent liability had to be liquidated, and the demand on the companies to produce cash was at its greatest when business was at its worst.

Costs per man-hour, the most significant measure of cost, may be reckoned in terms of contributions and of benefits. Under the steel plan, the man-hour cost of contributions, including the accrual of contingent liability, averaged about 6 cents, while the cost of benefits averaged less than 4 cents. For the auto and agricultural implement companies, contributions cost 4 to 5 cents per man-hour, while benefits cost about 3 cents. The rubber companies had lower man-hour costs than any of the other core plans. Contributions amounted to less than 3 cents, and benefits were about 70 percent of contributions. Under all plans there was considerable variation over time and between companies. For example, in 1961, one auto company had a benefit cost of 17.6 cents per man-hour.

The experience of the Alan Wood Steel Company is particularly interesting because this company has had, since 1965, the most liberal SUB plan of all those studied. During the first 20 months (July 1965 through February 1967) under the new provisions, the plan paid out in benefits only 1.33 cents per man-hour (0.19 cents in regular benefits and 1.14 cents in short-week benefits). This favorable experience illustrates once again that, under relatively favorable economic conditions, even a very liberal SUB plan does not necessarily result in high costs.

The steel plan had a problem with fund adequacy during the early period of its operation (1956–1962). Most companies paid reduced benefits in at least some months during this period. The amendments to the plan negotiated in 1962 strengthened the financial structure considerably, and it is not likely that the previous experience will soon be repeated. Although the auto plans have been especially well financed, the Studebaker Corporation was able to pay only a small fraction of its SUB obligations when it closed. Moreover, Chrysler saw its fund go as low as 10 percent of maximum funding; and toward the end of 1965 the American Motors Corporation had to reduce duration of benefits because of the condition of its fund. Only a system of reinsurance — perhaps established by a union with its own funds — could provide protection against these extreme risks. The other core plans have had no problems with fund adequacy.

Operation: Multi-Employer Plans

The experience of the multi-employer plans is interesting for several reasons. The technique of bringing together a number of small employers enables SUB to flourish where it could not otherwise function. The number of these plans has increased notably in recent years, and they have penetrated new industries; hence they may have a significant growth potential. Also, of all SUB plans, these are the most similar to UI in their eligibility and disqualification provisions and hence their experience is most relevant to a comparison of the private and public programs.

As of mid-1966, after two and a half years of operation, the plan of the Detroit Electrical Workers (IBEW) had not made a single SUB payment. The complete absence of payments is striking evidence of administrative control of claims in a tight labor market. The control is all the more significant because administration was closely connected with the union and because the plan provided for considerable freedom from indirect control by UI.

Under the plan of the Buffalo Carpenters (CJA), union members have participated widely in the benefits of the plan: each year from one third to one half of the covered employees have drawn some benefits from the fund. The cost of contributions has been the highest of any SUB plan. As of 1965, covered employers were paying about 30 cents per man-hour into the SUB fund. Administrative costs have been moderate — about 6 percent of benefits.

The plan of the Retail Clerks (RCIA) employed in the food stores of southern California has been one of the least expensive of SUB plans. Employers have been required to contribute about 1 cent per man-hour, and this has been sufficient to pay benefits and build up a reserve fund. The relatively inexpensive operation of this plan is even more noteworthy because the plan's disqualification provisions have been identical with those in UI. The low cost of SUB payments under this plan is explained chiefly by the relatively high California UI benefits and by the low unemployment rate which characterizes retail food stores generally. Administrative costs for this plan averaged something less than 5 percent of benefits.

The SUB plan of the Brewery Workers (BFLSD) in New Orleans provides an example of how experience with unemployment may determine the choice between alternative kinds of unemployment benefit plans. The union members who had experienced a significant amount of unemployment chose a pooled SUB plan, while the others chose an individual-account plan. The contributory cost for each fund was originally the same, 5 cents per hour worked. The SUB plan paid out 29 percent of the contributions it collected, while the individual-account plan paid out only 11 percent. Moreover, in the SUB plan the entire 29 percent consisted of unemployment benefits, while less than 1 percent of the contributions made under the individual-account plan was paid out in the form of unemployment benefits.

Administrative costs as a percentage of benefits have been remarkably high for both plans, over 100 percent in the case of the individual-account plan and about 50 percent in the case of the SUB plan. For both plans, the chief reason for this high proportion has been the relatively few benefits paid out.

External Relationships

Effect of SUB on the Allocation of Labor

Whatever effect SUB plans may have had on the demand for labor by their contribution to "purchasing power," it has been too small to be measured. The more significant impact of the plans on the level of employment has been through the contributions required of the employer. Contributions to the plans represent an additional labor cost, which could have, and probably has had, two effects on the demand for labor. First, it has reinforced the employer's incentive to stabilize employment. To some extent both regular SUB and the short-week benefit seem to have had this effect. Second, SUB has probably contributed in a minor way to the recent tendency of employers to work a smaller labor force for longer hours.

Abandonment of experience rating has given SUB a relationship to employment stabilization the opposite of that originally intended. Where SUB has become a fixed cost, it has provided an incentive for the employer to accept more unemployment than would otherwise have been economical. But all effects of SUB on the demand for labor have been obscure and probably small.

SUB has had several effects on the supply of labor. It has helped maintain the employer's workforce intact during temporary layoffs. This desirable effect is only partially attributable to SUB, however, for in high-wage industries workers cling tenaciously to their seniority and gladly leave other jobs when they receive their call-back notices. SUB seems also to have lessened, without entirely removing, union opposition to technological changes that were expected to cause layoffs. Some liberalizations of SUB plans were negotiated with the explicit understanding that the employer was to have more freedom to introduce changes.

The net effect of SUB on labor mobility has probably been to decrease it. SUB programs often come into being in industries affected by serious unemployment problems, some of which call for movement of labor out of the industry and, at times, out of the locality. When the combined unemployment benefits of UI and SUB almost equal the wages paid in other available jobs, they can easily have the effect of delaying needed adjustments in the labor force.

One of the clearer and more significant effects of SUB has been the change, in some circumstances, in the relative desirability of working and not working. There have been situations in which the availability of SUB has induced employees to choose a temporary layoff rather than a lower-paying job. This tendency is most apparent in the new phenomenon of "reverse seniority." The major unions with SUB plans have begun to insist that in some circumstances workers with the highest seniority be laid off first or, preferably, that they be given a choice between moving into an available job and taking a layoff. Where the union already had this option, SUB has resulted in workers' choosing the layoff over the job much more frequently than before. In the industries covered by SUB, the seniority provisions are almost certain to be revised to make layoffs more readily available to the high-seniority employees.

By increasing the desirability of not working relative to working, SUB may have increased the size of the labor force needed for a given level of production, but for at least two reasons the increase up to the present has been so slight as to be insignificant. First, the exercise of the employee's option is in practice limited to situations involving either temporary layoff or permanent retirement. Second, the exercise of the option usually results, not in the hiring of an additional employee, but merely in the substitution of one employee for another in a given job.

Although the exercise of the option has on occasion limited the employer's freedom to deploy his workforce as he thinks best, on other occasions the availability of SUB has increased his freedom to make temporary layoffs according to the requirements of efficiency rather than according to rigid seniority rules. In the rubber industry, at least, the latter effect has probably offset the former.

SUB makes seasonal swings in employment less objectionable to labor. It may even make them desirable. Employees may work at overtime rates during the rush period and then draw UI and SUB during the slump period. In this way they may actually make more money — and have more leisure in addition — than if they had been employed steadily at regular hours. This possibility has application especially in the building trades.

SUB reinforces the effect of UI in enlarging the freedom of a union to strike. A strike often causes unemployment among workers other than those actually striking. This secondary unemployment generates pressure on the strikers to settle. The pressure is lessened to the extent that additional unemployment benefits are available to the nonstrikers.

Effect of SUB on UI

The expectation that SUB would change the attitudes of labor and management toward UI has not been fulfilled in either case. The more likely change, a lessening of labor's interest in liberalizing UI, if it has occurred at all, has not been noticeable.

During the early debates on SUB, the charge was frequently made that it would increase the costs of UI by weakening the incentive of beneficiaries to find other work promptly and by causing some employees to choose a layoff when they might otherwise have chosen a job, thus increasing the number of claimants for unemployment benefits. In all probability SUB has somewhat increased the costs of UI in both ways, but not to a measurable or significant extent.

Since the negotiation of SUB is proof that the negotiating employer can afford to pay more for unemployment benefits than the state requires him to pay in the UI program, there is a basis for raising the UI tax ceiling (the potential maximum tax rate) for employers with a SUB plan. Such an arrangement would remove the anomalous situation which exists when an employer who is not paying his way in the UI program but is being subsidized by other employers negotiates a private unemployment-benefit plan to pay his employees higher total unemployment benefits (UI plus SUB) than are being received by the employees of the subsidizing employers.

From the beginning of the negotiations which led to SUB, some unions, especially the Auto Workers, wanted to make the private program completely independent of the public program of UI. In particular, they wanted SUB to be independent of any disqualifications imposed by UI, so that if an employee were disqualified under the public program — for example, because he refused a job offer — he might still be eligible to collect full benefits, equal to UI plus SUB, from the SUB fund.

Although none of the core plans has fully achieved this objective, there has been a trend in its direction. A dozen or more exceptions have been negotiated to the original requirement that to be eligible for SUB a claimant must be eligible for UI. There has been a tendency, also, to increase the amount of SUB that is payable when UI is not received. As of 1965, the can companies and Allis-Chalmers had gone farthest in this direction (but see Appendix B). As liberalized SUB plans became more independent of UI, the decline of union interest in UI that had been predicted at the beginning of SUB may begin to appear.

The unions have been almost completely successful in using SUB to achieve another long-sought objective. By means of SUB payments they have eliminated the effect of differences in the UI benefits paid by the various states. Where a state pays a relatively low UI benefit, the SUB payment is correspondingly increased, so that almost every union member, regardless of the state in which he works, receives the same benefit in relation to his wage.

Has a decade of experience under SUB thrown any light on the feasibility of liberalizing UI benefits to the point where they equal those paid by SUB plans? To liberalize UI to that extent would greatly increase, possibly double, UI taxes. It would also increase the number of improper payments in UI and probably lessen somewhat the mobility of labor. For all of these reasons, there is little immediate likelihood that UI will be liberalized to that extent. Nevertheless, the example of SUB has not been without its influence on UI. The knowledge that these higher benefits have been available to large numbers of workers for over a decade inevitably prepares the mind to accept UI benefits at least somewhat higher than have been paid traditionally. This influence of SUB on UI is likely to grow as the liberalization of SUB continues and as its successful experience becomes more widely known.

Although it is not likely that UI will ever actually absorb SUB, the question may be raised whether it should. This writer is inclined to think that it should not, partly for the philosophical reason given in the first quotation below and partly for the practical reason given in the other quotation. The first is from a statement in 1955 by Murray W. Latimer, the father of SUB: "I believe strongly in the social insurances operated by the government, but I believe equally strongly that the government ought not to have a monopoly in any of them. I think it would be a sad day for this country if all the old age insurance were provided under the Social Security Act. . . . There is now a government monopoly of unemployment insurance, to all intents and purposes. I do not believe it ought to continue. I think and I hope that the year 1955 has marked the end of government monopoly in unemployment insurance. I do not believe that SUB has meant a drive towards socialism, but the opposite" [11]. The other quotation is from David Lasser, research director of the Electrical Workers (IUE):

> *Question:* Mr. Lasser, you condemn present unemployment compensation benefits as inadequate. . . . If benefits were raised to the level you consider desirable, would you still believe in private supplementation?
>
> *Mr. Lasser:* Our attitude is similar on that with regard to the Federal

pension plan and private pensions. We do not suggest that the Government do everything. Government, whether it be national or State, has a certain lack of flexibility. We believe this dual system . . . is a good idea. . . . If, for example, all employers, right now, had to contribute 8 percent of their payroll to an unemployment compensation fund, some might not be able to do it. . . . We would introduce it first among those who are able to pay and let the thing spread from that point on. [66]

The chief limitation on the potential scope of all private programs is the limitation common to the whole system of private property, the inequality that results. Supplementary benefits generally appear in the industries that can better afford them, not necessarily in those that most need them. In a job-oriented society, where unemployment is a major and universal threat, the benefits provided by the public program should be as adequate and as widely available "as possible." In the debate over the dimensions of that possibility, any reasonable doubt among prudent men should generally be settled in favor of the public program. Private programs should be only supplemental to a truly adequate public program. Nevertheless, since our society has always preferred the system of competitive wages and private property, properly modified by a concern for the public interest, and since this preference inevitably involves the acceptance of some inequality of income, it would be inconsistent to demand equality of unemployment benefits. In our society, there is and probably will continue to be an established place for private unemployment-benefit programs.

Relation of SUB to Other Private Plans

Other private plans to aid the unemployed represent alternatives or complements to SUB. The individual-account type of plan, such as prevails in the glass industry, is one such alternative. As compared with SUB, the individual-account plan keeps clearer the distinction between the public and private spheres, is simpler to administer, and of course more directly encourages individual initiative and responsibility. This latter characteristic is particularly prominent in plans — such as that set up by the Egger Steel Company in 1956 — in which the employer matches the employee's contribution.

On the other hand, the individual-account plan provides the least protection for those who need it most, the low-seniority employees who have had the shortest time in which to build up their account and who are most liable to layoff. After a year of contributions at 5 cents per man-hour, a laid-off employee could receive $1,800 in a year from SUB but only $100 in a year from an individual-account plan. This type of plan is really nothing more than a form of forced savings and raises the question of whether such a plan is necessary for adults. Those connected with such plans, both labor and management, felt strongly that a significant proportion of the workforce would not save as they should without such compulsion.[8]

As compared with other unemployment-benefit plans, the individual-account plan has a further disadvantage: the individual may draw on his fund for purposes other than unemployment benefits. As a result the available resources are often dissipated among a variety of expenditures, leaving little for unemployment benefits. As a protection against the threat of unemployment, SUB is a much more effective instrument than the individual-account plan.

Severance-pay plans may be an alternative or a complement to SUB. In the airframe industry, for example, the Extended Layoff Benefit Plan, which provides a lump-sum payment to any employee who has been laid off for as long as four weeks, has functioned as an alternative to SUB. The industry contends that it rarely recalls workers who have been laid off and that therefore SUB is not an appropriate unemployment benefit.

Some SUB funds provide severance payments in place of or subsequent to SUB payments. In some plans, the employer may require the laid-off worker to take severance pay rather than SUB. Some plans subtract from the severance pay otherwise due any SUB payments that have been made.

To encourage labor mobility, it would seem desirable that there always be an adequate severance-pay plan operating concurrently with SUB and that, at least in some situations, such as the closing of a plant, the employer have the right to designate which benefit will be paid. High benefits payable over long periods are not the most appropriate provision for unemployed workers who have been permanently separated from their usual employment and who can draw the benefits only on condition that they remain unemployed.

The drive for employment security which culminated in SUB began as a demand for something called the "guaranteed annual wage." The guaranteed annual wage (GAW) and SUB have many points of similarity. Both seek to assure the worker a substantial proportion of his regular wage for a predictable period of time. Neither of them necessarily extends this assurance to the entire workforce nor for the full amount of wages. One difference is that the protection provided by a guaranteed annual wage

---

8. As one of the workers at the Nunn-Bush Company, which has had the equivalent of a forced savings plan for many years, put it: "I know a guy who made 60 bucks a week a year ago and now he makes $160 in a new business. A couple of nights ago he was so broke he couldn't pay for a beer. It's the same story. You got it coming, you spend it. You ain't got it, you don't spend it."

begins at the time of hire, while the protection of SUB begins at the time of layoff. Another difference is that SUB liability is confined to the resources of a fund built up by limited contributions. Although SUB was, as a matter of fact, negotiated as an alternative to GAW, the two could be complementary. An employee protected by both programs would be guaranteed a year of employment measured from the time of hire and a year or more of unemployment benefits payable after separation from employment (see Appendix B).

Conclusions

Internal Relationships

The original decisions, the fruit of intensive study by the steel and auto unions and by the Ford Motor Company, have proved sound. No fundamental changes have had to be made in the structure of the core SUB plans.

Many modifications, however, have been made in the plans in order to liberalize them further and to tailor them more closely to the particular circumstances of individual firms and industries. It is one of the advantages of private plans that they can be adapted to the individual situation.

In their operations, the core SUB plans must be judged as having been generally successful in achieving their principal objectives. A great majority of covered workers have had the necessary seniority and have been eligible for benefits. On the average, SUB has supplemented the UI amount by at least 50 percent, and very few SUB claimants have exhausted their benefits. In general, the core plans have been adequately financed, especially in recent years, and have been able to pay the covenanted benefits.

The multi-employer plans, which came into existence later than the core plans, have undergone fewer changes, but have been equally successful in attaining their objectives. The spread of SUB to the construction industry is the most noteworthy development in this area.

External Relationships

Judged by the norm of its relationship to other social objectives, again SUB would seem to deserve a favorable verdict.

SUB's net effect on the allocation of labor is slight. It has probably exercised a slight favorable effect on the demand for labor and a slight unfavorable effect on the labor supply. In any case, it is clear that, in certain types of situations, SUB has significantly affected the worker's choice between working and not working.

SUB has not notably changed the attitude of labor or of employers toward UI, nor has it notably increased the costs of UI. SUB is too different from UI to serve as an exact model for the further development of the public program. Nevertheless, as SUB grows more liberal and as its favorable experience becomes more widely known, UI is likely to be affected by the incontestable fact that for a decade it has been possible to pay large groups of workers in various industries relatively high unemployment benefits without causing any discernible disturbance in the labor market.

As a protection against unemployment, SUB would seem to be a more adequate instrument than either the originally proposed guaranteed annual wage or the individual-account plan.

Overall Appraisal

Although based on only a "scouting expedition" into the land of SUB — to repeat the warning of the Preface — the conclusions of this study are, on the whole, favorable. By both internal and external norms SUB's first decade must be judged a success.

APPENDIXES

APPENDIX A

Tables

Major Aspects of One Year's SUB Experience, Auto Company B,
April 1, 1960–March 31, 1961

Percentage Distributions

Layoffs by reason for layoff		*Laid-off employees by full weeks of*	
Model change	27.8	*layoff during the year*	
Reduction in force	31.1	1 or less	20.0
Inventory	10.1	2–5	45.7
Strikes	3.1	6–26	29.6
All other reasons[a]	27.9	Over 26	4.7
Total	100.0	Total	100.0
Layoffs by duration			
3 days to 1 week	56.5	*Laid-off employees by years of*	
2–5 weeks	27.6	*seniority at time of layoff*	
6–26 weeks	14.3	Less than 1	11.4
Over 26 weeks	1.6	1–5	16.7
Total	100.0	5–10	32.6
		10–15	20.7
Full weeks of layoff, by application		15–20	6.5
experience		Over 20	12.1
None filed	46.0	Total	100.0
Filed and SUB paid	51.0		
Disqualified	3.0	*Laid-off employees by credit units*	
Total	100.0	*accrued at time of layoff*	
		26 and over	74.4
Applications disqualified, by reason		17–25	11.1
for disqualification		1–16	5.0
State UI plus other compensa-		None	9.5
tion equaled more than 65 per-		Total	100.0
cent of after-tax straight-time			
pay	27.6	*Laid-off employees by participation*	
Failure to present UI check or		Did not file application	30.7
substitute document	38.1	Filed application but did not	
SUB calculated as less than $2.00	9.0	receive any SUB	1.5
Earnings for week equaled or		Filed more than one application,	
more than 65 percent of after-		but did not receive SUB on all	
tax straight-time pay	6.1	of them	14.0
Credits exhausted	4.5	Filed application(s) and received	
All other reasons	14.7	SUB on all of them	53.8
Total	100.0	Total	100.0

Other Major Aspects

Average amount of SUB benefit paid	$17.12
Average amount of state UI benefit paid	$39.79
Average amount of 65 percent of after-tax straight-time pay	$58.06
Percent of total laid-off employees who received one or more SUB payments	67.8
Percent of total weeks of layoff for which SUB benefits were paid	51.0
Average number of SUB payments per laid-off employee	3.5
Average number of SUB payments per laid-off employee who received SUB	5.1

SOURCE: Summary prepared by Company B.
[a] Includes shutdowns to adjust inventories.

297

APPENDIX TABLE 2

Contributions and Benefits, Twelve Auto-Type Plans, 1956–1965

Contributions and benefits, by plan[a]	1956	1957	1958	1959	1960	1961	1962	1963	1964	1965	1956–1965
					(thousands of dollars)						
UAW and American Motors											
Contributions	297	961	1,369	2,163	2,548	844	2,206[b]	2,154	794	1,777	15,113
Benefits	0	62	199	51	168	754	628[b]	1,147	3,516	3,538	10,063
UAW and Chrysler											
Contributions	12,306	10,625	3,616	6,496	7,259	3,794[c]	5,313	6,621	7,992	9,882	73,904
Benefits	1,899	1,603	8,134	9,741	5,223	3,385[c]	2,802	2,664	2,539	3,019	51,009
UAW and Ford											
Contributions	21,309	14,403	6,395	9,744	9,830	8,879	12,695	12,886	14,596	17,234	127,971
Benefits	793	1,388	13,256	5,309	5,512	8,492	5,125	7,820	4,174	4,521	56,390
UAW and General Motors											
Contributions	34,881	32,924	12,906	6,373	33,482	15,086	39,088	37,011	27,617	32,082	271,450
Benefits	1,545	4,121	16,313	22,515	8,942	21,930	10,950	11,910	11,936	13,804	123,966
UAW and Allis-Chalmers											
Contributions	1,895	1,746	1,382	738	114	425	1,003	1,162	1,181	1,202	10,848
Benefits	50	500	1,203	460	1,380	1,482	484	942	629	502	7,632
UAW and Caterpillar Tractor											
Contributions	2,060	2,132	827	240	1,063	1,511	33	774	28	1,836	10,504
Benefits	82	87	774	701	464	560	64	21	4	6	2,763

UAW and International Harvester											
Contributions	4,160	2,981	2,424	233	2,182	2,578	3,022	3,249	3,168	3,343	27,340
Benefits	408	352	580	498	2,776	1,604	1,676	528	449	1,151	10,022
UAW and Deere & Co.											
Contributions	1,448	1,185	1,325	1,371	1,444	852	1,059	1,454	1,728	1,834	13,700
Benefits	41	54	65	198	1,045	1,223	1,278	454	357	434	5,149
URW and Firestone											
Contributions		1,807	1,010	877	896	917	336	118	787	1,122	7,870
Benefits		47	1,038	130	215	1,081	338	273	871	954	4,947
URW and Goodrich											
Contributions		1,219	763	677	144	438	66	253	846	520	4,926
Benefits		7	378	35	250	566	182	390	850	533	3,191
URW and Goodyear											
Contributions		2,065	1,246	1,449	109	636	240	172	72	840	6,657
Benefits		10	562	219	396	819	322		325	392	3,217
URW and Uniroyal											
Contributions		2,464	1,466	1,567	793	944	304	95	603	884	9,120
Benefits		65	1,234	168	503	949	342	510	930	792	5,493

SOURCE: Data supplied by the companies.
a The companies are identified in this table because the data have been reported to the U.S. Department of Labor under the Welfare and Pension Plans Disclosure Act and are a matter of public record.
b Through November 1962.
c Through October 1961.

APPENDIX TABLE 3

Trust Fund Position,[a] Eleven Auto-Type SUB Plans, by Month, 1956–1965

Year and month	Auto companies-UAW				Agricultural implement companies-UAW			Rubber companies-URW			
	A	B	C	D	A	B	C	A	B	C	D
1956											
June	28	28		22							
July	30	31		23							
Aug.	32	33		25							
Sept.	34	36		26	24	31	21				
Oct.	32	37		25	25	33	22				
Nov.	34	36		28	27	36	24				
Dec.	35	37		27	7	38	25				
1957											
Jan.	38	39		30	29	40	28				
Feb.	40	42		32	30	41	29				
Mar.	43	46		35	32	43	33				
Apr.	46	49		37	34	45	37				
May	49	53		42	36	48	42				
June	51	55		42	37	50	45				
July	52	57		45	39	52	48		33		
Aug.	53	60		49	41	54	49	34	37	32	33
Sept.	54	63	21	51	43	55	51	37	39	35	36
Oct.	59	64	19	57	46	59	51	40	41	38	39
Nov.	59	61	20	55	48	62	51	43	44	91	42
Dec.	61	59	21	57	50	65	53	45	45	43	45
1958											
Jan.	66	64	21	58	51	68	55	48	49	46	48
Feb.	69	69	22	61	53	71	57	51	52	48	n.a.
Mar.	73	72	25	61	55	73	57	54	50	51	55
Apr.	74	76	28	59	58	74	59	55	48	50	57
May	71	77	30	59	59	75	58	57	48	51	57
June	116	128	30	100	61	75	60	56	44	49	57
July	109	129	38	104	61	74	78	55	46	46	56
Aug.	106	128	41	103	73	75	81	54	46	44	57
Sept.	102	123	50	102	77	74	84	56	49	45	59
Oct.	96	117	39	98	80	73	86	58	49	45	60
Nov.	94	154	40	98	84	73	86	61	51	47	62
Dec.	93	109	36	95	87	77	85	63	53	49	64
1959											
Jan.	94	107	37	104	117	79	82	66	56	47	68
Feb.	97	107	39	89	117	79	81	68	58	51	69
Mar.	100	109	42	n.a.	104	80	83	70	63	53	71
Apr.	99	109	44	82	100	105	84	74	67	56	75
May	97	109	45	86	99	108	87	77	67	58	80
June	98	109	47	87	100	99	89	79	69	n.a.	n.a.
July	99	107	66	n.a.	98	96	95	81	69	60	79
Aug.	100	109	70	99	100	98	98	83	74	58	79
Sept.	76	83	114	69	103	101	100	87	77	61	83

APPENDIX TABLE 3 (*Continued*)

Year and month	Auto companies-UAW				Agricultural implement companies-UAW			Rubber companies-URW			
	A	B	C	D	A	B	C	A	B	C	D
1959 (Cont.)											
Oct.	75	75	76	63	106	91	83	90	77	64	85
Nov.	76	79	74	61	108	104	86	93	84	66	89
Dec.	79	76	75	61	114	98	92	94	87	68	91
1960											
Jan.	81	66	78	60	87	98	91	98	87	70	95
Feb.	84	67	79	60	85	134	90	100	90	73	97
Mar.	89	72	82	62	87	135	86	101	93	78	101
Apr.	94	77	88	65	88	127	84	102	95	80	101
May	95	81	92	n.a.	88	126	86	103	98	84	111
June	97	83	97	68	91	129	87	102	98	89	110
July	98	87	76	71	92	124	84	103	100	89	105
Aug.	100	93	80	75	91	124	82	102	100	93	105
Sept.	97	97	102	74	90	134	80	102	101	96	107
Oct.	97	89	88	75	88	128	81	102	100	99	105
Nov.	99	90	82	77	86	125	82	103	100	100	102
Dec.	101	93	81	78	85	108	84	100	101	98	101
1961											
Jan.	102	95	84	76	81	107	86	100	101	98	94
Feb.	102	101	96	70	80	103	89	99	100	99	94
Mar.	100	101	105	63	80	105	96	98	99	97	95
Apr.	97	99	104	51	80	100	99	97	98	96	94
May	92	96	100	45	77	98	104	96	95	93	92
June	92	96	95	41	80	94	107	95	94	90	97
July	94	98	129	41	82	95	107	95	95	90	98
Aug.	96	102	133	41	82	112	105	97	99	92	114
Sept.	97	96	141	30	85	109	106	98	99	92	101
Oct.	97	144	138	29	88	109	101	101	100	94	101
Nov.	99	90	128	30	90	100	98	101	103	97	102
Dec.	99	90	128	32	91	109	94	100	103	98	100
1962											
Jan.	100	92	n.a.	35	73	92	90	100	102	100	100
Feb.	101	69	n.a.	35	74	104	87	99	104	99	102
Mar.	104	68	n.a.	34	73	52	87	101	104	99	101
Apr.	104	66	n.a.	33	71	58	n.a.	100	102	98	100
May	b	64	n.a.	32	71	51	n.a.	100	100	99	99
June	b	64	n.a.	32	66	47	n.a.	99	99	97	100
July	b	64	n.a.	32	65	45	n.a.	99	100	96	99
Aug.	b	68	n.a.	32	57	45	n.a.	101	104	98	101
Sept.	b	73	n.a.	31	59	45	n.a.	99	104	100	101
Oct.	b	68	n.a.	31	72	46	n.a.	98	103	102	100
Nov.	b	69	n.a.	31	76	49	n.a.	98	103	101	100
Dec.	75	66	n.a.	10	50	53	56	99	101	99	105

APPENDIX TABLE 3 (*Continued*)

Year and month	Auto companies-UAW				Agricultural implement companies-UAW			Rubber companies-URW			
	A	B	C	D	A	B	C	A	B	C	D
1963											
Jan.	76	68	78	11	51	54	56	100	101	99	100
Feb.	76	71	79	12	52	55	55	100	104	101	100
Mar.	77	74	76	14	52	51	55	102	103	101	99
Apr.	80	76	78	15	52	54	57	102	103	101	100
May	82	78	80	16	52	51	61	102	102	99	98
June	83	80	81	16	53	54	62	102	102	99	100
July	82	83	82	18	53	54	64	101	102	98	109
Aug.	83	87	83	20	55	54	66	102	103	100	107
Sept.	83	87	95	17	55	57	63	101	133	101	96
Oct.	81	79	104	18	58	54	65	101	132	101	99
Nov.	81	80	108	19	59	54	56	102	118	101	91
Dec.	82	81	110	20	61	51	59	102	112	101	93
1964											
Jan.	84	82	111	21	62	50	58	101	104	96	90
Feb.	87	84	114	23	61	47	58	101	105	99	91
Mar.	88	86	119	24	63	47	60	103	101	98	90
Apr.	89	88	117	26	62	49	62	102	99	96	92
May	100	89	118	27	62	51	64	102	101	97	91
June	88	90	116	28	63	51	65	101	98	98	92
July	89	94	100	69	64	50	67	99	99	97	94
Aug.	89	99	93	71	65	55	65	100	103	99	97
Sept.	87	93	94	62	67	58	63	100	101	99	101
Oct.	87	91	91	57	69	60	61	100	101	99	96
Nov.	86	95	93	57	71	62	61	100	100	99	98
Dec.	88	97	95	58	73	63	62	99	99	98	100
1965											
Jan.	90	93	98	59	77	65	61				
Feb.	91	99	99	61	72	67	61				
Mar.	90	99	90	62	75	68	62				
Apr.	91	99	91	62	77	68	65				
May	91	98	91	63	78	71	62				
June	91	99	89	65	76	70	62				
July	89	98	79	66	75	72	63				
Aug.	89	98	73	68	75	80	63				
Sept.	88	90	69	68	77	81	65				
Oct.	88	91	69	63	79	88	60				
Nov.	90	88	71	63	81	86	60				
Dec.	91	87	71	65	82	89	61				

SOURCE: For some dates and companies, calculations supplied by the companies or the unions; for other dates and companies, calculations made by the writer.

[a] Amount of fund as percent of maximum financing.

[b] Data not available. It may be assumed, however, that the fund was below maximum financing because the latter was increased substantially, effective during this period.

APPENDIX B

Changes in SUB Plans, 1967

The SUB changes negotiated during 1967 were among the more dramatic in the program's history, notably extending the previous trends toward greater liberality and increased differentiation. These changes have come close to completing the evolution begun in 1955. Moreover, while still only skirting anything that could properly be called a "guaranteed annual wage," the 1967 amendments moved the SUB plans substantially closer to supplying equivalent protection.

The major changes are shown in the table below. It is not so completely self-explanatory as might be desired, but this Appendix, which had to be written when the rest of the manuscript was in galleys, presumes that the reader is already familiar with the body of the report, where the basic explanations have been given.

As in 1955, in 1967 the drive for greater employment security was begun by the Auto Workers (UAW). More than a year in advance of negotiations, the union had announced that its next contract would have to include salaried status and some form of guaranteed wage for the hourly-paid worker. These goals were stated only in general terms which left much room for adaptation in the course of the bargaining process.

The Rubber Workers (URW) adopted the same slogans of "salaried status" and "guaranteed wages," but they were even less specific in their pre-bargaining explanation of the terms. Since contracts in the rubber industry expired in the spring of 1967, the Rubber Workers had the first opportunity to move toward these goals. On July 14th, after a three-week strike, the union reached an agreement with General Tire & Rubber Co. The other major companies, some of which had been strike-bound since April 21st, followed suit. When the dust had settled, the result was seen to be a simple but dramatic liberalization of the SUB plan.

As shown in the table, the regular benefit was increased to 80 percent (from 65 percent) of gross weekly wages.[1] At this high level of benefits, equivalent to 90 percent or more of net wages,[2] there seemed to be little room for the addition of dependents' allowances, so these were eliminated. As a result, however, claimants with dependents now receive a smaller percentage of net wages than do claimants without dependents.

The limit on the maximum benefit was removed. This change, important in itself, altered the significance of other parts of the plan. A claimant eligible for SUB is now entitled to receive 80 percent of his gross weekly wage under all circumstances. Since this includes the circumstance of a claimant's not being eligible for UI, it enhances the significance of all the "Arabs" (Table 4-3). For example, a claimant who has exhausted his UI benefits — usually after 26 weeks — will no longer experience a reduction in his benefit amount but will

1. Weekly straight-time pay before taxes. Net wages are gross wages after taxes.
2. A worker subject to federal, state, and municipal income taxes could receive more than his net wages. For example, such a worker living in Detroit and earning $3.65 per hour would receive unemployment benefits equal to 104 percent of his net wages. However, he would have to pay some taxes on the SUB part of these benefits.

303

APPENDIX B
Major Changes Negotiated in Selected SUB Plans during 1967[a]

Plan	Regular benefit amount		Dependents' allowance	Waiting week	Short-week benefit	Contribution rate per hour	Maximum funding (approx. amount per employee)[c]	Experience rating
	Percentage of wages[b]	Maximum						
	(1)	(2)	(3)	(4)	(5)	(6)	(7)	(8)
URW and rubber companies	80% of gross wages	None	None		80% of gross wages lost[b, d]	5¢ or 6¢[e]	$300	Partially restored
UAW and auto companies[f]	95% of net wages, minus $7.50	None[g]	None[g]		80% of gross wages lost[b, d]	5¢, 6¢, or 7¢[e h]	$900	Restored
UAW and Deere & Company	95% of net wages for first 3–7 wks. depending on seniority; thereafter as in auto plan	None	None	None	95% of net wages lost[b, d]	5¢, 6¢, or 7¢[e h]	$800	Restored

[a] Exclusive of new provision for guaranteed annual income credit units (see text).

[b] Gross wages, average weekly straight-time pay; net wages, gross wages minus taxes withheld.

[c] In most plans, these approximate amounts change as the average benefit changes in response to changes in wages and/or UI benefits. (The average benefit is a factor in the funding formula.)

[d] "Wages lost": straight-time pay for each hour less than 40 not compensated or made available by the company. In the rubber and auto plans the same benefit is paid for both scheduled and unscheduled short weeks. In the Deere plan only unscheduled short-week benefits are paid from the SUB fund; scheduled short-week benefits are paid, at 100 percent of gross wages lost, as part of the Income Security plan.

[e] 6¢ until plan is at maximum funding; then the company continues to contribute 5¢, which, while the fund remains at maximum level, "spills over" into a special account for an annual bonus.

[f] Provisions shown in columns (1), (2), and (3) become effective Dec. 1, 1968.

[g] Except in the case of the claimant who has been denied UI because he has refused suitable work offered by the company or who, having exhausted his UI credits, continues on layoff after refusing such work. In such cases the maximum amount payable is $70 plus $1.50 for each of not more than 4 dependents.

[h] Dependent on whether the fund is at least 13/16, 1/2, or less than 1/2, respectively, of maximum funding.

continue to receive 80 percent of his gross wage (all in the form of SUB) over an extended period — up to four years for long-seniority employees. Since the benefit approaches or exceeds take-home pay, there is thus a marked increase in security for the victims of structural long-term unemployment. On the other hand, there are obviously some implications for work incentives and labor mobility (see Chapter 11).

The elimination of the maximum also affects Arab No. 7 (Table 4–3), which allows a claimant to receive SUB even when he has refused a job offer by the company and has therefore been disqualified by the UI agency. Such a claimant may continue to receive 80 percent of his gross wages for as long as he has credit units. Because of these liberalizations in the benefit formula and because the rubber plan has always operated under a seniority system of more than average liberality, it has probably replaced the plan of the can industry in providing "the most instructive testing ground for the relationship of SUB to labor mobility and availability" (p. 117).

The rubber plan increased the amount of the short-week benefit to 80 percent of lost earnings[3] for scheduled and unscheduled short weeks alike. By this change the hourly-paid employee almost achieved the "salaried status" sought by the union, at least as far as security against layoffs is concerned. An employee laid off for a day or two could still count on receiving over 90 percent of his gross weekly earnings.

To finance these liberalizations, maximum funding was raised to $300 per employee and the maximum contribution rate was increased from 5 cents to 6 cents.[4] It was further provided that when maximum funding had been attained, the employer's contribution would revert to 5 cents, which would — as before — go into a special account for the financing of an annual bonus. Insofar as the employer is thus given the opportunity to save 1 cent of his total contribution, a bit of experience rating has been restored to the rubber plan.

When the auto contracts expired in the summer of 1967, the Auto Workers selected Ford as the target company. The choice of Ford was dictated by many of the considerations which had led to the same choice in 1955 (see Chapter 1). At the beginning of the negotiations, the union demanded more security than had been won in the rubber settlement, while the company refused to grant even that much. The result was a compromise, achieved in October,[5] in which the SUB plan was liberalized to a lesser extent than in the rubber industry but now included a new form of security, Guaranteed Annual Income Credit Units (GAICU). Subsequently, Chrysler, General Motors, and American Motors[6] adopted essentially the same settlement. The net result of negotiations in 1967,

3. "Lost earnings": straight-time pay for each hour less than 40 not compensated or made available by the company.

4. General Tire & Rubber Company, the first rubber company to agree to the new benefits, did not increase maximum funding or the maximum contribution in its plan.

5. The Ford strike, which began on September 7, 1967, was formally settled 46 days later on October 22d. The strike did not end at all locations until November 11th, thus lasting a total of 66 days.

6. The American Motors settlement, reached in mid-March 1968, provided that the higher contribution rate of 7 cents would go into effect immediately but that the higher benefits would not be payable until the SUB reserve had reached 50 percent of maximum funding. It was not expected that this level would be reached during the life of the two-year contract.

as in 1955, was something less than seems to have been envisaged in the union's original statement of objectives ("guaranteed income and salaried status"), but it still represented a very substantial gain.

The Ford negotiations produced an increase in the benefit amount from 62 percent of gross wages to 95 percent of net wages. The company insisted on returning to the base of net wages for the same reason that had led it to prefer this base originally, namely, the better to maintain an adequate work incentive. For this reason also, the company and union agreed to subtract an average amount, estimated at $7.50 a week, for expenses normally incurred by the employee only when working. Since the usual result of the use of net wages is that the worker with dependents receives a larger payment than one without dependents, there was no need to retain the separate provision for a dependents' allowance, and it was dropped. As compared with the previous formula, which paid 62 percent of gross wages plus a dependents' allowance, the new formula is calculated to yield an average benefit equal to about 68 to 77 percent of gross wages, varying positively with the number of dependents.[7] The formula for the short-week benefit was liberalized to pay, as in the rubber plan, 80 percent of lost gross wages.

The benefit formula used in the auto plan thus differs in two respects from that used in the rubber plan: it pays a benefit representing a lower percentage of wages (gross and net), and it favors the claimant with dependents instead of the claimant without dependents. For both reasons, the auto plan poses less of a problem with respect to the maintenance of work incentives. This is particularly true for the claimant without dependents. Where such a worker is eligible for 80 percent of gross wages under the rubber plan, he is eligible for only about 68 percent of gross wages under the auto plan.

The auto plan is also less liberal than the rubber plan in the benefit it pays to the claimant who has refused an offer of work. The auto plan, as negotiated by Ford, followed the rubber plan in abolishing the limitation on the maximum amount of SUB payable — with one exception. A benefit of $70 plus $1.50 for each of not more than four dependents is the maximum amount payable to the claimant who is laid off or continues on layoff because he refused an offer of work by the company[8] and who is not receiving UI because he has refused such work or has exhausted his UI benefits. The limitation on the maximum in this circumstance reflected Ford's concern with the possible effect of the increased benefits on labor availability and mobility. The same concern caused the company to write into its SUB plan (Art. V, Sec. 1[c]) more stringent reporting requirements to be fulfilled by claimants who had exhausted their UI benefits and would therefore no longer be exposed to offers of jobs by the state employment security agency.

To provide a reserve adequate for the liberalized benefits, maximum funding was increased to about $900 per employee,[9] and the employer's maximum con-

7. As before, health insurance for the worker and his dependents and life insurance for the worker are continued without worker contribution for a period corresponding to SUB duration. Thus the laid-off worker is receiving the equivalent of about $8 per week more than his SUB check would indicate.

8. As in previous contracts, the skilled trades men are exempt from this limitation: they may refuse an offer of production work without penalty.

9. In determining the amount of maximum funding, all the auto companies now use a 12-month moving average mancount.

tribution rate was raised to 7 cents per hour. The company was successful in achieving the restoration of experience rating. The employer need contribute only to the extent that the fund is below the maximum and may thus save up to the full 7 cents. The previous "Christmas bonus" which had been financed by the "spill-over" from the SUB fund was eliminated. The union did not seriously oppose the restoration of experience rating, probably for two reasons. First, the union saw some value in experience rating: in both 1955 and 1967, in explaining its demand for guaranteed income, the union had stressed strongly the advantages of providing the employer with an added incentive to avoid unemployment. Second, the union expected that the new level of maximum funding would not be reached during the term of the present agreement. In the auto plan, the effective date for the higher maximum contribution was postponed until October 1968 and for the higher SUB benefits, until December 1968.

As compared with the pattern established in previous negotiations, the agricultural implement companies followed the auto settlement less closely; they also differed more among themselves. Although not identical in all details with the SUB plans of the other companies in this industry, the plan of Deere & Company illustrates the deviation of the agricultural implement plans from the auto pattern.[10] As is shown in the table above, the benefits provided by this plan are somewhat more liberal than those of the auto plan. For example, during the early weeks of each layoff (the first three to seven weeks, depending on seniority), the estimated working expenses ($7.50) are not subtracted from the benefit amount. Thereafter, the benefit is calculated as in the auto plan.

The Deere plan was amended to eliminate the waiting week; that is, SUB (the full amount, unaffected by a maximum) has become payable when UI is not payable because the week involved is the first week in the benefit year. This change is the more expensive because it affects every eligible employee who becomes unemployed for even one week in the course of a year.

The Deere plan retains a distinction between scheduled and unscheduled short weeks. Scheduled short weeks have been taken out of the SUB plan and made a part of the new Income Security plan. For such weeks, the employee is guaranteed his full (gross) weekly wage. The unscheduled short-week benefit is paid from the SUB fund at the same rate as the regular benefit, 95 percent of lost net wages. (Unlike the Deere plan, the plan of International Harvester follows the auto formula, paying 80 percent of lost gross wages for any kind of short week.)

The Deere plan resembles the rubber plan in its complete elimination of the maximum benefit and dependents' allowances. In this plan, maximum funding has been set at about $800 per employee,[11] and the maximum contribution rate is the same as that in the auto plan. Also, as in the auto plan, experience rating has been restored.

10. The plan of Caterpillar Tractor differed from the Deere plan somewhat more than did the plan of International Harvester. As of February 1968, negotiations had not been completed at Allis-Chalmers, which, like American Motors, was asking for special provisions in view of its particular circumstances.

11. The plan of International Harvester does not use the formula for calculating maximum funding used by the other plans; instead, it directly specifies a dollar amount ($800) per employee, which will remain constant over the life of the contract. The plans of International Harvester and Caterpillar provide for a somewhat different contribution schedule, requiring maximum contribution of 10 cents per hour when the fund is below 55 percent of maximum funding.

In many of the 1967 negotiations, seniority provisions came in for discussion in connection with the liberalization of SUB provisions. Some employers asked for a loosening of seniority restrictions in exchange for increased income security; these demands seem to have been granted only to Deere & Company and Caterpillar Tractor Company. On their side, the unions demanded more options for high-seniority employees to choose a layoff rather than available work. In both the rubber and agricultural implement industries, some companies agreed to try to work out provisions, on a plant-by-plant basis, that would permit the exercise of such an option in specified circumstances.

The Steelworkers negotiated a new contract with the can companies in February 1968 but made no change in the benefit formula, which had already been considerably liberalized in 1965. The only substantial change made in this SUB plan was in the method of financing. Previously, several different kinds of benefits, including sickness benefits, had been paid out of a single fund financed by a contribution of 17 cents. But payments for sickness benefits out of this joint fund had been so heavy as to jeopardize the availability of the fund for unemployment benefits. To guard against this danger, the company and the union decided to establish a separate fund for unemployment benefits. By the 1968 amendments, 7 cents of the previous total contribution of 17 cents were allocated to this independent SUB fund. Beginning in early 1969, the maximum contribution to this fund will be raised to 8 cents.

As of this writing (February 1968), the Steelworkers have not commenced negotiations with the basic steel companies. Since the SUB plan in the basic steel industry has remained substantially unchanged since 1962, while plans in other industries have been greatly liberalized, the 1968 negotiations may produce significant changes in the steel SUB plan.

GUARANTEED ANNUAL INCOME

"Since these two benefits [SUB and GAW] are not exact substitutes for one another but are distinct programs fitted to perform distinct functions, labor may seek to add the guaranteed wage to supplementary unemployment benefits. An employee protected by both programs would be guaranteed a period of employment measured from the time of hire and a period of unemployment benefits after separation from employment" [31, p. 136]. In 1967, something not entirely unlike this anticipated development occurred when the Auto Workers and the Ford Motor Company negotiated the plan of Guaranteed Annual Income Credit Units (GAICU).

GAICU is what eventually came of the union's 1967 drive for "guaranteed wages." Just as the demand for GAW in 1955 resulted in SUB, so the similar demand in 1967 was answered by the further development of SUB. GAICU is essentially an extension of SUB. Its closest analogue is perhaps to be found in the way SUB credit units are restored to long-seniority employees in the 1965 can plan (see Table 5–6, n. h). In the auto plan, GAICU works this way: at a given date each year (the first pay period ending in December), every employee who is on the active employment rolls and has at least one year of seniority is given outright a specified number of credit units without having had to earn them in the usual way. The number of these free credit units is determined by two factors — the number of units he needs to bring his total to 52 and his years of seniority.[12] Employees with seven or more years of seniority receive 100 percent of the number of credit units needed to raise their total to 52. At the beginning of each guarantee year, therefore, such employees are assured[13] of a guaranteed annual income paid at the weekly SUB rate (95 percent of net wages, minus $7.50).

Employees with less than seven years of seniority are given a smaller percentage of the credit units needed to bring their total to 52, according to the following table.

Years of seniority	Applicable percent
1 but less than 2	25
2 but less than 4	50
4 but less than 7	75

For example, suppose that an employee comes to the end of November with 32 units remaining to his credit. Such an employee would need 20 more units to be certain of a full year's protection. If he is a seven-year man he will be given the entire 20 units, but if he has less than two years of seniority he will be given only 25 percent of 20, or 5 units, leaving him with 37 weeks of assured protection as he begins the year.

The additional benefit payments generated by the GAICU provisions are paid out of the SUB fund and are in every respect indistinguishable from other SUB payments.[14] They are thus liable to the uncertainties that attach to all SUB payments. For example, when the fund drops below a specified level, more than 1 credit unit may be required in exchange for each SUB payment, so that 52 credit units may not guarantee 52 payments. In all but the most abnormal circumstances, however, the guarantee will be effective. GAICU thus represents an ingenious use of SUB to move closer to that perpetually beckoning goal, "the guaranteed annual wage."

GAICU seems to have been the product of the combined efforts of union and company. In its proposal made in July 1967, the union clearly envisaged that the guaranteed wage (then called Income Maintenance Supplement) might be paid through the SUB trust fund and that the employer's liability might be limited in much the same way as his liability for SUB. On its side, Ford had taken the union's early announcement seriously, had done its homework, and was in a position — once again — to make constructive proposals of its own as to how the union's objectives might be reached in ways acceptable to the company. As a result, the final product bore the imprint of the company to a significant extent.[15]

As currently constituted, GAICU is not likely to prove very expensive. An extension of duration has always been one of the less costly forms of liberaliza-

12. Claimants who fulfill the requirements at some time later than the accounting date are not entirely excluded from the plan but are given proportionately fewer free credit units.

13. As explained below, the assurance is only as strong as the SUB fund.

14. In its November 1967 quarterly report to the stockholders, the Ford Motor Company stated: "The revised plan provides greater income security for employees, but still at a limited and predictable cost."

15. The rubber settlement does not seem to manifest the same degree of union and company inventiveness.

tion, and GAICU is very similar to an extension of duration. To see this, let us take the example of the seven-year man, who has the fullest guarantee. Suppose that such a man has experienced ten weeks of unemployment during the year and has thus used up ten credit units. Unless these ten weeks of unemployment occurred immediately before the accounting date (the first pay period in December), he will have had subsequent employment and will have thus regained some or all of the lost credit units. Even in the unlikely situation that he has regained none of the lost credit units, there may be no actual cost involved for the fund because he will use the free credit units only in the event that he eventually exhausts his earned credit units. The free units will actually all be used only if he becomes unemployed immediately after the guarantee date and stays unemployed throughout the entire ensuing year. Employees with lesser seniority are slightly more likely to use the free credit units, but they are also the ones who receive a smaller percentage of the credit units needed.

Essentially the same plan of increasing SUB duration for long-term employees was adopted by the agricultural implement industry. It differs from the auto plan chiefly in its definition of the guarantee date. Instead of restoring credit units on a fixed day of the year, this plan restores them on an individual basis, that is, on the Monday following the completion of two calendar weeks following the date of the individual's recall to active employment. It is too early to tell whether this difference will turn out to be important or not.

In its original proposal, the UAW had asked for a guaranteed monthly wage at full pay. They obtained this goal in only one contract, that negotiated with the Caterpillar Tractor Company.[16] This company was willing to grant the monthly guarantee in exchange for some revisions of seniority provisions which it felt were badly needed. International Harvester Company seems to have offered the same monthly guarantee, also in exchange for changes in seniority provisions, but the Auto Workers rejected this proposal (*Wall Street Journal*, November 2, 1967).

Appraisal of the new provisions must wait upon experience. It is clear that the security of the individual worker has been substantially increased. It would seem, also, that the companies which offer such liberal benefits should have less difficulty in retaining their workforces intact over periods of layoff and should be able to attract new workers more readily because of the great security represented by the SUB plans. On the other hand, the gap between the rewards for working and not working has been narrowed to a point where it may affect the availability and mobility of labor. Social scientists have a fertile field here in exploring the relative advantages and disadvantages of the new provisions. Certainly, if experience reveals no serious disadvantages, the horizons of industry and government will have been greatly expanded as to the possible extent fo unemployment-benefit programs.

16. This monthly guarantee covers scheduled layoffs only, and only if the company fails to give notice of layoff as required by the plan.

LIST OF REFERENCES

1. U.S., Department of Labor, Bureau of Labor Statistics, *Severance Pay and Layoff Benefit Plans*, Bulletin 1425–2 (Washington: Government Printing Office, 1965).
2. Stewart, Bryce M., and Associates, *Unemployment Benefits in the United States* (New York: Industrial Relations Research Counselors, Inc., 1938).
3. U.S., Office of War Mobilization and Reconversion, *Guaranteed Wages* (Washington: Government Printing Office, 1947).
4. Rowntree, B. Seebohm, *The Human Factor in Business* (Boston: Longmans, Green & Co., 1938).
5. Letter to author from H. Metcalf of Rowntree & Company, Ltd., November 9, 1966.
6. Letter of D. H. Mason to author, July 28, 1965.
7. U.S., Wage Stabilization Board, *A Guaranteed Wage Plan for Workers in the Steel Industry*, Case No. D-18-C (Washington: Government Printing Office, n.d.).
8. United Automobile Workers, CIO, *Progress Report on Guaranteed Annual Wage Preparations: Prepared for the UAW–CIO Full Employment Conference, Washington, D.C., December 6 and 7, 1953* (Washington: United Automobile Workers, 1953).
9. The Bureau of National Affairs, *Views of the UAW's Public Advisory Committee on the Guaranteed Annual Wage: Special Report No. 2, Daily Labor Report, May 17, 1955* (Washington: By the Bureau, 1955).
10. United Automobile Workers, CIO, *Preparing a Guaranteed Employment Plan That Fits UAW Members like a Glove: Prepared for the Delegates to the 6th International UAW–CIO Education Conference, Chicago, April 8–11, 1954* (Washington: United Automobile Workers, 1954).
11. Latimer, Murray W., Address given at Pueblo College, October 28, 1955, *Radio Reports, Inc., Transcript Service*, October, 1955.
12. Denise, Malcolm L., "The 1955 Ford-UAW Contract," Address to the Fall Conference of the American Management Association, September 26, 1955 (New York: By the Association, 1955) (mimeographed).
13. Ford Motor Company, *The Ford Supplemental Benefit Plan* (Dearborn, Mich.: Ford Motor Company, 1955), p. iii.
14. *Detroit Free Press*, June 15, 1955, p. 1.
15. U.S., Department of Labor, Bureau of Employment Security, Unemployment Insurance Service, *Supplemental Unemployment Insurance Plans and Unemployment Insurance*, BES No. U-172 (Washington: Government Printing Office, 1957).
16. U.S., Department of Labor, Bureau of Labor Statistics, *Monthly Labor Review*, February 1959, p. 187.
17. U.S., Department of Labor, Bureau of Employment Security, *Comparison of State Unemployment Compensation Laws*, BES No. U-141 (Washington: Government Printing Office, 1965).

18. Letter to author, July 23, 1965.
19. *Proceedings of the Sixth Annual Meeting of the Industrial Relations Research Association, December 28–30, 1953* (Madison, Wis.: By the Association, 1954), p. 88.
20. *The NMU Pilot*, November 17, 1960.
21. *The NMU Pilot*, July 7, 1955, p. 2.
22. Neufield, Maurice F., *Day In, Day Out with Local 3, IBEW*, New York School of Industrial and Labor Relations Bulletin No. 28 (Ithaca, N.Y.: New York School of Industrial and Labor Relations, 1955).
23. Contract between Local 58, IBEW, and the Southwestern Michigan Chapter, National Electrical Contractors' Association, August 21, 1963, p. 6 (mimeographed).
24. California Department of Industrial Relations, *California Industrial Relations Report No. 27* (Sacramento: By the Department, 1965), p. 8.
25. U.S., Bureau of Labor Statistics, *Major Collective Bargaining Agreements— Supplemental Unemployment Benefit Plans and Wage Employment Guarantees*, No. 1425-3 (Washington: Government Printing Office, 1965).
26. Bell, Daniel, "Beyond the Annual Wage: The New Economy," *Fortune*, May 1955.
27. Chernick, Jack, and Berkowitz, Monroe, "The Guaranteed Wage: The Economics of Opulence in Collective Bargaining," *Journal of Business*, July 1955.
28. Stieglitz, Harold, "Labor Leaders View SUB," *Management Record*, April 1956, pp. 124ff.
29. Letter to author, May 10, 1965.
30. Johnson, Richard L., "Ford Supplemental Unemployment Benefit Plan," Paper presented at the 1957 spring meeting of the Financial Council of the Machinery and Allied Products Institute, *Proceedings of the Machinery and Allied Products Institute* (New York: By the Institute, 1957).
31. Becker, Joseph M., S. J. (ed.), *In Aid of the Unemployed* (Baltimore: The Johns Hopkins Press, 1965).
32. Kaplan, A. D. H., *The Guarantee of Annual Wages* (Washington: The Brookings Institution, 1947).
33. Letter to author, June 19, 1965.
34. Letter to author from General Manager of the company, August 9, 1965.
35. Letter to author, May 18, 1965.
36. Letter to author from Manager, Industrial Relations, September 27, 1965.
37. U.S. Bureau of Labor Statistics, *Monthly Labor Review*, July 1966.
38. Letter to author, May 21, 1965.
39. Letter to author, February 28, 1966.
40. United Steelworkers of America, "Explanation of 1962 SUB Amendments," April 2, 1962 (Pittsburgh, Pa.: United Steelworkers of America, 1962), p. 8 (mimeographed).
41. Kelly-Springfield Tire Company and United Rubber Workers, 31 LA 707 (October 31, 1958).
42. Lukens Steel Company and United Steelworkers of America, 36 LA 1309 (June 22, 1961).
43. Dayton Malleable Iron Company and United Steelworkers of America, 38 LA 776 (June 4, 1962).

44. *Agreements between Ford Motor Company and the UAW-AFL-CIO, October 20, 1961* (Dearborn, Mich.: Ford Motor Company and United Automobile Workers, 1961), Article V, Section 2 (a) (2).

45. Budd Company [Detroit, Mich.] and United Automobile Workers of America, Local 306, 32 LA 510 (April 16, 1959).

46. Ideal Cement Company and International Union of United Cement, Lime & Gypsum Workers, *Supplemental Benefit Agreement* (Denver, Colo.: Ideal Cement Company and International Union of United Cement, Lime & Gypsum Workers, 1959), p. 6.

47. Report of union members of subcommittee to Human Relations Research Committee in connection with 1962 negotiations between USWA and steel companies (unpublished).

48. *Proceedings of the 19th Annual Meeting of the Interstate Conference of Employment Security Administrators, September 22-25, 1955* (St. Louis, Mo.: Von Hoffman Press, 1955).

48a. Letter of Agreement between USWA and United States Steel Corporation, 1958.

49. U.S., Department of Labor, Bureau of Labor Statistics, *Monthly Labor Review*, April 1956.

50. Letter to author from Murray W. Latimer, July 6, 1967.

51. Weinberg, Nat, Discussion of SUB (separately issued), *Proceedings of the Sixth Annual Meeting of the Industrial Relations Research Association, December 28-30, 1953* (Madison, Wis.: By the Association, 1954).

52. Weinberg, Nat, "The Future of Guaranteed Pay Plans," Address delivered at the Annual Meeting of the State Bar of Michigan, Detroit, September 14, 1955, *Proceedings of the Annual Meeting of the State Bar of Michigan* (Detroit, Mich.: By the State Bar of Michigan, 1955).

53. United Steelworkers of America, *Insurance, Pensions and Supplemental Unemployment Benefits; Industry Conferences, Washington, D.C., January 1958* (Pittsburgh, Pa.: United Steelworkers of America, 1958).

54. United Steelworkers of America, *Special Report on Insurance, Pensions and Supplemental Unemployment Benefits: Submitted to the 10th Constitutional Convention, Atlantic City, N. J., September 1960* (Washington: United Steelworkers of America, 1960), p. 54.

55. U.S., Department of Labor, Bureau of Labor Statistics, *Monthly Labor Review*, October 1965, p. iv.

56. Pittsburgh Steel Company and United Steelworkers of America, 42 LA 228 (February 3, 1964).

57. United Engineering and Foundry Company and United Steelworkers of America, 47 LA 164 (August 2, 1966).

58. United States Steel Corporation, American Steel and Wire Division, Worcester Works, and United Steelworkers of America, Local 1895, 31 LA 988 (January 20, 1959).

59. *Proceedings of Annual Meeting of Interstate Conference of Employment Security Administrators* (New Orleans, La.: By the Conference, 1954), p. 85.

60. Slichter, Sumner H., Address to the American Management Association, Chicago, February 15, 1954, p. 10 (mimeographed).

61. McConnell, John W., "Supplementary Unemployment Benefits," *Proceed-*

ings of the Eighth Annual Meeting of the Industrial Relations Research Association (Madison, Wis.: By the Association, 1955), p. 181.

62. Bugas, John S., "The Future Course of Industrial Relations," *Monthly Labor Review*, April 1956, p. 412.

63. Becker, Joseph M., S.J., *The Problem of Abuse in Unemployment Benefits* (New York: Columbia University Press, 1953).

64. Wickersham, Edward D., "Repercussions of the Ford Agreement," *Harvard Business Review*, January–February 1956, p. 61.

65. *New York Times*, June 7, 1955, p. 24.

66. *Proceedings of the Society for the Advancement of Management, Special Executive Conference on Guaranteed Annual Wages, March 10–11, 1955* (n.p.: By the Society, 1955).

INDEX

315

281; compared with UI, 270; disqualifications, 86–87, 89, 95, 281, 286; eligibility, 34–35, 82–83, 84, 103, 105, 229, 231, 239, 241, 259, 281, 286; funding, 32, 34, 153n, 156–57, 230–31, 233–34, 235, 237, 238–39, 240–41, 247–48, 281; and labor mobility, 249; origins, 32–41; and size of firm, 64; and UI, 34; and unionization, 63

Murray, Philip, 10, 12, 68

Myers, Charles A., 14n

N

National Association of Manufacturers: and GAW, 6

National Electrical Contractors' Association, 35–36

National Maritime Union of America (NMU): causes of unemployment in, 34; employment security plan, 34–35, 83, 132, 228–31; and GAW, 9

Net wages. See Benefits, SUB: and wage ratio; Wages

Neufeld, Maurice F., 35

New Hampshire: SUB and UI payments in, 23

New Mexico: SUB and UI payments in, 23

New Orleans Brewers and Brewery Workers Welfare Plan, 241–44

New York: Disability Insurance, 35; simultaneous public and private benefits, 8; SUB benefits, 216; UI benefits, 216, 236; Workmen's Compensation, 35

New York Commercial Photoengravers' Unemployment Fund, 41, 41n

"Nonworking violators": of SUB, 269

North Carolina: SUB and UI payments, 22

Nunn-Bush company: and GAW, 3

O

Office and Professional Employees Union (OEIU): and SUB, 54

Office of War Mobilization and Reconversion, Advisory Board, 10. See also Latimer Report

Ohio: Bureau of Employment Security, 23; SUB and UI payments, 22, 23, 23n

Oil industry: contributory pension plans in, 4–5

Operating Engineers (IUOE), 38

Opinion Research Corporation, 54

Overtime: "banked," 84; and SUB benefits, 106, 246; and unemployment, 272

P

Pacific Maritime Association, 70

Packing House Workers (UPWA), 70, 95

Paper industry: and SUB, 54–55

Pattern bargaining, 66

Pattern Makers' League of North America, 51, 59, 73

Pension plans: contributory, 4–5; and SUB, 268n

"Permanent employee": and SUB, 83

Phares, Burl, 68

Plant closings: and SUB, 28, 32, 33–34, 130

Platt, Harry: quoted, 146n–47n

Plumbers and pipefitters. See United Association of Journeymen and Apprentices of the Plumbing and Pipefitting Industry

Political factors: and SUB, 6, 57; and UI, 22

Pooled-fund plans: adequacy, 286, 287; BFCSD, 40–41, 241–42, 244, 286, 287; described, 5, 35–41, 241–42, 244, 287; IBEW, 35–36; PPF, 37, 236; and taxes, 61; and UI, 36

Post War Contingency Fund (General Motors Corporation), 13

Post War Security Fund: proposed by UAW, 13

Private sector: early plans, in relation to public sector, 7, 8, 10–11; in Europe, 7–8; limitations on plans of, 291; and SUB, 5–6; types of programs in, 3–5. See also Supplemental unemployment benefits (SUB)

Profit-sharing plans, 5

Public sector: in Europe, 7; and GAW, 15, 16, 18; in relation to private sector, 7, 8, 12, 13, 291; SUB and, 6. See also Unemployment insurance (UI)

Public utility industry, 4–5

Puerto Rico: SUB and UI payments, 23

Pulp, Sulphite and Paper Mill Workers (PSPMW), 55

Q

Quaker Oats Company: plan of 1934, 8
Quits: and disqualifications, 239, 241, 241n; and eligibility, 86–87, 88, 103–4, 277, 281; as employment, 84; and seniority, 80; and UI, 86–87

R

Radio Corporation of America: Income Extension Plan, 31
Railroad industry: Washington Job Protection Agreement (1936), 129
Raushenbush, Paul A., 264
Recall: and costs, 120; rights, 169; and seniority, 80, 96, 129n, 287
Reduction of workforce, 3–4
Refusal of suitable work: and benefits, 129–30, 235; and disqualification, 90–95, 104; and eligibility, 36, 267, 277, 305, 306; and labor mobility, 252, 253, 256; and unemployment, 85
Registration lists: for laid-off employees, 256
Reinsurance: and pre-SUB plans, 17; and SUB, 226, 285–86
Relocation allowances, 150, 155, 156
Reserve fund: adequacy, 225–27; and cyclical work, 169; depletion, 136, 137; development, 147–50, 151–53, 155; management, 159; original provisions, 137, 143–47; percent used, 284–85; principles of, 142–43; reports on, 161, 162; tax status, 143. See also Funding, SUB
Retail Clerks International Association (RCIA). See Retail food industry SUB plans
Retail food industry SUB plans: adequacy, 286; described, 39–40, 68, 83, 87, 132, 134, 157, 239–41, 281
Retirement, early, 4
Reuther, Walter: Daniel Bell on, 50; on GAW, 276n; rivalry with David McDonald, 18; and SUB, 16, 51, 60, 68
Reverse seniority, 247, 271, 288
Riegel brewery, 40
Rowntree and Company, 7
Rowntree plan, 7–8
Rubber industry: cyclical aspects, 206, 208, 283; and SUB, 56; and UI, 114n

Rubber industry SUB plans: adequacy, 282, 283, 284, 285; administration, 160, 161, 162; benefits, 90, 108, 110, 111, 114n, 117, 118, 119–21, 123–24, 125, 129, 130, 131, 206, 208, 209, 210, 212–14, 216–17, 220, 267, 278, 283, 284, 304, 305; disqualifications, 88, 89, 94; eligibility, 90, 94, 95, 101, 102, 197–98, 220, 253–54, 266n; funding, 137, 142, 146, 147, 148, 153, 155, 157, 221–22, 223, 224–25, 226–27, 247, 279, 285, 304; liberalized, 252, 304; percent of beneficiaries, 29, 282
Rubber workers. See United Rubber, Cork, Linoleum and Plastic Workers of America

S

Sabbatical leave, 5, 82
"Salaried employee": goal of labor, 118, 121, 123, 202, 278, 303, 305, 306. See also Guaranteed Annual Wage (GAW)
Savings fund plans: as alternative to SUB, 25
Scheduled short week, 119–22, 202–4, 205, 305, 307
Schlesinger, Arthur, 67
Seafarers International Union (SIU), 70
Seasonal unemployment. See Unemployment, seasonal
Seniority, non-SUB: as factor in GAW, 11, 12, 14, 15, 17
Seniority, SUB: and ability to work, 85, 86; and age of employees, 62, 63; of beneficiaries, 211–12; and benefits, 279; and "bumping" rights, 57; and credit units, 125, 130n; and discharge, 80; and duration, 125, 129, 130, 131; in first SUB plan, 20, 211; and job preference, 129; and layoffs, 80, 81, 84, 96, 97, 100, 168, 197–98, 200, 220; limited use of, in multi-employer plans, 82–83, 87; lowering requirements for, 103, 167, 222, 308; male versus female, 258; and preferential layoffs, 254–59; and quits, 87; ratio to workforce, 169, 197; and recall, 96, 287; "reverse," 247, 271, 288; seasonal workers and, 82; and Wagner Act, 254n; and work sharing, 120, 122
Severance-pay plans: advantages and dis-

V

W

Designed by Edward D. King

Composed in Times Roman by Monotype
    Composition Company

Printed offset on Perkins and Squier GM
    by Universal Lithographers

Bound in Riverside Linen RL–3375 by
    L. H. Jenkins

Soc
HD
7096
U5
B39